**Susan J. Blackmore** is a disti\_ \_ known for her books exploring consciousness, memetics, evolution and spirituality. Her first book *Beyond the Body* (1982) was hailed as a classic and the life-changing experience detailed in that book is revisited and explained in *Seeing Myself*. Susan is a Visiting Professor at The University of Plymouth but now mainly works freelance, giving lectures all over the world both at academic conferences and to the public.

# Seeing Myself

## The New Science of Out-of-body Experiences

Susan J. Blackmore

ROBINSON

ROBINSON

First published in Great Britain in 2017 by Robinson

1 3 5 7 9 10 8 6 4 2

A CIP catalogue record for this book
is available from the British Library.

Every effort has been made to trace the copyright holders and to obtain their
permission for the use of copyright material. The publisher apologizes
for any errors or omissions and would be grateful if notified of any
corrections that should be incorporated in future reprints or
editions of this book.

ISBN: 978-1-47213-736-4

Typeset in Adobe Jenson Pro by SX Composing DTP, Rayleigh, Essex
Printed and bound in Great Britain by Clays Ltd, St Ives plc

Papers used by Robinson are from well-managed forests
and other responsible sources.

Robinson
An imprint of
Little, Brown Book Group
Carmelite House
50 Victoria Embankment
London EC4Y 0DZ

An Hachette UK Company
www.hachette.co.uk

www.littlebrown.co.uk

To everyone who has had an out-of-body experience
and not known what to make of it.

# Contents

# List of Figures

# A Note on the References

I have chosen to use an academic referencing system for this book. The way it works is that I put the author's name and year for each book or article I am writing about in parentheses. Then all the publications are listed in alphabetical order at the end of the book. By convention, a maximum of two authors are given in the text. If an article has more than two I insert *et al* which, in Latin, means 'and others'. All authors are shown in the list at the end unless there is a really huge number. The system I am using is the APA; American Psychological Association system. Following the main reference list is a list of websites that I have quoted from.

I am doing this because I hope the book may be useful to other OBE researchers in the future. When I read any science book I want to see immediately which research is being referred to. Sometimes, from the author and date, I know already and this helps me assess whether the discussion of it is correct. Sometimes I recognise the authors but don't know this particular paper. And sometimes I know that the work is new to me and I must look it up. Only then do I have to turn to the list at the back.

Many popular science books use end notes. Personally this drives me up the wall. I do not want to keep interrupting my reading to look at a confusing list at the back, especially when the notes are presented by chapter and I've forgotten which chapter I am currently reading! The other is that I sometimes want to check whether the book includes a given piece of research and for that I need an alphabetical list, not one listed by order of appearance in the book.

If you are not familiar with this system I hope that once you've been reading for a while you'll get used to skipping straight over the names in parentheses and that this full referencing system will be helpful.

# Acknowledgements

I could not have completed this book without the help of many friends and colleagues who have sent me images or copies of their work, explained difficult procedures or analyses, and answered my persistent questions. I would especially like to thank Carlos Alvarado, Jason Braithwaite and Ken Ring for their generous help, and my son, Jolyon Troscianko, for his delightful cartoons of the aura test and the rubber hand illusion. Thanks too to my agent, Donald Winchester, who has provided steady help and reassurance throughout. My husband, Adam Hart-Davis, has put up with me during my obsession with trying to understand the OBE, as well as helping in practical ways including acting as my editor, reading the entire book and providing invaluable suggestions. My thanks to you all.

CHAPTER 1

# Leaving My Body

I was just nineteen when everything I thought I knew was overthrown and my life changed direction. If I had imagined a future in some sensible university job, that was now impossible for I was determined to understand what had happened to me. For just a couple of hours I was no longer confined to a slow, heavy, physical body but escaped through a tunnel into a world of flying, exploring the world from outside my body and finally entering the mystical experience of oneness, of unity with the universe.

How could an enthusiastic first-year student of psychology understand any of this? I couldn't. There was nothing in the narrow 1960s science we were learning at Oxford that had any bearing on such adventures. Indeed, our lecturers made it quite clear that we were not there to think about (or even mention) such woolly topics as the nature of mind or the meaning of consciousness, but to study measurable behaviour and only measurable behaviour. I had never heard of tunnel experiences, and the phrase 'near-death experience' (NDE) had not yet been invented. So I jumped to my own conclusions. I was sure that my spirit had left my body and would survive after death. I was convinced that telepathy and clairvoyance must be possible and that ghosts were real. From that day on I became determined to devote my life to parapsychology and to prove all my closed-minded lecturers wrong.

1

I failed; of course I failed. The conclusions I had jumped to so quickly were ill-thought-out and superficial. But never mind. The vivid memories of those few hours kept driving me on. Nearly half a century later I can look back and see the way my intellectual life has been shaped, pushed and pulled by the experience, and how my spiritual life might never have even begun had I not found myself disappearing into selflessness without having a clue what that was.

So that failure has shaped the story of my life. I did become a parapsychologist, hunting for paranormal phenomena and failing, time and again, to find them (Blackmore, 1996). That repeated failure, over months and years of experimentation, drove me back again and again to my own experience, the memory of which I could never shake off, but nor could I induce it to happen again. At first, I tried to understand it by studying the occult, sitting with mediums, learning to read Tarot cards and training as a witch. I still have my beautiful crystal ball that I learned to peer into. I studied mystical theories of spirit separation and astral projection and found they led only to confusion and wild, untestable conjectures.

But if my spirit had not left my body then what had happened? Could there be a more down-to-earth explanation than astral projection? I soon discovered there was a more neutral term, 'out-of-body experience' or OBE. I studied what little academic research had been done on OBEs, and began to do my own experiments. Then I wrote my first book, *Beyond the Body* (1982), doing my best to find a psychological account of what I, and so many others, had experienced. But the science I needed was simply not there.

By that time there were just a few scientific studies mapping the nature, circumstances and details of spontaneous experiences (e.g. Green, 1968, Morris et al., 1978, Palmer, 1979). It was clear that OBEs were surprisingly common and were reported by people of many ages and cultures, regardless of sex, age or education. In 1975, the term 'near-death experience' (NDE) was coined by the American physician Raymond Moody and OBEs close to death were widely documented and widely taken as proof of a surviving spirit or soul. But what caused them still seemed utterly mysterious.

Almost no one seemed to want to understand these experiences scientifically. Instead a popular movement began in which tales of guardian angels, surviving spirits and trips to a loosely Christian heaven captured the public's imagination and were taken as proof that consciousness survives death. As an increasingly sceptical parapsychologist I was invited on to numerous TV and radio shows, where a hundred people who had been to the other side were pitted against one 'materialist, reductionist, atheist, unspiritual sceptic' (me) to be a lone voice suggesting there might be better explanations.

Popular enthusiasm for such tales waxes and wanes. After relative calm, a new flood arrived in 2011 with the experiences of two doctors, Eben Alexander with *Proof of Heaven* and Mary Neal with *To Heaven and Back*, books which spent months on bestseller lists. Then came the book *Heaven Is for Real* that was turned into a popular film about a young boy's experiences. Once again their claims of heaven – an exclusively Christian heaven – were widely accepted at face value despite such peculiarities as spirit clothes and shoes, and heavenly cities, streets, trees and pets. Claims of survival make for bestselling books regardless of such tricky questions as which of my lovers might greet me at heaven's gate and whether my parents will be as deeply demented as they were when they died.

Several of us tried, back in the 1970s, to frame psychological theories without other worlds or travelling minds but with only a handful of us taking the experiences seriously, progress more or less fizzled out. Then, finally, with the turn of a new century, everything changed.

This is why I am writing this book. This is why, after so many years, I have come back to the first love of my working life, trying to understand what happened to me during those few hours in 1970. It is a great pleasure to see the details finally falling into place, even the strangest and most disturbing of them. It is a joy, after such long struggles, to come to accept the very different notion of a self and consciousness that emerges from this new understanding. So where else can I begin but with an account of what happened on the evening of Sunday 8 November 1970.

## Bright and vivid memories

My memories of that night are curiously vivid, as people often say about their memories of NDEs, OBEs and mystical experiences. It is as though they have a brightness, immediacy and intensity of feeling that other old memories do not, and studies of NDE memories confirm this (Thonnard et al., 2013). But are they accurate? Are they reliable over such a long time? Possibly they are. Among NDE researchers, Bruce Greyson (2007a) contacted seventy-two of his surviving patients after two decades to find their accounts had hardly changed. Another team re-interviewed NDErs twice. After two years they could 'retell their experience almost exactly' and after eight years survivors still had clear memories (van Lommel et al., 2001).

Or could my memory be selective and distorted by wishful thinking? It was hard enough to make sense of what had happened immediately afterwards, and since then I have had a lifetime of strange experiences; spontaneous visions, drug-induced states and insights arising through long practice of meditation. Could I be mixing these memories together or twisting them to fit with my later experiences? Possibly, but I am encouraged by research showing that NDE memories behave more like memories of actual events than memories of imagined ones (Thonnard et al., 2013).

And I'm getting old. These memories now reside in an ageing brain and we know how unreliable even recent memories can be. We also know that when you tell and retell any story, what you remember is more often the latest version of what you said rather than any reliable details of events. This is often how false memories are formed (Loftus & Pickrell, 1995, French, 2003). So perhaps I still shouldn't rely too much on those glorious memories.

Happily, I have two other sources to go on. The first is my diary, which I began writing in 1964. I scribbled 'I love Paul' or 'I love Ringo' in the margins and every page was decorated with little pictures of beetles to enliven my boring accounts of the tedium and misery of life in a girls' boarding school. Descriptions of my first term at Oxford are far more exciting, full of challenging lectures and scary tutorials, music, painting, rehearsals and eclectic new friends. Even so, the entry for 8 November stands out. It begins: 'I have the most amazing thing to tell. Really the most fantastic thing that ever happened in my life. I went astral travelling. I was thousands of miles away – not in my body at all'.

The rest of that entry tells of a typical day, being exhausted from a previous late night while struggling with my work, having my new friend Kevin to supper in college and then hosting one of our regular séance evenings. I had met Kevin in Freshers' Week after I'd signed up to join, among other clubs, the Oxford University Society for Psychical Research (OUSPR). I had no deep interest in or knowledge of the subject, but having read a single book on psychic powers, I thought the idea rather exciting. Then Kevin turned up in my room one morning and said he was the only remaining member of the OUSPR from the previous year and asked whether I would like to join him in setting it up again. He was not only a second year but had long, dark, wavy hair, bright eyes and hippy clothes. I immediately agreed.

So this is how we ended up inviting mediums and psychics to give us lectures, running experiments to test for ESP (extrasensory perception), reading about astral projection and having regular sessions with a Ouija board in my college room. We wrote the letters of the alphabet on scraps of paper, along with the words 'Yes' and 'No' and the numerals 0–9, arranged them in a circle on a table and placed an upturned glass in the centre. Then we all placed one finger on the glass, half-closed our eyes and asked the spirits to appear. Typically the glass would soon start moving and, ever faster, spell out answers to our questions. We got terribly excited whenever a door creaked or a curtain moved with no sign of a breeze, but we were also sceptical and curious to find out the truth.

On one occasion we decided that spirits ought to be able to see through paper with no trouble so we turned all the pieces over and wrote numbers on the back. Then we recorded which numbers the glass pointed to and only at the very end turned over the papers and decoded the answers. The sequence they made, unlike all our attempts with visible letters, was total gibberish.

As our society became increasingly popular I used to cycle around Oxford pinning handmade posters for all our events on college notice boards. Sometimes we even had too many participants to sit comfortably around one small table, so we used another student's room and used two or three tables simultaneously. In my diary for that day I wrote of our séance in barely legible writing:

> The other room had a very light-hearted, fun one. Ours was terribly intense. Robin, Dugald, Brian, Kevin, Paul L ... + I. We had some very dubious contacts and got a little scared! We packed it in and I was exhausted – absolutely exhausted and no-body would leave. Finally they left at 11.30, or 11.15 anyway. We 3, Kevin, Vicki and I went up to her room to smoke. I don't think I really got high at all. I started off seeing all these hallucinations. They thought maybe I was tripping I think and after I don't know how long I realised and Kevin realised that I was Astral travelling. The white shining cord was there and I went all over the world, and out of the world – or the universe etc. it was fantastic. I must write a whole thing on it, where I went etc. I won't do it now; if I do it at all I'll do it properly.

And so I did, at least as 'properly' as I could. Two days later, when I began to feel well enough to set my fingers to my little portable typewriter, I wrote a much fuller account. I still have the grubby original and it has also been online since 2001 when American parapsychologist, Charles Tart, asked me if he could post it on his 'Scientists' Transcendent Experiences' website. It is also on my own site but makes for an odd and tedious read, so I'm using that, my diary and my still vivid memories to write a more concise account. This seems like a rather selfish and indulgent thing to do – to drag up this old experience as though it were the most important thing in the world – but it was this, after all, that inspired my research. Explaining it, and other experiences like it, is really the whole point of this book. I'll try to keep it simple.

**Figure 1.1: Tunnel of trees.** I drew this 'tunnel of trees' to try to convey the sense of moving through a tunnel that was made of autumn leaves all round – both on the trees and on the ground below.

## One night in November

I was sitting cross-legged on the floor late one evening. Sleep deprived and tired after hours of holding out my arm on the Ouija board, my mind was already wandering when the hallucinations began. Unlike later events, these drifting visions didn't feel real, which means they should technically be called 'pseudo-hallucinations'. Music was playing on a portable record player, although I've forgotten what it was; probably Pink Floyd, Led Zeppelin or Grateful Dead. Whatever it was, it turned into multi-coloured patterns pulsing with the rhythms, interspersed with incredibly sharp and detailed images of different places that came briefly and disappeared. Then a tunnel formed and I began rushing along it, accompanied by a thunderous noise as though I were a horse galloping down a tree-lined avenue towards a distant light.

I wrote that all this lasted '... for about half an hour – 12:00 to 12:30 – and then the transition came.' So it's clear that I immediately sensed the difference between what I took to be familiar drug effects and something quite new. My feet seemed to be far away and I sensed a wall of drifting whiteness passing right through me. What I saw with my eyes open ceased to make sense, so I closed them and kept them closed as I felt as though I was rising up to the ceiling and gently drifting about. I could still hear the music and the others talking but they seemed ever so far away, and when Vicki asked if I'd like some coffee I couldn't reply. So she left the room.

Alone with Kevin, he asked me the strangest question, 'Where are you, Sue?' As I tried to work out where I was, everything suddenly cleared. I was near the ceiling and looking down. I could even watch myself – the body down below – reply. I seemed able both to control that lumpen body and to watch it as though it were someone else, and I continued speaking like this for most of the next three hours. I wrote, 'I was somehow quite able to conceive of being in the two places at once, or rather to be in one place but to still have the knowledge and perception of the body in another.' My vision now was nothing like those hallucinations of colour and shape or even the tunnel of leaves: it was real. Looking down from up there the scene felt as real, even more real, than looking out of my eyes had seemed all my life.

Soon I saw the silver cord, a shiny greyish-white thread, slowly bending and moving. The 'me' up there seemed to be made of a similar substance, only denser and more solid, and the cord stretched away from my tummy down to the neck of the body below. Everything in the room seemed clear and normal and, with Kevin's encouragement, I set off to explore the world outside. I whizzed up through another room and out into the night sky. As I flew over the college roofs a tiny flicker of scepticism urged me to take a good look at the ancient gutters, downpipes and chimneys and then I was off.

Some of my travels are rather tedious to recount as I flew about for ages in what I took to be the astral planes – even then wondering whether this was the real physical world or some kind of mind-created astral version that looked like the physical world. But my encounter with an island in the Mediterranean stands out in my memory.

> As I approached the island I could see its shape, which was almost star shaped with very sharp points, but the shape seemed to be changing all the time and pulsating with the music. I became even more excited and tried to tell the others what I was seeing as I got closer and closer. It was at this point that I discovered what was to be of such importance later on – that I could change shape at will. So far I had been aware that I could produce hands at will, but now I was able to lose my bodily shape altogether and become any shape I wanted. I stretched out over the island and watched it changing shape. Then from being a flat thin shape, I thought my way down in among the trees. For the first time I got a little scared as I thought the cord might get tangled up and broken in the trees: however I soon found that it could pass among or through the trees with no difficulty whatsoever and that I wouldn't have to worry about it at all. I was then again a little scared because it was all dark and . . . treacly, under the trees. Feelings of pleasure and displeasure were very exaggerated and the feeling of being in that thick darkness was intense. However as soon as I discovered that I could move up again at will, I lost the fear and was enjoying going into and out of trees. Another impression I had of the island was that it had one hundred trees. I was really excited by the funny idea of there being exactly that number.

Learning to control my shape and size meant that I could float flat on the surface of water, lie on sharp rocks, or leap up crumbling cliffs without touching them. And all the while I could still hear the music back in Vicki's room. This didn't seem odd, 'nor did it seem at all difficult to concentrate on so much at once.'

At one point I had the powerful impression that everyone below me on the ordinary earth was working terribly hard – that they were striving needlessly. This new world of thought seemed so much more real than the world of dragging bodies around and getting exhausted.

I felt overwhelmingly sorry for them while also realising that I would have to work like that again one day. If I hadn't written this down I might have forgotten this little oddity because it seemed to have no significance at the time. Now I see it differently.

At times I grew frightened. When I dropped down among trees or between tall buildings the atmosphere was dank and dark; I feared I might never escape. Buffeted by waves, I thought I might drown. Yet I was gradually learning how to control my movements and escape anything I didn't like. There was a sense of effortlessness about all this: all I had to do was think of something or somewhere and I would be there. Yet there were oddities about this 'travelling by thought'. If I looked down, I moved upwards and if I looked up, I moved down. But to move horizontally I had to look where I wanted to go. For shorter distances I could just think about where I wanted to be and arrive there almost instantly or in short hops. For longer distances I flew way up high and at great speed with very little control.

On one such journey I arrived back in Oxford and said 'hello' to Vicki and Kevin, who were still there, patiently listening to my rantings. I briefly opened my eyes but the conflict with my inner vision was too great. Somewhat reassured that I could get back if I wanted to, I set off travelling again.

It was on the second return to my body that everything changed again. I could see Vicki, Kevin and the room quite clearly but when I looked at my own body, I was shocked. It was a strange brown colour and had a jagged edge around the neck where the head had been. Intrigued, I found myself landing on the edge like a fly, before slipping inside. All this, as far as I can remember, was great fun. I swooped about, exploring what seemed to be an empty shell, zooming up and down the legs and into the feet. I made so much noise that Vicki got angry and told me to shut up, whereupon I told her to take 'that body' away. By now I had lost any sense that this body was really mine or that I could control it.

I suppose it was the desire to get back to normal that led to me trying to get bigger, to fill up that empty shell and regain control. But this attempt failed spectacularly. Instead of growing to the right size and taking control of my body again I simply grew and grew, and kept on growing. I expanded out through the room and through my friends, through the building and the streets, through the underground places of Oxford, all of England, and ultimately the earth. I wrote that I 'had the wonderful experience of being able to look at the earth from being all round it', an ability I can only vaguely imagine in retrospect. And from there I just kept on expanding until there was nowhere to go. Expanding ever faster but going nowhere, I was simply everything that was, and nothing else existed.

It is hard to describe these final stages. They are, as so many mystics say, ineffable. But I can try to say something and hope that it isn't too much affected by other experiences that have happened since. Being everything was more like being a vast space than a collection of things – more like being everywhere and nowhere as an unknowable spaciousness in which everything happens but nothing happens. If that sounds odd, I can say that neither time nor space had their ordinary meanings any more. Things happened but they did not happen in any recognisable framework of time and location. It was as though everything were just as it should be and complete, yet still ever changing. I had the sense of knowing things or being taught things which I can now say nothing at all about. I had the sense that this was obviously how things should be even though I had never realised it before – a sense of rightness and peace; nothing to be done, nowhere to go.

By now Kevin was worried and started asking questions. What was I doing? Could I see anything else? What came next? They seemed silly questions – after all, this was 'it'. Yet somehow they changed everything. As I struggled to answer it seemed as though I was swimming up through some kind of white mist or cloud to gain the slightest glimpse of another world. Through this veil there seemed to be a great wide open plain and from all around I sensed that someone or something, or some kind of awareness was observing my pathetic little struggles with mild and kindly amusement. The words 'However far you go, there's always somewhere further,' echoed in my mind as the plain disappeared. And that was that.

Exhausted, I could take no more. Vicki was longing for bed but there was no way I could just snap back to normal. With Kevin constantly urging me on, I struggled and struggled to get back inside the body. At first it seemed easy but as soon as I opened my eyes I seemed to shoot out of the body again and end up wherever I had been looking. Then I had to start again to get back in, try again, fail; try again. Corners presented a special challenge as I seemed unable to understand how three dimensions could meet in one place. I kept talking to myself, saying, 'Wherever you go you have to take the body with you.' Or, 'You can only be in one place at a time.' Then gradually, after about three quarters of an hour, I found this other 'me' was more or less coincident with my physical body and I carefully stood up.

The room looked very strange and so did my friends. So did my own body. Looking down at myself, I could still see the whitish stuff I had been made of. It was more or less coincident with my body but not quite and still slightly moving. Round the others was a similar pale glow, as though they too had another body or a living aura. And further out than that was another body that I could feel with my hands but not see. Around Kevin it stretched a long way; around Vicki, rather less. Was this the occultists' aura that psychics could see and ordinary people could not? Had my third eye been opened? I played around with these sensations for some time before cautiously taking a few steps and setting off back to my own room. Vicki was greatly relieved.

Kevin said it would be dangerous to go to sleep because my astral body might leave again and be unable to return so he kept me awake until well into the next morning. I did finally sleep and as far as I know my astral body did nothing of the kind. But I felt very weird indeed. As I cycled around Oxford I seemed to be watching myself from one side and almost fell off my bike. In a tutorial two days later my rather strict tutor told me to pull myself together and pay attention. As I recorded in my diary, she said, 'You seem to be floating off on a cloud somewhere,' and I blurted out, 'I am!' and then felt I had to give some kind of explanation. She seemed genuinely interested, so I told

12

her more or less all about it, until eventually she said we were rather stupid to be messing around with drugs at such an unstable age.

So that was the experience that changed my life. That was the experience whose memory kept nudging me for decades to come; reminding me that I didn't understand; making me dissatisfied with our scientific understanding of the world and the mind. That was the experience that kept me asking questions and more questions. It still does.

## First questions

Had I really travelled on the astral planes, I wanted to know. And what was the relationship between this astral world and the actual physical world I could see with my real eyes?

The next morning I went out enthusiastically to inspect the roofs and gutters and chimneys. I was shocked: the gutters were not the old-fashioned iron ones I had seen from above but modern plastic, and there were no chimneys at all. I cursed myself that I hadn't thought to look into rooms where I had never been so that I could check what they looked like. I was furious with myself for not having had the presence of mind to ask Kevin or Vicki to try ESP tests; to hide cards or numbers or anything at all in the next room or out in the corridor to test my psychic vision. Instead I had stupidly gone flitting off across the oceans to see distant cities that I could never check. I was angry that I'd not once thought to ask them to find a tape recorder and record what I said.

How I'd like that now. And we did have such things: as well as my Dansette record player, that could stack six LPs one above the other and play them with a scratchy needle, I had a small Philips cassette recorder, the latest technology from the 1960s. But no one thought to use it that night. So I checked what little I could around college and found it most frustrating. Much of what I had seen was exactly right while some small details were wrong. And there were other anomalies too. I remembered having passed up through another room above Vicki's as I would have had to do from my own ground-floor room. But Vicki's room was on the top floor, with no other room above it. I remembered it all so clearly yet I was wrong.

Yes, I was disappointed, but somehow I accepted these discrepancies. The vividness and clarity of the experience and my powerful memories of flying free meant I could not believe this was all hallucinated. There had to be some other explanation. Perhaps psychic powers work in strange ways; perhaps the astral world is made of other people's thought forms that go on existing without them; perhaps psychics can pick up on thoughts created by others and so see the world as others see it. In this case there might really be a kind of telepathy but it would not be perfect, as I knew it was not. Seeing others' thoughts would always mean extracting them from the jumble of endless thought forms in the astral world. Clairvoyance would not be perfect either as it is thoughts that are seen, not physical objects.

And so I brushed off the many little anomalies and went on running the OUSPR for the rest of my three years at Oxford, reading more and more about psychics and occultism, Jung's theory of synchronicity, Madame Blavatsky's Theosophy and the idea of the Akashic records that store everything that ever happens. I studied the evidence for survival after death in the classics of early psychical research like *Human Personality and Its Survival of Bodily Death* (Myers, 1903) and *Phantasms of the Living* (Gurney et al., 1886). I studied the work of modern parapsychologists J. B. and Louisa Rhine, who invented the field of parapsychology and coined the phrase 'extrasensory perception' (Rhine, 1935). When offered the chance to do a PhD at Surrey University, I began another such society and invited more students to join Ouija board sessions, Tarot reading evenings, crystal gazing, table tipping, metal bending and other such fun pursuits. And all the time I was trying to work out how seeing the astral worlds could fit with science.

## Mind beyond the brain?

My best idea, and the foundation for my PhD, was my very own 'memory theory of ESP'. It looks completely implausible now we know the basics of how memory depends on neural networks, dendritic growth and changes to synapse strengths, but I like to think it was at least a little more plausible back in the 1970s.

My idea was that memory is not stored in the brain at all but in some kind of psychic field potentially accessible to everyone; memory would then turn out to be a special form of the more general process of ESP. We find it easier to remember what happened to us because our brains now are more similar to our own brains in the past than they are to other people's brains, and similarity is what counts. This is why memory is easier and more accurate than ESP, even though they are essentially the same process. This is also why twins and close friends or lovers are better at ESP than unrelated people. It might even be why so many ESP experiments fail to find any effects and why the astral plane is not identical to the physical world.

I set to work with great enthusiasm, and some initial success, but my optimism and self-confidence were soon knocked by reality. As I delved into more reading, I discovered that my great theory was far from original. Lots of people had explored similar ideas before me. There was Henri Bergson's (1896) idea that the brain is more like a filter than a memory store; H. H. Price's (1939) 'psychic ether hypothesis' accounting for hauntings, Whateley Carington's (1945) 'psychons' that are created by thought but not confined to the person who created them; and William Roll's (1966) 'psi field theory'. And I wasn't the last: Rupert Sheldrake's (1981) highly popular 'morphic resonance theory' is yet another example and we'll meet several more new ones in the murky world of NDE research. But they all face enormous theoretical difficulties, not least in determining their physical basis and finding ways to test them.

Then there was my own evidence, or rather the lack of it. My PhD research focused on the similarities between memory and ESP but when, year after year after year, I failed to find any ESP, I could not even test for this comparison (Blackmore, 1980a, 1980b, 1981a). I sub-mitted my thesis, *Extrasensory Perception as a Cognitive Process*, in 1979 (Blackmore, 1980c). It described nearly thirty experiments which provided no evidence whatsoever for ESP and no solutions to the dilemmas presented by psychic claims. Of ESP, it concluded 'that which appeared so difficult may not after all exist' (p.350). In other words I had neither proved nor disproved anything, had made no progress at all with my theory, and still had no idea how to explain my experience.

But I did know something: I could still remember vividly the sensations of flying above the world, of leaving my heavy body behind, of being light and flexible and moving by thought alone, of ceasing to be separate from the universe. I had thought I could understand this by devoting myself to parapsychology but I was wrong. Parapsychology had, after all, proved to be a red herring (Blackmore, 1986a). I was left with my memories and even more unanswered questions.

CHAPTER 2

# Defining the OBE

A s luck would have it, my chance to look for answers came out of the
blue. The Society for Psychical Research was celebrating its
centenary. Founded in London in 1882 at the peak of the craze for
spiritualism, its aim was to investigate, in a scientific and unprejudiced
manner, mediumship, hypnotism, life after death and claims of telepathy and clairvoyance. One hundred years later they hoped to publish
a small collection of new books and asked me to write one on out-of-
the-body experiences. I welcomed the challenge and the result was
*Beyond the Body*.

I began by trying to organise the most important questions and
these are still relevant now:

1.  How should we define an OBE?
2.  How common are the experiences, and what are they like?
3.  Who has them and under what circumstances?
4.  Can they be induced at will and controlled?
5.  Are they the same as dreams, hallucinations or any other
    well-known phenomena?
6.  What is happening in the brain during an OBE?
7.  Can people see or hear things that they could not otherwise
    have known about (paranormal perception or ESP)?

8. Can people affect others or influence distant events (psychokinesis or PK)?

9. Is there any evidence for the existence of a 'double'?

10. What do OBEs tell us about human nature and the possibility of life after death?

Most of these questions are fairly straightforward and in the intervening years research has answered them. But these answers only lead inexorably to the last, horribly contentious, one. From reading most popular accounts you would believe that OBEs are certain proof of the wondrous nature of human consciousness; that we humans are not confined to our gross physical bodies but have some kind of double – a spirit or soul that is the real source of our individuality and consciousness and can travel outside of its mere physical shell. This implies that individual consciousness can exist beyond the brain even though this flies in the face of everything that neuroscience seems to be telling us.

This is a profound challenge to science. If dualism is true – if mind and body are separate – then our current science needs completely overhauling. Most philosophers and scientists today reject dualism of any kind, partly because they see no good evidence for it and partly because it makes little sense. How could a non-material mind that is truly distinct from its body influence that body? And how could a physical brain and body create or provide a home for a non-material mind? If mind is distinct from brain, why would brain damage have the effects it does? Why would drugs that affect the brain change consciousness in the dramatic ways they do? For these and many other reasons dualism seems like a dead end, which is why so many scientists opt for some kind of monism – most of them choosing materialism, the view that ultimately everything is made of matter. This means that compelling evidence for consciousness beyond the brain would force a massive scientific upheaval. It is hard to imagine many discoveries that would have such an impact.

On the other hand, if the evidence does not uphold these claims we are left with a different mystery: how can a science that rejects dualism account for these dramatic and life-changing experiences? Some scientists seem afraid of trying to find out and dismiss accounts of OBEs as 'just hallucinations' or 'nothing but dreams' but, as we shall see, OBEs are not like most other hallucinations and they are certainly not dreams. So what is going on? Can science yet provide an explanation that does justice to the experiences themselves? From my own selfish point of view I just want to understand what happened to me but the implications of any explanation reach far beyond that.

## Am I alone?

This question is easy to answer. I am not alone – far from it. There are plenty of books and websites describing strange and wonderful experiences. After I wrote *Beyond the Body* and spoke about OBEs on radio and television, I received floods of letters and then emails describing similar, or at least related, experiences. Here is an account sent to me by a 23-year-old man.

> About 7 years ago I found myself hurtling upwards through an incredible black void propelled at a fantastic speed, I was very frightened and thought that if I carried on this 'journey' I would not be able to get back. I then fought against the direction I was going and it was at this point that I felt I was in the presence of two beings (I couldn't see anything) then I hurtled back and 'crashed' into my body lying in bed. It took a tremendous amount of effort to move and open my eyes, and as I was 'falling back' and trying to gain full consciousness I could hear tremendous roaring sounds, like I imagine a tornado to sound like. . . .
>
> Last summer I decided I would face up to this fear of the experience and see if I could have a self induced OBE and prove certain things to myself. Then early one morning I became aware I was dreaming at that moment the dream vanished and I was aware that I was lying in bed, the vibrations started. I imagined myself floating upward and incredibly I began to feel myself floating upwards as light as a feather. I suddenly opened my eyes, for an instant I could 'see' the ceiling as if it was next to my face, then as if a camera was zooming backwards the ceiling got further

19

away to where it should be from the viewpoint of lying on the bed. I was very excited by this, but it was over so quickly.

Does this count as an OBE? He tells of a journey into what seems to be another world and specifically refers to an OBE. He sees his bedroom ceiling close up and describes floating 'light as a feather'. Yet he also mentions a black void, roaring sounds, powerful vibrations and the sense of two other beings. Were the roaring sounds like my galloping hooves? Are these other details typical of such experiences?

What about this account, from a young woman whose letter also described her having vivid hypnagogic images, seeing coloured balls of light floating round her bedroom, being paralysed and hearing a 'screeching, whirling noise'?

When I was twelve I got into trouble in the water at the swimming pool. I was under the water, struggling and choking, etc. When I felt suddenly separated from it all, as if I were watching someone else, I felt nothing. That same day, later on while playing with friends in the park, I was running, and I suddenly began to float up out of my body. I felt like I could go up and up. It was when I thought to myself, 'This is weird', that everything went back to normal.

Approximately 14 months ago I decided to try this astral travel lark, just to see if it worked. I lay on my bed in the afternoon and waited to see what would happen. I am certain that I did not fall asleep during this. After about an hour or so I began to see little dots of coloured light gather at the centre of my vision (my eyes were closed). A tiny black dot appeared at the centre of these lights and began to grow bigger. As it grew I began to hear high-pitched beeps, or digital-type noises in my head. The black dot grew very big until it resembled the tunnel experience which I have read about. It was surrounded by a beautiful ring of spinning glittery lights. It was then that I felt a sucking sensation and I panicked. It felt like I was being pulled towards this tunnel and I only got out of it by fighting the paralysis. I must admit that I was absolutely terrified and it took me a few days to get over the fright.

This story includes floating 'up out of my body'. She mentions attempting 'astral travel' and describes a tunnel experience and noises, suggesting similarities with both my own experience and the young man's account. She also says she was paralysed, which I did not experience, as does this final example from a 33-year-old man, who writes about his fear of being wide awake and unable to move.

> I do not like the feeling I get. I try to fight against it, but it is useless – I can't scream as no sound comes out of my mouth, but I know what is happening. I had a very strange experience a few weeks ago, but I'm not sure whether I dreamt it or whether it really happened. I know it sounds crazy as since it happened you are the only other person that I have tried to explain this to.
>
> I was lying down on my sofa watching television. It was late night and I felt myself dropping off to sleep. I also felt myself going into the sleep paralysis state – which I don't like, as I've explained before. But this one was not like the others. I felt myself sort of rolling off the sofa and then sort of floating round the living room, but for the life of me I cannot remember whether I dreamed it or whether it really happened. One thing that came across was the fact that I seemed to be aware of my surroundings and that I could move anywhere within my living room. Another thing I seem to remember was that as it was happening I enjoyed it. You know the sensation of floating round.
>
> I know it sounds mad and crazy but that is what happened to me. The next thing I remember I woke up back on the sofa again. . . . I have decided not to go to a doctor because he would think I'm crazy.

How are we to bring order to all these differing accounts? With just four so far (these three and my own) there is already great variety. Are the ones that involve paralysis different from those that do not? Are those on the verge of sleep, or possibly in deep sleep, the same or different? Should those that involve drugs, like mine, be dismissed as irrelevant or 'fake'? Are any of these features essential for an experience to be called an OBE?

We need a definition. Fortunately there are lots. Unfortunately many are confusing and misleading.

## Ignorance, confusion and terrible advice

The worst problem is that some definitions already assume what we want to find out. Here is an especially bad example from a popular website: 'An occasion when an individual separates from and views from above his or her physical body'.

This not only assumes that something actually leaves the body but that the body must be seen 'from above'. In our last case the man seemed to roll off the sofa, presumably to a point below, not above, his body. He says he floated around the living room but not whether he looked at his body so his experience does not fit this definition even though it sounds to me like an OBE. Even some scientists unnecessarily include seeing one's own body as a requirement, as in 'experiences in which a person seems to be awake and sees his body and the world from a location outside his physical body' (Bünning & Blanke, 2005). But as we shall see, not everyone does see their own body.

Several websites add further confusion, defining astral projection as 'the intentional act of having the spirit leave the body, whereas an out-of-body experience will happen involuntarily'. This distinction is completely unjustified. It means that in our first case, only one of the man's experiences counts as an OBE because the other was deliberate. As we shall see, there are differences between spontaneous and deliberate OBEs but not ones that could justify such an arbitrary definition. Most importantly, both these definitions and many others demand that the 'individual' or 'spirit' separates from the body. The implication is that there are 'real' OBEs in which something really separates from the body and that all the others are 'fake' or 'imaginary' and don't count. This might not matter if it was easy to find out whether something has actually separated but – as we shall see again and again – it is not. This means that in none of our four cases could we decide whether the experience was an OBE or not because we have no proof of separation. This kind of definition is useless.

Things get even worse when religions are involved. A Christian website (Christian Apologetics and Research Ministry) describes an OBE as 'the phenomenon when a person's consciousness is detached from the physical body and travels or exists outside of the body', warning that the Bible forbids occult practices, OBEs amount to divination and sorcery, and 'dabbling in the spiritual realm in a manner not approved by scripture' may 'open up individuals to demonic oppression'. This is not very helpful.

For Muslims seeking advice, the situation is equally dire. One asked whether it is permitted in Islam to have an OBE knowingly because he'd been having OBEs after morning prayers for many years. A mufti replied that such 'futile and vain' activity should be stopped. Others warn that the astral realm is full of Jinns – supernatural fiery entities described in the Koran that can help or harm human beings: 'Who knows in what manner they could attack you. Maybe even possess your body when you are away.' Another response cites the Koran's teaching that the soul leaves the body in sleep and returns only by the permission of Allah. 'The soul roams away from the body at sleep and may do so also when awake,' says Shaykh Gibril F. Haddad. His advice is that Awliya (believers close to Allah) may deliberately become disembodied if the purpose is to help others but, 'There is a very important difference between Muslims and non-Muslims in such phenomena. Muslim spirits are clothed with light while non-Muslim spirits are clothed with darkness and vulnerable to dark forces. Another danger is that the disembodied soul may "lose" its way back or be prevented from its body, which results in death.' It seems that Muslims who seek help are meant to be scared by their experiences rather than find helpful information from the science of sleep, dreaming and altered states of consciousness.

So how do we gain that helpful information? To begin with what we need is a neutral definition that clearly describes the basic experience without making any assumptions about how to explain it. We can then explore the great variety of OBEs, learn as much as we can about them, find out whether there really are any dangers and only then ask, with an open mind, how to explain them.

## A neutral definition

The few scientists who have investigated OBEs have had to be very careful about definitions. The origin of the term 'out-of-body experience' or sometimes 'out-of-the-body experience' is often attributed to Charles Tart, an American psychologist who pioneered some of the earliest laboratory studies of OBEs (Tart, 1967, 1968). But in fact the term is much older, going back at least as far as 1918, when it was used as a section title in a book by psychical researcher, J. Arthur Hill (1918, p.67), who wrote that humans 'seem to be spirits in prison' (Alvarado, 2007). G. N. M. Tyrrell's 1943 book *Apparitions* has a similar section. For these men, as for other psychical researchers, OBEs suggested a spirit or soul that could survive bodily death. Yet Tyrrell was admirably cautious, writing, 'Such experiences do not, of course, prove survival; but they are very surprising on an epiphenomenalist view of consciousness' (Tyrrell, 1943, p.149). I wish that modern best-selling authors on near-death experiences were equally cautious.

The first person who carefully separated the definition of an OBE from dualist assumptions was probably the American psychical researcher, Hornell Hart, whose surveys of OBEs we will meet later. Like his predecessors, he wanted evidence of survival after death and this is why he collected cases of what he called 'ESP projection' and 'ESP travel'. Both required evidence that something – a soul, spirit, conscious mind or astral body – had left the body and either was seen by someone else or had obtained 'veridical' (truthful, correct) information. Hart treated these 'veridical' phenomena as a subset of the more inclusive term 'out-of-body experience'. This term, he said, can be 'used to include ESP projection and ESP travel, without rigorous insistence upon veridicality' (Hart, 1954, p.122).

This broader meaning is just what we need, and is the theory-neutral sense in which most scientists and parapsychologists have used the term ever since. For example, British researcher Celia Green (1966, 1967) published a classic collection of cases in the 1960s, defining an OBE or 'ecsomatic experience' as 'one in which the objects of perception are apparently organised in such a way that the observer seems to himself to be observing them from a point of view which is not coincident with his physical body' (Green, 1968, p.xvii). This hardly trips off the tongue but the principle is clear and her questionnaires simply asked people, 'Have you ever had an experience in which you felt you were "out of your body"?' This could not be simpler; it assumes nothing beyond the way it felt.

Green's studies were the first real research that I learned about and I was thrilled to discover that her 'Institute of Psychophysical Research' was right there in Oxford. So one day I plucked up the courage to contact her and ask whether a small group of us from our OUSPR could come and meet her. We were very excited about the visit and set off hopefully up the Banbury Road, only to be slightly surprised that the 'Institute' turned out to be just her house. I guess we had naively expected some kind of academic building or laboratory. We had also hoped, or perhaps even assumed, that she would encourage our interest in OBEs and even ask us to help with her research but we were to be disappointed by this self-proclaimed 'genius' and 'academic exile'. It is fair to say that we were young, ignorant and probably rather arrogant, but we were not invited back.

Many definitions have been used since Green's pioneering work. Some state that the experience must not be a dream (Alvarado, 1982) or that the person must 'seem to be awake' (Bünning and Blanke, 2005), but this just adds complications. To my mind the best definitions are the simplest. For Harvey Irwin, an Australian parapsychologist and author of *Flight of Mind* (1985), 'An out-of-body experience is one in which the center of consciousness appears to the experient to occupy temporarily a position which is spatially remote from his/her body' (Irwin, 1985, p.5) and for others it is, 'An experience where you felt that your mind or awareness was separated from your physical body' (Gabbard & Twemlow, 1984, pp.3–4). Both mean that if people 'feel' they are out of the body, this counts as an OBE.

Finally, John Palmer is an American parapsychologist who, like me, has worked on OBEs since the 1970s. He defines them as 'any experience where the person believes that his consciousness is localized in space outside his physical body' (Palmer, 1978a in *Rogo*, p.35), stressing that the experience of being out of the body is not equivalent to the fact of being out and 'the OBE is neither potentially nor actually a psychic phenomenon' (1978b, p.19).

This statement has often been misunderstood but what Palmer says is a natural consequence of all these experiential definitions. A personal experience can take any form imaginable and be as bizarre as you like, but it cannot – of itself – be paranormal or psychic. It is only in relation to other external events that an experience becomes psychic, such as when a dream 'comes true', an apparition coincides with a person's death, or an OBEr sees correct details at a distant place. So we are dealing with an experience that may turn out to be associated with ESP and paranormal events – that may turn out to imply consciousness beyond the body – but may not. With these definitions we are free to find out.

So I stick to the definition I gave in *Beyond the Body*: 'An experience in which a person seems to perceive the world from a location outside their physical body'. This is simple and sufficient. It means that if someone claims to have been on the ceiling looking down, then they have, by this definition, had an OBE. It means all our four examples, including mine, are OBEs.

This also means that we can exclude many kinds of visions, apparitions and other hallucinations because they do not entail seeing or hearing the world from outside the body. For example, when someone wakes in the night to see the ghostly form of a friend hovering at the end of their bed, or feels the approach of an alien abductor, who whisks them away to a distant planet, this would not count, nor would feeling dissociated without changing location, nor would the common hallucinations of hearing voices, feeling bugs under the skin, or seeing rows of animals, imps, fairies or mechanical creatures.

Ordinary dreams don't count either because on waking we don't typically think we were seeing the real world; 'it was just a dream,' we say. People do not say that after an OBE. They say, 'This was real' or even, 'This was more real and I felt more alive than I've ever felt in my life before.'

More relevant are lucid dreams in which we know we are dreaming. As we shall see, these turn out to be closely related to OBEs. Even so, they do not count as OBEs because with lucidity comes the knowledge that the dreamer is asleep and the sights, sounds and feelings make up a dream world; a world that dreamers can even manipulate, control and have fun with. The lucid dreamer is a player in this dream world, not an observer that seems to have left its body.

Some other experiences are more easily confused with OBEs.

## Doppelgängers and bilocating saints

Tales of someone appearing in two places at once abound in popular mythology. The Norwegians tell of the Vardøger, a kind of spirit or duplicate person that can arrive at a destination before the flesh-and-blood one gets there. In Cumberland, in the north of England, such apparitions of the living were called swarths and revealed a double that could only be seen by those with 'second sight'. Then there are the old English wraith, the Scottish taslach, the Irish fetch, the German doppel-gänger and the Finnish etiäinen or 'first comer'. Sometimes these doubles have sinister overtones, predicting death or calamity, but more often they are said to be harmless.

Although these phenomena may suggest a double, they are not OBEs. In the folk tales of fetches and wraiths the double is an unconscious automaton, and its 'owner' may know nothing about it. For example, if my fetch were to arrive at the pub before me I would not be aware of the fact. I might turn up later to find it had already ordered a pint of bitter and a packet of peanuts and the barman was waiting for his money. In OBEs it is the conscious, observing self that seems to be outside the body, not a visible but mindless duplicate.

In rare cases a double is seen alongside the real person. In a famous, though uncorroborated, story from the 1840s, a 32-year-old French schoolteacher called Mademoiselle Emilie Sagée was sacked from her nineteenth post because of double trouble. Apparently, girls at the school saw two Mlle Sagées writing on the blackboard, two at din-ner and two walking around the school. When parents began to remove their daughters from the school, the director chose instead to remove Mlle Sagée.

The most dramatic tales of bilocation appear in religious contexts, as miracles promoting the supernatural powers of saints, yogins or sufis. The Catholic Church is especially fond of such tales. For example, on Holy Thursday in 1226, Saint Anthony of Padua knelt to pray in the Church of St Pierre-du-Queyroix at Limoges, pulled his cowl over his head and at the same moment appeared at the other end of the town at another service. Saint Alphonsus Liguori was said to have gone into a trance while preparing to celebrate mass in 1774. When he awoke he said that he had been at the deathbed of Pope Clement XIV in Rome, four days' journey away. The news came later that not only had the Pope died, but those at his bedside had seen and talked to the saint and joined him in prayers.

In Hinduism are many accounts of gurus and swamis bilocating, levitating, materialising objects out of thin air and performing other supernatural feats, some of them in recent times. In one case, the popular spiritual teacher known as Dadaji emerged from his prayer room and instructed one of his followers to ask her sister-in-law in Calcutta whether he had been seen there. The report came back that the Mukherjee family had all seen Dadaji appear in their study and ask for tea. Later he had vanished from the room, leaving a half-eaten biscuit and a still-burning cigarette. Of course the story was told some time after it happened and many interpretations are possible. The vision might have been a collective hallucination, an example of ESP, a trick staged by the swami for his own reputation, or it could have coincided with Dadaji having an OBE.

Parapsychologists have long been interested in these potential proofs of paranormal powers and in the 1970s Karlis Osis and Erlendur Haraldsson (1977; Haraldsson, 1988) investigated claims that both Dadaji and Sathya Sai Baba had appeared in two places at once. They concluded that Dadaji had indeed had an OBE but the evidence is weak and no other cups of tea have ever been drunk by a person 'out of the body'. As for Sai Baba, once hailed a living God by millions of followers worldwide, time has revealed a depressingly long trail of fraud, deceit and sexual abuse, though many of his followers remain faithful.

Finally, there is the pathological experience of autoscopy, which literally means 'seeing oneself' but should not be confused with an

OBE – although, sadly, it often is. In an OBE, as we have seen, a conscious, observing self seems to be outside the body and able to see it. Quite the opposite happens in autoscopy, in which patients seem to remain inside their own body, observing the world in the normal way but seeing their own double as though it were another person. I say 'patients' because this kind of autoscopy is nearly always associated with mental illness or brain damage and the experience itself is rather creepy. Just imagine getting up in the morning and seeing a duplicate of yourself sitting in your bedside chair, or walking down to the shops and seeing another 'you' coming towards you.

Such experiences have a long history in literature. Aristotle writes of a madman called Antipheron, who could not go for a walk without seeing a reflection of himself coming towards him. In *The Double*, Dostoyevsky tells of a man who found his double sitting at his own desk. The fact that almost everyone can appreciate the terror of such an experience indicates the potency of the story. But does it tap a deep and poorly understood truth, that we really have a double, or is there some other explanation?

In a related, and perhaps even weirder, experience called heautoscopy, the patient is unclear about which of the two selves is the real one. Having never experienced this, I can barely imagine what that would be like, yet it is widely reported in the psychiatric literature. It turns out that all these different experiences are connected and I will return to consider them later.

One of the many unanswered questions that I'd love to investigate is why OBEs are typically reported by perfectly healthy people, with no history of mental illness, while autoscopy and heautoscopy are almost exclusively pathological. For the moment let's just note that, like bilocation, all these experiences are suggestive of a human double. So what is going on? Is there really some other part of ourselves that sometimes emerges during life and then survives after death?

## The human double

The idea of the double has a long and colourful history in philosophy, as well as folklore and religion, and this itself needs explanation.

Does it reflect the reality of human nature or could there be other explanations for its popularity? Mead (1919), a classical scholar writing a century ago, traced the 'doctrine of the subtle body' as it runs through Western tradition. He found that other bodies appear in many forms and there are schemes with up to seven, or even more, other bodies. If it is not the physical body which sees, but the spirit or some other kind of subtle body, then it seems to follow that the spirit would be better able to see without its cumbersome body.

Plato, in the fourth century BC, describes this intuition so well. In *Phaedrus*, he describes us poor mortals as 'enshrined in that living tomb which we carry about . . . imprisoned in the body, like an oyster in his shell', seeing only a dim reflection of reality. Imprisoned in a gross physical body, our spirit is restricted; released from that body, it could join with the spirits of the departed and see more clearly. In his famous allegory of the cave, chained prisoners see only shadows cast by a great fire behind them that they cannot see. Escaping the cave is painful and hard but is like the soul rising into the world of the mind, where everything is clearer and brighter, healthier and happier. In this purer environment those liberated from their bodies live in bliss and see with true vision. Could this be the clear vision so many OBErs describe?

The ancient Egyptians had complex schemes involving several other bodies apart from the gross physical one. The soul was said to be made up of five parts called the Ren, Ba, Ka, Sheut and Ib. Among these the Ib, or heart, was supposed to survive death, as was the Ba, or personality, which is sometimes depicted as a bird flying out of the tomb to join the Ka, or vital spirit, in the afterlife. The Ka was said to resemble the physical body and stayed near it at death.

Christianity and Islam both teach the existence of a soul or spirit that survives death, as does Judaism, although it places far less emphasis on the afterlife. In modern Hinduism humans are often described as 'embodied souls', but the early Advaita Vedanta tradition rejected this dualism. Advaita literally means 'not-two' in Sanskrit and this spiritual tradition, now increasingly popular, is a form of monism that does away with separate spirits and emphasises non-duality.

Buddhism too has both dualist and nondual traditions. Many followers of Tibetan Buddhism believe in personal reincarnation and hence in some kind of continuing soul, mind-stream or consciousness that passes from one life to the next, and the famous *Bardo Thodol*, or *Tibetan Book of the Dead*, provides guidance to the dying as they pass through the 'bardo' states between death and the next birth. In September 2011, in a message on his website, the fourteenth Dalai Lama declared, 'as long as you are a Buddhist, it is necessary to accept past and future rebirth.' Yet the Buddha himself rejected the idea of a human double, teaching the notion of *anatta*, or no-self, and declaring that there is no permanent, unchanging self or soul, but only streams of phenomena dependently arising and passing away. He likened the self to the collection of parts that make up a carriage. We give it a name even though we know it is just a collection of wheels, chassis and so on. We are the same, he taught – a collection of bones, muscles, blood and brain, with no extra 'self' inside. This ran contrary to all the popular beliefs of his time, as it does to those of our own time. I guess it has always been hard to relinquish the intuition that our precious 'self' is more than a collection of bodily parts.

Having an OBE just makes this harder. Indeed the German philosopher, Thomas Metzinger, believes the whole concept of the soul, and even of the mind, originated from people throughout the ages having such experiences. 'For anyone who actually had that type of experience it is almost impossible not to become an ontological dualist afterwards,' he says (Metzinger, 2005, p.78). This perfectly describes my own reaction: my travels seemed so utterly real, my consciousness so clear, and my flying self so free and alive, that I couldn't see any other explanation than that my soul had left my body.

So what is the truth? There are at least two possibilities here. One is that we have these experiences because there really is a soul. The other is that we invent a mythical soul because we have these experiences. This provides us with the two main, and completely opposed, theories of the OBE:

(a) Duality. *Something leaves the body.* That 'something' might be a soul, a spirit or an astral body, but whatever it is this theory is dualistic. Mind and brain, or soul and body, are separate entities, normally tightly entwined but able to separate briefly during life and permanently upon death.

(b) Nonduality. *Nothing leaves the body*. Dualism is false; mind and brain are not separate and there is no soul. The powerful sense of leaving the body has to be explained some other way, perhaps in terms of biology, psychology or neuroscience.

Here I will add one more possibility, even though it is just a compromise, that there are two kinds of OBE:

(c) A compromise. There are two distinct kinds of OBE: one is the 'real' thing, in which a soul or spirit really does leave. The other is a hallucination or 'fake' OBE.

I want to find out which is true.

CHAPTER 3

# Astral Projection

Astral projection is such a wonderfully exciting idea – implying travel to the stars. When I had that dramatic experience it was the only idea I knew about that could account for it. No wonder I confidently wrote in my diary, 'I went astral travelling'.

By then, in my few weeks of student life and running the OUSPR, I was lapping up ideas about occultism, divination and the magical Order of the Golden Dawn. I read about the Victorian occultist and spirit medium, Madame Blavatsky, who claimed to have travelled the world, studied with Tibetan gurus, contacted the dead and reached higher planes with Hindus and Buddhists. She believed that a hidden spiritual hierarchy called 'the Masters of the Ancient Wisdom' oversaw cosmic evolution, leading humanity inexorably towards the conscious attainment of perfection. In 1875 she co-founded the Theosophical Society, which still exists today.

I loved books by Blavatsky's Theosophical followers, such as Annie Besent and C. W. Leadbeater, who wrote of the 'ancient wisdom', the power of 'thought forms' and 'the seven principles of man'. They always spoke of 'man' even though Besent herself was a feminist, atheist and campaigner for marriage reform.

The idea of thought forms enchanted me and a version of it lurked for many years in my (ultimately abandoned) theories of consciousness and the paranormal. According to this 'ancient wisdom', every thought creates a form and these forms have a life of their own, attracted by similar thoughts, repelled by opposites, making up our dream life, forming apparitions of the deceased and facilitating telepathy and clairvoyance. By learning to concentrate deeply we can produce powerful thought forms that leave behind the mind that created them and continue to exist on another plane. The idea was supposed to have come from Blavatsky's studies in Buddhism but took on a new significance in the Western Occult tradition and especially in the theory of astral projection. So here it is.

## The seven bodies of man

We human beings are not just physical creatures living out our lives like every other animal that has evolved on earth. Instead, according to Theosophy, we are 'that continuing individual who passes from life to life, who comes into bodies and again leaves them, over and over again, who develops slowly in the course of ages, who grows by the gathering and by the assimilation of experience, and who exists on that higher mânasic or mental plane' (Besent, 1896, p.90).

As for those 'bodies', they are seven 'vehicles of consciousness' and we merely use them to function in different regions of the universe, from the grossest physical world to the subtlest and most spiritual realms beyond. Our big mistake is to identify with one or other of these 'outer garments' when really we are the Self that dwells in them (note the capital 'S' for this ultimate self). We must learn, says Besent, to understand this Self as the owner of the vehicle, so that we can step outside of its temporary casing and drop the illusion that we are what we wear. We can exist in far fuller consciousness outside the vehicle than we ever could within it.

Tempting, isn't it? I'm not surprised that I lapped up this stuff at the time.

So what are these seven bodies and their corresponding seven great planes of existence? Schemes vary, which is not surprising given there is no empirical way of detecting or checking them, but a typical list includes:

1. The physical body.
2. The etheric body or vehicle of vitality.
3. The astral body.
4. The manasic or mental body.
5. The causal body.
6. The Buddhic, diamond or cosmic body (there is much less agreement over the higher levels).
7. The celestial, eternal or nirvanic body.

The physical body is, as you would expect, composed of 'ordinary matter' which confines consciousness to physical limitations and the laws of space and time. Closely interwoven with this is the etheric double or 'vehicle of vitality', which is visible to adepts as violet-grey in colour. This, curiously, is an exact duplicate of the physical body, particle for particle, but made of ether. It acts as a kind of transmitter of energy, keeping the lower physical body in contact with the higher bodies and is 'the medium through which play all the electrical and vital currents on which the activity of the body depends' (Besent, 1896, p.6). Because this etheric body interpenetrates the physical, the two separate only rarely, in illness or when close to death. After death the double becomes redundant and dissipates, perhaps briefly forming ghostly wraiths like those sometimes seen in churchyards.

If some of this seems completely mad we should at least remember that in the early days of Theosophy the idea of an interpenetrating ether seemed far more plausible than it does today. Annie Besant tells us that wherever there is electricity there must be the ether, and probably readers of her books would have thought so too, if they knew anything about the physics of the day. This was a time when most scientists still believed in the need for a 'luminiferous ether' to explain the propagation of light because it seemed incomprehensible that waves of light could travel from the sun and the moon through empty space without any medium to carry them. This view remained common until the great Michelson-Morley experiment of 1887 disproved the existence of the ether and presaged a revolution in physics.

Despite this discovery, the idea of the ether persisted in the popular imagination and seemed to provide a haven for the higher planes of Theosophy and spiritualism. A popular book of 1931, by spiritualist Arthur Findlay, was called *On the Edge of the Etheric or Survival after Death Scientifically Explained*. I bought my second-hand copy in 1976 for twenty pence in a Yorkshire bookshop. The forty-first impression, it was printed in 1945 and already translated into eighteen other languages as well as Braille. It was prefaced with gushingly positive reviews from over seventy newspapers. To my amazement it is still for sale today and in 2017 has five-star ratings on both Amazon.com and Amazon UK – why?

The science is appalling and should have seemed so even in the 1930s. Findlay crammed the etheric worlds into then undetected parts of the electromagnetic spectrum, claiming that the etheric world begins just beyond the ultraviolet, depending on 'higher vibrations' that most of us cannot detect. In this 'universe of ether', Mind (note the capital 'M') is King, and all sorts of mental entities survive. Through a spiritualist medium called John Sloan, he spoke with 'Whitefeather' or 'Whitie', who claimed to have been a Red Indian when alive. (And yes, it's no myth that many of the early 'spirit guides' were 'Red Indians' and in the twenty-first century 'Native American' spirit guides are as popular as ever.) Findlay assures us these feats 'are not produced by any means of trickery' and that he heard the voices of 'friends who, in my ignorance, I had looked upon as dead' (Findlay, 1931, p.12). These spirits, he explained, can reach us by borrowing a 'certain excretion' from the medium's body, by which they 'materialise their vocal organs and thus vibrate our atmosphere'. This 'ectoplasm' can even be seen with our own physical eyes when exuded from the orifices of the medium to create a misty shape or even a fully formed human apparition! Reading about all this I longed to see ectoplasm for myself and, full of hope, joined many séances.

## A physical séance

At the London Society for Psychical Research several senior members swore they had seen ectoplasm with their own eyes. I came to know them well, being elected to the Executive Council and attending many meetings at their offices in the delightfully named 'Adam and Eve Mews'. Arthur Ellison was a professor of Electrical Engineering and twice president of the SPR. He said he had seen ectoplasm, felt spirit touches and even seen a complete human figure that walked around and then disappeared into the floor. Could this highly intelligent man have been tricked or deluded?

Over the years, as I gradually became more sceptical, I was often excluded from finding out for myself. I was dubbed a 'psi-inhibitory experimenter', meaning that psychic phenomena disappeared when my sceptical 'vibrations' were around. So psychical researchers became reluctant to have me come and ruin their experiments or researches into spiritualism. The psychologist David Fontana (1991) refused to let me near the site of the famous Cardiff poltergeist because my presence would inhibit the unexplained stone throwing, changes in temperature, objects and money going missing, overpowering smells and clattering noises he was investigating there.

Others took the opposite view and over the years I received invitations from many psychics and mediums hoping to prove me wrong. But it was not until 2011 that I joined my first 'physical séance' – that is, a séance meant to demonstrate such 'physical phenomena' as objects moved by spirits, things appearing or disappearing, disembodied voices speaking from the 'other side' and materialised spirits touching our arms or hair.

We convened in a specially converted garden shed with total blackout and, as in the heyday of spiritualism, there was a 'cabinet' in one corner where the medium could sit behind a curtain while his spirit guide, 'Yellow feather' (yes, it really was another Native American), took control of the medium's voice. Before we began I was encouraged to inspect the whole place. I checked for obvious tricks like trapdoors, removable arms on the chair or useful objects hidden in the cabinet, but I'm no magician and I did not find anything suspicious.

Really, I needn't have bothered. What was amazing was the nonchalance with which the assembled group of regular séance-goers took the whole event. There was no chanting or singing or holding hands to start us off; no deep breathing or relaxation; there was nothing to encourage an altered state of consciousness or group hallucinations. Yet there we sat as the medium was tied to his chair with ropes, the curtain was closed and the lights extinguished to leave us in total darkness. Then – and this is the bit I remember most clearly – to 'raise the vibrations' the music was turned on. For several hours we strained to hear the croaky voice of spirit guides above the jolly tunes of ABBA.

It is true that objects moved in the dark. A small table, a box and a cardboard 'trumpet' had been marked with luminous paint so they could be seen dancing about in the air. It is true that the medium was said to have disappeared, as confirmed by one of the sitters, who reached into the cabinet and declared he could feel only an empty chair. It is true that at times the spirit voice seemed to be coming from the ceiling (was the medium levitating?). It is true that Yellow Feather told us about life in the beyond, but I never saw any ectoplasm and nothing I witnessed was remotely convincing.

Then, as now, I mused on the fact that if any of this were true, most of science would be overthrown. The discovery of etheric matter, ectoplasm, or spirits of the dead would change for ever our understanding of the universe and I have always admired those few great scientists who have taken the possibility seriously and put it to the test. One such was Michael Faraday, who was intrigued by spiritualist claims of 'table tipping' in which tables slid about, tipped up or even lifted into the air when mediums and their circle of sitters placed their hands lightly on the surface. With ingenious experiments involving little pieces of card and slippery glue, Faraday (1853) showed that the sitters' hands were pushing the table, not the table pulling the hands. He promptly went back to studying electricity and magnetism.

There are no great scientists trying to find evidence of spirit forces today, only little groups of keen sitters like the one I attended. When all the excitement was over, the lights turned on and ABBA thankfully turned off, our little band of friendly folk retired to the house for tea and cake and a pleasant chat.

Why do these shows continue? Is it just the longing for evidence of life after death that makes for such enduring popularity? This is certainly a powerful motivation and we'll find it again in modern accounts of near-death experiences. Whatever the reason, the idea of communicating with dead spirits has continued to thrive despite the fact that physics quickly filled in those parts of the electromagnetic spectrum that Theosophy had adopted, and neuroscience began to understand the workings of the human brain.

But back to the theories; beyond the etheric lies the realm most relevant to our quest, the astral world and its associated astral body. According to Theosophy, these are finer than their etheric counterparts and correspondingly harder to see. There are seven grades of astral matter and in addition all physical atoms have 'astral envelopes'. This means that all objects in the physical world have a replica in the astral. Yet the astral world is more than just a replica. It has seven subdivisions containing things that have no counterpart in the physical. There are the colourful and variously shaped thought forms created by human minds; there are elementals, given form by human thought and animated by desire and emotion; there are vampires, werewolves and animal spirits; there are fairies and guardian angels; and there are the lowest and most miserable of the dead, who have risen no further than the astral world since they left their physical body for good. All are ably described in lurid detail by Leadbeater in *The Astral Plane: Its Scenery, Inhabitants and Phenomena* (1895).

Some of these entities can be summoned for use in ritual magic and thought forms can be specially created to carry out tasks such as healing, carrying messages or gaining information. It's strange to remember now but back in the 1970s I not only sat with spiritualist mediums and joined séances to summon up the dead but began training in magic. In early lessons we practised honing our imagination to create stable thought forms. We learned chants, rituals and spells to direct healing powers from the astral. I even, briefly, joined a coven and took part enthusiastically in pagan rituals. But when it came to making my own sandals and sewing my robe I decided not to become a witch after all. Perhaps it was not just a dread of sewing but a growing scepticism combined with increasing distrust of the young man who acted as teacher and High Priest and terrified me with lifts on the back of his speeding motorbike.

Yet the ideas remained tempting in many ways. For example, there's the whole concept of the human aura. I could not forget that shimmering, ghostly shape that I had seen around my own body and the bodies of my friends. Nothing I had learnt in my school science or degree courses came near to providing an explanation, nor even an admission that such things happen, but astral projection theory does: the various higher bodies can be seen by those who have the gift. And apparently lots of people have the gift.

## Seeing auras

The spirit medium Ursula Roberts, who died (I mean 'passed over') in 1996, channelled the teachings of her 'Red Indian' spirit guide Ramadahn (yes, another Red Indian to join the 'highly evolved spirits' from Atlantis or ancient Egypt). She described auras as like the skins of an onion, one inside the other. The etheric body forms just an outline around the physical, appearing as silvery radiance in the healthy but a dull grey in those who are tired or ill; the astral or psychic aura is larger, colourful and flame-like in shape; the even greater spiritual aura is 'radiated by souls who consciously send out healing, light, and loving thoughts, through their spiritual will' (Roberts, 1975, p.8).

The etheric, she claims, is most commonly seen. Was this the whitish, gently moving stuff that I saw? Could I have seen my friends' etheric auras and then touched, though not seen, their larger astral auras? Psychics and mystics often describe the astral aura as like a glowing flame, small and nebulous in an undeveloped and materialistic person but larger and brighter in a highly developed or spiritual person, even to the point that the aura of the Buddha or of Jesus Christ could fill the whole world. Would this mean that my friend Kevin was more spiritually developed than Vicki? Surely not.

In addition to its size, trained psychics claim to use the colours of a person's aura to read their personality, emotions and thoughts. According to Besent and Leadbeater, clear blues are the colours of spirituality and yellows reveal intellectual development. Pride shows up as bright red, while selfishness and depression are various shades of brown. There are two problems here. First, not everyone agrees about what each colour means. Second, as with other forms of divination, aura reading usually provides vague and mainly positive statements that most people believe are true of themselves but not of others – this is the so-called 'Barnum Effect'.

I recently looked into just one colour, yellow, in a variety of books and websites. One site divides yellow into different shades that can mean spiritual inspiration, fear of loss or latent psychic abilities. Another claims that 'Yellow Aura people are analytical, logical and very intelligent'. A Reiki healing site relates yellow to the spleen and 'life energy' and, echoing some of the first site I visited word for word, lists so many possible characteristics that any reading becomes meaningless. Everyone can find something true about them in this list: 'emerging psychic and spiritual awareness' (I cannot count how many times psychics, Tarot readers and clairvoyants have told me that I have latent psychic powers), 'optimism and hopefulness' (another good one), 'awakening, inspiration, intelligence and action shared, creative, playful, optimistic, easy-going', 'struggling to maintain power and control in a personal or business relationship; fear of losing control, prestige, respect and/or power' (is there anyone who doesn't like to be told they are intelligent and creative or sometimes fears losing control?).

Delving more thoroughly into aura colours, psychologist Andrew Neher (2011, pp.188–9) found incompatible claims about both size and colour. For example, the famous psychic Edgar Cayce describes red as increasing with over-work to the point of nervous breakdown, while Ursula Roberts claims that 'the colour of earthly love is red'.

In principle, if auras could reliably be seen, these claims could be tested. Aura-seers could record the colours and sizes of the auras of a group of volunteers and then psychologists could test those volunteers for personality type, stress, happiness, intelligence and so on. For example, IQ tests could show whether people with yellow in their auras score higher. The results might reveal that some of the psychics were right and others were wrong and we could then rely on the ones who got it consistently right. We might even be able to train people to see auras more clearly, and so turn aura-reading into a useful psychological tool.

But none of this has happened.

## Testing aura-seeing

A different kind of aura test has been damning. This is Charles Tart's 'doorway test' – designed to find out whether there is any sense in which auras are actually present in the space around a person's body. The idea is very simple: if a psychic can see a person's aura sticking out around their body then they should be able to see that aura whether or not the body is visible as well. So Tart (1972) suggested the following test, shown in Figure 3.1.

First, a psychic (let's call him Jim) is asked whether he can clearly see the aura of a target person (we'll call her Julie). If he confirms that he can, he stands facing an open doorway while Julie goes through the doorway and stands behind the wall. She then takes up one of two positions: In position (A) she is well away from the edge of the doorway and so neither her physical body nor her aura should be visible to Jim; at position (B) she stands very close to the edge of the doorway, so Jim still cannot see her physical body but he ought to be able to see her aura protruding past the side of the doorframe. For a good experiment Julie should take up each position several times, an experimenter choosing the position randomly so that Jim cannot guess where she is likely to be. All Jim has to do is say whether or not he sees Julie's aura. Tart and Palmer (1979) tried this test with the well-known psychic healer, Matthew Manning, but in ten trials he was no more accurate than would be expected by chance.

I have tried this test informally without success, as have others (Neher, 2011). Among proper experiments, one study tested ten people who claimed to see auras, along with a control group who did not (Gissurarson & Gunnarsson, 1997). Four screens were placed in a row and an experimenter stood behind one of them. The aura-seer then came into the room and had to say which screen had someone hidden behind it. Each group completed eighteen sessions of forty trials each. So if anyone could see the 'auric emanations streaming out

**Figure 3.1: The doorway test for auras.** The psychic claimant, Jim, says he can see Julie's aura around her body. For the test he stands facing an open doorway while Julie takes up one of two possible positions. At position (A) Jim cannot see either her or her aura; at position (B) Jim cannot see her body but should still be able to see her aura sticking out past the side of the doorframe. On each trial Jim must say whether he sees the aura or not. The test should be done many times with Julie's position randomly chosen. There is no published evidence that anyone has ever passed this test, suggesting that whatever auras are, they are not physically present in the space around the body.

from behind the screen' they were given ample opportunity. The results were clear: the aura-seers chose the correct screen 185 times and the control group 196 times. Neither of these totals is significantly different from the 180 that would be expected by pure chance guessing. The aura-seers who took part were mostly surprised and upset by their failure. They genuinely seemed to be seeing colours around people and could not understand why they failed. Something is going on here, but what?

The same idea has been used in those glitzy television shows where mediums and psychics perform their miracles on brightly lit stages with spooky music and special effects. In 1991 I took part regularly in a TV series called *James Randi: Psychic Investigator* in which Randi, ex-magician and perhaps the most famous sceptic ever, would stride onto the stage in his flowing black cape and put various psychics, including aura-seers, to the test.

Randi was then offering huge prizes to anyone who could prove their psychic ability, starting in 1964 with a prize of $1,000, rising to a million dollars in the 1990s and finally ending in 2015. In all this time over a thousand people were tested but none won the million dollars and Randi was frustrated by the many famous psychics who refused to apply. Some said that he cheated, preventing people from winning when they had genuine powers, but this is not how it appeared to me.

One show tested an aura-seer. First, Randi asked her to look at a group of people and say whether she could see their auras around and above them. She confirmed that she could and agreed that the test was fair. This step is crucial, as I learned from Randi, because there's no point testing a claim that the psychic does not make. In this case a row of screens just taller than the people being looked at was placed on stage. Out of sight of the psychic, some of the people went and stood behind screens while other screens were left empty. Then Randi asked the psychic to come on stage and say which screens had auras rising over the top. She was sure that she would succeed, but she did not.

In a similar TV show in the US, the Berkeley Psychic Institute sent their top aura-reader to try the same test and again she failed, claiming to see auras above twenty screens when only six had someone standing behind them (Carroll, 2003). Once again auras do not seem to be physically present in the way that most aura-seers say they are.

One final claim is that auras can be captured with Kirlian photography. This method, invented in 1939 by the Russian engineer Semyon Kirlian, involves placing photographic paper or film over a metal plate connected to a high-voltage, high-frequency power supply. With brief exposures this method does indeed produce auras surrounding, for example, a finger, a hand or even a coin or a leaf.

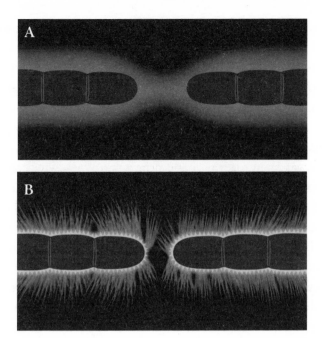

**Figure 3.2: The Kirlian aura.** Claims are often made that Kirlian photography detects the aura purportedly seen by psychics. In fact the Kirlian effect is due to corona discharge, a well understood effect of connecting a photographic plate to a high-voltage source. An additional reason for doubting the claims is that when two psychics reach out their fingers towards each other they claim that the auras stretch across the gap (A) as happened in my own experience. In the Kirlian photographs that I took it is clear that the corona discharges repel each other (B), as would be expected from two similarly charged objects.

This effect is, however, the well-understood phenomenon of corona discharge caused by the ionisation of an electrically charged conductor.

In 1975, before I knew anything about the physics involved, I bought a Kirlian machine and took dozens of pictures, developing them myself in our bathroom 'darkroom'. I was gradually disillusioned by what I found. The final straw came when I thought to photograph two fingers pointing towards each other. I remembered that when I had seen auras after my OBE, I could reach out towards Kevin or Vicki's hands and their auras would stretch out towards mine. It was a rather nice feeling and I subsequently discovered that mediums and aura-seers describe a similar effect. But Kirlian photography does not. Place two fingers pointing at each other on the plate and the 'aura' of each repels the other – just as would be expected from two negatively charged objects coming together (Figure 3.2). The corona discharge is not the etheric or astral aura.

So what did I see and touch? I am happy to believe that, like all the psychics and mediums tested, I would fail the doorway test. Yet this experience of seeing my own and others' auras was vivid, as was the sense of feeling it with my hands around Kevin's body. And I am not alone. In a survey in Iceland, 5 per cent of the public said they had seen auras (Haraldsson, 1985), and in the US, 5 per cent of the public and 6 per cent of students did (Palmer, 1979). Many OBErs claim to see objects as transparent or glowing, or with auras around them so there is some connection here, but if the aura is not a physically existing emanation around the human body, what is it?

Could it be imaginary, even though it appears so realistic? The failure of doorway tests led some researchers to think so (Gissurarson & Gunnarsson, 1997) and others have tried to find out. Carlos Alvarado and Nancy Zingrone at the University of Edinburgh compared nineteen aura-seers with a control group who had never seen auras and found they scored higher on both the Vividness of Visual Imagery Questionnaire and the Inventory of Childhood Memories and Imaginings. They more often saw apparitions, had mystical experiences and 'seeing with eyes closed' – a strangely interesting experience I shall return to many times; they also had more OBEs. So this confirms a link between OBEs and auras, and gives a clue that imagination is involved, but why are auras typically seen as right there in physical space? Tart concludes that an imagined aura with no objective existence is projected beyond the seen body, but how?

The most promising idea involves synaesthesia, a mixing of the senses, in which sounds can become colours or tastes have shapes. Many children experience the world this way but lose the ability with age, leaving some adults with weak synaesthesia and just a few (about 4%) as true synaesthetes. In the most common type of synaesthesia, colour-grapheme synaesthesia, one person might see the number two as green and three as orange, while another sees two as blue and three as lurid pink. These colours leap out from written text and have been shown to last for decades, if not a lifetime (Ramachandran & Hubbard, 2001; Cytowic & Eagleman, 2009). Some synaesthetes associate colours with human faces but a study of four such people found that their experiences were not like seeing auras (Milán et al., 2012). Even so, others do report aura-like experiences. So could the colours of the aura come about through synaesthesia? Might the aura-seer look at a person and involuntarily convert their impressions into colour?

In their classic study of LSD, a psychedelic drug with a reputation for inducing synaesthesia (Luke & Terhune, 2013), Masters and Houston found 'a fairly common experience where the subject seems to himself to project his consciousness away from his body and then is able to see his body as if he were standing off to one side of it or looking down on it from above'. Some LSD users said they could 'move about in something like the "astral body" familiar to occultists' and 'Some identify this astral body with an "aura" they earlier had perceived as radiating from them, an "energy force field" surrounding the body'. The researchers concluded that the 'perception of the aura by psychedelic subjects is very common' (Masters & Houston, 1967, p.86).

There does seem to be a link between OBEs and auras but I am far from satisfied that we understand the aura.

## On to the astral planes

What then of astral projection itself? According to the theory, the astral body is the 'vehicle of consciousness', not our physical body with its nervous system and senses. This is why it can leave the lower bodies behind to go travelling on the astral planes. But if the astral body can see without using physical eyes, we have to wonder why we need them in the first place. And conversely, if we do need them, how is the astral body supposed to see without them?

The distinguished Cambridge vision scientist, William Rushton, provides a delightful objection. Writing in a letter to the Society for Psychical Research in 1976, he asked,

What is this OOB eye that can encode the visual scene exactly as does the real eye, with its hundred million photoreceptors and its million signalling optic nerves? Can you imagine anything but a replica of the real eye that could manage to do this? But if this floating replica is to see, it must catch light, and hence cannot be transparent, and so must be visible to people in the vicinity. In fact floating eyes are not observed, nor would this be expected, for they only exist in fantasy.

Rushton, 1976, p.412

Is his argument as damning as it appears? I think so. For why, if there is such a useful, mobile, light and invisible perceiving double, should we bother with all the complex, evolved paraphernalia of eyes, muscles, nerves and a massive brain, with nearly a quarter of its cortex devoted to vision?

The answer, from believers in astral projection, is that the astral body is not seeing the physical world at all but is travelling in the astral world. It therefore sees not physical objects, but their astral counterparts, as well as all the thought forms and non-physical beings that live there. It sounds like a crowded place and because of the effect of thought on the astral is sometimes known as the 'world of illusion' or 'world of thought'. Mediums may warn that the unwary astral traveller can become lost or confused by the power of his own imaginings. If all this is true it means that we do need our brains and nervous systems after all; they see the physical world, while astral vision sees the higher realms.

There remains the question of how these different bodies and worlds are connected and why our astral bodies don't get lost. This is where the silver cord comes in. It is said that in life the astral body is connected to its physical body by an infinitely elastic but strong cord, of a flowing and delicate silver colour. In spontaneous astral projection the traveller sometimes sees this cord stretching back to his body and can use it to return to the body, while experts can often do without it. As one approaches death, the astral body gradually loosens itself, rises above the physical and then the cord breaks to allow the higher bodies to leave. Death is therefore a form of permanent astral projection, and one in which the essential Self survives and goes on to higher worlds. The task of a true student of Theosophy is to progress through all of these many incarnations until the highest spiritual state is achieved.

Some people have seen references to astral projection in the Bible. For example, Paul's conversion on the road to Damascus has been claimed as evidence that Jesus was able to project at will, as have Christ's ascent into heaven and resurrection; but most often cited is Paul's reference to a spiritual body (1 Corinthians 15, 35–38) and this short passage from Ecclesiastes (12.6): 'Or ever the silver cord be loosed, or the golden bowl be broken, or the pitcher be broken at the fountain, or the wheel broken at the cistern'. Others claim the bowl refers to the skull and the cord to the spine, or to other completely different metaphors.

So did I really see and feel the silver cord? Would I have died had it broken, leaving me lost and unable to find my way back to Oxford? There are enormous problems with the whole idea. First, as we shall see, very few OBErs actually report any connecting cord and those who do tend to write in terms of astral projection theory. That theory can account for the rarity of silver cords but only by claiming that some people's astral sight is weak, or their cord was very thin and nearly invisible, or they were sufficiently spiritually advanced not to need it, but a theory this stretchable becomes so weak as to be useless.

Nevertheless, cords are reported often enough to require some kind of explanation. Perhaps they represent the person's fear of losing their way home, but in this case why are they always said to be a shimmery grey or silver, as mine was? Perhaps they are a self-fulfilling prophecy with those who read about astral projecting inventing them in their imagination. In my case, since I had already read about silver cords, this is possible. Also, I have weak synaesthesia. So perhaps the cord, like the aura, becomes visible through this synaesthetic combining of the senses. Even so, there is surely much more to find out about the origins of the silver cord.

## Another world?

Underlying all these questions is confusion over whether the astral body and world are part of our familiar physical world or are evidence for a non-physical world that few of us can see. In *Beyond the Body* (1982) I tried to make sense of three possibilities.

The first is that the astral body travels in the physical astral world but this is fraught with problems and I concluded that the only form in which it could survive would be something like this:

> There is a second physical body that we all possess but that only some people can see. It can leave the body and travel on its own seeing the world around it, but it cannot be detected because it is made of some kind of matter that is as yet unknown and it travels by some unknown energy and it sees rather poorly using a mechanism about which nothing is known except that it does not use light, or any other readily detectable form of energy.
>
> Blackmore, 1982a, p.229

A second possibility is that the astral is a non-physical or mental double that travels in the physical world. But this is just a form of mind-body dualism and faces all the same problems. How could a non-physical body interact with the physical world? If it is to observe the physical world then it must interact with it and so be detectable. If it does not interact with it, then the whole theory of astral projection collapses into subjective experience.

Finally, could a non-physical double travel in a non-physical world? For this to be anything more than a private, subjective world, as in dreams or hallucinations, this non-physical astral world must somehow be shared, but how? In traditional astral projection theory the astral eyes see replicas of physical things. Yet all the problems of interaction beset these replicas too.

Astral projection and all its associated worlds are tempting if you want to progress to the highest spiritual realms and survive after death. But if you do, you have to take on a set of theories that are self-contradictory, illogical, scientifically illiterate and so flexible that almost anything can be encompassed within them.

So should we despair of astral projection? No, not entirely. These famous adventurers were trying to describe their experiences as best they could with the tools available. Even if their theories are completely unconvincing we still have much to learn from the experiences they describe.

CHAPTER 4

# The Astral Travellers

S ome stories of astral projection are so bizarre that it is tempting to dismiss them as fantasies concocted by deluded occultists but this would be a mistake. Their accounts may be annoyingly entangled with astral projection lore but then no experience is ever completely free of our attempts to explain it. My own OBE was influenced not only by the science of the time but by what little I knew about astral projection, and it was to these famous tales of astral projection that I first turned for help. Even if the theories are implausible, the sheer courage and adventurousness of these astral travellers has to be admired.

## Muldoon and Carrington

Hereward Carrington was a well-known psychical researcher and author of books about spiritualism, ghosts, psychic photography, plant and animal souls, and evidence for life after death. In *Modern Psychical Phenomena* (1919), he wrote confidently about 'the voluntary projection of the "astral body" of man – the expulsion of the human "double" or etheric counterpart of the physical body – by methods under control of the human will' (Carrington, 1919, p.146). He included photographs and sketches of projected astral bodies showing their structure and 'vital radiations', but with no experiences of his own his account was based entirely on the work of a French occultist, Dr Charles Lancelin.

Then in 1927 he received a powerful letter from a young American called Sylvan Muldoon, saying, 'you make the remark that M. Lancelin has told practically all that is known on the subject. Why, Mr Carrington, I have never read Lancelin's work, but if you have given the gist of it in your book, then I can write a book on the things that Lancelin does not know!'

Muldoon went on to provide a wealth of details about the astral world, the silver cord and the formation and movement of the double, and Carrington was hooked. He contacted Muldoon, and together they wrote two classic books. *The Projection of the Astral Body* (1929) was mainly an account of Muldoon's own experiences while *The Phenomena of Astral Projection* (1951) was a collection of cases sent in from around the world.

Muldoon's first conscious projection happened when he was twelve years old. He awoke in the middle of the night to find himself fully aware, but not knowing where he was, and apparently unable to move. Later he referred to this as 'astral catalepsy' and it is presumably what we now call 'sleep paralysis'. Gradually he felt a sensation of floating, then a rapid up-and-down vibration, and finally a tremendous pressure in the back of his head. Out of this nightmare of sensations his hearing gradually began to return and then his sight, until he could see that he was floating above his bed. A force took hold of him and pulled him up from horizontal to vertical. Looking down, he could see his body lying quietly asleep on the bed, with an elastic cable joining the back of his head to a spot between the eyes of the body six feet or so below him. Swaying and pulling against the cord, he tried to walk to another room to wake someone up, but found that he passed right through the door and when he tried to shake or clutch at other sleepers he passed right through them as well.

Frightened, he roamed the house for about fifteen minutes until the pull of the cord increased, he was dragged back to his body and everything went in reverse. He tipped back to horizontal, became unable to move again, felt the same vibrations and then, with a jerk, dropped back into his body.

After this, Muldoon had hundreds more projections but his levels of consciousness varied and not every projection included all the features he wrote about. First he described the astral catalepsy which lasts until the phantom, or double, has become vertical. Then there is the astral cord, or cable, which is much thicker when the phantom is close to the physical body and can exert a powerful pull. This he called 'cord activity range' which stretches from about eight to fifteen feet. Only when the astral body escapes cord activity range can it move about freely and then the cord is stretched as thin as a sewing thread.

Once away from the physical body, he described three moving speeds, which feel rather familiar to me. At slow speed the astral body simply walks about in the immediate environment. At intermediate

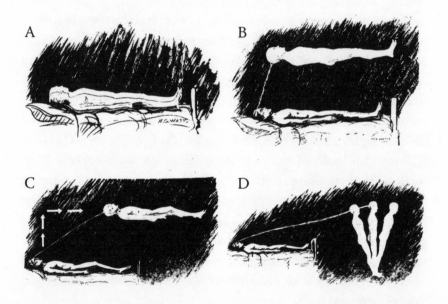

**Figure 4.1: Projection of the Astral Body.** In *The Projection of the Astral Body* (1929), Muldoon and Carrington illustrate the stages that the astral body goes through as it separates from the physical. A. The phantom is slightly out of coincidence with the body, B. The phantom rises above the body, C. The route the phantom takes when projecting, D. The phantom is projected, upright and able to move.

speed it moves without effort and seems to stay still while everything else moves backwards through and past it. 'The phantom does not seem to pass through the door; the door seems to pass through the phantom' (Muldoon & Carrington, 1929, p.13). This is rather like being in a fast train but with streaks of light or phosphorescent 'scintillations' trailing behind the astral form. Finally, at its fastest the phantom can cover great distances without being aware of them, faster than the mind can imagine.

Others have described similar ways of moving. For example, in *Practical Astral Projection* (1935), Yram (presumably a pseudonym from 'Mary' backwards) mentions moving just as in the physical body when in the house or walking about the streets, but moving by thought alone when projected into space. At first he did breaststroke, like swimming, then floated on his back and finally discovered that he could move from place to place instantaneously. Those descriptions make me reflect on how we 'travel' in our imagination. If I now think about the other end of this room, I seem to turn around, leave my desk and slowly move there. If I think about the kitchen, I seem to slide there much faster. And if I think about Oxford, there's a moment of blur, a faint sense of a map and north-easterly direction, and then I am there. None of this seems real, as it does in an OBE, but this similarity might give us a clue.

Both Muldoon and Yram thought in terms of energy and 'vibrations', although not in a way that makes any sense in terms of physics. The reason the astral body can pass through objects, Muldoon says, is because of its high vibration rate, and the further from the physical it moves, the higher this rate becomes. He argued that projection, or partial projection, is far more common than most people realise, explaining all sorts of ordinary experiences this way. Anaesthesia and fainting force the astral body out; falling and flying dreams are a kind of projection. And among the signs of leaving the body are the muscle twitches and jerks we now know as myoclonus, or 'hypnic jerks' when they occur on falling asleep. Even car sickness, he thought, happens because the astral body keeps on moving when a car stops suddenly.

Critics then, as now, had many objections to the whole idea. Why can astral bodies walk on floors without falling through when they can so easily pass through doors and walls? Why do they often have clothes and even glasses and walking sticks? His reply was that it is not the actual, physical floor that holds the astral up, but habits of thought.

> One thing is clear to me – the clothing of the phantom is *created*, and is not a counterpart of the physical clothing ... Thought creates in the astral, and one *appears* to others as he *is* in mind. In fact the whole astral world is governed by thought. ... As I have observed it, the clothing seems to form out of the coloured aura which surrounds the astral body; that is, when one sees the clothing form ... it seems to form by the aura growing very dense, close to the body.
>
> Muldoon & Carrington, 1951, p.46

I appreciate the care with which Muldoon tries to describe his own experiences, and his conclusion that 'thought creates in the astral', but in so doing he lays bare that fundamental confusion that lurks in all accounts of astral projection. Are the contents of the astral world physical or non-physical; material or mental; objective or subjective? Like many authors before and since, Muldoon tried hard to find evidence of an objective astral world and astral body, as though he feared no one would take his accounts seriously unless he could provide evidence of this kind.

He describes one occasion on which he produced raps that were heard by other people, and another on which he believed his astral body contacted his mother, even though he had fainted and was unconscious. Yet most of his attempts failed. The idea that 'thought creates in the astral' might suggest that the experiences are purely subjective and private but Muldoon remained convinced of the objective reality of the astral world and used the ideas of vibration rates and different kinds of consciousness to explain the many failures. Asking, 'hallucination or reality?' (1936), he was convinced that astral projection is for real.

## Oliver Fox

'Oliver Fox' was the pseudonym of Hugh George Callaway, who was born in northeast London in 1885 and became a short story writer, poet and journalist. Presumably he wanted to keep his occult studies separate from his 'real' work but it is for these that he is known today. *Astral Projection* became a classic, describing his lifetime of explorations into lucid dreaming and OBEs, and the methods he discovered for inducing them.

Fox describes a miserable childhood progressing, as he puts it, 'from illness to illness', dreading sleep because of the frequent nightmares it brought and the frightening apparitions he saw. 'Sometimes, just before falling asleep, I would see through my closed eyelids a number of small misty-blue or mauve vibrating circles ... somewhat resembling a mass of frog's eggs, and only just on the borderline of visibility' (Fox, n.d.. p.19). Then either grinning faces would appear inside them, presaging a nightmare, or little inkpots, saving him from one. So he learned to call on the inkpots to avoid the terror of a bad dream.

The daytime was not all happy either. He especially feared those times when he might be playing with his toys and fall into a reverie. Then a subtle change would come over the room and things would 'go wrong', leaving him feeling temporarily paralysed and afraid.

> I might have, say, one hand resting on the table and one on the back of my chair. The illusion was that I could not remove my hands and that the table and chair were very slowly separating and stretching me, yet at the same time I knew with one part of my mind that they were not *really* moving.

He would then struggle to remove his hands and just as suddenly everything would 'come right' again and he was free (Fox, n.d., p.17).

One night, in the early summer of 1902, when he was sixteen and studying science in Southampton, he had the dream that sparked his life in the occult. He dreamt that he was standing on the pavement outside his house but there was something odd about the scene; the 'little rectangular stones' that made up the pavement seemed to have changed position in the night, and were now parallel to the kerb. This mystery was solved when, in a flash of inspiration, he realised that although the sunny morning seemed as real as anything, he was dreaming. At that realisation the quality of everything around him changed: the house, trees, sea and sky all became vivid and alive, and he suddenly felt powerful and free; but the next moment he awoke.

Not knowing anything about such dreams, he called them 'dreams of knowledge', because he had the knowledge of dreaming. This is rather a good name for them, and possibly better than their more common name of 'lucid dreams' because it is the knowledge of dreaming that makes all the difference, not the lucidity or vividness of the dream. Fox found this realisation exhilarating and went on to practise and practise, frustrated at how difficult it was until eventually he mastered the skill.

It was in one of those dreams that Fox found himself both walking along a beach on a sunny morning, and conscious of himself lying in bed. He struggled to maintain this 'dual consciousness' but failed and instead ended up with a terrible pain in his head. As he fought against the pain, suddenly there was a 'click': he was on the beach and free. Once there, he could see other people but they did not seem to be aware of him. Then he began to get frightened. What was the time, how long had he been there, and how was he supposed to get back? Was he dead? A fear of premature burial gripped him. He willed himself to wake up, felt the click in his head again and was back. But he was paralysed. He preferred this to being away from his body, but it took a desperate struggle to move one little finger until he could break the trance and move again.

Starting from these dreams of knowledge Fox began to explore what he knew as the astral planes. The places he visited varied from familiar and ordinary street scenes to countryside of stunning beauty, or buildings unlike any ever built on earth. Sometimes conditions were like those prevailing physically at the time; other times he was enjoying warm sunshine in the middle of the night, or blue skies when it was actually raining. These travels, he concluded, were on the astral plane, while those coinciding with reality were on earth.

Here he forestalls criticism with this comment, 'People who cannot forget or forgive poor Raymond's cigar will get very cross with me when I say that there are electric trams on the astral plane; but there are – unless there is no astral plane, and my trams run only in my brain' (Fox, n.d., p.90).

One of his most interesting observations is that when projected he could never see his physical body. This seems odd because in most spontaneous OBEs people see their own body, usually from above. But Fox had a rather convincing rationale for this: he argued that if he was seeing the astral world when projected, then what he saw should be the astral counterparts of physical objects, including that of his own body. Since his astral body was out travelling, he could not expect to see it still lying in bed.

Why has no one else used this argument? Perhaps some people can see both astral and physical bodies at once but this raises other difficulties. Things are said to look slightly different, or even grossly different, when 'out of the body', and this is supposed to be because one is seeing the astral, not the physical world. But you cannot have it both ways. It seems to me that this clever observation presents yet another challenge to the traditional theory of astral projection.

For many years Fox assumed that he could leave his body only by starting from a dream of knowledge. But one day he was lying down in the afternoon when he found that he could see the pattern on the back of the sofa with his eyes closed. Although still awake he seemed to be in a trance condition. He left his body, found himself in some beautiful countryside and then went back along a street, passing through a horse and van on the way – an experience reminiscent of Muldoon's 'intermediate' speed of travelling.

Like Muldoon, Fox describes different ways of moving in the astral. Arduous flapping of the arms or paddling with the hands seemed to be necessary in a dream of knowledge, but when projected, he could move by will alone. He speculated that the clumsy dream movements might be needed only as an aid to concentration. I find this fascinating because during my own experience I gradually shed many things and actions that I'd originally assumed were necessary, ultimately losing even the sense of having, or being, a body. If my experience had not lasted so long I would probably never have discovered this freedom. If Muldoon is right that, 'Thought creates in the astral', this is only to be expected. If I assume I must have a body, then a body I will have. If I assume flying means flapping my arms, then flap my arms I will. The question, as ever, is whether this reveals the properties of another world, or is a product of how the mind works.

Both Muldoon and Fox desperately wanted to prove that the astral world is more than that. In one of his early travelling dreams Fox apparently succeeded in seeing an exam paper the day before he sat the exam. He remembered only two of the questions because the print kept changing or becoming blurred. This inability to read in lucid dreams is very common, although seeing an actual exam question is not (LaBerge, 1985). One of the questions was unexpected and therefore suggestive of actual travelling but he decided against repeating the experiment because he felt uneasy about the morality of what he was doing. Later, however, he made deliberate experiments, trying the best he could to convince critics of the reality of his adventures. On one occasion he and two college friends tried to meet on the Common in a dream. Two succeeded, dreaming that they met each other, but their third friend was absent. Another time a friend said he would visit Fox one night. That night Fox awoke to see his friend in an egg-shaped cloud of bluish-white light with other colours inside. Yet this was not the success they had hoped for because the friend recalled no matching experience. Fox's explanation was that a 'thought form' may have been unconsciously projected by his friend but the obvious alternative is that Fox saw what he was expecting, and hoping, to see.

Most of Fox's attempts at proof were failures. For example, much later in his life he often seemed to see and speak to his wife when projected but in the morning she denied recalling anything of the meeting. On just one occasion, though, it was different. One of Fox's sweethearts, Elsie, disapproved of his experiments, saying they were evil and offensive to God, but she was even more incensed at his calling her 'a narrow-minded little ignoramus' and said she could visit him that night if she wanted to.

He didn't take her boast seriously but sure enough, that night he saw a large egg-shaped cloud and in the middle of it was Elsie with her hair loose and in a nightdress. He watched her as she ran her fingers along the edge of his desk but when he called her name she vanished. The next day she was apparently able to tell him the layout of his room, and the details of objects in it, although she had never been there. She specifically mentioned a gilt ridge running along the edge of the desk, which Fox himself had not realised was there.

This seemed to Fox to be evidence that could prove his critics wrong, but to me it tells an all too familiar tale. It reminds me of the many psychics who say things like, 'I can see you have a scar on your left knee'. Their client denies having any such scar, takes a look at their knee and discovers, to their great surprise, that they do. There seems to be something about the surprise that makes the claim all the more convincing – 'I didn't know it myself but this psychic knew!'

This is why I included the question, 'Do you have a scar on your left knee?', in a large survey carried out in the *Daily Telegraph* in 1994, exploring people's estimates of probabilities and their belief in the paranormal. Thirty-four per cent of the thousands who replied said they had a scar on their left knee. I wonder how many Edwardian gentlemen's rooms had desks in them and how many of those desks had a gilt ridge. This incident was important for Fox as it seemed to be one of the few occurrences that had to be more than just subjective. But as evidence goes it is hardly spectacular and this event has to be set against his lifetime of failed experiments.

I can understand why Fox, Muldoon and many others so badly wanted to prove that their travels were not just in their own minds, but to me it is their own minds that are more fascinating. In my own OBE I saw chimneys that weren't there and places that didn't exist. Had I really seen verifiable things, either then or later, I might still be pursuing parapsychology, but it was years of repeated failures that eventually made me give it up as leading nowhere (Blackmore, 1996). Instead I want to understand why my experience happened at all and why it took the form it did. For this purpose Fox's stories and discoveries are a wonderful resource, but his rare claims of veridical vision are unimportant.

Having discovered that he could project directly from waking, Fox began to experiment whenever he found time to lie down quietly by himself. He discovered that if he concentrated very hard on a spot in the centre of his forehead, just above the eyebrows, he would eventually hear a click in his head, as though a door had closed behind him. Once that happened he found himself in the astral world with much greater clarity and freedom of movement than he had in his lucid dreams. From this he developed what he called the 'Pineal Door' method of astral projection (Fox, 1920).

## The pineal doorway and third eye

Fox is clear that he uses the term 'pineal' metaphorically but it has long had mystical and occult connotations. The pineal gland is a small structure near the centre of the brain between the two halves of the thalamus. One of its main functions is to produce melatonin, a hormone related to the neurotransmitter serotonin, which is involved in modulating sleep patterns and circadian rhythms. This connection with states of consciousness may have inspired occult ideas but so might René Descartes' choice of the pineal gland as the connecting point between mind and brain.

Descartes, the sixteenth-century French philosopher, developed what must be the most famous dualist theory ever, known as Cartesian dualism. He really struggled to understand how mind and brain, which seem so very different in nature, could relate to each other. His theories of how the body worked were remarkably prescient for the time. He described the body as a machine and the function of nerves and blood vessels in mechanical terms. But when he asked himself how all these machine-like processes gave rise to consciousness he was stumped, as we still are today. In the end he went for duality. There are two kinds of substance, he claimed: extended or material substance, and thinking substance. Unable to understand how the two could interact he chose the pineal gland to connect them, primarily because there is just one pineal gland in the centre of the brain rather than one in each half, like most brain structures. He called the pineal 'the seat of the soul'. It was a brave attempt, but of course this gland is a physical structure itself and gives no clue as to how it might connect brain to mind or consciousness.

But back to the pineal door; in occult theories the pineal gland equates to the 'third eye', or 'eye of Shiva', or 'eye of Horus', located in the middle of the forehead, the spot that Fox concentrated on. In schemes that use the idea of the seven chakras, or energy vortices of the body, the pineal is associated with the seventh chakra, the crown chakra at the top of the head. In related schemes there is a special energy called kundalini. This is normally confined to the base of the spine but the right kind of meditation or spiritual practice can 'awaken kundalini'. Energy then rushes up through the spine like a serpent, releasing its power in the form of heat, tremors and bodily movements as it reaches the crown chakra. This can then lead either to psychological troubles or to spiritual awakening.

The third eye is supposed to give rise to the sixth sense and psychic abilities, and serves a similar function to Descartes' seat of the soul. That is, it connects the lower or grosser physical planes with the higher, finer or more spiritual planes. Pure energy, or prana flows through the pineal gland, allowing the astral body to raise its vibrations and leave through the top of the head, sometimes making a popping sound as it goes. Sadly, none of these occult theories solves the mind–body problem – they just gloss over it with invented 'energies' and non-physical planes and do no better than Descartes did.

We still struggle with the mind–body problem today and with its modern version, the 'hard problem of consciousness', that is, how an objective brain with all its measurable neural processes can give rise to the subjective experiences we call consciousness (Chalmers, 1995). The difficulty of bridging the gulf between the objective world and subjective experiences is so great that few philosophers now accept dualism, especially Descartes' substance dualism, but there is no obvious solution and the problem remains what some have called the 'greatest mystery facing science today'. It is a mystery that has long entranced me and still does (Blackmore, 2010, 2011).

## Robert Monroe

Born in Indiana in 1915, Robert Monroe was a businessman working in radio and communications, who later founded the highly successful Monroe Institute where, for a hefty fee, you can learn how to experience OBEs for yourself using, among other methods, his patented system for producing brainwave synchronisation and binaural beats called 'Hemi-Sync'.

Monroe's first book, *Journeys Out of the Body* (1971), tells how one Sunday afternoon he was lying down for a rest when suddenly a beam of light seemed to come out of the sky, his body began to vibrate and he felt powerless to move, as though held in a vice. The sensations lasted only a moment and stopped when he forced himself to move. Over the following six weeks the same thing happened many times. He always felt the shaking but could not see any actual movement, and it always stopped when he moved. Initially frightened, he decided to face up to the sensations instead of fighting them and found he could stay calm and come to no harm. Then one night the vibrations began again when his arm was hanging out of the bed. As his fingers brushed the rug on the floor they seemed to pass through it and then through the floor to the rough surface of the ceiling below. There he felt a triangular chip of wood, a bent nail and some sawdust before his arm emerged and then touched water. He yanked his arm back and the vibrations faded away. Another time he found himself bouncing against the ceiling, looking down on himself and his wife in bed before diving back into his body.

As Monroe dared to explore further he learned how to induce the experience at will and how to move when out of his body. He claimed that he sometimes succeeded in visiting friends and could describe where they were, what they were doing and even the clothes they were wearing. In his three books he describes in detail the three distinctly different 'locales' in which he travelled.

The first locale corresponds more or less to the normal physical world and it is here that he claimed to see people and events as they happened. Yet, as with so many OBEs, the details were a confusing mixture of right and wrong. In the introduction to Monroe's book the psychologist Charles Tart (1971b) gives a good example. After completing a series of laboratory experiments with Monroe, Tart moved to California, from where he tried a more informal experiment. He telephoned Monroe one afternoon and told him that he and his wife would try to help him to have an OBE that night and come to their home, which he had never seen. That evening Tart randomly selected the time of 11 p.m. California time (2 a.m. where Monroe lived). At the appointed hour Tart and his wife began concentrating, continuing for half an hour and ignoring a phone call at 11.05 p.m.

The next day Tart rang Monroe to ask what had happened. Apparently he had left his body and travelled, with someone guiding him by the wrist, to Tart's house. On returning, he rang to report what he saw. The call Tart had ignored was indeed Monroe, so the time was an excellent match, but Tart adds, 'his continuing description of what our home looked like and what my wife and I were doing was not good at all: he "perceived" too many people in the room, he "perceived" me doing things I didn't do, and his description of the room itself was quite vague' (Tart, 1971b, p.21).

Locale 2 is a further step away from ordinary reality and includes heaven and hell, and all sorts of strange entities who were once in the physical world but now recreate their own familiar environment. 'As you think, so you are' applies in Locale 2, and 'thought is the well-spring of existence'. Moving is entirely brought about by thought, and where you go depends on your innermost desires rather than your conscious plans. Monroe describes some areas as 'closer' to the physical and unpleasant to pass through, while the 'further' places are more pleasant. In traditional occult lore these would be referred to as the lower and higher astral planes. By long experimentation Monroe learned how to navigate them, and on the way fought hostile creatures, willingly and unwillingly indulged in sexual adventures, and was guided by 'Helpers'.

Locale 3 Monroe discovered when he once turned over 180° and found himself looking into a hole in an apparently limitless wall. When he finally got through the hole he found a world much like the physical, but here things get truly bizarre. He describes a world with trees and houses, people and cities, but no electricity. There are vehicles quite different from any on earth (like Fox's astral trams?). The 'second body' in which he travels has weight, is visible and touchable under certain conditions, and able to adopt any form. It uses a 'third force' in addition to electricity and magnetism and he speculates that it might even consist of antimatter – a rather curious suggestion since antimatter would immediately be destroyed on encountering any ordinary matter. Whether anyone else has ever travelled in these three locales is impossible to say.

## Where have we got to?

The adventures of these travellers are fun and fascinating to read but their theories are plain daft: they are not only internally inconsistent and illogical but they contradict each other too. They invoke 'energies' that bear no relation to the make-up of the universe we know about – electromagnetism or gravity, for example. And this conclusion seems inescapable, having considered only three of the most famous astral travellers.

I could add the theories of Yram, who invokes 'radioactivity' to claim that the higher doubles inhabiting the higher planes are more radioactive than the lower ones and their atoms are finer, less dense and more sensitive (though to what I cannot fathom, although that may be because I, too, am less sensitive). Or there are the 'nonphysical dimensions' of Robert Bruce, an Australian psychic who visits the spirit world regularly, has raised kundalini over fifty times, sees auras and has been empowered with clairvoyance. His website and book, *Astral Dynamics* (Bruce, 1999), claim to teach you how to visit these 'levels of existence vibrating at a higher frequency than the known physical universe', which of course makes them 'invisible and undetectable to all scientific means available today'. For him, the etheric is the 'extra factor' that biases quantum jumps to offset the forces of entropy. The etheric realm with its etheric thought forms and 'hyper-dimensional entities' is a superset of the physical, and the astral planes are part of 'an incredibly complex nonphysical dimensional level'.

I can see why so many sceptics dismiss astral travelling as nonsense but in the process they may be dismissing something important. That something is the consistencies to be found in the experiences described. Among ideas that stand out are the paralysis before or after the experience, along with 'vibrations' or shaking, bodily distortions and loud noises. There is the association with lucid dreaming and the sense of being able to 'see with eyes closed'. There is the feeling of passing through a doorway, hole or narrow space, sometimes with a click or popping sound. There may be a silver cord or at least the sense of being pulled back to the body. There are the different ways of 'travelling' and the sense that the worlds seen are created and controlled by thought. And finally, there is the overwhelming vividness and clarity of the experience. Surely we can try to make sense of these consistencies without becoming embroiled in gobbledegook.

# CHAPTER 5

# The Varieties of Astral Experience

It happened on the 18th March 1995, I went to bed at around 10:30 pm and I managed to go to sleep quite quickly. During the night I woke up or should I say opened my eyes and I felt a bit of cramp in my right toes . . . My whole body then stiffened up and I couldn't move any part of my body. . . . it felt as if my whole body was vibrating at a high frequency and I could even feel my teeth vibrating together.

When I was in this paralysed state I tried shouting for my Mum who was only in the next room but I also discovered that I couldn't call for help; the words were there but they were not coming out. I didn't understand what was happening to me at this time and then suddenly I found myself 'floating' out of my bed in a sought [sic] of curled up sleep position (this is the only way I can think of describing it) and from what I can remember the vibrating sensation seemed to have lessened but I still felt strange. I didn't actually float upwards out of my bed, but it seemed as if I was pulled out of my bed from the side and when I expected to hit the floor I seemed to just stop in mid-air approximately seven inches from my bedroom floor and then I began to travel towards my bedroom door and eventually out of my room totally and on to the upstairs landing.

When I started to travel out of my room I got very scared as I knew I had no control over which direction I was travelling or even where I was going, so I began saying even shouting to myself "I want to go back ... I can't go" continuously. My emotions or thoughts were extremely strong to return to my room. The next thing I knew I was sat on my bed in an upright position, still no control over my movements. My legs were then manoeuvred on to my bed and I felt myself lean back into a normal lying down position, but as my head was about to hit the pillow. My eyes opened but it was as if I had just woke up from sleep because I was lay [sic] down in bed, lay [sic] flat on my back and what I saw was the back of my own head coming towards me and it went straight though me and I could then control my own movements, everything was back to normal and I felt fine. It was as if I had returned to my own body and I actually saw the final stages of myself returning with my own eyes.

This account comes not from another famous astral projector but from a letter written to me by 19-year-old man. After all these years of studying OBEs I still get a thrill in reading, and rereading, accounts like this one. What must it have felt like to see the back of your own head zooming towards your own eyes? Or is that what he meant? Perhaps it is impossible to describe such a strange experience to someone who has not experienced anything like it.

Such cases confirm that it is not just well-known astral projectors who experience paralysis, vibrations, floating and the sensation of leaving the body. Ordinary people do too, but this raises a host of new questions. How common are the experiences? Do these features always occur together? Does any feature always accompany an OBE or are all OBEs completely different? In other words, what are OBEs really like?

## What is it like to have an OBE?

The answer is that there is no single answer. OBEs vary widely and this makes it hard to develop good theories. Even so, it will help if we can discover which features are most common and whether any always occur together or follow each other. Then there might be different types of OBE – for example, induced by different means or happening to different kinds of people in different circumstances. Exploring the variety of OBEs should help us begin to understand them.

There are two main ways to do this. One is just to collect cases as they come along and try to learn what you can from each one. The other is to carry out systematic surveys using a properly selected sample of the population and asking specific questions. Each has distinct advantages and disadvantages.

Researchers have been collecting cases since the early days of the Society for Psychical Research in the nineteenth century and still do so. The main advantage of this method is that you get rich descriptions of people's experiences in their own words without asking any leading questions; the main disadvantage is that the sample is self-selected and so is probably biased. Only some people are willing or sufficiently motivated to send in their accounts. Many people have no idea where to send an account or don't even realise that anyone would be interested if they did.

Descriptions may also be biased with more dramatic experiences more often being reported. And people will choose which aspects of their experience to include and which to leave out. Many people describe their OBEs as the most memorable experience of their life. Yet this does not make their memories invulnerable, especially if they are recounting events from years or even decades before. Because of these biases it is not possible to determine, for example, how common the OBE is among different groups or what circumstances most often precipitate it.

Another limitation is that case collections can rarely settle questions about paranormal claims even when people try. The early SPR collections were specifically aimed at finding evidence of survival after death and so they emphasised any apparently psychic aspects rather than looking into the nature of the experiences themselves. Among the most famous are *Phantasms of the Living* by Edmund Gurney, Frederic Myers and Frank Podmore (1886), all founder members of the Society, and *Human Personality and its Survival of Bodily Death* by Myers (1903). Both are massive two-volume works containing hundreds of cases of mediumship and trance, deathbed apparitions, sensory automatisms, dream visions and the effects of hypnosis, but very few OBEs.

Among these few is the famous Wilmot case, still frequently cited today. Parapsychologist Douglas Stokes writes that it is 'almost obligatory to cite the Wilmot case in an introductory work on parapsychology' (Stokes, 2007, p.115). I didn't include the Wilmots' adventure in *Beyond the Body*, perhaps precisely because it was so famous and I thought there was little more to say. I did study it a few years later (Blackmore, 1983a) and revisiting it now, I think it has even more to reveal than I thought then.

## Mrs Wilmot visits the ship

The Wilmot case first appeared in the 1891 *Proceedings of the Society for Psychical Research* in a paper called 'On the evidence for clairvoyance' by the editor Eleanor Sidgwick (1891). It begins with an account sent in to the SPR by a certain Mr W. B. H. that was investigated during the years 1889/90 by one of their leading researchers, Richard Hodgson. The whole was then reprinted in Myers' *Human Personality and its Survival of Bodily Death* (1903, Vol. i, pp. 682–5).

Mr W. B. H.'s report begins: 'The incidents were related to me by Mr. S.R. Wilmot, a manufacturer of this city, several years ago, and I wrote them down from memory, and he afterwards revised the manuscript.' He adds: 'If published, please do not give my name, as I have simply acted as scribe, and have no personal knowledge about the incidents' (Myers, 1903, p.682). Since the incidents in question happened in 1863 this means that more than twenty years had elapsed before they were written down.

On 3 October 1863 Mr Wilmot set sail from Liverpool to New York on the steamship *City of Limerick*. On the second day out a severe storm blew up and lasted for nine days. The conditions must have been truly awful, as he recounts: 'During this time we saw neither sun nor stars nor any vessel; the bulwarks on the weather bow were carried away, one of the anchors broke loose from its lashings, and did considerable damage before it could be secured, and several stout storm sails, though closely reefed, were carried away and the booms broken' (Myers, 1903, p.682).

Not surprisingly his wife, waiting for him in America, was concerned for his safety, as he probably was himself. When the storm finally abated he slept well for the first time since leaving port, and towards morning he dreamed that his wife came to the door of his stateroom clad in her night-dress. She hesitated a little on seeing the other passenger there but then kissed and gently caressed him and quietly withdrew. In the morning he was surprised to find his fellow passenger, Mr Tait, staring fixedly at him. 'You're a pretty fellow,' said his companion, 'to have a lady come and visit you in this way.' When pressed for an explanation he 'related what he had seen while wide awake, lying in his berth. It exactly corresponded with my dream' (p.683). Mr Tait, he explained, was 'a sedate and very religious man, whose testimony upon any subject could be taken unhesitatingly.'

The day after landing, Mr Wilmot took a train to Watertown, Connecticut, where his wife was staying with her parents and the children. 'Almost her first question when we were alone together was, "Did you receive a visit from me a week ago Tuesday?" "A visit from you?" said I, "we were more than a thousand miles at sea." "I know it," she replied, "but it seemed to me that I visited you."' He says that his wife then explained that on that same night she had lain awake a long time thinking of him, 'and about 4 o'clock in the morning it seemed to her that she went out to seek me. Crossing the wide and stormy sea, she came at length to a low, black steamship, whose side she went up, and then descending into the cabin, passed through it to the stern until she came to my state-room.' She described the room, the two berths, the man looking at her and said that she had bent down, kissed him, embraced him and went away. He concludes, 'The description given by my wife of the steamship was correct in all particulars, though she had never seen it. I find by my sister's diary that we sailed October 4th; we reached New York, 22nd; home, 23rd. With the above corrections I can very willingly subscribe my name. S.R. Wilmot.'

Mr W. B. H., who originally sent in the story, searched the newspapers but could find no report of a severe storm. He did ascertain that the ship sailed on 3 October (Wilmot's sister might have been referring to leaving a second port in Ireland en route). Trying to find corroboration, Mr Hodgson contacted Mr Wilmot and obtained an account from his sister, Miss Wilmot, who was on the ship with him. Writing in 1890, she says that she remembered Mr Tait asking her one morning, when 'the cyclone was raging fearfully', whether she had been in last night to see her brother and she was astonished at the question. He also obtained a signed statement from Mrs Wilmot herself, apparently answering some of his questions, but oddly only part of the document is reprinted. She says, 'I think that I told my mother the next morning about my dream; and I know that I had a very vivid sense all day of having visited my husband' (p.685). But all these accounts were written in 1890, twenty-seven years after the events in question.

What should we make of this story? It is surely hard to assess it fairly at such a distance in time. For a start, just imagine trying to reconstruct from memory a conversation that someone else said he had with his wife twenty-seven years ago and told you about 'several years ago'. Remember, this is the only account we have of that conversation in which the details given were 'correct in all particulars'. Yet the case keeps on being repeated as though it is evidence for veridical perception in an OBE and if it is then the implications are staggering. I want to say this as clearly as I can: if Mrs Wilmot really did see details of the ship, the cabin and Mr Tait, and if two people really did see her appearing at exactly the same moment, even though she was far away, then much of science as we know it must be overthrown.

This overthrowing would not just be another example of normal science, in which we repeatedly adapt or abandon theories in the face of the evidence and build new and better ones in their place; that happens all the time. Indeed this is what I am trying to do here and have done often before when I have had to reject my own failed theories about consciousness, memes and other topics to replace them with better ones. It is not even like the radical paradigm shifts that periodically rock a whole branch of science, such as the abandonment of phlogiston with new theories of heat, the huge changes in biology after the discovery of the structure of DNA, or the shift from Newtonian mechanics to relativity theory in physics (Kuhn, 1962). All these were dramatic changes of direction, forced by the evidence on sometimes unwilling scientists who wanted to stick with what they already believed. If the Wilmot case is true, as claimed, then the implications would be even more dramatic. They would force a completely new understanding of space, time, mind and consciousness. Wouldn't that be exciting? Wouldn't it be amazing? We therefore have a duty to assess this case carefully, setting aside our own prior beliefs or scepticism about the paranormal. So here goes.

Paring away the details, the critical claims that make this story so impressive are these:

1. Mrs Wilmot seemed to travel, out of her body, across the sea to her husband's ship.
2. Her experience happened at exactly the same time as both Mr Wilmot and Mr Tait saw her appear in their stateroom.
3. The details Mrs Wilmot saw were correct and she could not have known about them beforehand.

Does the evidence back up these claims? We need to answer some questions:

First, was this an OBE? Writers and researchers from the nineteenth century to the present have treated it as an OBE or 'OBE projection' (Charman, 2013). Yet all we have from Mrs Wilmot herself is the statement, 'I think that I told my mother the next morning about my dream; and I know that I had a very vivid sense all day of having visited my husband: the impression was so strong that I felt unusually happy and refreshed, to my surprise ...' (the document ends with these three dots). People do not usually confuse dreams with OBEs and Mrs Wilmot gives no description of having seemed to leave her body, let alone of travelling across the sea or seeing the ship. This is told to us only by Mr Wilmot himself via his scribe, presumably based on the conversation he had with his wife more than twenty years before. Could errors have crept in?

Second, when did the experiences happen? The crucial claim is that the two coincided, but for us to be convinced of this we would need at least two independent mentions of the date, and preferably the time; one from Mr Wilmot alone is not enough. For example, Mrs Wilmot might have described her experience in a diary, or told someone else, who made a note of the date. But this did not happen. As we have seen, she says only, 'I think I told my mother' but she does not say on which day she told her and we have no confirmation from the mother herself.

We know that Miss Wilmot (who was on the ship) kept a diary. So if the conversation with Mr Tait had struck her as especially odd she might have noted it in her diary, so revealing the date, but she did not. Her recollection, twenty-seven years after the voyage, was that one morning Mr Tait asked her whether she had visited her brother's room that night. She does not say which day this was and clearly had trouble remembering the events for she adds, 'but in the imminent danger that loomed over us, I did not fix my mind on their after conversations.'

Reading this case again and again I did notice one odd little detail. Mr Tait asked her this unexpected question, 'when assisting me to the breakfast table, for the cyclone was raging fearfully' (p.684). Yet Mr Wilmot writes that the events occurred on the first night that the storm had abated and he 'enjoyed refreshing sleep', which implies that by now it was no longer 'raging fearfully'. Mr Tait himself might have noted the date this happened or told someone else who did, but we have no statement from him. By the time the case was investigated he was long dead.

So when did it all happen? Mr Wilmot says that almost his wife's first question when he saw her was, 'Did you receive a visit from me a week ago Tuesday?' and that she concurred. By my calculation this would have been Tuesday 13 October, but no one else mentions a date and we have no corroboration that this conversation ever took place, or if it did that Mrs Wilmot agreed it happened on that Tuesday. So really we have no evidence that the events happened on the same night other than Mr Wilmot saying they did.

Third, Mr Wilmot says, 'The description given by my wife of the steamship was correct in all particulars, though she had never seen it.' Yet she never describes what she saw of the ship, nor does anyone else other than Wilmot himself. On being questioned by Mr Hodgson she says, 'In reply to the question, Did I "notice any details about the man I saw in the upper berth?" I cannot at this late day positively say that I did, but I distinctly remember that I felt much disturbed at his presence, as he leaned over, looking at us' (p.685).

I so wish we had more information and have long wondered what was in the rest of the document containing Hodgson's questions and Miss Wilmot's answers. When I first studied this case I searched the extensive SPR archives, hoping to find the whole document but in vain, and I have recently checked again but there is nothing more there than what is printed. So we are left with this brief statement beginning and ending with . . . (three dots).

Thoroughly reexamining the whole case in the *Journal of the Society for Psychical Research*, Robert Charman explores some further possibilities. He points out that even if Mrs Wilmot had never seen this particular ship, whose maiden voyage was earlier that year, she had probably seen many other similar vessels because her husband frequently travelled between England and New York, and it was common then to have staterooms with the upper berth set back against the outward angle of the stern of the ship.

He also wonders whether another passenger, returning from the toilet, might have entered the wrong cabin, briefly woken both Mr Tait and Mr Wilmot, who then went back to sleep and incorporated the event into a dream of being visited by his wife. Although there are no plans of that ship in existence, there are plans of her sister ships and the upper berth would have been about 1.7m high. In that confined space Mr Tait would surely have been very close to the woman's face yet although he was convinced it was a real woman and not a phantom, he did not describe her appearance.

As for the coincidence in timing, Charman says that given the storm lasted some nine to ten days, there was a one-in-ten chance of the days coinciding, and once the couple had compared their dreams it would have been natural for them to assume that both occurred at the same time. 'Repeated retelling of their experience would inevitably have shaped and reshaped memory over the twenty-seven years of what exactly they had said to each other on Mr Wilmot's return' (Charman, 2013, p.174). He concludes that the verdict must be 'not proven'.

I have been accused of having 'grossly misrepresented this case' (Carter, 2012). I have been accused of not reading the reports carefully enough, even though they are only four pages long and I have read them very, very many times. Indeed the original article is lying right in front of me now, along with my much-loved first edition copy of Myers' 1903 book, whose pages have been well-thumbed since I bought it, back in the 1970s. I have been accused of 'offhand dismissal' of testimony that conflicts with my beliefs (Kelly et al., 2007). Yet all I have done is try to work out just how evidential this most famous case is.

I want to scream! I fear I may bore people by going into such elaborate detail and becoming so obsessed with this ancient case, but that is what you have to do if you want to get to the bottom of psychic and paranormal claims. Time after time they appear compelling at first sight and crumble on closer inspection. Read any account of the Wilmot case in a parapsychology book and you will likely be convinced that Mrs Wilmot left her body, travelled across the sea, saw the cabin and appeared to Mr Wilmot and Mr Tait in their beds.

Do you still think so?

## A visit to London

I have often wanted to scream, but that never seemed to stop me searching for evidence in obsessive detail. Perhaps it's the potential importance of these claims, perhaps it's a suppressed desire on my part for them to be true – or alternatively *not* to be true, or perhaps it's just that I really do want to understand the OBE – properly understand it – and if that means checking on paranormal claims then I will.

I know, to my cost, that investigating a claim can take a great deal more hard work than making it ever did. This was so in such cases as Betty Markwick's heroic attempt to exonerate Samuel Soal from accusations of cheating in telepathy experiments. Her efforts finally led her to uncover just how he did cheat (Markwick, 1978). It was so in my dispiriting investigations into Carl Sargent's unwarranted claims of ESP in the Ganzfeld and the ways in which his work was open to fraud or error (Blackmore, 1987b). It is so in many cases of OBEs.

As a simple example, I once helped with the case of a Canadian architect who thought he had left his body and flown across the Atlantic to London (Blackmore, 1983a). When he arrived, his vivid visions of the environment and people's clothes suggested that he was in the mid-nineteenth century. He described in great detail a shop window with leaded panes and wares for sale outside, a cobbled street with people hurrying along to a nearby square and three-storey houses with narrow windows and tidy front yards. From his clear recollection of the flight he could identify the bends in the River Thames and so from a map was able to pick out a particular street in the west London area of Fulham. Having never been there, he says he asked an English colleague to describe the area, and the colleague, 'proceeded to describe the character of the street, the buildings, the style, the building setbacks and entrance yards – all exactly as I had seen them!' (Does this remind you of Mr Wilmot's confident claim that, 'It exactly corresponded with my dream'?)

At the time, some forty years ago or so, I was excited enough by being sent this story to go up to London and try to find the area. As I wandered around Fulham for ages on a cold, dreary day, I was getting increasingly despondent. I visited the local library (no Internet in those days, of course) and found old maps of London to check what was there a hundred years before. The answer was simple: a map of 1862 shows green fields where the architect thought he saw his street. Fulham was built up only when the railways reached that far and then it was with two-storey workmen's houses. They are still there now and are nothing like the houses he described. I even went so far as to take photographs of various areas of London, get them developed and post slides to him. From these he matched his visions with eighteenth-century townhouses of a type that never existed in Fulham or in any area near any other bend in the river similar to the one he described.

Looking back, I cannot really remember whether I was more surprised or disappointed by my failure. I only know that I did my best to check the details I was sent and the effort came to nothing, as it did so many other times. If the outcome had been different I would doubtless be chasing paranormal theories of the OBE. I might now be trying to develop astral projection theory into a workable form, or inventing a completely new theory about mind leaving the body or consciousness existing outside of the brain. I might be trying to overthrow all of conventional science with my new discoveries, as I long ago hoped to do. But I am not. Instead I think all these theories and the paranormal claims made to back them up are red herrings. We need to start again from the basics, asking what OBEs are like, how they vary and all the other questions that case collections can help us answer.

## Muldoon and Carrington

The first major collection of astral projections was by Muldoon and Carrington (1951), who included published cases as well as those sent to them after *The Projection of the Astral Body* was published. They categorised nearly a hundred according to whether they were produced by drugs or anaesthetics, occurred at the time of accident, death or illness, or were set off by suppressed desire. They listed cases involving spirits, some occurring during sleep, and some induced experimentally or by hypnosis, interpreting them in the light of their theories of astral projection. For example, they believed that in cases of anaesthesia or accidents the astral body was forced out of the physical, often violently, spinning or spiralling, as shown in their drawing (Figure 5.1).

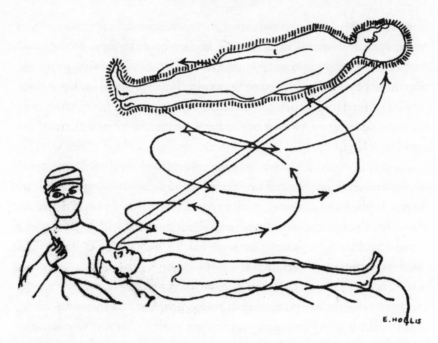

**Figure 5.1: Violent exteriorisation.** In *The Projection of the Astral Body* (1929), Muldoon and Carrington claim that when the phantom is forced from the physical body by shock, accidents or anaesthesia it leaves abruptly, spinning or spiralling out of control.

An example is that of Mr Landa, who was very nervous before an operation. On being given the anaesthetic he briefly became unconscious, then felt he was being torn apart by a sudden violent reaction and saw his physical self lying there on the operating table with the doctor holding an instrument. He said he could see very clearly, it all seemed real, and he would never forget the experience.

In the illness category was the case of Mr Johnson who got out of bed one night and fell to the floor in pain. He had 'severe cramps in his legs', rather like the young man's experience at the start of this chapter. The next thing he knew was that he was watching his wife and daughters trying to lift him up, and there seemed to be two of him, the conscious part watching the body on the floor. He writes, 'While I knew it happened, it was not until I read of a similar experience, described by Sir Arthur Conan Doyle, that I realized what the explanation was' (p.75). And what was the explanation? Conan Doyle, despite creating the character of Sherlock Holmes, probably the most logical man in literature, was a spiritualist who was convinced of the existence of other worlds and even of fairies.

His wife, Lady Doyle, also reported an experience. After her husband's death in 1930, when dangerously ill, she seemed to travel to a realm of 'light and calm, the portals of a marvellous other world'. There was her husband with another figure, both of them happy and loving, and showing her the wonderful life that awaited her there, but she remembered her three children and decided to go back to them instead. In other cases people met spirits or were helped by loving beings, Muldoon and Carrington suggesting this might lighten grief or teach people necessary lessons.

Other cases begin from the borders of sleep, starting with falling and flying dreams or the paralysis they called 'astral catalepsy'. They noted cracking or snapping sensations in the head, momentary blanking of consciousness when entering and leaving the body, sensations of floating or flying, looking down on the body from above and seeing an astral cord uniting the two bodies. Sometimes people described feeling pressed down before projection and 'repercussion' on returning.

Muldoon and Carrington conclude that these characteristics are repeatedly found and surely require some explanation. I totally agree. But I disagree that they prove the truth of astral projection, or of a double that can separate from the physical body and survive death. We do not need to agree with their conclusions to learn from the consistencies they found.

## Hornell Hart

The same emphasis on looking for evidence of the paranormal was clear in another famous case collection, that of Hornell Hart (1954). He was a sociology professor at Duke University in North Carolina, where J. B. and Louisa Rhine had their parapsychology laboratory.

Hart collected cases of what he called 'ESP projection' and was very specific about what he would include. The observer had to acquire extrasensory information from a location outside of his own body, and experience 'consistent orientation to the out-of-the-body location'. In other words, this had to be an OBE with information obtained without the use of the normal senses. He collected 288 cases from the literature, including Muldoon and Carrington's, some collected by the American Society for Psychical Research, the Wilmot case and many other famous ones. Just ninety-nine passed his stringent requirements. He divided them into two groups depending on whether they occurred spontaneously or experimentally. Experimental induction could include hypnosis, drugs, concentration or other deliberate induction methods, and he gave each case an 'evidentiality rating' from 0 to 1. Many obtained very low scores while the best cases scored up to 0.9, with an average around 0.3 to 0.4. He scored the Wilmot case just 0.28.

As an example of the deliberate kind, Mr Apsey tried to project to visit his mother. He concentrated on her for five minutes.

> I then saw my mother in a flesh-colored nightdress sitting on the edge of her bed. A peculiar fact which I particularly noticed was that the nightdress was either torn or cut so exceptionally low in the back that my mother's skin showed almost down to her waist.
>
> Hart, 1954, p.127

He wrote down what had happened and told his wife about it the next day. Then later in the day his mother told his wife that she had indeed been wearing such a nightdress but it was a gift and did not fit very well, being too low at the back. She said she had been woken up by someone but he did not look like her son. She had screamed and opened her eyes, whereupon the figure faded away.

This sounds rather impressive, and Hart gave it a score of 0.72 on his evidentiality rating scale. Yet no specific times were recorded and we would need evidence from the other people involved to be convinced there was ESP. As so often with OBEs, the details are a curious mixture of right and wrong. Mr Apsey saw his mother sitting on the side of her bed but she says she was woken by the apparition. So unless she was sleeping sitting up he was wrong, and the figure she saw did not look like her son.

Hart divided all his cases into the two groups and then compared them against a list of eight features that he thought important for a 'full-fledged ESP projection': that the person made careful observations of people, objects or events; that the apparition was seen by others and he was aware of being seen; that he saw his own body from outside; occupied a 'projected body' which could float and pass through physical matter; and that he travelled swiftly through the air. He argued that the spontaneous cases and those induced by more complex methods had more of these features and concluded that hypnosis was the most promising method for inducing ESP projection.

Whether or not there is really a distinction to be made, the problem with Hart's scheme was that he determined in advance what the essential features of the experience were. This made sense given that he was trying to find proof of ESP and life after death but we already know that few OBErs claim to see details at a distance, and even fewer are seen as an apparition by someone else. If we want to try to understand the full range of OBEs we need impartial data on what most are like, how they vary, who has them and so on. Although Hart did some valuable pioneering work, he cannot answer these questions.

## Robert Crookall

The largest collection of all was amassed by the British geologist Robert Crookall, who wrote books on mystical experiences and life after death as well as astral projection (1961a, b, 1964, 1968, 1969). Most of his cases were from the literature of spiritualism and psychical research, others from newspapers and biographies and, in his later books, from cases sent directly to him. He classified hundreds into groups and listed recurring features but was criticised for his haphazard methods of collecting cases, lack of clear criteria for classifying them and circular definitions (Alvarado, 2012).

Crookall emphasised sensations on leaving the body, including blackouts and tunnels; cracking, clicking and tearing sounds; and different ways of leaving the physical body, such as directly up through the head or in spiral fashion. Once 'out' the double, he claimed, is usually horizontal for some time before righting itself when it can move by the power of thought or will alone, sometimes leaving a trail of light behind it. Then there is the mysterious light with which surroundings are often illuminated, the shining double, its inability to influence material objects and the silver cord joining the two bodies which is not always seen but may be felt as a pulling sensation. Crookall noted emotions, including peace and happiness, clarity of mind and the 'realness' of everything seen. He was convinced these recurring features did not match any known hallucinatory experiences and so provided evidence for genuine projection.

Crookall also distinguished two types of experience but in a different way from Hart. Rather than contrasting spontaneous with deliberate experiences, he contrasted natural with enforced. His 'natural' category, rather oddly, included OBEs occurring near death or during illness and exhaustion. These, he said, are more gradual and pleasant. 'Enforced' ones could occur with drugs, anaesthetics, accidents and hypnosis, and are sudden and less pleasant, sometimes trapping travellers on the earth plane or even in Hades, the final destination for the souls of the dead.

This distinction was important to Crookall because of his theory of astral projection. He believed there are three bodies, all familiar from Theosophy: the physical body, the body of vitality (equivalent to the etheric double) and the higher soul body (equivalent to the astral body). In natural OBEs, he argued, only the soul body leaves the physical, which is why perception is usually clear and the experience heavenly, but in enforced OBEs some part of the body of vitality may also be projected, enshrouding the soul body, causing clouding of consciousness, misty or foggy perception and fewer OBE features.

Decades later, Alvarado (1984, 2012) tried to test this distinction using two predictions: first, that natural OBEs have more phenomenological features than enforced ones; second, that natural OBEs are more pleasant. To estimate the number of features, he designed a questionnaire to count such details as sensations on leaving the body, vibrations, floating sensations, tunnels, lights, seeing the body and connecting cords. This score makes up the 'OBE Features Index'.

Using both Crookall's data and his own survey of sixty-one OBErs, Alvarado found no confirmation for Crookall's distinction. Indeed many differences were in the opposite direction to that predicted. Other claims failed too. For example, Crookall argued that when more of the body of vitality is projected, OBErs see mist and fog and cannot move far from the physical. Yet Alvarado found that the distance travelled was unrelated to seeing mist or fog.

In my early attempts to understand the OBE I also compared spontaneous with deliberate OBEs but with a different rationale from either Hart or Crookall. I suggested that spontaneous OBEs would result from disrupted sensory input, such as happens on the verge of sleep, during accidents or near death. By contrast, deliberate OBEs would need to use relaxation or meditation to cut off sensory input intentionally (Blackmore, 1982, 1986c). Using my theory, Alvarado and Zingrone predicted they would find more features during deliberate than spontaneous OBEs and also amongst frequent OBErs. They confirmed both these predictions in two studies (Alvarado & Zingrone, 1999, 2015).

## Mistaken logic

Crookall asks his readers 'to compare the accounts given in this book, to note the comments made and to consider whether the concordances and coherences that occur can be explained except on the assumption that the narratives are, in fact, descriptive of genuine experiences' (1961a, p.1).

This same false logic appears time and again. We find it not only in the history of astral projection, but as we shall see, with depressing regularity in interpretations of near-death experiences said to 'prove' that heaven is real. The mistake is simple: only two possibilities are given and a third is ignored:

1. The experiences are proof of a Christian heaven, an Islamic Paradise, the astral planes or whichever theory is preferred.

This is compared with:

2.  The accounts are not 'genuine experiences' at all. They never really happened or are just dreams or flights of imagination.

The third possibility is that they are indeed 'genuine experiences'; there really are multiple 'concordances and coherences'; people really do seem to leave their body and fly around – but the reason their experiences are so similar is that we all have similar bodies and brains.

We need to keep an open mind about these three possible explanations until we know just what consistencies do need explaining. To some extent these great case collections have helped, but if we really want to know what it's like to have an OBE we can learn a lot more from the systematic surveys that followed.

CHAPTER 6

# What Is It Like?

I was working as a waitress in a local restaurant and had just finished a 12 hour stint ... I was terribly fatigued ... However I started walking ... I remember feeling so fatigued that I wondered if I'd make it & resolved to myself that I'd 'got to keep going'. At this time I was where the Playhouse is today. The next I registered, was of hearing the sound of my heels very hollowly and I looked down and watched myself walk round the bend of Beaumont St. into Walton St. I – the bit of me that counts – was up on a level with Worcester College chapel. I saw myself very clearly – it was a summer evening and I was wearing a sleeveless shantung dress. I remember thinking, 'so that's how I look to other people.'

Green, 1968a, p.1

I love that phrase 'the bit of me that counts'. Others might say, 'the real me', 'the thinking I' or the 'conscious self'. But the gist is always the same and that is certainly how it was for me. I felt that whatever might count as 'really me' was outside my body and more alive and aware than ever, while the body simply didn't count. It was just a shell that had once housed the 'the bit of me that counts'. This feeling is central to what we have to understand about OBEs. It brings us to that deep philosophical and spiritual question – who, or what, am I?

If we could answer this question, what happens in an OBE ought to be obvious but we cannot. Not only have great thinkers pondered this one for millennia but so have meditators, mystics and psychonauts exploring the realms of hallucinogenic drugs. I have spent many Zen retreats engaged with the koan, 'Who am I?', sometimes in organised retreats, struggling along with a group of other meditators; at other times alone on solitary retreat in the mountains or at home. I have let that question hover hour after hour and day after day, letting it seep right into me while feeling the duality of self and other slipping away (Blackmore, 2011).

My hope is that one day we can bring together the personal approach – the strange experiences, heart-searching questioning, insights and transformations – with the academic approach – the psychology and neuroscience of how the sense of self is constructed in the brain. Even more optimistically, I hope that studying the OBE might help us understand the self as well as the other way around. But before I get too carried away, we need to get a clearer idea of just what typical, and not so typical, OBEs are like.

## Surveying the experiences

The research that really began this task started in the 1960s. That decade marked a new attitude towards altered states of consciousness. Behaviourism, which had dominated and even oppressed experimental psychology, was being abandoned and at last it was possible to study thinking, imagination and dreams, even if the naughty word 'consciousness' was still taboo. The 1960s was also the era of hippy culture and adventures into psychedelic drugs, meditation and new ways of expanding the mind. In this climate, OBEs became of interest again, not just as evidence for life after death, but as a phenomenon in their own right, and this is when the first systematic case collections began.

The first and most significant of these were by Celia Green of the Institute of Psychophysical Research in Oxford. Her books, *Lucid Dreams* and *Out-of-body Experiences*, both published in 1968, were the most extensive and useful reviews available when I was an undergraduate and I read them avidly. Unlike early psychical researchers, Green tried to collect cases from a wide range of people. She did not use random sampling methods as many later surveys did, so there were many questions she could not answer. But the wealth of her material and careful analysis provided rich detail about OBEs and the people who have them which, along with data from subsequent surveys, gives us a pretty full picture. It turns out that some of Crookall's 'concordances and coherences' stand up to these tests while others certainly do not.

In September 1966, Green put out an appeal 'by means of the Press and sound radio', asking for 'first-hand accounts of experiences in which the subject had appeared to himself to be observing things from a point located outside his physical body' (Green, 1968a, p xiii). She called these 'ecsomatic experiences'; but note the wording. Unlike Muldoon's 'astral projection' or Hart's 'ESP projection' she used a modern definition of the OBE with no requirement either for ESP or for evidence of anything being projected. This meant she could study the phenomenology of the experiences without imposing any theory on them.

She received replies from about 400 people to whom she sent two further questionnaires. Three hundred and twenty-six people replied to the first and 251 to the second. She then collated all the data on punched cards and using this novel method, which seems horrifyingly laborious to us now, she was able to analyse the cases in ways that had never been attempted before. The results were published in her book, *Out-of-the-body Experiences*, which begins with the story that opened this chapter. Other collections followed (e.g. Poynton, 1975, Osis, 1979, Blackmore, 1982b) and then many more surveys which I'll describe in the next chapter, all of which provide a much clearer idea of what OBEs are really like.

## The circumstances of the OBE

Under what circumstances do OBEs occur? Is there some necessary requirement, such as lying down or being ill or stressed? Or is there some condition that usually sets them off despite the differences? If

OBEs all occurred in similar circumstances there might be simple answers, but they do not.

The most common circumstances are, on the one hand, sleep or deep relaxation, and on the other, highly stressful situations, including accidents and near death. These might seem almost to be opposites. So any theory has to account for both. But OBEs can also occur in almost any situation, including when people are just getting on with their ordinary lives and nothing is apparently amiss. There are accounts of people having OBEs while serving breakfast, putting on make-up, or going for a walk. Among the stressful situations perhaps taking one's driving test is an especially unnerving example.

> . . . as I settled myself, switched on the engine, let in the gear, I seemed to fill with horror because I simply wasn't in the car at all, I was settled firmly on the roof watching myself and despite a fearsome mental struggle to get back into myself. I was unable to do so and carried out the whole test, (30 mins.?) watching the body part of me making every sort of fool of myself that one could possibly manage in a limited time.
>
> Green, 1968a, p.64

I wish she'd said whether she passed. One can only guess not, but at least she lived to tell the tale, as did the young man in this even more scary-sounding case:

> I was riding my motorcycle home from school (with girl passenger). While I was operating all the controls (of the motorcycle), I was watching my motorcycle with the girl and me from a distance of about six to eight feet above our physical existence. I had no noticeable physical sensations such as feeling while operating the motorcycle, though I seemed to be functioning fairly well. Physical sound didn't register either. I thought I was hearing wonderful, powerful, colorful, emotional, free music. The whole experience was remarkably enjoyable.
>
> Tart, 1971a, pp.103–4

In another of Green's cases a vicar was delivering his sermon when he suddenly found himself watching from the west end of the church and hearing his own voice. When the service was over he asked some of the congregation, without explaining why, whether they had noticed anything amiss but was assured they had not. Others have had OBEs when acting on the stage or giving a presentation to a challenging audience.

Such situations suggest an element of self-consciousness or worrying about oneself. Some people have even induced OBEs by asking, 'Who am I?'

> I used to achieve this by saying to myself, 'who am I, what am I' and really concentrating on the questions...
>
> I willed myself to do it . . . What am I? Who am I? I would repeat this several times, concentrating on the questions and forgetting my surroundings. Then I would feel as if I was separate from my body which was still on the earth. I felt as if I was up in the clouds. I can remember doing it on a bus going to school. And the last time was in bed, when I seemed to have difficulty in 'getting back' I became frightened and never tried it again. It all occurred during my childhood, it could have been any time up to the age of 13.
>
> Green, 1968a, pp.13–14

Other people begin asking such questions after finding themselves out of the body.

> This is me. Who am I? What is 'me'? I am ME. Why in all the world should I be in this body? Why am I this person called D –
>
> Green, 1968a, p.14

I am particularly touched by these questions. I too remember lying in bed at night, with my younger sister asleep in the next room, and wondering why I was me and not her, and what would happen if we swapped places so that I became her and she was me and . . . My earnest questioning never led me into an OBE but I have gone on asking such questions all my life. They have motivated not only my academic research but my long training in Zen, my experiences with drugs and thirty years of daily meditation. It is wonderful to see a kind of symmetry emerging here. Questions about self can provoke OBEs and now research on OBEs brings us back to asking about self.

Green looked further into the circumstances, finding that most of her single cases (when a person reports only one OBE) occurred under stress of some kind, some during sleep (12%) and others when anaesthetised or unconscious (32%). Then on the other side of the Atlantic, in 1976, the American psychiatrist, Stuart Twemlow, had an interview with a national periodical and asked people to write in if they had OBEs (Twemlow et al., 1982, Gabbard and Twemlow, 1984). About 700 did so and 339 people completed his questionnaires. The vast majority (79%) said they were physically relaxed and mentally calm. About a third were dreaming and most of those dreams were falling or flying dreams. Some were meditating and, like Green, Twemlow found that another quarter were under emotional stress, while only a few were near death, taking drugs, in severe pain or involved in an accident.

By the time I had completed *Beyond the Body* there was not much more information available than this so I set about conducting a proper survey of OBEs myself, as I'll describe in the next chapter (Blackmore, 1984a). Of the thirty-nine people who had had at least one OBE nearly 60 per cent said they were resting and only 10 per cent carrying out waking activities. About a quarter had had an accident or operation, while others had migraines or were taking drugs or medicines. Only 10 per cent had induced an OBE deliberately. Comparable results come from a more recent study by Alvarado and Zingrone (2015), who found that nearly 30 per cent of OBEs took place during sleep, rest, or on the edges of sleep and 12 per cent during illness but the categories used by each survey are different and, much as I'd love to make a clear table of them all, this makes it impossible. I think we are best to use these figures only as a rough guide and conclude, along with Green, that 'Ecsomatic experiences may occur in a great variety of external circumstances' (Green, 1968a, p.1).

One curious, but possibly significant, factor to emerge concerns people's physical position and posture. In pathological cases of autoscopy people are usually standing upright when they see their double but most OBEs happen lying down. Among Green's cases, 73% were lying down, others were sitting (18%) and the rest standing, walking or doing something else. Some people who reported multiple OBEs claimed they had to be relaxed. In a South African survey by researcher John Poynton (1975), most of his 122 respondents were physically relaxed and either lying or sitting. And of Alvarado's 88 accounts, 59% were lying down, 14% sitting and 9% standing, while the rest changed position or could not remember (Zingrone, Alvarado & Cardena, 2010). Using the OBE Feature Index revealed that people who were lying down when their OBE began had a much deeper experience than those who were standing or walking and relaxation also seemed to help. As for the double, that is more often horizontal above the physical body (32%) than vertical (11%, Alvarado & Zingrone, 2015). According to Crookall (1964) it usually remains horizontal for some time before righting itself and being able to move, and Green (1968a) noted that it need not be in the same position as the body.

Note there are potentially two separate influences here: activity and posture. Could the precise position of the body matter? The trouble is that so few people are precise about this. Even so, images of astral projection nearly always show the physical body lying supine and while a few show the person meditating or sitting, I don't think I have ever seen an illustration with the physical body lying face down. Muldoon occasionally notes that he was lying on his back and the diagrams in his books all show that position, as do many books and websites telling you how to project your astral body. Could this be a clue to something important?

Strange things are said to happen when you lie on your back, and many people try to avoid sleeping this way because they find it unpleasant or even scary. Could there be something special about this position that affects our experience? If so, what kind of explanation might help? Could it be that the astral body finds its escape easier this way? Or could there be some physiological effect to do with our vestibular system and balance, or muscular relaxation or blood flow to the brain? Zingrone and her colleagues (2010) suggest that lying down induces more vivid imagery and that hypnotic states are deeper for people lying on their backs. This may seem a tiny detail to try to explain but sometimes it is tiny details that point to something important. So this is just one little clue to bear in mind.

## In the process of separating

The great astral projectors, Muldoon, Fox and Yram, all emphasised weird sensations on leaving and re-entering the body: shaking, vibrating, head-pulling, zig-zagging, sounds in the head, catalepsy or paralysis, momentary blanking of consciousness, and travelling down tunnels or through dark spaces. If they are right about the way the astral body separates from its lower bodies then we might expect most OBEs to involve at least some of these sensations, but the evidence on this is completely confusing.

Green found that most people had no awareness of a transition. Some mentioned noises at the beginning or end of the experience and one or two noted a momentary blacking out, but this was not the rule, and paralysis or catalepsy was rare. When experiences started from sleep or unconsciousness people typically said they just awoke or 'came to' in the ecsomatic state. When starting from waking most just 'found themselves' out:

> I was lying on my back, with the light out, when suddenly I found myself in mid-air, looking down at myself.

> I was laying on my side in bed. Then I was standing by the side of the bed looking down at myself in bed.

> I suddenly realized I was flying around my bedroom right up against the ceiling going round and round and I looked down on body lying in bed . . .

> Green, 1968a, pp.123–4

Only nine of Poynton's 122 cases reported paralysis, but a quarter had 'peculiar sensations', including strange noises, tingling, shivering and shaking. In a good example of how a sceptical hypothesis can be tested with survey data, Poynton worried that these strange effects might be symptoms of illness rather than part of the OBE itself. So he compared the frequency of these sensations in healthy versus ill people. When he found the sensations *less* common in people who were ill, he rejected the idea.

When I was writing *Beyond the Body* (1982) I scoured the Society for Psychical Research archives for OBE reports but found only forty-four, of which twenty-five were 'single' cases, i.e. had had only one such experience. Only one mentioned catalepsy, one felt 'thrills of sensation' and another 'rushing winds'. One describes dropping endlessly, and one passed through something like a TV screen, but most just found themselves 'out'. In my 1984 survey, when more specific questions were asked, 12 per cent reported shaking or vibrating and 10 per cent heard strange noises. Again, the majority (67%) just found themselves out with no weird sensations at all.

Over a third of Gabbard and Twemlow's 339 OBErs reported noises (37%) or vibrations in the body (38%), with noises being mostly buzzing, roaring, music and singing. In Alvarado and Zingrone's more recent study (2015), a third reported paralysis and another third sensations on leaving the body (35% and 33%). Rather fewer felt vibrations or tingling (17%) or heard sounds (26%). The variation between these studies is enormous, which is frustrating for trying to understand the OBE. If there is any consensus here it is that most people simply find themselves outside their body even if a substantial minority experience some of the weirder accompaniments.

As for the tunnels, which feature so prominently in astral projection lore and in modern near-death experiences, Green mentions none at all and nor does Poynton. In the SPR cases there is just one mentioning 'funnels of darkness'. Yet just over a quarter (26%) of Gabbard and Twemlow's sample ticked, 'Experienced being in a dark tunnel with a white light at the end of it'. And in Alvarado and Zingrone's collection 18 per cent passed through a tunnel or enclosure on leaving the body and 5 per cent on returning. In mine just 8 per cent went through a tunnel or doorway on leaving and another 8 per cent on returning.

It's hard to know what to make of these confusing findings because they span more than a century and use very different methods for collecting cases. They also begin with very different populations. People writing to the SPR in the late nineteenth century are likely to be very different in knowledge and expectations from those in South Africa responding to Poynton's questions and different again from respondents to the British and American questionnaires. Even so, noises, vibrations, paralysis and tunnels are reported often enough to demand explanation even if they are far from universal.

## Flying free

Once 'out', what is it like? The most obvious feeling is one of having the freedom to float, fly and soar in the air. Many of Green's respondents describe looking down on their own body as they flew, some being fascinated by seeing it in a new way, not at all like looking in a mirror. Most of Alvarado and Zingrone's respondents saw or felt their physical body (65%) but the findings are not consistent. In my survey less than half (46%) saw their own body, although among my cases from the SPR, twenty-five had had just one OBE and of these eighteen saw their own body. One tried to see it and could not. One man was disgusted at his unshaven appearance and another '... thought how funny I looked with a sheet pulled up over my clothes and my arms on top of the sheet with my navy blue dress ...' One woman even thought, 'Just fancy having dragged that heavy body about all this time! How awful!'

How I sympathise with her sentiment. I remember looking down on people from above and wondering how they could go on carrying those heavy bodies about and working so hard when, it seemed to me, there was no need. I think this powerful feeling of freedom from the body is another reason why the astral projection idea is so tempting. If 'the bit of me that counts' is so free to move and see and feel, the body seems to be just an unnecessary encumbrance. I say 'seems to be' because in most cases the physical body was functioning perfectly well at the time. So there is no good reason to give in to this tempting conclusion – although I have to admit that I did.

# What Is It Like?

For astral projection there has to be an astral body because this is what leaves to go travelling. What then of OBEs in which there seems to be no other body? Green separated OBEs into those she called 'parasomatic' (with a second body) and 'asomatic' (without). One woman wrote,

> I wondered if I could wake my husband and tell him but I seemed to have no hands to shake him or touch him, there was nothing of me, all I could do is see.
>
> Green, 1968a, p.24

Green's surprising claim was that 80 per cent were asomatic, with many describing themselves as disembodied consciousness. Yet it is not clear that all these people really had no second body. Some claimed not to but then mentioned stretching their feet, or reaching out to touch something. One woman had 'astral' hands but when she tried to touch her 'astral head', she found she hadn't one! This suggests that some cases are not clearly either, or perhaps they change. In his early writings Robert Monroe described projecting in a second body, but later said he thought of himself as more like a spot or point of light. My own experience began with a duplicate body complete with arms, legs and head, but over the course of an hour or more this second body changed into various different shapes and finally disappeared altogether.

The results of case collections have been wildly variable, with some finding that three quarters of OBErs had another body (Poynton, 1975, Gabbard & Twemlow, 1984), while others found far fewer. In one collection someone saw two bodies from a third position (Rogo, 1976), which may sound a very odd experience but it cannot be unique because Alvarado and Zingrone's (2015) list of features included, 'Saw both the physical body and the second body while located in a third position', and four of their seventy-nine respondents ticked it. Strange.

In 1979, American parapsychologist Karlis Osis gave a questionnaire to a group of mainly parapsychology teachers, who would be expected to know a lot about OBEs. Of the OBErs among them, a third had a double (36%), while others were just a 'spaceless body' or a ball or point (22% and 14%). My 1984 survey gave as options, 'a complete body', 'a different body', 'another shape', 'a point', or 'other' and a full 69% ticked 'a complete body' and only 12 per cent 'a point', which is almost the opposite of what Green found.

It is impossible to draw any firm conclusions from this muddle, other than that the OB form varies dramatically and no more than three quarters of OBErs even see one. Yet perhaps that in itself is a potential clue. We can at least conclude that astral bodies are not universal and then try to find out why.

What then of the famous silver cord? If we find that nearly all OBErs see or feel a connecting cord, this might strengthen the case for traditional astral projection theory. At the other extreme we might find that the only people who see silver cords are those who have read about or already believe in astral projection. Sadly the evidence is just as confusing.

Green asked a vague question, whether people felt any connection to their body, and about a third said yes, but only 4 per cent had a visible or tangible connection. One of Poynton's respondents described 'an elastic cord with [sic] tightened and slacked off as I moved up and down'; another, 'an invisible, but tangible, cord'; and a third 'a thin silvery cord . . . shiny like quicksilver and quite opaque', but only 9 per cent reported any connection at all. Rather more were found in my 1984 survey (24%) and in Gabbard and Twemlow's (21%).

What of the silver cord that figures so heavily in Robert Crookall's writings? Alvarado and Zingrone found only 2 per cent 'saw ray of light, cord, ribbon or rope connecting OB self to the physical body' and just one of the twenty-five SPR cases described a 'long silver thread attached to my earth body' and one other a 'rubber cord'. What strikes me here is that although cords are far from universal, when mentioned at all they are usually 'silver', elastic and flowing; they grow thinner the further out they go, yet never break. Why? If this were due to prior knowledge we would expect cords to feature only for those people who knew about them already. This was something I thought a lot about myself: did I see and feel that silvery cord only because I'd been reading about astral projection beforehand?

I wish there were more evidence on this but what little we have suggests this is not the explanation. Poynton asked whether respondents had previously read anything about OBEs and found this made no difference to their reports. Alvarado and Zingrone (2015) found no correlation between people's prior knowledge and their score on the Features Index, and those who were found through parapsychology-related sources did not have higher scores either. Yet their research did not break this down specifically for the silver cord, so there is much more to find out here.

The silver cord is thus a bit of a mystery. We must accept that it is rare – with perhaps around 5 per cent of OBErs seeing it – but the consistency of descriptions invites explanation. Perhaps there really is a silver cord but most people fail to see or even feel it. Perhaps the idea is so popular because people can easily imagine it even if they have forgotten hearing or reading about it. Or it could be that there is some psychological, neurological or physiological explanation which, for the life of me, I cannot yet imagine.

## Seeing another world

> I could see as I had never seen before.... And I could hear, as I had never heard in my life before.... And I could breathe, as I dimly remembered breathing as a boy.
>
> Oxenham & Oxenham, 1941, pp.3–4

The first thing many people say about their OBE is that it felt completely real, or even realer than real. This is exactly how I felt about mine. Nothing, I would say, had ever seemed so vivid and bright and immediate as the world I saw from outside my body.

Many books on OBEs mention this special clarity and some suggest it helps to demand 'clarity now'! Green reports how 'objects and places showed brilliant colours', or colours 'clear and bright and very stereoscopic'. One man asked himself, 'is my hearing acute, without ears?' Some of the SPR accounts describe seeing things in very small detail, and with a vividness never to be forgotten. Yet this reported clarity does not necessarily imply either supernormal visual ability or a normal-looking world. In my 1984 survey only 21% said their vision was clearer than normal, half said it was normal and 31% that it was dimmer. Others note small differences from normality, such as things seeming exaggerated or having a strange quality. One of Green's OBErs said, 'I am tempted to say just as normal, but there is a qualitative difference, there is something about the colour that is too vivid and sparkly …'

When looking for OBErs to test for ESP, parapsychologist Janet Mitchell (1973) found that OB perception 'seems to be different from physical perception in several ways. One experient reported that it was like looking through a fish-eye lens'. Others noted distortions and 'a circular visual capacity' (p.158). Osis asked his knowledgeable parapsychology teachers about their perceptual experience and 40% of them said that normal perspective broke down, producing 360-degree vision. In Gabbard and Twemlow's study half the OBErs said they could pass through objects.

Lighting can also be very strange with the surroundings looking bright without any obvious light source. Objects may glow with a light of their own, just as Fox and Monroe had noticed. Half of Osis's OBErs saw objects glowing or transparent, while others said that objects had auras around them. One of Poynton's wrote, 'I could see the garden with all its normal surroundings. The thing that surprised me was the fact that the garden was so clearly visible, even though my mind told me it was nearly midnight and there was no moon' (Poynton, 1975, p.121).

Most people seem to stay in their familiar environment (Gabbard & Twemlow's, 62%, Alvarado & Zingrone's, 69%, and my 1984 survey, 75%), but often it is distorted or vaguer than usual. Others visit entirely impossible or strange worlds of 'heavenly scenes' or 'other realms of existence'. Some meet 'non-physical beings' such as angels, spirits, demons or monsters of various kinds (37% in Gabbard & Twemlow's study). These are variously interpreted as inhabitants of higher or lower realms, beings from other planes, or the spirits of people who have died. In one SPR case, a woman travelled through a pleasant world of fields and trees observing people walking around and heard one of them say, 'Oh, she's from the earth.'

Astral projection theory has no problem with these other worlds; they are said to be other planes created by thought forms. But even if we accept that theory we must still ask whether each of these worlds is accessible to anyone who has an OBE or whether different people would see different collections of thought forms and hence travel in different worlds or astral planes.

Something else odd is worth noting. That is how rarely people mention any senses other than vision and hearing. Nearly all of Green's cases included vision (93%) and a third also had hearing, but touch, temperature, taste and smell are rarely mentioned. This might be a clue because the same is true of apparitions (Green, 1968a) and of dreams and hypnagogic imagery (the vivid visual and auditory images experienced just before falling asleep). Does this imply that the whole weird out-of-body world is some kind of dream?

Absolutely not, say most experiencers. Only 4% of Osis's respondents said theirs was like dream imagery and Gabbard and Twemlow found that nearly everyone (94%) ticked 'Experience was more real than a dream'. Yet given what we have learned about vision often being distorted or dim, and the places visited being so very strange, it is a little hard to understand what this huge majority means by 'more real than a dream'. They must mean something, but what?

## Just a dream?

How can we answer this question? Some pioneering experiments of the 1960s recorded brain activity using the EEG (electroencephalogram, with electrodes on the scalp) and eye movements using a polygraph (popularly known as a 'lie detector') to approach this question in two ways (Tart, 1967, 1968).

First, the EEG patterns associated with waking, deep sleep and REM (rapid eye movement sleep, the state most often associated with dreaming) were well known. If volunteers' OBEs were dreams they would be expected to show REM-like EEG as well as muscular relaxation, variable breathing and heart rate and rapid eye movements.

Second – and this was the controversial part – some researchers argued that if OBErs could see something at a distance during OBEs this would prove they were not just dreaming. But would it? There is the alternative possibility that ESP could occur during dreams of leaving the body; so this wouldn't prove anything. Even so it would still be a very exciting discovery. So there was a lot riding on these experiments.

The first step was to find someone who could have an OBE at will in the laboratory, and such people are rare. Charles Tart found two (Tart, 1967, 1968). Miss Z was in her early twenties after a difficult childhood with many psychological problems. Since she had all her OBEs at night she was invited to sleep in the lab in a small room while Tart watched the output of instruments in an adjoining room and observed her through a window. She was asked to speak through an intercom when she had an OBE so that Tart could mark the time on the charts. She slept there on four nights and had several OBEs, including one dramatic one in which she visited California and saw her sister. The records showed that she was clearly not in REM sleep at the time, but nor was she in any other well-defined state. Her EEG, heart rate and other measures showed something like a relaxed or borderline sleep state. So Miss Z was not dreaming.

The fourth night was even more important. To test for ESP, Tart had first asked Miss Z to do simple tests at home, writing the numbers 1 to 10 on pieces of paper. Each night she put them in a box beside her bed, took one out without looking and placed it where it could only be seen from above. Then during OBEs she tried to see it. She told Tart that she succeeded on every occasion, thus encouraging him to try experiments in the lab. For this he placed a randomly chosen five-digit number on a shelf more than five feet above her head, assuming she could not sit up or leave the bed without disconnecting the electrodes. The first three nights she did not manage to look at the shelf but on the fourth and final night she did. She had an OBE, saw the number and at 6.04 a.m. reported that it was 25132 – and she was right!

This one event might have counted as a convincing piece of evidence for perception beyond the body, and is often reported that way, but it has also been thoroughly torn apart. Tart (1968) mentioned, in the original paper, that he sometimes dozed off during the night and there was a Venetian blind over the window. So Miss Z was not continually watched. If she had tried to climb up to see the number she might not have been seen but we would expect to see the effect on the EEG recordings and we do. The recording was obscured by a sixty-cycle interference at the time of her OBE (Parker, 1975).

Tart himself pointed out that the number was very faintly reflected in the base of the clock above it, but he thought it was impossible to read without more light. He suggested that she might have hidden mirrors and reaching rods in her pyjamas but thought this unlikely. Even so he did not check for such possibilities before the experiment began. He checked afterwards, reporting that, 'The set-up of the room was changed slightly in preparation for a fifth laboratory night, and the shelf was extended so that no reflection could be seen off the clock from the subject's position in bed' (Tart, 1968, p.18). So what happened on that fifth night? Nothing. Sadly, Miss Z had personal problems that prevented her from taking part in any more experiments.

Canadian psychologist James Alcock (1981) analysed the case in detail, pointing out how reports have changed over the years to sound more conclusive. Even Tart himself stopped mentioning the poor experimental design and possible cheating, while others have reported the experiment as definitive evidence for ESP. I will end by quoting what Tart said in his original article: 'reading of the target number cannot be considered as providing conclusive evidence for a parapsychological effect' (Tart, 1968, p.18). I think he was right.

What then of his second participant? Referred to as Mr X in the research report, he turned out to be Robert Monroe, of *Journeys Out of the Body* fame (Tart, 1967). Monroe's OBEs happened when he was awake; so he came to the lab in the daytime. He completed nine sessions but finding the electrodes uncomfortable, was able to have only two OBEs. Tart found it hard to match these up with the data but concluded that the OBEs coincided with Stage 1 sleep (the lightest sleep) mixed with some REMs, an unsatisfactory conclusion since Monroe insisted that his OBEs were quite different from dreaming.

Tart suggested that they might be a mixture of dreams and 'something else', perhaps ESP as Monroe claimed. This time Tart had placed the shelf in the equipment room, not the subject's room, but Monroe never managed to look at it and so no ESP test was possible.

Other studies with OB experts followed (Hartwell et al., 1975, Osis & Mitchell, 1977). Blue Harary, a frequent OBEr as well as researcher, was found to be deeply relaxed but awake during his OBEs. He also attempted ESP tests but, according to the researcher Scott Rogo (1978), was only 'sporadically successful' and research turned to other aspects. Another expert OBEr, Ingo Swann, showed a flattened EEG with decreased alpha and 'a speed-up of the brain waves in the visual, occipital region of his brain' (Mitchell, 1973, p.160), but was otherwise in an alert waking state.

Does this answer our question? The results, once again, are confusing but I think we can give the answer 'no'. OBEs do not typically happen during dreaming sleep; they are not 'just dreams'. Nor is there any special, identifiable OBE state. If anything, these OBEs occurred on the edges of sleep or during waking states. But remember, these tests were done in the artificial environment of a lab and with experts who could induce OBEs at will, so they may differ from other OBEs.

Many people claim that lab experiments are artificial and unfair so could there be a way to test for ESP during spontaneous experiences? I was delighted when a visitor who told me he had frequent OBEs said he would visit my kitchen one night by travelling in the astral. He asked me to put some numbers, words and small objects next to the fridge and out of sight of the window. I carefully chose the targets, randomised them correctly and changed them every week, then every month, and finally even less often. Every time I met someone who said they could project at will I asked them to visit and many said they would. Only two said they reached my kitchen, saw the words and objects, and neither was correct.

# CHAPTER 7

# Can Anyone Have
# an OBE?

I was around 9 years old, at home alone, bored. My mom had a hippie book with games and suggestions of things to do. One thing that interested me was 'making energy balls', and I did that for a while... I turned a few pages and read about simple yoga poses for kids. My mom had already shown me some. I lay down and did the sponge pose for a good while. I think I felt 'electricity' and I 'opened my eyes' to see the ceiling tiles right in front of my face. I was flying. I could control it a bit, and I 'explored' my house from the new vantage point. Then I realized that this wasn't a dream and I probably shouldn't be doing this. I went back to my body.

## How common are OBEs?

You might have the impression that OBEs happen only to special people – whether you think that means they are spiritually developed or mentally unhinged. Yet tales of leaving the body seem to come from perfectly ordinary people who have OBEs in all sorts of circumstances, like the woman above who sent her account of a childhood OBE to one of my students (Jones, 2016). As a rough estimate, somewhere between

8 and 25 per cent of the population claim to have had at least one OBE. This is a lot of people. But precisely how many, and who are they?

The great case collections cannot answer such questions, despite all their fascinating stories, because by their very nature they contain whatever cases researchers can find. Instead, surveys are needed – surveys that take properly chosen samples from specified populations.

Ideally you would ask every single person in the world but in practice you have to use a manageable sized sample, and that sample needs to be representative of the population you are interested in. For example, if men are less likely to have OBEs than women but your sample includes more men, the result will not be valid, and the same applies to many other variables such as age, socioeconomic status, education, religious belief and so on, and it is hard to know which variables are important before you start. Then even if you begin with a good sample, not everyone will respond. So if women are more inclined to reply than men, or the other way around, again the answer will be skewed. These difficulties apply to all surveys and we just have to do the best we can.

Before I had my own experience in 1970 Hart (1954) had already done a small survey but he asked only 126 students and did not say how they were selected. He also changed the question halfway through, so his estimate of 27 per cent is unreliable. Some early studies used special samples, such as students on particular courses, marijuana users or members of spiritual societies (Blackmore, 1986b, Green, 1967, Kohr, 1980, Tart, 1971a). Others were designed to investigate the nature of the experiences rather than their incidence and for that purpose randomness is not so important and semi-random or opportunity samples are adequate (Braithwaite et al., 2011, Irwin, 2000, Terhune, 2009, Twemlow et al.,1982).

The first survey to use a properly balanced sample from a specified population was by parapsychologist John Palmer (Palmer & Dennis, 1975, Palmer, 1979) in Charlottesville, Virginia, a town of about 35,000 people from whom a thousand were selected. The University of Virginia at Charlottesville accounts for much of the population and so townspeople and students were sampled in the appropriate ratio of 700 and 300 and sent a forty-six-item questionnaire about psychic experiences, with non-responders followed up twice more. Fifty-one per cent of the townspeople responded and 14 per cent said 'yes' they had had an OBE; 89 per cent of the students responded and 25 per cent said 'yes'.

Why the big difference? Since the students were younger we might expect them to have had fewer OBEs in their shorter lives. On the other hand perhaps those who have odd experiences are more likely to go to college. Or perhaps the students had taken more drugs and this caused some of their experiences. This was a good survey but, like any other, it raised as many questions as it answered.

In Iceland a national survey was carried out by parapsychologist Erlendur Haraldsson and his colleagues (1977). Although Iceland's population is over 300,000 now, it was then only about 210,000 and from these, 1,157 people aged thirty to seventy were randomly selected from the National Registry and sent a questionnaire on psychic experiences. After follow-up mailings and even phone calls and visits, a high response rate of 80 per cent was achieved. Just 8 per cent claimed to have had an OBE – much lower than Palmer's estimate. So are Icelanders different from Americans? Were the questions different? Does the language matter? There are many possible reasons other than a genuine difference in numbers of OBErs. These figures, and those from other random surveys, are shown in Table 7.1.

| Authors | Sample | Number surveyed | Response rate % | Percentage reporting OBE |
|---------|--------|-----------------|-----------------|--------------------------|
| Palmer & Dennis 1975 | Townspeople Charlottesville, VA, USA | 700 | 51 | 14 |
| Palmer & Dennis 1975 | Students Charlottesville, VA, USA | 300 | 89 | 25 |
| Haraldsson et al 1977 | Residents of Iceland | 1157 | 80 | 8 |
| Blackmore 1984 | Residents of Bristol, UK | 593 | 55 | 12 |

Table 7.1: The incidence of OBEs in the general population, from four studies using random samples.

In the early years of my OBE research I too wanted to do a proper survey, perhaps not realising how much work it would be. I had already tested students at the University of Surrey, where I was doing my PhD. Thirteen per cent of 132 students claimed to have had an OBE and I got similar results with other student groups, but these samples were far from random. Later, when I was living in Bristol, I set about getting the best sample I could by randomly selecting 593 Bristol adults from the Electoral Register (Blackmore, 1984a). I sent questionnaires by post and then follow-up letters to non-responders, getting a final response rate of 55 per cent.

Mine was a long questionnaire asking about psychic and mystical experiences, dreams, imagery skills and beliefs. The OBE question was 'Have you ever had an experience in which you felt that "you" were 'located "outside of" or "away from" your physical body; that is the feeling that your consciousness, mind or centre of awareness was in a different place from your physical body? If you have trouble answering this question then you probably have not had the experience so please answer "no".' Twelve per cent answered 'yes' and were asked more than twenty further questions about their OBEs.

Note the wording of the question I used. For any survey the precise wording can be crucial because different ways of asking the same question can lead to different results. Palmer was equally cautious, asking, 'Have you ever had an experience in which you felt that "you" were located "outside of" or "away from" your physical body; that is, the feeling that your consciousness, mind, or center of awareness was at a different place than your physical body? (If in doubt, please answer "no")'. There is a good reason for adding, 'If in doubt, please answer "no"'. Someone who has had an OBE will probably understand the question easily and so answer 'yes' but someone who hasn't may misunderstand it and think that a very vivid or flying dream counts and so give a false positive. On the other hand, adding this rider may put people off and push them in the opposite direction.

Because it's hard to know how people interpret such questions, Australian parapsychologist, Harvey Irwin, tried to find out (1980, 2000). He gave questionnaires to 177 students, of whom 20% initially said 'yes' but when he asked them to describe their experiences he concluded that only 12% had really had OBEs. When I asked 187 Bristol students, 50% claimed OBEs, but after a more detailed OBE questionnaire this dropped to 23% (Blackmore, 1986b). This is why some researchers now routinely use detailed questionnaires to distinguish OBErs from non-OBErs (e.g. Braithwaite et al., 2011).

I also tried to find out whether different levels of knowledge would make a difference. The Surrey students on my parapsychology course should have understood the question, 'Have you ever had an out-of-body experience?', but I could not be sure that the Bristol students would. Yet the percentage reporting OBEs was very close (14% and 13%, Blackmore, 1981b). In 1980 I worked for a few months at the parapsychology laboratory at Utrecht University in The Netherlands, and with psychologist Dick Bierman at the University of Amsterdam, we gave one group of students no information about OBEs and another definitions and descriptions. In both groups 18% reported OBEs (Blackmore, 1982b). So apparently this information did not affect their replies.

Does any of this matter? Up to a point, yes, but it is probably not worth making any further effort trying to get an even more precise answer. Taking all this evidence into account, my best guess is that about 15% of the population has had an OBE.

## Can anyone have an OBE?

In broad terms the answer is probably 'yes' but some people are more prone to having OBEs than others. This is not because of such basic variables as age, sex, or education. Almost all surveys asked about age and sex. Indeed some surveys have found that more women claim OBEs while others found the opposite. Some looked at personality variables such as extraversion, psychoticism or neuroticism and again found no consistent differences (Gabbard & Twemlow, 1984; Irwin, 1985; Alvarado, 2000) and the same seems to be true for educational level, religious background, occupation and income. There is no clear pattern.

Far more obvious is a strong relationship between having OBEs and many other unusual experiences. In Palmer's Charlottesville survey the OBErs were more likely to have had mystical experiences as well as to practice meditation and take drugs. Those in Green's and Tart's were more likely to have psychotherapy or engage in spiritual practices, and in these and many other surveys OBErs were found to have more sleep-related experiences and hallucinations. In my Bristol survey I went into more detail, asking about dream recall and vividness, flying and lucid dreams, hallucinations, imagery skills, and having a profound or moving mystical experience. The result was that most of these experiences were highly correlated with each other; some people reported lots of these experiences while others reported none. Dream recall and vividness were related only weakly to having an OBE, but mystical experiences, lucid dreams, flying dreams and waking hallucinations were all strongly related, and OBErs were more likely to believe in ESP and survival after death. The statistical analysis showed that the relationships between mystical experiences and OBEs, and flying dreams and OBEs had a probability of less than 0.0000001 of being due to chance. So we can be confident that these are reliable relationships even if we don't yet know why.

The reason I asked all these questions was because of things I had experienced for myself, and I included other questions directly inspired by my own OBE. I asked about seeming to grow very large or small, seeming to shake, turn or float when the body is not moving, and seeming to see with closed eyes. This last one fascinates me and I wish I could understand what is happening in the brain when it happens. Sometimes, very rarely, when on the verge of sleep it suddenly feels as though my eyes are open when I know they are still closed. I can even reach up and feel my closed eyelids, but I can see a scene, usually something very simple like a stretch of grass or stones, or a simple pattern, and I can move my eyes as though scanning the picture. This is an extreme form of hypnagogic imagery that might give a clue to what is seen during OBEs. Thus I was pleased to find that the OBErs in my sample were far more likely to report having had this experience, as well as that of floating. I was surprised, though, to find that changing size was only weakly related to having an OBE and shaking or turning not at all.

Sometimes it is surprising negative results that prove the most interesting. I had included two questions about people's vividness of imagery because of the way I was theorising about OBEs at the time. That same year, 1984, I published my 'psychological theory of the OBE' (Blackmore, 1984b). By then I'd become disillusioned with occult theories of astral projection and was trying to understand how it was possible to have such a vivid, realistic and convincing experience of being out of the body if nothing actually left the body.

I was also not convinced by John Palmer's (1978b) psychoanalytic theory of the OBE, which was the only psychological alternative at the time. He began by noting that OBEs almost always occur in a hypnagogic state with reduced proprioception – that is, the sense of one's bodily position and movement that comes from sensors in the muscles. This threatens the self-concept and the threat activates deep unconscious processes that try to re-establish the sense of individual identity. It is this attempt to regain identity that precipitates the OBE and explains why it seems so real. Palmer, like me, was trying to do the best he could with what was known then, but psychoanalytic ideas of the unconscious have been more or less abandoned in psychology and even if you accept them it is hard to know why seeming to be outside the body would be less threatening than losing a firm sense of your bodily position as you fall asleep. Also, although popular at the time, Palmer's theory did not lead to any testable predictions.

The best idea that I could come up with, given the science available, was that the OBE is an 'illusion of reality'. In the absence of strong sensory input the normal input-driven model of reality could break down and be replaced by a model from memory and imagination. If this was more stable than the failing input-based model then it would take over and seem real. This idea was viable as far as it went. As Palmer noted, OBEs often occur in conditions that would destabilise the input model, including on the edge of sleep as well as in accidents or near death. My theory needed no psychoanalytic concepts but depended on the idea that what seems real at any time is the brain's most stable model of self in the world – our current 'model of reality'. Theories are useful only if they can be tested by making specific predictions. So I came up with several, including predictions about the relationship between imagery ability and OBEs.

My simplest prediction was that people with good imagery skills should be more likely to have OBEs. This was why my survey included the following two questions. You might like to try answering these for yourself, by circling the answer that best applies.

1. Close your eyes and try to imagine standing outside your own front door. How clear is the image that comes to mind?

Totally vivid – very vivid – average – vague and dim – cannot imagine

2. Close your eyes and try to imagine you are floating near the ceiling and looking down at the room. How clear is the image that comes to mind?

Totally vivid – very vivid – average – vague and dim – cannot imagine

It seemed odd that the imagery scores were only very slightly higher for people who had had OBEs, but in fact other researchers found a similar lack of evidence using more detailed imagery questionnaires (Cook & Irwin, 1983). This led me to thinking more deeply about the role of imagery and to several rather different experiments (Blackmore, 1987b). I reasoned that if the OBE world is constructed from imagination and memory then those who often dream or remember events as though from a bird's-eye view should be more likely to have OBEs, as should people who are better at switching imaginary viewpoints.

In one experiment I asked people about their perspectives when remembering or dreaming. I found that those who often dream in birds-eye view, as though looking down on themselves, were more likely to have had OBEs. In a second experiment I asked students to imagine the room they were in from various different positions and then to switch positions – for example, between imagining the room from above their head to imagining it from by their feet. Imagining it from foot level turns out to be surprisingly difficult, but those who had had OBEs had more vivid images from these odd positions. They were also better at switching between them.

One surprise in this task was that many of them said that when they imagined the room from above they also saw themselves sitting there down below, as is so common during OBEs. And 15 per cent said they seemed to imagine another body at their imagined, floating location. I guess this was not an astral body they were seeing, but it suggests that it is easy and natural to imagine a floating, observing self. Of course these imaginations did not seem real, as they so often do in OBEs, but they might give us some clues to what is going on. Even so, the imagery research hardly provided a stunning explanation for the OBE, and it was decades before I was able to make any further progress.

## Am I going mad?

Imagine you have an OBE and no idea what is going on. You might easily be frightened and even think you are going mad. Over the years I have had many letters and emails from people worrying they were going out of their mind because they had felt they were out of their body. Among the most upsetting were those from people who had visited a doctor, been told there was something wrong with them and then prescribed medicine or psychological treatment because of their OBEs, even though they were perfectly healthy. This happens much less often now, partly because doctors are more aware than they were, but mainly because it is so easy for people to find online information that reassures them. Even so, there is a serious question here.

On the one hand we know that perfectly ordinary, healthy people have OBEs, but we also know that having OBEs correlates with some kinds of dissociation that can be pathological, and with a tendency to hallucinations, especially auditory hallucinations (Parra 2010, de Foe et al., 2012). OBErs have also been found to score higher on a scale measuring anomalous perceptions, including various kinds of hallucination (Braithwaite et al., 2011). So could the OBE be a sign of mental illness?

There are some superficial similarities between OBEs and the symptoms of schizophrenia. For example, in schizophrenia body boundary disturbances are common. Schizophrenics often describe their body as feeling diffuse and fragile, and sometimes even missing hands or feet. They tend to over- or underestimate the size of parts of their body and underestimate their own height; they may feel their body is unreal or doesn't belong to them. This is a kind of 'depersonalisation'; a dissociative disorder that most often occurs after trauma, in extreme anxiety, or with various other mental illnesses. It often goes along with 'derealisation', the horrible feeling that the whole world is unreal or dreamlike.

Is this like anything we know from OBEs? Are the schizophrenic changes in body size the same as my experiences of becoming first very small and then as large as the whole universe? Not at all. The bodily distortions of schizophrenia are ongoing, disturbing and threaten the person's whole identity. OBEs are brief, intense and feel completely real. Indeed this is something that many OBErs stress, as I did myself – that this feels as real as everyday life – no, it feels even more real than everyday life. There was no derealisation during my OBE.

Even so, it could still be the case that OBErs have tendencies towards mental illness and that their experience is a sign of incipient problems. To find out, psychiatrists Glen Gabbard and Stuart Twemlow gave a variety of tests to their large group of OBErs as well as to several other groups for comparison. These included a questionnaire called the 'Profile of Adaptation to Life' that includes questions about negative emotions, psychological and physical well-being, money management, drug abuse and close relationships. After detailed analysis of all these data they concluded that, 'the "typical profile" of the OBE subject is remarkably similar to the average, healthy American ... His or her psychological health is generally excellent, ranking with the healthiest groups in the population' (Gabbard & Twemlow, 1984, p.40).

This is extremely encouraging for us OBErs but I still wanted to find out whether OBEs can be a symptom of serious mental illness, and in particular of schizophrenia. Gabbard and Twemlow's sample came from letters sent in by the public and might not have included many people living with the difficulties of schizophrenia or confined in mental hospitals. So I still needed to find out about these people. Do they have unusually frequent OBEs, or perhaps more pathological kinds of OBE? If so, do schizophrenics suffering the most serious symptoms of schizophrenia also have more frequent OBEs?

I was lucky enough to have a colleague in Bristol doing a study of perceptual distortions with members of the National Schizophrenia Fellowship and he was happy to include my questions about OBEs in his research. So we gave questionnaires on perceptual distortions, symptoms of schizophrenia and OBEs to seventy-one volunteers with a history of schizophrenia and forty patients in a hospital accident ward to act as a control group (Blackmore & Harris, 1983, Blackmore, 1986c). The OBE question was from Palmer (1979), 'Have you ever had an experience in which you felt that "you" were located "outside of" or "away from" your physical body; that is the feeling that your consciousness, mind or center of awareness was in a different place than your physical body?'

At first sight it seemed that significantly more of the schizophrenics (42%) reported OBEs than the control group (13%). But we then gave them a follow-up questionnaire, asking the schizophrenics to describe their OBEs, and from the thirty who replied, it was immediately clear that the experiences varied wildly.

Here are two that both involve theatres, though in rather different ways. The first is described by a 43-year-old man, who reported no visual distortions but suffered thought interference and hearing voices (one of the most common symptoms of schizophrenia). He wrote that it happened,

> ... on stage in the middle of a play at Her Majesty's Theatre, Barrow-in-Furness. It didn't affect my performance in any way at all. I went on acting while my centre of consciousness (I) floated about 15 feet above the scene I was in. I'm not making this up: it was a very exhilarating experience and an absolute mystery to me.

This must have been strange and disturbing, but it fits the usual definition of an OBE and is like many others I have come across. By comparison, this next one, from a 31-year-old man with many symptoms of schizophrenia, does not.

115

During my last schizophrenic breakdown I was transported, through music, to Titan (Saturn's moon), on which the gods had erected a theatre in which the fate of the earth was to be determined. I travelled without a body—as an idea or thought or some intangible aspect of consciousness.

Others described apparitions, déjà vu, lucid dreams, experiences of fusion with other people and various bodily disturbances. When I separated these experiences out, I found that only 14 per cent of the schizophrenics had had 'typical' OBEs in which a change of viewpoint was reported. This is almost exactly the same as the 13 per cent in the control group. Also, those who reported typical OBEs did not suffer from more symptoms of schizophrenia although those who had the atypical experiences did.

This suggests that OBEs are not a symptom of mental illness. Yet there is still a possible connection here. This concerns the concept of schizotypy, which is based on the idea that schizophrenia is not an all-or-none disease but lies at one end of a continuum from normal dissociative and imaginative states through to extremely pathological ones. High schizotypes tend to have four main characteristics: lots of unusual experiences, disorganised thoughts, flat emotion and unstable mood and behaviour, but they are also more creative and include many writers, artists and poets, suggesting that there are both positive and negative aspects to schizotypy.

Charles McCreery and Gordon Claridge (2002), at Celia Green's Oxford Institute, divided schizotypy into several different factors and found that OBErs scored highly on only one subset of questions, leading them to the idea of healthy schizotypes who function well in spite of, or even because of, their anomalous experiences. Argentinian researcher Alejandro Parra (2010) also found correlations with more positive aspects of schizotypy. This is very encouraging for OBErs. We may have experiences that other people find weird or hard to understand but these are related to the ability to imagine vividly, to dissociate ideas and bodily feelings, and to conjure up creative other worlds. We may be different, but we are not just mad.

## An OBE-prone personality?

Associations like the one I found between OBEs and paranormal belief may be pointers to some kind of difference between OBErs and other people. But we must be very careful about drawing unwarranted conclusions. This finding was just a correlation, so it's impossible to tell whether it means that people who already believe in ESP are more likely to have an OBE or whether having an OBE increases people's belief because they are convinced they had a paranormal experience. After all, this is precisely what I thought after my experience (Blackmore, 1982a, 1996).

Much more interesting is the psychological dimension of 'absorption' which is the tendency to become wrapped up in other worlds; in books, films, deep thought or day-dreaming. Absorption is closely related to fantasy-proneness and adults differ widely in their capacity for absorption. Many children invent other worlds and play with imaginary friends. Some are encouraged in this kind of fantasy play while others are discouraged or even punished for it, and others resort to it as an escape from loneliness, trauma or abuse.

Originally the idea of psychological absorption came out of attempts to measure susceptibility to being hypnotised and is usually measured using the Tellegen Absorption Scale (Tellegen & Atkinson, 1974). If you are high on absorption this means you can apply total attention to what you are doing to the exclusion of everything else. You are likely to experience synaesthesia in which the senses cross over, as in hearing colours or seeing shapes in sounds. You may be good at summoning up mental images and have vivid memories of the past, as well as responding strongly to meditation and to drugs such as cannabis and psilocybin.

Back in the 1980s when I was struggling with my psychological theory of the OBE, Harvey Irwin became interested in absorption. In early studies he showed that OBErs scored higher in absorption than non-OBErs and later developed his 'dissociational theory of the OBE' (Irwin 1980, 1985, 2000). It might seem obvious that OBEs are a kind of dissociation and indeed they have often been dismissed as 'just dissociation' but this tells us nothing. More interesting is that there are three different kinds of dissociative tendency that can be measured using questionnaires. First, there is pathological dissociation, which includes depersonalisation; the unpleasant sense of feeling unreal, unimportant or detached. Second is non-pathological dissociation, which is closely related to absorption. Third is somatoform dissociation, which relates more closely to bodily than mental dissociation, and includes disturbances in physical sensations and even difficulty moving or walking normally. Irwin found that the bodily type of dissociation most closely predicts whether someone will have an OBE and if so, how many OBEs. Other researchers have since confirmed the connections between fantasy proneness, absorption and somatoform dissociation (Gow et al., 2004), as well as to body dissatisfaction and self-consciousness (Murray & Fox, 2005).

Irwin's theory is rather hard to understand but I will do my best. Strong absorption can be induced deliberately, or by very high or very low cortical arousal, especially in people who score high in absorption capacity. This, along with bodily dissociation, produces an OBE. If the bodily dissociation is gradual, innate biological warning signals occur, forming the OBE onset sensations. Keeping attention away from external and bodily sensations 'effectively suspends support for the socially conditioned assumption that the perceiving self is "in" the physical body, fostering the impression that consciousness no longer is tied spatially to the body' (Irwin & Watt, 2007, p.189). This produces the abstract idea of a disembodied consciousness and corresponds to an asomatic OBE. Then by synaesthesia this may be transformed into a visual image, so producing a somatic OBE. Finally, strong absorption leads to the OBE's perceptual realism.

Phew! Does this help? Well, in some ways it does. It led to predictions about dissociation and absorption that proved to be correct, and any viable theory of the OBE needs to fit with these findings as well as the others I have been amassing here. But I am left with many unanswered questions. Are those vivid sensations on leaving the body really accounted for by saying they are 'biological warning signals'? I want to know specifically why there are drifting and floating feelings, why the vibrations and shaking, why the occasional popping and other sounds, for these don't make sense as warning signals. What are they warning of? Do we really know that both high and low arousal lead to absorption? I don't think so, although they might. Above all, is the sense that 'I' am inside my body really a 'socially conditioned assumption'? This would imply that there could be societies that condition people in other ways, perhaps to feel they are located in their feet, or floating above their heads, or distributed throughout their houses. Is the sense of 'where I am' so arbitrary?

The answer is no. People seem naturally to believe in a single point, or at least a specific area, inside the body where 'I' am located, and they are quite consistent about where this is (Mitson et al., 1976, Limanowski & Hecht, 2011). When encouraged to explore their sense of self in carefully structured interviews, 83 per cent of people confidently located 'the I-that-perceives' in their head, midway between the eyes. This was true for both Chinese and Italians, sighted or blind (Bertossa et al., 2008) and, using different methods, in both adults and children (Starmans & Bloom, 2012). In general, the research suggests that people locate their 'self' either in their upper head or upper torso, with a preference for the head (Alsmith & Longo, 2014) or, to put it in more friendly terms, they live in their brain or in their heart (Limanowski, 2014).

Does this mean there is literally something sitting there inside your brain or heart? Could there be a soul or spirit or centre of consciousness that lives inside the body and is really located where it seems to be? That seems unlikely. We know that the brain is a massively parallel processing system with multiple processing going on all the time and all over the place. So it seems far more plausible that the powerful sense of being a located self is constructed somehow by all this activity. This thought led me to look at OBEs slightly differently and to ask a different question: if I normally feel I'm located inside my head looking out through my eyes, what could make me feel I was located somewhere else?

Once again the OBE throws us back to fundamental questions about the nature of self. Is my self a separate, conscious entity inhabiting a physical body, or is this an illusion? And if it is, what sort of illusion is it and why do I feel so firmly embodied?

## Whatever next?

Much of the OBE research I have described so far was done by nineteenth-century psychical researchers and a few brave souls in the late twentieth century. From all that work we learned a great deal about the phenomenology of the OBE and answered many questions about how common they are, who has them and so on. Progress was certainly made, yet in terms of theoretical understanding nothing really moved on and the whole idea of OBEs remained baffling and contentious. Those who believed in astral worlds or separating souls stuck firmly to their beliefs, parapsychologists kept looking for signs of ESP during OBEs and sceptics had little to offer other than feeble assertions that OBEs are 'just hallucinations' or the tentative attempts by Irwin, Palmer and myself to develop psychological theories. Meanwhile, mainstream science completely ignored the OBE.

Then in 2002 everything changed.

CHAPTER 8

# Inside the Brain

I wouldn't be writing this book if research on out-of-body experiences had just carried on as before, amassing small details to answer our simpler questions but never making any theoretical breakthrough. I am writing it now because, finally, things have changed. In 2002, a paper on OBEs was published, not in an obscure fringe journal or a specialised parapsychology journal, but in *Nature*, arguably the most prestigious science journal in the world. It declared, 'The part of the brain that can induce out-of-body experiences has been located.'

This discovery came about almost by accident, with the work of the Swiss neurosurgeon, Olaf Blanke, and his colleagues in Zurich (Blanke et al., 2002). He and his team were operating on a 43-year-old woman who had suffered frequent epileptic fits for eleven years. Her condition would not respond to drugs and she could not be treated until the surgeons found the epileptic focus, that place in the brain where seizures begin before they spread to the rest of the brain. But they had so far failed. As a last resort they used an advanced technique that allowed them to stimulate, with great precision, many places on the brain's surface and then measure any resulting seizures. This meant opening up enough of the skull to insert an array of electrodes right on the surface of the brain. These are called 'subdural electrodes' because they are spread out underneath the dura, the brain's tough outer membrane.

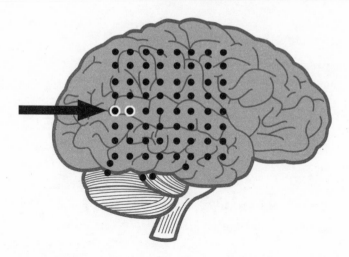

**Figure 8.1: Array of subdural electrodes in Blanke's patient.** The part of the brain that induced OBEs in Blanke's epileptic patient is shown in this three-dimensional surface reconstruction of the patient's right hemisphere from magnetic-resonance imaging. The dots show the position of the subdural electrodes. The two dots indicated by the arrow are the positions that, when stimulated at low intensity, induced bodily distortions and at high intensity produced OBEs.

The brain itself has no pain receptors and the scalp is not sensitive, so while tiny electrical currents were passed through the array, the patient could remain wide awake, answering questions and reporting what she experienced. As the surgeons stimulated different areas in turn they found many of the effects they would expect, including various sensations and muscle movements. They were able to track down the seizure focus and remove it, leaving her free of seizures. What they did not expect was the woman's reactions when they stimulated a spot on the right side of her brain (Figure 8.1).

With a gentle current she reported 'falling from a height' or 'sinking into the bed'; she felt her arms or legs moving or being shortened, and a feeling of lightness. With increasing current she said, 'I see myself lying in bed, from above, but I only see my legs and lower trunk'. Finally, she had the sensation of floating close to the ceiling above the bed, just as people describe in spontaneous OBEs. The place in the brain that can induce an OBE had indeed been found.

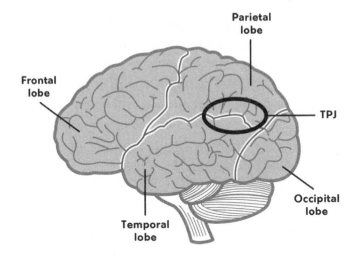

**Figure 8.2: The location of the temporoparietal junction (TPJ).** The brain has four main lobes: occipital, parietal, frontal and temporal. The TPJ, as its name implies, is an area around the junction between the temporal and parietal lobes.

The crucial spot was in the right angular gyrus, a small area of the brain at the temporoparietal junction, or TPJ, in the right hemisphere (Figure 8.2).

This finding was a great surprise although there were already a few tantalising clues. Back in the 1930s, without effective drugs to treat epilepsy, pioneering Canadian neurosurgeon, Wilder Penfield, operated on epileptics when no other treatment was possible. Opening up the skull and using electrodes that were very crude by today's standards, he stimulated patients' exposed brains to try to locate the epileptic focus. On one occasion, when touching a patient's right temporal lobe, she cried out, 'Oh God! I am leaving my body' (Penfield, 1955, p.458). Sadly, he was unable to investigate further and did not report exactly where he had probed. It was not until Blanke's discovery that the precise location was found.

Of course further confirmation was needed, and this duly followed. Belgian neurosurgeon Dirk De Ridder implanted electrodes in the brain of a 63-year-old man in the hope of suppressing his long-lasting and intractable tinnitus (a continuous ringing or buzzing noise in the ear).

Sadly, the tinnitus remained but when he stimulated the patient's right TPJ, 'An out-of-body experience was repeatedly elicited' (De Ridder, 2007, p.1829) with the patient feeling he was located to the left and about 50cm behind his body. The experiences lasted an average of seventeen seconds, measured by asking the patient to press a button at the beginning and end of each episode. A PET (positron emission tomography) scan showed 'highly significant increased activity in a cluster at the temporoparietal junction on the right side' (p.1831). The researchers suggested that activation of the right TPJ is 'the neural correlate of the disembodiment that is part of the out-of-body experience' (p.1829).

Note that this man did not see his own body as happens in most (though not all) spontaneous OBEs. So was his electrically induced experience a 'real' OBE? We might dismiss this idea altogether, or we might accept De Ridder's implication that OBEs are an amalgam of two or more different effects and this feeling of disembodiment is just one part occurring without the rest.

Further evidence pointing to the TPJ comes from patients with epilepsy or brain damage. Swiss researchers compared nine patients who reported OBEs with eight others who did not. In eight of the nine OBE patients the damage was in the right temporal and/or parietal cortex and most often at the TPJ (Ionta et al., 2011).

Swiss neuroscientist Lukas Heydrich even caught an OBE as it happened, and measured the associated brain activity, while a 10-year-old boy had an epileptic seizure in hospital. The boy was able to say when the seizure was beginning because his left hand began to hurt and when the hand began moving by itself he asked his mother whether it was his own, 'Look, the arm is moving. Who is moving the arm?' he asked. After two minutes he became unconscious but later told the doctors that before he lost consciousness he felt lightness and floating. He had the vivid sensation that he was outside his physical body and floating just below the ceiling from where he could look down and see his mother and the room but not his own body. Finally, he seemed to fly above the hospital and then even higher. 'It feels like I am flying way above the world but I know this can't be true. I feel light, very light!' (Heydrich et al., 2011, p.584). Studying the boy's brain, the electroencephalogram suggested a focus in the right temporal lobe, while an MRI scan revealed a lesion in the right angular gyrus – the same place that Blanke had identified before.

It seems there's plenty of evidence to home in on the right TPJ, but what does it mean to have found this special place in the brain?

## Back to the big question

Perhaps it means nothing at all. You might argue that we still cannot explain the OBE just because scientists have found the spot that can induce one. Indeed this finding could work either way. Some will claim this as proof that the OBE is perfectly natural, while others may claim that disturbing the brain releases the true spirit from its bodily shell. And perhaps there's a third possibility: that there are two totally different kinds of experience; the artificially induced, brain-based OBE, which is a hallucination, and the truly spiritual sort, which is not. In that case we should not make the mistake of confusing them.

This brings us back to the two main theories I outlined in Chapter 2, and we can now set them more firmly in the context of what we know about the brain. Here are some suggestions for different versions of the two main types:

A. *Something leaves the body* (dualist theories in which we all have a soul, spirit or astral body).

    1. The brain always releases the soul after death and if stimulated in the right way during life, it can do the same.

    2. The brain is a container or conduit for the soul and prevents it leaving until death but in some circumstances the soul can be accidentally released during life.

B. *Nothing leaves the body* (dualism is false; mind and brain are not separate and there is no soul, spirit or astral body).

    1. The brain can sometimes create the sensation, or hallucination, of leaving the body and when stimulated in the right way it does so.

2. The brain constructs our normal sense of being inside the body and when it malfunctions we have the illusion of leaving the body.

C. *There are two different kinds of OBE:* 'real' OBEs in which something leaves the body, and 'fake' ones which are illusions or hallucinations.

How can we find out which is right? Simply finding the 'OBE spot' in the brain is not enough to settle the issue. Indeed this discovery reminds me of the delightful arguments over the so-called 'God spot'.

## Interpreting the God spot

When brain scans were used to show that spiritual experiences have a basis in brain activity, the media were quick to proclaim that the 'God spot' had been found. Arguments soon polarised into those who thought this showed there is no need for a God (Ramachandran & Blakeslee, 1998), and others who claimed the opposite – that God uses this spot in the brain to make his presence felt, or that 'we' use our brains to contact the divine (Newberg & D'Aquili, 2001). Others went even further, claiming the 'seat of the soul' had been found; or 'the part of the brain that literally communicates with God'; 'the place where the material and the spiritual worlds meet' (Morse, 1990, p.110).

Among experiments that provoked the 'God spot' debate and laid the foundations for the new field of 'neurotheology' was one in which Carmelite nuns lay in a scanner while 'subjectively in a state of union with God' (Beauregard & Paquette, 2006, p.186). Another tested Franciscan nuns deep in prayer and Buddhist meditators in their deepest state of meditation (Newberg et al., 2003). Using a method called SPECT (single-photon emission computed tomography), neuroscientists Andrew Newberg and Eugene D'Aquili found 'a sharp reduction in activity levels' in part of the posterior parietal lobe. They called this the 'orientation association area' because it orients the person in physical space and distinguishes their own body from the rest of the world. They speculated that when deprived of sensory input during deep meditation or prayer this area would no longer be able to distinguish self from other and the person would feel at one with all, or with God (Newberg & D'Aquili, 2001). The experience is 'biologically, observably, and scientifically real,' they declared (2001, p.7).

To me this suggests the beginnings of a naturalistic explanation for the mystical sense of oneness or nonduality, but this is not what Newberg and D'Aquili meant. For them the experience is not 'a delusion caused by the chemical misfirings of a bundle of nerve cells'. Rather, these brain processes evolved 'to allow us humans to transcend material existence and ... connect with a deeper, more spiritual part of ourselves' (p 9). They seem to want to have it both ways.

I mention this because the connections between OBEs and spiritual experiences run deep. Whether you have a brief OBE or a profound religious experience you are likely to wonder about the self: am I a spirit that can leave my body? Am I one with God or with the universe? If not, what am I?

In OBEs the self is still a separate conscious entity even if it seems to have left the body, while in mystical and religious experiences the sense of self can be completely lost in one-ness or non-separation. Religious people may interpret this as merging with God or the divine. Buddhists may see it as a realisation of anatta or 'no-self' – the idea that the self is not an eternal essence or persisting entity but impermanent like everything else. The non-religious may think their experience reveals the interconnectedness of everything in the universe or is a realisation of nonduality. Long-term meditators, whether in religious or secular traditions, often report that their sense of being a persisting self is radically transformed by their practice. My own experience, all those years ago, culminated in this same oneness, my self dissolving into the world and leaving no distinction. So we return to wondering about the self.

These experiences have long been associated with the temporal lobes. For example, people with temporal lobe epilepsy more often report mystical experiences, are more responsive than others to religious words and symbols (Ramachandran & Blakeslee, 1998) and sometimes have OBEs associated with their seizures (Greyson et al., 2014). And

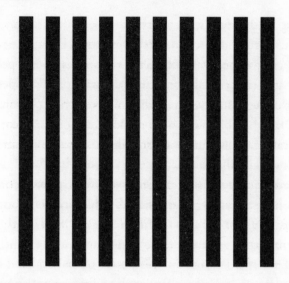

**Figure 8.3: The pattern-glare test.** A typical stimulus from the pattern-glare test. When I look at high contrast black and white stripes like this they quickly start to flicker and scintillate in disturbing ways. If I force myself to keep looking, pale coloured shapes and diagonal patterns drift across the stripes. The effects are extremely unpleasant. Images like this are used in the pattern-glare test. People who are highly susceptible, like myself, are more prone to migraines as well as to OBEs and the effect is thought to be associated with cortical hyper-excitability.

spirituality is associated with decreased functioning of the right parietal lobe after traumatic brain injury (Johnstone & Glass, 2008).

Some people have much more labile (variable or unstable) temporal lobes than others, and are more likely to have paranormal, religious and mystical experiences (Persinger & Makarec, 1987) as well as OBEs (Braithwaite et al., 2011). This connection with the temporal lobe has been used as the basis for a neurobiological model of near-death experiences (Saavedra-Aguilar & Gómez-Jeria, 1989) and Canadian neuroscientist Michael Persinger claims to be able to induce religious experiences by magnetically stimulating the temporal lobes (Persinger et al., 2010), referring to all 'religious and mystical experiences as artifacts of temporal lobe function' (Persinger, 1983).

Does this mean there is something different about the brains of OBErs? Previous findings were based only on questionnaires but British psychologist Jason Braithwaite tested a group of students with the 'pattern-glare test'. This involves looking at striped patterns at different spatial frequencies (the distance apart of the stripes). Some people find that stripes at an intermediate spacing (about three cycles per degree) jiggle about, causing unpleasant movement and visual illusions (Figure 8.3). The OBErs in the group not only showed the usual correlations with temporal lobe signs but were also more susceptible to pattern-glare (Braithwaite et al., 2013a).

Why could this be? Being upset by such patterns is common in people who have migraines and visual illusions, and is thought to be due to cortical hyperexcitability (Wilkins et al., 1984). In other words, OBErs might have a more excitable cortex in general (Braithwaite et al., 2015). I was thrilled when I read about this because I too have migraines and when I look at Figure 8.3 I can't help seeing illusory colours and annoying movements. I see flickering in ordinary black and white text and even on my kitchen worktop! Could a hyper-excitable brain be a clue to why I had that OBE?

But back to the God spot – these associations between brain and experience can be interpreted in totally opposite ways. So if we don't want to end up in the same impasse over OBEs, we need to do far more than discover the spot that can induce them: we need to know why it does so. So what is the function of the TPJ?

## Self and the TPJ

The answer brings us back to that fundamental question about self. Am I a thinking, conscious entity inhabiting a physical body, or is this an illusion?

It turns out that the TPJ is deeply implicated in building up our sense of self. The areas where the two lobes meet are ideally placed to bring together multisensory information from our eyes, ears, skin and muscles to construct a body-schema and body-image (Decety & Lamm, 2007). They incorporate information from emotions, memory and the senses via the limbic system, thalamus and parts of the cortex, and especially the prefrontal cortex, to build up an impression of where our body is and what it is doing; they contribute to our ability to imagine being in someone else's position and hence our capacity for empathy.

Note that the terms 'body image' and 'body schema', although often used interchangeably, can be distinguished. The body image describes your appearance; how you think others see you, how your body looks and how attractive you feel. The body schema refers to the constantly updated model of the body with its posture, actions and position in space. This model of our own body is essential to behaviour, as it is to any creature that moves around, whether a cat, a dog, or a blackbird. It needs to be detailed, reasonably accurate and rapidly updated.

Also essential is our vestibular system. Walking, sitting down and even standing still requires complex coordination to prevent us from falling over. The vestibular system begins with structures in the inner ear that signal rotation, directional movements and acceleration. This information is used at high speed to control eye movements and posture, to adjust breathing when lying down or standing up, and to make quick reflex reactions. Then it feeds up to higher areas of the cortex including the TPJ, to be combined with somatosensory input, including touch, temperature and signals from muscles, bones and joints. When something goes wrong with the vestibular system, whether an ear infection or brain damage, we feel unstable, with disturbing floating, spinning or flying sensations.

I have only once suffered from an ear infection and remember crawling helplessly along the floor of my bedroom with my eyes closed, trying to reach the phone. Every time I opened my eyes the world whirled around me, nausea welled up and I had to shut them again. There was no way I could stand up without falling over. I learned to appreciate the vestibular system from this (happily brief) episode.

You may, as you read this, be sitting in a chair and looking at a book or screen. Take a moment to shut your eyes and feel your body. You will probably have a clear sense of where your arms and legs are, the angle of your neck, the position of your fingers and the sensation of pressure on the chair or your elbows on the table: this is your body schema. It works automatically all the time but you can deliberately sense it, if required, because of the way the TPJ brings the information together and connects with other parts of the cortex. You can also use it flexibly when you imagine turning round or standing up, or being in some other position.

This body schema is combined, at the TPJ, not only with hearing, sight, taste and smell, but with thoughts, imaginings and memories sustained in other parts of the temporal and parietal lobes, and with intentions and control functions handled in the frontal lobes to create a rich sense of self that goes beyond just the body, providing the sense that you are an integral human being, in this position, carrying out these actions, having these intentions and thinking these thoughts right now.

Does this knowledge help us understand the OBE? I think so. Presumably, if the TPJ is disturbed, some of the functions needed to create an accurate body schema and self-image fail. This explains why Blanke and his colleagues refer to OBEs as caused by 'disturbed self-processing at the TPJ' (Blanke & Arzy, 2005), concluding that 'out-of-body experiences may reflect a failure by the brain to integrate complex somatosensory and vestibular information' (Blanke et al., 2002, p.269). In other words, when parts of the TPJ are not working properly, the body schema goes haywire and an OBE results.

If Blanke and his colleagues are right then activity in the TPJ might also be disturbed when people imagine being out of their body. They claim to have shown this by asking volunteers to imagine themselves 'in the position and visual perspective that generally are reported by people experiencing spontaneous OBEs' (Blanke et al., 2005, p.550). Using a method called evoked potential mapping, they found selective activation at the TPJ about a third of a second later.

This finding bothered me for a long time. It reminded me of my own research, described in the previous chapter, in which I asked students to imagine looking at the room from positions outside their body and found that OBErs were better at this and better at switching viewpoints (Blackmore, 1987a). Yet doing this task demands time and effort. You can't just instantly conjure up a different viewpoint, so how could Blanke's team have measured the precise time to an accuracy of a fraction of second? The answer is that they couldn't, and didn't.

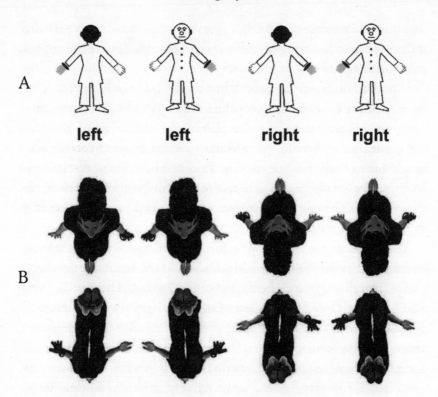

**left**   **left**   **right**   **right**

**Figure 8.4: Own Body Transformation Tasks (OBTs).**
A. The original OBT task. Participants are shown each image many times in random order and have to say, as quickly as possible, whether the grey glove is on the right or left hand. The task is meant to involve imagining one's own body transformed into the perspective of the drawn figures but there are other ways of getting the right answer. The HOBT was designed to solve this problem.

B. Human Own Body Transformation Task (HOBT). Unlike the OBT, these avatars involve two transformations. The two top left and two bottom right require a rotation of the body as well transformation of plane. Also the perspective of those seen from above is more similar to that in OBEs (Braithwaite et al., 2013b).

In fact they didn't actually ask volunteers to imagine being out of body at all, they gave them the 'own body transformation' test (OBT) shown in Figure 8.4 (above).

You can try this for yourself. Look at each outline person in turn and decide whether the grey glove is on the right or left hand. In the experiment eighty of these pictures were shown, in random order, for two hundred milliseconds (a fifth of a second) each, which means the experimenters could accurately time the activity in TPJ. I don't know how this task seems to you, but I have always imagined that I'm looking at a man standing up in front of me and I have to rotate either him or me to decide which hand is which. Others might not even do this but simply take the outline as a mirror image and say 'left' if the glove appears on the right, and vice versa. In that case no imaginary rotation is involved at all.

Leaving aside these problems for a moment, another prediction was that if the TPJ is involved in bodily rotations and perspective-taking then disrupting it should make the OBT task harder. To test this Blanke and his team used transcranial magnetic stimulation (TMS); a non-invasive method in which electrical pulses are passed through a coil placed close to the head. The pulses induce tiny electric currents in small regions of the brain below the coil and this interferes with normal functioning. As predicted, TMS at the TPJ (but not at other brain areas) made the task harder but did not affect imagining other objects moving. So the effect was very specific.

This helps us understand the role of the TPJ but we still have those niggling worries about what the OBT task actually measures and its relevance to OBEs. One argument goes like this: if OBEs are caused by disturbed processing at the TPJ, and if the OBT depends on having a well-functioning TPJ, then OBErs should do worse at the OBT. But what if the OBE requires a positive skill, as I was thinking when I did my imagery experiments all those years ago (Blackmore, 1987a)? Kessler and Braithwaite (2016) take this view. Rather than implying failure, 'genuine OBEs should not be regarded as a flaw in the system of certain individuals but as "the other side of the coin" of full-blown perspective taking', as part of the uniquely human ability to take another person's viewpoint. If this is right, OBErs should do better at perspective taking tasks. So which is true?

Two early studies found that OBErs did worse at the OBT (Easton et al., 2009, Braithwaite et al., 2011), but because of uncertainty about the task, Braithwaite and his team (2013b) devised a new test using avatars seen from different perspectives, including some seen from above (Human Own Body Transformation task, HOBT, Figure 8.4). In their experiment, as in mine, the OBErs performed better.

These arguments may hang on the minutiae of experimental methods. Yet underlying them is the vital question: are OBEs a sign of failure or of skill?

## Bodily illusions and autoscopy

The discovery of the role of the TPJ was a great leap forward but I have many more questions about the idea of 'disturbed self-processing' at the TPJ. Why does it lead specifically to our familiar kind of OBE, to such an integrated and realistic experience rather than, say, a muddled body schema, no schema at all, or perhaps one exploding into fragments? Why do we read again and again of the particular sensations of leaving the body and floating or flying? Why the common viewpoint above the body, looking down? Why the travels and visions? Why is there sometimes a phantom body and sometimes not? Why the silver cord, the strange sounds and other rarer features? Above all, why the extraordinary vividness and realness of the experience if it's caused by 'disturbed self-processing'? And if disrupting the TPJ with TMS makes it harder to *imagine* being out of the body, why should disrupting it some other way make people feel they *really are* out of the body? Indeed, why doesn't disrupting the TPJ lead to all sorts of other distortions and errors as well as to OBEs?

The answer is that it does. Disruption or damage to the temporal and parietal lobes leads to a whole range of strange and interesting experiences. Some can precede a full-blown OBE, as in my own experience, including vestibular sensations of floating, flying or sinking into the bed. Less often people feel as if they are rotating, or that their limbs are being distorted, shortened or pulled out to enormous length. When Penfield induced an OBE back in the 1950s, his patient reported different experiences according to where the electrode was placed; when Blanke did so in 2002, his patient experienced various bodily distortions depending on the strength of stimulation and looking down at her body, she saw only her legs and lower trunk.

We might think these were pathological oddities and nothing to do with OBEs, but if that is true, my own experience begins to sound like one too. Although I have always regarded mine as a classic OBE, reading about Blanke's case reminded me of a curious fact: on two occasions I tried to reunite with my physical body. The second time I saw the body it was no longer whole. There was no head and a jagged edge around the hole in the neck. This seems very odd if you think that a soul or astral body is looking down on the world, but makes much more sense as a distortion of the body schema. Must I reject my experience as not being a real OBE?

I keep coming back to this question: have I deluded myself all along that I had a profound, long-lasting and classic type of OBE? Should I instead consider my experience as some kind of pathology? If so, then those truly classic cases of astral projection must be put in the same dubious category. Monroe felt his arm going right down through the floor and the ceiling below him, and Fox had horrible sensations of being 'stretched' before his astral body projected.

In the psychiatric literature, the OBE is often classed as one of four types of full-body or whole-body illusions. The other three are autoscopy, heautoscopy and the sense of presence or feeling of a presence (FP). Understanding these may help us think more clearly about where the OBE fits in.

The pathological experience of autoscopy is often confused with an OBE but you will remember that the difference is quite clear. In an OBE the experiencing self or centre of consciousness seems to be outside the physical body, while in autoscopy it remains inside with a double outside. Autoscopy was long ago defined by the psychiatrist, Macdonald Critchley (1950), as 'delusional dislocation of the body image into the visual sphere' and by the Ukrainian neurologist, Narcyz Lukianowicz (1958), as 'a complex psychosensorial hallucinatory perception of one's own body image projected into the external visual space'. More recently, Olaf Blanke and Shahar Arzy (2005) define it as 'the experience of seeing a double of oneself in extrapersonal space without leaving one's body'. They give a simple example.

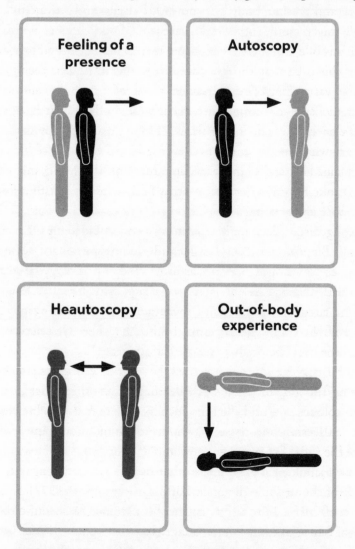

**Figure 8.5: Four types of full body illusion.** OBEs should not be confused with the pathological experiences of autoscopy or heautoscopy. Here each experience is illustrated with black depicting the physical body and light grey indicating the position of double that is typically seen or felt. Dark grey suggests the uncertainty felt in heautoscopy. The arrow indicates the direction in which the person seems to be looking.

'The patient suddenly noticed a seated figure on the left. 'It wasn't hard to realize that it was I myself who was sitting there. I looked younger and fresher than I do now. My double smiled at me in a friendly way' (from Kölmel, 1985, case 6).

It seems odd that the nomenclature is still often confused today but perhaps this is because the term 'autoscopy' literally means 'seeing oneself'. So various full-body illusions are referred to as 'autoscopic hallucinations' or 'autoscopic phenomena' and in OBE research the ability to see one's own body is sometimes referred to as autoscopy since that is literally what the word means. Nevertheless, the difference has been well explained in much of the recent literature on OBEs (e.g. Blanke et al., 2004, Blanke & Arzy, 2005, Brugger, 2002, Brugger et al., 1997, Lopez et al., 2008), along with helpful diagrams (see Figure 8.5, opposite).

Having discovered the apparent connection between OBEs and the TPJ, Blanke and his colleagues (2004) used modern scanning techniques to study six neurological patients who had experienced both OBE and autoscopy. Some of them also reported floating, flying or rotating, and illusory movements or shortening of their limbs. In five of the six patients the brain damage or dysfunction was found to be in the TPJ, some on the right and some on the left side.

Peter Brugger, a neuroscientist in Zurich, points out that in autoscopy the double appears as a mirror image and includes clothes, natural colours and other details such as wearing glasses. He cites a classic 1901 case of an old man who used to smoke his pipe leaning against the right side of his window and regularly saw a man identical to himself smoking a pipe in his other hand and leaning against the left side of the window (Brugger 2002, Brugger et al., 1997). This is not true of OBEs. In some OBEs there is a double at the out-of-body location, but it is not a mirror image. In other (parasomatic) OBEs the self seems to be just a disembodied out-of-body location or floating point of view.

During my own, long OBE I experienced both; starting with a ghostly double that could fly before dispensing with it and becoming just a moving point of view. I wish now that I could remember more about that double: was it a mirror image as in autoscopy? I know that

I reached out with my hand to touch the silver cord and in my memory this was my right hand as it would be in ordinary life, but sadly I did not record this little detail.

## Neither here nor there

The third category of full-body or whole-body illusions, heautoscopy, is the hardest to imagine. Patients not only see a double but may feel they are in both places at once or be unsure which one is 'me' or which position they are looking from. So both body and self seem to be duplicated and sometimes perception alternates rapidly between the two positions. This means that self-localisation, first-person perspective and self-identification may all be experienced as 'split in two parts' (Blanke et al., 2004, Furlanetto et al., 2013). The experience of heautoscopy can occasionally be so distressing that some people resort to suicide (Brugger et al., 1994).

One patient:

> ...felt as if she were 'standing at the foot of my bed and looking down at myself'.... Asked at which of these two positions she thinks herself to be, she answered that 'I am at both positions at the same time.'
>
> Blanke et al., 2004

A 40-year-old Italian woman with an epileptic focus in the right parietal lobe used to see:

> ... the image of her entire body as in a mirror or from an external point of view. She saw herself not from an elevated visuo-spatial perspective, as in out of body experience, but in front of her in normal size and colour without a definable facial expression. The patient could not clearly define her localization in space.
>
> Anzellotti et al., 2011

One man described a bizarre two-stage experience of rising up in his living-room chair and then having a second duplicate body leave the floating chair. He could see this 'second own body' from behind as it sat still. In rapid alternation he heard and saw his wife from above and from in front of him, as though he was still sitting in his chair on the ground. As well as feeling lightness and floating, he was elated and happy. If this is difficult to visualise, his drawing makes the experience clear (see Figure 8.6, below).

Even rarer are the weird phenomena of negative and internal heautoscopy. In negative heautoscopy, people report failing to see their own bodies. They can look down and see no legs; they may even look into a mirror and see no one there.

Internal heautoscopy means seeing inside the body, sometimes seeing one or more inner organs (Blanke & Mohr, 2005). This was originally reported in the early days of hypnosis and it seems that the organs people 'saw' were not anatomically plausible. Brugger gives a vivid example which he translated from a 1920s account of a healthy man who suffered a severe attack of vertigo.

**Figure 8.6: Two-stage OBE with two duplicate bodies.** This series of drawings was made by one of Blanke's patients to illustrate his two-stage OBE. He divided his experience into two periods (A,B). In the first he felt he was lifted about 3 meters into the air in his living room chair in the direction of the arrow (A). In the second period, a 'second' body left his body from the elevated position in the chair (B). (C) depicts the visual scene as he saw it from his elevated position in the chair. The position of his wife is indicated by (A) and his own successive locations by (B), (C) and (D). From Blanke et al 2004.

I approached myself, or rather my body which I already considered dead. A scene which I did not grasp immediately attracted my attention: I saw myself breathing and then I saw the interior of my torso, saw my heart slowly and regularly beating there. I saw the blood circulating in the vessels.

Brugger et al., 1997, p.27

I might have thought this irrelevant to OBEs until I remembered another oddity of my own experience. When I returned to my body, I found myself entering through the neck with its jagged edge and going inside. What happened next, I described as follows:

It was all varying shades of brown, a little greenish in some places and shaded almost like a drawing. . . . it appeared to have no contents whatever, to be just a hollow shell. I went down one of the legs, balanced on the knee joint and then, as if under the influence of gravity, whizzed down the leg into the foot, like going down a slide. . . . There I could look into any one of the openings made by the toes and see light streaming in through the window-like toenails.

I guess a psychiatrist might call this internal heautoscopy. The odd thing is that it seemed absolutely clear, vivid and realistic at the time. I thought that my soul had separated from its body and then gone down inside.

## There's something there

Finally, there is the sense of presence or 'feeling of a presence' (FOP). This may appear too different from an OBE to be worth mentioning but the connection is that, like OBEs and autoscopy, it entails a second body. The difference is that the other body is not seen, but only sensed.

Could this 'presence', this feeling of someone being close by, be a version of oneself? Psychiatrists have long thought so. For example, in the 1950s, Critchley described an elderly patient who used to wake in the night with a very intense feeling that there was somebody in the room. It was ' . . . a person she knew; indeed, with whom she was very familiar. Sometimes, she was at a loss to decide who this could be, but on many occasions, it would dawn on her that this person was none other than herself' (Critchley, 1953, p.242).

Perhaps the invisible presence is like a phantom limb, only it's a phantom whole body. Brugger (2006) notes the similarities and the fact that the double usually walks along with the person and mimics their posture and movements. He suggests that postural and kinaesthetic parts of the body schema are projected outside the body and the double is 'an extension of corporeal awareness into extracorporeal space' (Brugger, 2006, pp.187–8). The presence is 'one's invisible *doppelganger*' (Brugger et al., 1996), one's own body schema projected outside the body.

If this is the right interpretation, it should be possible to induce the invisible presence with brain stimulation, and it is. Once again this was discovered by accident when Shahar Arzy and his colleagues in Lausanne were evaluating a 22-year-old patient with epilepsy. She had no history of mental illness and had never sensed a presence before yet when they electrically stimulated her left TPJ she felt another person close by. When lying down she said, 'He is behind me, almost at my body, but I do not feel it' (Arzy et al., 2006, p.287). When she sat up with her arms around her knees the man hovered right behind her, clasping her in his arms. His position imitated hers and when she tried to read words on a card he appeared to her right, trying to grab the card. There are suggestions that the right TPJ is more concerned with self-processing and OBEs, and the left TPJ with other-processing and the sense of presence, but whether this turns out to be correct or not, this case adds to the evidence that the sensed presence is a displaced body schema.

Happily, an exposed brain is unnecessary because transcranial magnetic stimulation (TMS) can be used, as can a much weaker form of magnetic stimulation. Persinger has long claimed to create the whole range of experiences using a specially adapted motorcycle helmet, sometimes called the 'God helmet'. This has solenoids fixed on either side, just above the ears and right against the temporal lobes. Persinger claims that different patterns induce different experiences when he applies 'complex, physiologically-patterned weak magnetic fields' (Persinger et al., 2010, p.808). However, he has not published the precise details of these patterns and his work has provoked much doubt and controversy. Even so, many people have had strange experiences inside the helmet, including me.

In 1994 the idea of alien abductions had captured the public imagination with wild claims of tall grey aliens with almond-shaped eyes who whisked abductees away to distant planets and operated upon them to steal eggs or sperm and create half-human, half-alien babies. In the midst of all this I was invited to present a BBC TV documentary called 'Close Encounters' for the *Horizon* series (available online, see References, page 346), and this is how I ended up at Persinger's laboratory in Sudbury, Ontario.

Persinger planned to give me an experience similar to alien abduction, leading me into a small soundproof room, where I lay back in a dentist's chair while the helmet was put on and the wires fixed in place. Then the heavy double door was closed and I lay there, fearing I might inadvertently imagine things even if the helmet had no effect. For ten minutes or so absolutely nothing happened. Then suddenly I felt a swaying, rather like the start of an OBE except nothing lifted out of my body. This is how I described it soon afterwards:

> Then it felt for all the world as though two hands had grabbed my shoulders and were bodily yanking me upright. I knew I was still lying in the reclining chair, but someone, or something, was pulling me up. Something seemed to get hold of my leg and pull it, distort it, and drag it up the wall. It felt as though I had been stretched halfway up to the ceiling
>
> Blackmore, 1994, p.31

I would say this was one of the strangest experiences of my life. I've had spontaneous experiences of many kinds, taken many different drugs and tried many kinds of relaxation or imagery procedures, but this was somehow different. Emotions came and went; I suddenly felt terribly afraid, though of nothing, and just as suddenly the fear stopped. I felt suddenly angry and once again the feeling disappeared as suddenly as it came. My body felt pulled and distorted this way and that. I felt controlled by something outside myself, as indeed I was.

We do not know precisely what the helmet does but it certainly affects areas around the TPJ, and I have no doubt it can induce weird experiences that are highly relevant to OBEs. Persinger himself believes that in religious experiences people interpret the sense of presence as a spirit, an angel or even God. He famously invited the evolutionary biologist Richard Dawkins to see whether he could have a religious experience but Dawkins reported nothing unusual happening at all!

Although invisible presences appear with epilepsy, schizophrenia and even migraines, you don't need to be ill to sense one. Perfectly happy and healthy children can be afraid of the monster under the bed or the creature that lives in the wardrobe. Parents may worry that there's something wrong or dismiss these fears as overactive imagination and tell their child not to be silly. Yet these children are not being silly. Their monsters seem completely real, and are even more frightening when combined with waking up unable to move. These are just some of the strange experiences that haunt the edges of our sleep.

There are more.

CHAPTER 9

# Paralysed!

My morning alarm had gone off as scheduled, but then I drifted back to sleep – face up. After a few minutes I seemed to wake once more . . . only to be aware of something or someone sat on my chest, pinning me down, while a second entity ran around my bedroom, mocking me.

The whole experience must have lasted less than a minute, but when I finally awoke . . . (I was still face up and frightened as to what might be staring down at me), I was shocked and confused as to what had actually happened.

This is sleep paralysis (SP), that awful feeling of waking up unable to move. It's perhaps the least pleasant experience you can have on the verge of sleep, especially if you don't know what it is, although it can be fun if you do.

Every night we become paralysed several times to prevent us from acting out our dreams. Usually we know nothing about it, but just sometimes something goes wrong and either the paralysis comes on too quickly before we are fully asleep or it doesn't wear off quickly enough as we wake up. This is the experience known as 'sleep paralysis' (SP), a form of 'REM intrusion' in which the REM state intrudes into either light sleep or even waking (Nelson et al., 2006). When this

144

happens occasionally to someone with no history of sleep disorders it is known as 'isolated sleep paralysis' (ISP). A rarer form is inherited and runs in families.

REM sleep is the stage of sleep during which most dreams occur and most people have four or five periods of REM during a typical night's sleep. The stages are coordinated by signals from the brain stem and the very low muscle tone is induced by blocking the receptors of two neurotransmitters, glycine and GABA (*gamma*-Aminobutyric acid) (Brooks & Peever, 2012). This prevents motor neurons from sending signals to all the voluntary muscles, that is, the ones we can deliberately control. The ones that control eye movements and breathing are not affected. Meanwhile, brain activity is desynchronised and looks rather similar to the waking state except that primary visual cortex is suppressed while the higher visual areas remain very active. This means we cannot see using our eyes (even if they were open) but can still have vivid and realistic-seeming dreams driven by the rest of the visual system. And if REM intrudes into the waking state we get visual and auditory hallucinations. This happens to people suffering from narcolepsy who find themselves falling asleep unpredictably during the day, sometimes experiencing OBEs and hallucinations as well as SP. Sleep deprivation can also produce REM intrusion as the brain tries to catch up on lost REM sleep. For most of us, though, the only kind of REM intrusion we are likely to have is SP.

Needless to say, waking up unable to move can be unpleasant, and even terrifying, if you don't know what's happening, but it's surprisingly common (Spanos et al., 1995). Surveys suggest that anything up to 60% of us have experienced it, with estimates coming from Japan (40%), Nigeria (44%), Hong Kong (37%), Canada (21%), Newfoundland (62%) and England (46%) (Parker & Blackmore, 2002). One overview, synthesising data from thirty-five previous studies, estimated a lifetime incidence of 8% in the general population, 28% among students and 32% of psychiatric patients (Sharpless & Barber, 2011).

As with OBEs, it is hard to know whether people understand the questions as intended. To find out, researchers from Denmark and the US interviewed people as well as giving them questionnaires.

Rates of SP were much higher using questionnaires (38% in both groups) than interviews (25 and 26%) and apparently some people had confused SP with either 'dreams' or 'fatigue' (Jalal et al., 2014a). Shift workers and those with disturbed sleep patterns are the most susceptible, which explains one of its many other names – 'night nurses' paralysis'. In the days when hospital wards were quiet and dimly-lit at night, nurses on night duty might easily fall briefly asleep at their desks, only to wake unable to move when someone needed them.

Anxiety and terror are the most common accompaniments of SP, followed by pressure on the chest and the sense of presence. Less common, but still occurring in up to 30 per cent of episodes, are hallucinations and floating sensations (Spanos et al., 1995, Fukuda et al., 1987, Wing et al., 1994). But there may be several different types of SP.

Based on 196 examples of SP, my student Nicholas Rose developed a sleep paralysis questionnaire and gave it to nearly four hundred respondents (Rose et al., 2002). Using a statistical method called principal components analysis, he found four types: the 'Visionary' Experience, the 'Levitation Dream', the 'Spiritual Assault', and a final experience that resembles a panic attack, with the feeling of being about to die.

'Spiritual assaults' can be deeply unpleasant, like the one that opened this chapter, sent to me by a 25-year-old man who felt that he 'was being attacked by a pair of demons.' He said this had happened to him only twice in his life, adding, 'Both incidents occurred with me face up. I never sleep on my back and always seem to wake up face down. It can't be a coincidence that the two times in recent years I have awoken face up, this has happened.'

We already know that OBEs more often occur when people are lying on their backs, and SP does too (Cheyne & Girard, 2009). Spontaneous OBEs, like the one at the start of Chapter 5 (pages 68–9), often begin with paralysis, and this probably reminds you of Sylvan Muldoon's 'astral catalepsy' as well as the paralysis that Oliver Fox was so scared of that he taught himself astral projection to escape. There is clearly some connection here – but what?

## Sleep paralysis myths

The weird sensations of SP and the sense of presence have evoked a wonderful variety of myths about scary night-time creatures that attack people in their sleep, such as the medieval incubus that rapes women in the night and the female succubus that seduces men. Arabian mythology has its qarinah and Hinduism the voluptuous Yakshinis.

But it is not just ancient traditions that have their myths. Modern variations include 'ghost oppression' in China, *kana tevoro* or being eaten by a demon in Fiji, *Karabasan* in Turkey, 'Kanashibari' in Japan (Fukuda et al., 1987), and 'The Devil on your back' in Nigeria. There are '*Kokma*' attacks by the spirits of unbaptised babies in St Lucia, '*Phi um*' or being enveloped by ghosts in Thailand, '*Hexendruchem*' or passing witches in Germany and '*Ha-wi-nulita*' or being squeezed by scissors in Korea (Dahlitz & Parkes, 1993, Blackmore & Rose, 1997, Jalal et al., 2014b). Nearly every known culture has some kind of SP myth but people in traditional cultures are far more likely to believe they are under supernatural attack (Jalal et al., 2014b).

Until the early twentieth century the 'Old Hag' of English folklore was said to come and press on sleepers' chests, riding them like a horse, which may be how the term 'nightmare' originated (Hufford, 1982, Davies, 1996). Unlucky people who were visited were said to have been 'Hagridden' or 'hagged'.

Even today fear of being hagged survives in Newfoundland, and it was to this bleak but beautiful part of Canada that I went in 1994 as part of the 'Close Encounters' TV trip. In those days before digital cameras this meant travelling across North America with a crew of sound and cameramen, assistant and director, often driving the van myself with the cameraman crouching beside the passenger seat to film me from a ridiculous angle. But there I met abductees, their therapists and hypnotists who claimed to release hidden memories of being paralysed by alien creatures, deafened by engines and humming noises, flying through space and being operated on by evil aliens. Does this sound familiar?

Around that time, a widely publicised Roper Poll, with a well selected random sample, claimed that 3.7 million Americans had been abducted by aliens (Hopkins et al., 1992). Really? Whether many people believed this I do not know, but a look at how the poll was designed should raise doubts even if the figure of 3.7 million doesn't sound silly enough. The questions were compiled by Budd Hopkins, David Jacobs and John Mack, all of whom I met on my travels. On the basis of 'abductees' who 'remembered' their experiences under hypnotic regression, they included five 'indicator experiences'. These were – guess what – waking up paralysed with a sense of a strange person or presence (18%); feelings of flying through the air (10%); lost time of an hour or more (13%); seeing unusual lights or balls of light (8%) and finding puzzling scars on the body (8%). Anyone who ticked four or more was, said the authors, likely to have been abducted – that's how they arrived at 3.7 million.

After meeting so many of these people I was even less convinced that anyone has actually been abducted from earth by grey aliens, although I might be proved wrong in the future. Far more likely, as our TV programme concluded, is that the popular craze for alien abductions, which soon died down again, was a modern sleep paralysis myth, encouraged by films like *E.T.* and *Close Encounters* and part of the popular culture of space travel (Blackmore, 1998, Blackmore & Cox, 2000, McNally & Clancy, 2005, Spanos et al., 1993).

On this same trip I learned something much more interesting when I ended up in a Newfoundland bar, listening to the weird sounds of a band of didgeridoos, and chatting with a group of young people who all believed they'd been hagged. One young woman smiled, wondering whether she'd been visited by an old woman with a black cape only because she'd heard stories of hagging. 'My mind is awake,' she went on, 'and my body won't move. And I want to wake up. I want to scream. I try to scream and nothing comes out. Nothing at all.'

'Whoosh!' said a young man, waving his hands across his face. 'These two things came up in front of my face and it was like a swirly black, grey mass. There was all this weight, just couldn't move, couldn't breathe, just couldn't do anything at all.' They all knew people who had been hagged and worried that someone with a grudge against you might 'hag' you, magically sending the creature to frighten or even suffocate you. Oddly enough, no one admitted to hagging someone else.

One question continued to trouble me: when people are lying in bed paralysed, are their eyes open so that they are really looking at their own room, or are they closed and only dreaming their room? This sounds like an obvious question but we don't know the answer. It would be great if we could catch someone having an episode of SP in the lab and find out, but SP is hard to produce on demand. Even so, it has been done, by repeatedly waking people just after they have entered REM (Takeuchi et al., 1992, 2003). With this regime SP occurs in 'sleep onset REM' or SOREM, as people go straight from waking into dreaming. In one study, people who claimed they often experienced SP got more tired and miserable in the process, suggesting that those of us who cope less well with disturbed sleep may be more prone to SP (Inugami & Ma, 2002).

As for my question, the researchers did not say whether their subjects' eyes were open or closed, although they implied closed. But then SP induced in a lab might be different from spontaneous SP. The man whose story began this chapter said, 'After a few minutes I seemed to wake once more (I say "seemed" as the experience resembled a mixture of being half-asleep, dreaming and being fully awake).' Apparently he couldn't tell.

Yet the Newfoundlanders were quite clear about this.

'I can look around,' said one, 'Can you look around?' he asked the others.

'Oh yes,' replied another young man.

> My eyes are open. I've had the old hag and I've seen my mother walk in the room and walk out when I've had the old hag. And she has and she goes downstairs and, like, she'll yell to me, "Fred, supper's ready," and I'm there like, "Good, sure, it is, um, a bad time, Mum."

Another young man who wrote to me about frequent 'attacks' was just as sure.

... my heart was racing, I felt unable to breath [sic], I was trying to cry out but was totally helpless and unable to do anything. I was struggling and fighting inside the whole time. I really thought I was going to die. Throughout the attack my eyes were open and I was able to see my bedroom quite clearly.

But is this as clear as he implies? Compare his experience with this from a 25-year-old woman, who wrote to me about frequent and frightening SP.

One thing I am also sure about is that my eyelids can flicker open during the paralysis. Once I fell asleep in a lit room and my eyes were flickering open. I had this weird vivid dream that was enacted in a room (the same room I was asleep in) but the whole room was on its side. My head was facing the door of the room as I slept, and in my dream I was climbing up the room, towards the door, which was situated in the ceiling.

Could the man who heard his mother calling have still been in REM sleep and only dreaming of seeing her walk in? This might be like the 'seeing with eyes closed' I have mentioned earlier and we know very little about that so I still couldn't be sure.

A few years later my interest in SP was reawakened when, with my colleague Nick Rose, I advertised for experiences in which reality and imagination are confused. This was part of a project, funded by the Society for Psychical Research, to test the idea that ESP might lurk in the boundary between the real and imaginary (Blackmore & Rose, 1997). We received 201 letters (this was before the days of email) and, to our surprise, over 20 per cent reported OBEs and 128 (64%) mentioned feeling paralysed, even though we had not mentioned either OBEs or paralysis in the adverts. Nearly half included a malign presence and many mentioned vibrations, buzzing and humming noises and the feeling of being pulled or squashed (Rose et al., 2002).

We were then given nearly two hundred letters that readers had sent to *The X Factor*, a magazine about aliens and the paranormal. Twelve per cent described OBEs and many reported paralysis with malign presences, like this one:

> I have on at least a couple of occasions had sleep paralysis, combined with a terrifying dream of something unseen but truly awful that was trying to 'get' me. One 'thing' was in a large wooden chest beneath a window, and it was evil personified, and the other was something clawing away behind a curtain.

Another writes:

> It always happens to me at night when I am in bed, usually in the past when I am going to sleep, but recently it has been after I am asleep hours into the night.
>
> It comes on so quickly with no warning, and a sense of a terrible evil dark presence is there, if I give into it I feel I would never come back. I have to fight so very hard to move a limb and shake myself.

A different sample came from all the letters I received after *Beyond the Body* was published in 1982. These were from people who had read about OBEs and wanted to tell me their stories. Over 70 per cent mentioned flying or floating and nearly a fifth mentioned paralysis, with others describing strange voices and laughter. Almost a quarter (23%) included a sense of presence.

The nastiness of these presences was underlined in a study by my student in Bristol, Jenny Parker (Parker & Blackmore, 2002). She analysed the content of SP reports from sixty-four men and fifty-two women, comparing them with dream norms using Hall and Van de Castle's (1966) well-known scheme. Compared with typical dreams, SP was a more uniform state with more cognitive and auditory experiences and four times as many mentions of parts of the body. Attacks by aggressive creatures were common, as in this particularly revolting example from a 24-year-old man.

As I drifted off to sleep I felt someone climb up on the bed and lie spoon fashion against my back. I could feel this 'Being' against the full length of my body and with its hand resting on my right shoulder. I could also feel its breath on my neck as well as hearing it breathe. I had a large pimple on the back of my neck and I felt the 'Being' press its lips against this and begin to suck. As it did so my whole body, especially the muscles in my upper back, began to spasm and convulse. I was unable to move and found it difficult to breathe. The sucking would stop for a moment as the 'Being' took a breath. The spasms also stopped although I was paralysed, but would recommence along with the sucking. This lasted for what seemed like an eternity, during which time I tried to call for help but couldn't make a sound. I fought to break the paralysis by concentrating my will, after some time I snapped out of it. I felt my self almost immediately fall back to sleep, even though my heart was still racing from terror.

## Explaining sleep paralysis

Astral projection pioneer Sylvan Muldoon believed that physical catalepsy was caused by astral catalepsy. He thought that the astral body becomes paralysed first and only then can the phantom leave, controlled by the subconscious mind and swaying to and fro, until it rights itself into a standing position and becomes free to travel on the astral planes. Other occult theories followed his and even today you can find books and websites that tell you the paralysis occurs because the astral and physical are not properly aligned.

In her many best-selling 'spiritual' books, medium and psychic Sylvia Browne calls 'sleep paralysis' a simpler but less accurate name for astral catalepsy, which is always associated with astral trips. 'Obviously,' she says, 'astral travel can and does happen without an episode of astral catalepsy, but astral catalepsy doesn't happen and can't happen without astral travel.' So was the man mocked by two demons astral travelling? Is everyone who wakes briefly paralysed actually in the astral?

Browne, who was convicted of fraud in the 1980s and whose frequent psychic predictions rarely came true, goes on, 'We know that several times a week our spirits take brief vacations from our bodies while we sleep, to go visiting and exploring throughout the world, the universe, and The Other Side ... On the rare occasions when the conscious mind "catches" the spirit leaving or reentering the body, it panics.' There's no need to worry, though, she says. 'Think of the paralysis, the inability to breathe or scream, and all the other sensations of astral catalepsy as a kind of temporary mental and neurological "short circuit" in response to a realization that the spirit is in the process of either coming or going' (Browne, 2002). She is right to be reassuring but I'd rather understand what is really happening in my body and brain, and I don't think it's a spirit leaving.

If paralysis naturally accompanies REM sleep, we may wonder what causes those buzzing and humming noises that Rose and I read about in the letters we received (Rose et al., 2002). This example is from the same man who was sure his eyes were open (see also page 150).

> My first experience occurred when I was fifteen years old, I had gone to bed at the usual time and as I was about to fall asleep, I became aware of a slight buzzing-humming sound which increased and became more intense. The sound seemed to be heard internally inside my head ... as the sound intensified it seemed to take a grip and paralyze me.

A 26-year-old woman was deeply distressed by regular bouts of SP.

> My S.P. begins when I'm about to fall asleep or about to fall into deep sleep – something which I can't measure. It always begins with a loud 'buzzing' noise which I have also likened to a small electric charge – this always enters my body feet first and works its way up. . . . I am always deafened by buzzing noises and sometimes I hear voices in the background, I always keep my eyes open, I always try and scream for help.

Similar noises often precede OBEs but there is no deep mystery here. Indeed these noises are just what we would expect when the brain is shifting into REM but is still partly awake. Although our eyes can close to shut out light and vision, our ears cannot, yet activity in auditory cortex remains high. So what we are hearing is disorganised neural activity mixed with or provoked by actual sounds.

## Someone's suffocating me!

Imagine you are conscious but still in REM paralysis. Your breathing is under automatic control and is coordinated with bursts of rapid eye movements that correlate with what you are dreaming about. This irregular pattern of breathing will continue as long as REM lasts and there's nothing you can do about it. Even if you are frightened and want to take control you cannot; the automatic process just goes on. No wonder people believe they are suffocating. If only they could relax and let the normal REM breathing pattern continue they'd be fine, but of course this is easier said than done.

The fear experienced in SP is not only a natural reaction to feeling paralysed and unable to breathe but is exacerbated by activity in the amygdala, a part of the brain concerned with emotion and threat detection. The two amygdalae are located deep inside the temporal lobes and are highly active during REM sleep and therefore probably also during SP. This has consequences for memory too because of close links between the amygdala and the adjoining hippocampus, which is essential for laying down memories. This is why we tend to remember more vividly anything that happens when we are afraid.

Does any of this help us connect SP with OBEs and the sense of presence?

Yes, it does. And here we must return to the role of the temporo-parietal junction (TPJ) in managing the body schema. If you wake up paralysed, you may try to move. As happens with any physical action, the brain creates a copy of the intended movement (the efference copy), which enables it to predict the changed body position and check this against feedback from the muscles, somatosensory system and vestibular system to confirm that the movement has happened as planned. But during SP no actual movement occurs. This means there are two body schemas in different positions: one lying down, the other in whatever position you were trying to reach. This second one becomes the double. It has arms and legs and torso and head, but no connection with the body's actual position. This, I suggest, is why sleep paralysis so easily leads to an OBE.

Confirmation comes from the work of two Canadian psychologists, Allan Cheyne and Todd Girard, who investigated the relationships between SP, vestibular-motor sensations (V-M) and OBEs. Giving the 'Waterloo Unusual Sleep Experiences Scale' to thousands of people and using factor analysis on the results, they found three distinct factors. They called these 'Intruder' (a felt presence that can be elaborated into hallucinations of a threatening intruder), 'Incubus' (feelings of suffocation, pressure on the chest, pain and thoughts of death or sexual assault), and 'V-M hallucinations' (floating, flying, falling, illusory movement experiences (IMEs), and OBEs). Intruders were most common in SP novices, and V-M sensations in those who had frequently experienced SP. Some of these experts said that their V-M sensations had turned into interesting psychological or spiritual experiences for them (Cheyne, 2003, Cheyne & Girard, 2009, Cheyne et al., 1999).

But Cheyne and Girard wanted to understand the causal relationships between OBEs and sleep paralysis, proposing three hypotheses: illusory movement experiences might come first, leading to OB feelings followed by OB autoscopy (seeing one's own body as well as feeling yourself to be out); another possibility was that OB autoscopy comes before the OB feelings, as happened in some of Blanke's induced experiences; and finally, illusory movement experiences might directly cause both OB feelings and OB autoscopy. The results of analysing two samples and over eleven thousand cases showed that the first hypothesis was most likely. It is the IMEs – the illusory feelings of movement caused by vestibular and motor disturbance – that are the context in which first OB feelings and then OB autoscopy arise (Cheyne & Girard, 2009). Additional evidence comes from an online study of more than four hundred OBErs, in which Swedish researcher Devin Terhune (2009) found that 32 per cent of respondents reported 'out-of-body feelings' but without any visual content at all.

All this fits with our suspicion that the OBE double is a second body schema created when the muscles are paralysed, and explains why astral projectors so often report 'astral catalepsy' before projecting and why so many induction techniques make use of imagined bodily distortions and vestibular sensations (Chapter 11). These are all ways of inducing that first step – the illusory movement experiences that precede a full OBE.

So the close relationship between SP and OBEs is no coincidence. Being paralysed directly causes illusory movement experiences; this leads to the creation of a second body schema, and only after that can a full OBE occur, complete with visions and seeing one's own body. I would add that I believe that critical last step is not primarily about autoscopy but about vision itself. In other words, there is a flip into clear seeing, or OB vision, whether or not one's own body is seen.

## Flying and falling dreams

Illusory movement experiences are not confined to the awkward conditions of sleep paralysis. Flying, floating and falling are common in ordinary dreams too. Although flying can be exhilarating, falling is not so much fun. You might be rushing headfirst off the tallest building in the world, tripping over a cliff edge into a deep gorge, or dropping out of a dreamed helicopter without a parachute. Psychoanalysts have lumped falling dreams together with anxiety dreams and blamed them on 'separation anxiety'. Freud himself speculated that in women the falling dream may be a euphemistic reversal of the wish to yield to erotic temptation!

Even today, many popular 'dream interpretation' books and websites tell you that falling dreams represent a loss of confidence, a moral fall or a fall from power, or even (having it both ways) either the desire to let go of something or the fear of letting go. Yet somewhere between 58 and 80 per cent of people have falling dreams (Schredl et al., 2004), and there is no evidence that anxious people have more of them (Griffith, 1958). Astral projectors like Muldoon and Carrington (1929) thought falling dreams were the astral body dropping back into the physical at the end of its flight. This is why, they believed, you always wake before you hit the bottom.

# Paralysed!

Or do you? I can remember being told the old wives' tale that if you hit the bottom in a falling dream, you die. Happily, I discovered that it's not true when I dreamt I was standing on the top of a high cliff in a strong wind, looking down on the sea crashing onto spiky black rocks far below. Blown off the cliff, I found myself falling and falling until I hit the jagged rocks. Rather than instant death, I bounced several times and felt my body break apart into many large chunks. Then several ambulances arrived, men scurried over the rocks collecting body parts and packed them into the ambulances. Oddly enough I didn't seem to mind at all – nor to realise it was a dream.

So what are falling dreams? Sadly there is little research to help us. Even in the twenty-first century, mainstream dream researchers rarely stray into such quirky areas. Yet given what we know about the vestibular system and its changes during sleep we can be pretty sure this provides the answer. Even just lying down means adjustments in breathing, blood pressure and muscle tension, all of which require input from the vestibular system (Dharani, 2005). So perhaps it's not surprising if it erroneously signals floating or falling on the verges of sleep. Interestingly, the core region of the vestibular cortex is also located in the TPJ (Aspell & Blanke, 2009).

Another odd effect that happens on the verge of sleep is sudden twitching or jerking of the legs. Occultists say these are caused by the astral body dropping back into the physical. Psychoanalysts have attributed them to hidden fears or anxiety, but they are probably a natural side-effect of the muscles relaxing into sleep. Known as 'myoclonic jerks', 'hypnic jerks', 'sleep starts' or 'predormital myoclonus', they happen most often in the earliest stage of sleep while the muscles are adjusting to the relaxation. They are more common in children than adults and exacerbated by disturbed sleep or irregular sleep schedules. Although they can be a sign of epilepsy and other neurological problems, most healthy people occasionally have them. They too can happen along with the sense of falling, the whole disturbing pattern being just a sign of your body dropping down into deeper sleep.

Flying dreams are much more fun than falling dreams and many people enjoy them without even realising they are dreaming or taking control of where they fly. In my Bristol survey (Blackmore, 1994) a quarter of respondents reported flying dreams and most had had more than one, although only one person claimed to be able to fly at will. Other surveys have found between fifty and sixty per cent. As for who has them, research done after the financial crisis of 2009 found that flying correlated with financial stress (Kroth et al., 2010). More generally, flying dreams are slightly more common in men than women, in people who have frequent dream recall, and in those who score high on 'openness to experience' and low on neuroticism (Schredl, 2007, Schredl et al., 2004).

Over a hundred years ago there was a lively dispute over how to interpret flying dreams in the *Annals of Psychical Science* (de Vesme, 1906). The famous psychical researcher, Colonel Albert de Rochas, who had had flying dreams for half a century, collected cases from the public after publishing an article in a French magazine. A popular explanation of the time was that the flying resulted from the sleeper's inability, while lying down, to place his feet firmly on the ground. But de Rochas argued that on the contrary it resulted from actual astral flights. De Vesme then argued that real astral flights ought to be consistent but among the reports he found that some people flew diagonally, some vertically and some just dropped from place to place; some flapped their arms like wings while others floated on their backs, hopped, slid or swam as if in water, and one just moved by willpower alone. He concluded that flying dreams are not supernatural and provide no evidence for the existence of a soul or astral body.

On 22 April 1913, the Dutch psychiatrist Frederik Willem van Eeden read a paper to the Society for Psychical Research in London. He was a prolific writer and poet, and founder of an experimental commune. In 1896 he began studying his dream life and by the time of his famous paper had recorded five hundred dreams, classifying them into nine types. These included falling and flying dreams, false awakenings and a variety of depths of lucidity or 'mental clarity'. Indeed it was he who coined the term 'lucid dream' to mean a dream in which you have enough insight to know you are dreaming.

Not long after came Mrs Arnold-Forster's *Studies in Dreams* (1921). Like van Eeden, she classified her own rich and strange dreamlife, including many flying dreams. In some of these she flew around inside the British Museum, noticing how high the ceilings were and having to fly lower when she wanted to get through a door into another gallery. In those rather modest days she was worried that when she glided along the streets people would notice the odd way in which she moved and so she developed a special 'flying dress', which hid her feet from view. Presumably she was not aware enough to realise that these disapproving people were also part of her dream.

Does flying lead to lucidity, as van Eeden and Green had both claimed, or is it the other way around? Studying nearly two thousand dreams from 191 people, Harvard psychologist Deirdre Barrett (1991) found, as we might expect, that people who had flying dreams also reported more of other types of dream including lucid dreams. On the few occasions that lucidity and flying occurred in the same dream, lucidity more often came first, then flying. This makes sense because one of the delightful effects of becoming lucid is that you can often take control of the dream and do what you want, whether that is transforming a terrifying monster into a cuddly kitten, as some children learn to do to escape their nightmares, or simply taking off and gliding through the (dreamed) air for fun. But why are we so dim that we don't even realise we are dreaming? Indeed, why does the reverse sometimes happen and we discover we have been dreaming of being awake?

# CHAPTER 10

# Am I Awake?

I wake up and get out of bed I switch on the light, it appears to be dim, like the bulb is going to blow, I then realise I am asleep still, at this moment of thinking, shadows appear, you feel they are unfriendly and want to run, so you try to run, they chase you, and as they get a hold on you, you wake up.

These shadows are always there when I have these dreams, the background is where ever I am sleeping, I have flown in my 'dreams' to escape these shadows. I have no wings while this is happening, I tell myself to do so, the shadows can also fly and look demon-like.

I have fought with a shadow and have been fooled into feeling I have woken up from these dreams only to realise I haven't.

## False awakenings

How do we know whether we are awake or asleep? Two very different experiences prompt this question. One is lucid dreaming; the other is the false awakening, in which you think you've woken up only to discover you were dreaming, as in the description above sent to me by a 31-year-old man. He said it was an experience 'which I still have and which feels real'. You might say that in a false awakening you dream you are awake; in a lucid dream you dream you are dreaming. In one you are wrong; in the other you are right!

# Am I Awake?

In his classic book *Le Rêve: Étude Psychologique, Philosophique et Littéraire* (The Dream) a century ago the French zoologist, Yves Delage (1919), described a series of dreams in which his laboratory caretaker came knocking on his door, urging him to come quickly and attend to a friend who had suddenly fallen ill. He got up, dressed and started to wipe his face with a damp sponge, when the cold water woke him up for real and he realised that it had all been a dream. A little later he dreamt he heard the voice again, calling more urgently. Thinking he must have fallen asleep again, he hurriedly got dressed and once more the cold water woke him. He dreamt and woke up four times without ever getting out of bed, even checking to find a full water jug, empty bowl and dry sponge.

I was reminded of this famous story when a student of mine at Bristol University told me about an infuriating recurrent dream. She would dream that she got up, cleaned her teeth, got dressed, went out into the cold and cycled all the way up St Michael's Hill to the Medical School at the top, only to wake up and realise that she was late for lectures and would have to climb the hill again.

Green proposed dividing false awakenings into two types (Green, 1968b, Green & McCreery, 1994). In the more common Type 1 the surroundings seem quite normal, as they did for my student, although not necessarily where the person is actually sleeping. In Type 2 something is horribly wrong, as for the man above. Their familiar surroundings have an uncanny, or tense and stormy atmosphere with a feeling of suspense or foreboding. The lighting may look strange, with a greenish glow or objects seemingly lit from within – not an entirely pleasant state to find oneself in.

This sounds a bit like one of van Eeden's (1913) nine types of dream, the type he called the 'wrong waking up', described as 'demoniacal, uncanny, and very vivid and bright, with a sort of ominous sharpness and clearness, a strong diabolical light.' He blamed demons for the terror and found that the dream ended only when the demons were seen and the state realised. But he went on, 'the mind of the sleeper is aware that it is a dream, and a bad one, and he struggles to wake up.' So this is different from the majority of false awakenings

161

in which dreamers truly believe they are already awake until they really wake up.

The uncanniness of Type 2 pops up in other places too. Fox (n.d.) describes how he woke one night, or thought he woke, to find everything oddly strained and peculiarly lit. When he tried to move the strange light disappeared and he really woke up. It was during this peculiar state that he saw his beloved Elsie, but when he called her name, she vanished. For Fox the importance of a false awakening was the opportunity it provided for 'stepping out' of his body and into the astral. Many of his projections began this way and he trained himself to use false awakenings to good effect.

What is really going on in false awakenings? There is little research to guide us here although they have very occasionally been caught in the lab. In one study of lucid dreams (Holzinger et al., 2006) subjects were asked to move their eyes left and right, twice to indicate they knew they were dreaming and four times to say they were awake. On a few occasions the physiological measures showed they were fast asleep when they signalled four times, meaning 'awake', showing that false awakenings can happen, as they seem to do, during true sleep.

Most false awakenings end when the dreamer wakes up but sometimes the strange light, the greenish glow, or the curiously wrong details of the room alert them to what is wrong, to ask 'could I be dreaming?' and so, sometimes, to realise the truth.

False awakenings are closely related to lucid dreams. When Barrett (1991) studied nearly two thousand dreams she found that these two experiences were very likely to happen in the same dream or at least on the same night. Sometimes the lucidity came first, followed by a false awakening and then losing lucidity again. Sometimes the false awakening came first and acted as a cue to lucidity. Thus false awakenings, odd and distressing as they can be, can act as a gateway either to an OBE or to fully lucid dreaming.

## This must be a dream

I dreamt I was rummaging about in junk shops looking for something important (though I've no idea what) with my first husband (who's now dead, but I didn't remember this important fact). Setting off along a narrow street I suddenly saw my purse lying in the gutter, all wet. I stared for some time, wondering how it could possibly have fallen out of my bag, and then whether there was still any money inside. I grabbed it, opened it and all the money was there.

Something clicked. Oh yes, people dream of finding money, don't they? Could this be a dream? And with great joy and elation I realised I was dreaming. So I can fly! I flew out of the narrow town streets and along the side of a park where people were strolling with dogs and chatting or playing ball games. 'It's a dream. Don't you see? It's a dream!' I shouted out to them but they paid no attention. 'It's a dream, you can fly like me. Go on, it's wonderful. You can fly!' But no one joined me. They didn't seem to understand.

This was one of my rare lucid dreams; they remain rare, despite my trying every recommended method for inducing them, and despite decades of daily meditation, which is supposed to increase their frequency. Even so, the few I do have are always special, just as this, my most recent one, was.

Lucid dreams are intriguing not just because of the delightful sense of freedom and possibility but because of their deep oddity. In this dream I failed to realise I was dreaming while I went from shop to shop with my dead husband. Surely I should, even when asleep, remember that he is dead. When I did realise I was dreaming it was not because of this ridiculous transcendence of death but because I remembered something I read many years ago. Keith Hearne, one of the first researchers ever to study lucid dreams in the lab (Hearne, 1978), described how he dreamed of being on a Mediterranean beach. Seeing some shiny metal, he started digging in the sand and discovered it was coins. With that he realised he was dreaming. It was this small memory that provoked my own recognition. Finally, when I was lucid enough to enjoy the thrill, to know that I could fly and to control my flying extremely well, I still did not realise that the people in the park were also dream people, just like Mrs Arnold-Forster, with her modest flying dress. What a strange mixture of insight and lack of insight this is.

Equally perplexing is the dramatic change in self. Suddenly, in that moment of realisation, 'I' seem to wake up. But what on earth could this mean? Who is this 'I' that can be asleep in daft and confusing ordinary dreams and then reappear as 'conscious me' aware that I am dreaming? If there's a soul or astral body how would this help? If not, what could possibly be happening inside a brain that could correspond to 'me' waking up? This troubled me from the first time I ever had a lucid dream. I could feel this dramatic change in consciousness but couldn't even formulate sensible questions about what was going on. It is only now, in the twenty-first century that these questions begin to make sense and even find answers.

When he coined the term 'lucid dream' van Eeden (1913) wrote 'the re-integration of the psychic functions is so complete that the sleeper reaches a state of perfect awareness and is able to direct his attention, and to attempt different acts of free volition. Yet the sleep, as I am able confidently to state, is undisturbed, deep, and refreshing.' He remarked that of his five hundred recorded dreams about 70 per cent were lucid and most ended in a non-lucid dream from which he awoke. This is a remarkably high level of lucidity and his description is delightful, but sadly such 'perfect awareness', attention and volition, is very rare.

What does this have to do with OBEs? Lucid dreams and OBEs are linked in at least three ways. One is that many spontaneous OBEs start from lucid dreams and some of the best-known astral travellers have used lucid dreaming this way, including Oliver Fox with his 'dreams of knowledge' (see page 58). Another is that the same people tend to report both, as well as flying and falling dreams (Green, 1968b, Blackmore, 1982b, 1984a). A third is that it can be hard to draw the line between a lucid dream and an OBE (LaBerge, 1985). Becoming lucid is often described as like 'waking up in a dream', bringing with it a sense of being 'myself' again, of really being there, which sounds very much like OBE awareness.

Occasionally people have a lucid dream in which they visit their own bedroom and see their own body sleeping there. Is this then an OBE by definition? According to my definition it is because the person seems to see the world from somewhere outside their own body. According to Alvarado (1982) it is not because he specifies that an OBE is a *non-dream* experience. There is no point worrying about this conflict, better to conclude that the two experiences are closely related although one typically starts from waking and the other from dreaming sleep.

Can we define lucid dreams more precisely than just 'knowing you are dreaming'? The German psychologist Paul Tholey listed seven different signs that must be present, including awareness of dreaming, the ability to concentrate, make decisions, remember the past and be aware of the self. These are tough requirements. I don't think many – if any – of my lucid dreams would qualify on all these, and subsequent studies suggest wide variation. Even the ability to control the dream, so often associated with lucid dreaming, is not universal and may occur with or without lucidity (Kahan & LaBerge, 1994). So it's probably best to stick with the simple definition.

## Lucid through the ages

There are ancient Hindu and Buddhist texts that describe a variety of altered states, including awareness in dreams and learning to control them, but these are more directed towards spiritual development than scientific understanding and I will return to this theme later. Some believe that Mohammed's seventh-century 'night journey' was a lucid dream in which he flew to the furthest mosque on a great steed and then to heaven to gain teachings from God.

If it was, the pleasures of lucid dreaming are not for ordinary Muslims, for lucid dreaming is *'haram'* or 'forbidden'. One Islamic website tells readers that 'Controlling one's dreams means that the sleeper is in a state of awareness whilst he is dreaming! And this is something that cannot happen . . . claiming to have control of them is a figment of the imagination.' States in between waking and dreaming are impossible and, 'It is very unfortunate that this is a myth that is dressed up as science, like Darwinism. It may be opening the door to the shayaateen [devils] to toy with you'. Another advises that exploring your own dreams 'comes under the heading of spreading immorality and disbelief'.

Christianity too has a history of suppressing people's dream lives, which arguably explains why so little was written about lucid dreaming through the Middle Ages and until the Enlightenment. I doubt most Christians today believe that OBEs or lucid dreams are sinful, but some do. In reply to the question, 'Is having a lucid dream a sin?', the website 'The Bible has ANSWERS' replies that, 'Some researchers have identified a similarity between lucid dreaming, near-death experiences, transcendental meditation, out-of-body experiences, and other occult and New Age practices. God's Word forbids these practices (Leviticus 20:27; Deuteronomy 18:10-12).'

Aristotle, in about 350 BCE, wrote a treatise, *On Dreams*, in which he noted that 'often when one is asleep, there is something in consciousness which declares that what then presents itself is but a dream' (Mavromatis, 1987). René Descartes wrote briefly about his dreams and Samuel Pepys described a delightful dream in his diary of 1665, saying, 'I had my Lady Castlemayne in my arms and was admitted to use all the dalliance I desired with her, and then dreamt that this could not be awake, but that it was only a dream.'

Sometimes described as the father of lucid dreaming is the French academic and Chinese scholar Marie-Jean-Léon Lecoq, Baron d'Hervey de Juchereau, Marquis d'Hervey de Saint-Denys – I will call him 'Saint-Denys'. Although he wrote anonymously, he was soon identified as the author of an 1887 book, *Les Rêves et les Moyens de Les Diriger Observations Pratiques* (or *Dreams and the Ways to Direct Them: Practical Observations*) (de Saint-Denys, 1982). He had begun recording his dreams when he was just thirteen and included such comments as 'the dreamer is perfectly aware he is dreaming' or 'I was aware of my situation'. Presumably he published anonymously because the Church still opposed studying dreams and digging into what might be the work of the Devil. It was not until the early twentieth century that writing about dreaming became easier in the West, prompting a burst of research, debate and self-investigation, including Freud's dream theories, van Eeden's reports and the tales of the great astral projectors Sylvan Muldoon and Oliver Fox.

## Degrees of lucidity

Oliver Fox's ultimate hope was to find a route to astral projection, and lucid dreams were his stepping stone: 'I was tremendously bucked by my discovery that in a dream one could acquire, by observing some incongruity or anachronism, the knowledge that one was dreaming.' He described the ensuing change in the quality of the dream and how,

> ...it led to this exciting question: Was it possible, by the exercise of will-power, to prolong the dream? And I pictured myself, free as air, secure in the consciousness of my true condition and the knowledge that I could always wake if danger threatened, moving like a little god through the glorious scenery of the Dream World.

He told himself,

> Before going to sleep I must impress upon my mind the desirability of not allowing the critical faculty to slumber; it must be kept awake, ready to pounce on any inconsistency in the dream and recognize it as such. It sounds simple . . . but in practice I found it one of the most difficult things imaginable.
>
> Fox, n.d., p.34

I guess anyone who has struggled to become aware in their dreams will agree.

Fox gives a delightful example to illustrate four levels of awareness. He dreams he is sitting in a café when he notices at a nearby table a girl who would be very attractive except that she has four eyes. With little critical awareness he is hardly surprised during the dream but on waking has a faint feeling that there was something odd about her. Suddenly he gets it, 'Why, of course, she had four eyes!'

With a little more 'critical faculty' he might exhibit mild surprise, 'How curious, that girl has four eyes!' With still more he could understand that the eyes are abnormal but would reassure himself by thinking there must be a freak show or circus in town. Finally, at the fourth and highest level he refuses to be satisfied with this explanation and thinks, 'But there never was such a freak! An adult woman with four eyes – it's *impossible*. I am dreaming.' (Fox, n.d., p.36).

How can we learn to progress through these stages when most of us wake up in the morning after some completely stupid and impossible dream and think, 'Why on earth didn't I realise that Mum has been dead for years, my daughter is not the prime minister, and it's impossible for a volcano to erupt in the middle of my garden?'

Green listed four events that tend to coincide with lucidity: emotional stress in the dream, recognising incongruities, recognising a dream-like quality, and analytical thought, but, as she pointed out, we cannot conclude that the recognition itself causes the lucidity. It could be the other way around, or it might be that some change in bodily or brain state causes both.

Green described how we can sometimes get as far as asking, 'Is this a dream?', and still wrongly decide it is not. She called this a 'pre-lucid dream', giving an example from Delage, who was losing his sight but dreamt he could see again. In one dream he remembered how disappointed he had previously been to wake up and find it was not true so he asked himself whether he could be dreaming again. To test this, he asked his daughter-in-law to pinch him and when he felt the pinch he was very happy. But he didn't realise that the pinch, too, could be dreamed and so, yet again, woke up disappointed. It's so frustrating!

Others have invented better tests. P. D. Ouspensky, the Russian esotericist and follower of Gurdjieff, developed a method of maintaining awareness while falling asleep and observing the process as it occurred. He wrote, 'When one realises one is asleep, at that moment one is already half-awake.' He describes a dream of being in a room with a small black kitten. Deciding to test whether he was asleep or not, he commanded the kitten to change into a large white dog. Sure enough it transformed into a dog, but simultaneously the wall disappeared to reveal a landscape and he had to struggle to remember the most important thing, that he was asleep and conscious of himself. Even with all his practice he still found it hard to maintain lucidity.

# Am I Awake?

My favourite story of dream-testing comes, once again, from Oliver Fox:

> I dreamed that my wife and I awoke, got up, and dressed. On pull-
> ing up the blind, we made the amazing discovery that the row of
> houses opposite had vanished and in their place were bare fields. I
> said to my wife, 'This means I am dreaming, though everything
> seems so real and I feel perfectly awake. Those houses could not
> disappear in the night, and look at all that grass!' But though my
> wife was greatly puzzled, I could not convince her it was a dream.
> 'Well,' I continued, 'I am prepared to stand by my reason and put it
> to the test. I will jump out of the window, and I shall take no harm.'
> Ruthlessly ignoring her pleading and objecting, I opened the win-
> dow and climbed onto the sill. I then jumped, and floated gently
> down into the street. When my feet touched the pavement, I awoke.
>
> Fox, n.d., p. 69

Fox admits he was nervous about jumping because the atmosphere inside the bedroom seemed so real. He desperately wanted to know whether his dream-wife was only the creation of his own mind or was, as he hoped, 'functioning in her astral vehicle'. He seems to have been disappointed, concluding, 'Most unfortunately, my wife has never had any memory of dreaming on the occasions when I have seemed to encounter her either in a projection experience or in an ordinary dream' (p.70).

Van Eeden once dreamt of standing by a table with various objects on it and, knowing it was a dream, decided to experiment:

> I began by trying to break glass, by beating it with a stone. I put a
> small tablet of glass on two stones and struck it with another
> stone. Yet it would not break. Then I took a fine claret-glass from
> the table and struck it with my fist, with all my might, at the same
> time reflecting how dangerous it would be to do this in waking
> life; yet the glass remained whole. But lo! when I looked at it again
> after some time, it was broken.

169

It broke all right, but a little too late, like an actor who misses his cue. This gave me a very curious impression of being in a fake-world, cleverly imitated, but with small failures. I took the broken glass and threw it out of the window, in order to observe whether I could hear the tinkling. I heard the noise all right and I even saw two dogs run away from it quite naturally.

van Eeden, 1913, p.448

He proceeded to drink some claret, found it tasted quite like wine and thought what a good imitation this world of dreams was.

It is indeed – or can be. But why? And what is this world? Some occultists claim it is the astral world, while others disagree. Religious believers may think their soul travels during dreams, as do people from many varied cultures around the world (Sheils, 1978), but this throws us right back into all the problems that beset astral projection theory. Can we find better answers?

## The science of lucid dreaming

I have lots of questions. Why does lucid dreaming feel so wonderful? Why do I feel more like 'myself' once I realise I'm dreaming? Why can I sometimes control lucid dreams – even if I couldn't get those dream characters to fly alongside me? Above all, why does lucid dreaming feel more like being awake than ordinary dreaming, and what does that mean?

The first lucid dream I ever wrote down was on 16 March 1980, when I'd been recording my dreams for about two years. I wrote:

Lifted up on a chair lift but with no skis. Sun rising ahead over beautiful mountains, saying to someone how fantastic it was. It was! At first I was frightened but realised it was a dream and so felt terribly happy. Tried to imagine skis on my feet, since I was in control, but I don't remember any more!

I recounted this dream more fully in *Beyond the Body*, not long after it happened, describing the glorious mountain scenery, the snow lit by an orange glow as the sun came up and my shock at realising I had no skis on. How would I get off? And how did I get onto the lift without them? Then I worried that lifts don't run at dawn, in the dark and finally got to the solution, it must be a dream. For an instant everything was wonderfully clear; the mountains, the crisp clean air – van Eeden's 'change in the quality of the dream'. I wanted to fly, but instead found myself running across the snow and the lucidity was gone.

I didn't record another lucid dream for nearly a year after that. I was running back into a hospital to collect something I'd forgotten, but I couldn't find a way in. So I struggled up the fire escape but it began collapsing all around me. Terrified, I thought I was about to fall until I suddenly realised I wouldn't: it was a dream. I looked around at the falling bricks and stairs, thinking, 'This is a lucid dream, Wow!' and trying to see whether everything looked brighter. It did, but only a little and I felt somewhat disappointed. This, like van Eeden's lucid dreams, soon turned back into ordinary dreaming as I ran to the waiting van outside. But it prompted all those difficult questions.

Perhaps we must start with some easier ones though. First of all, we know not everyone has lucid dreams, although most people do. One online survey of 571 lucid dreamers suggested their lucidity most often began during adolescence (Stumbrys et al., 2014). Estimates among students include Green (73%), Palmer (71%), Kohr (70%) and my own students (Surrey 79%, Bristol 72%), with most having had more than one lucid dream. Yet representative samples of adults give lower figures such as Palmer's town sample (56%), my Bristol sample (47%) and another in Germany (51%, Schredl & Erlacher, 2011). This seems odd as you might expect older people to have had more time in which to accumulate experience. So are they forgetting the wonderful dreams of their youth?

A German study may provide an answer. Researchers interviewed nearly 700 students aged six to nineteen years in many German schools. As you might expect, the number who had ever had lucid dreams increased linearly with age, from a quarter of the youngest children to nearly three-quarters of the 18- and 19-year-olds. But when asked how often they currently had lucid dreams the result was the reverse. It was the youngest children, aged six and seven, who could more often change the dream plot at will and reported currently having more frequent lucid dreams. (Voss et al., 2012).

What about those harder questions; what does it really mean to become aware you are dreaming and how can we find out?

The route to finding answers began with a famous case of remarkable scepticism. Back in the 1950s the prominent American philosopher Norman Malcolm (1959) declared that lucid dreams were impossible and those who claimed them must have briefly woken up. Many dream researchers agreed with him, one arguing that lucid dreams are 'not typical parts of dreaming thought, but rather brief arousals' (Hartmann, 1975, p.74). This was more or less the accepted view when I was a student; lucid dreams were relegated to pseudoscience, if they were discussed at all.

The insight that proved the sceptics wrong came in 1978 with a brilliant discovery made independently by one researcher in Britain and another halfway across the world in California. The problem is this: we know that during REM sleep the voluntary muscles are paralysed so we cannot shout out, 'Hey, I'm dreaming,' nor press a button, nor wave, nor attract attention in any obvious way. In Liverpool, Keith Hearne, who was doing research for his PhD, did try. He was lucky enough to have discovered expert dreamer Alan Worsley, who could become lucid more or less at will and was willing to sleep in the lab night after night. Hearne tried many methods, such as taping a button to Worsley's hand for him to press when he became lucid, but Worsley only dreamed he pressed the button and even heard it click, but nothing actually moved.

However, we do keep breathing during REM sleep. So Hearne tried using breathing rate as a signal and this worked to some extent, but the real success came with eye movements. Obviously the eye muscles are not paralysed (there would be no 'rapid eye movements' if they were) so he asked Worsley to signal by moving his eyes left and right eight times in succession if he became lucid. It worked. Hearne could see the signal clearly on the recording polygraph and then the results kept coming. By matching up Worsley's signals with the EEG he discovered that a typical lucid dream lasted between two and five minutes, came at about 6.30 a.m., about twenty-four minutes into a REM period, and towards the end of a twenty-two-second burst of rapid eye movements (Hearne, 1978, 1981). The doubters were wrong: lucid dreams are not inventions, wishful thinking, micro-awakenings or brief arousals, they are true dreams.

Are they more than that? For example, could lucid dreams induce psychic powers? Fox said he saw his exam questions, van Eeden claimed to see the future and a few of Green's lucid dreamers claimed psychic abilities. Of course they could be wrong; the very vividness and controllability of lucid dreams might lead people to think they are seeing or influencing distant events. But what if they are right? This would open up a new avenue for parapsychology and change our entire understanding of dreams.

To find out, Hearne tried to transmit numbers to Worsley while he was dreaming. As soon as he saw the eye movement signals he picked a number from random number tables and concentrated on it. Sure enough Worsley saw numbers in his lucid dream; numbers on houses, numbers on gates, numbers in many other forms, but they were never the right numbers.

Meanwhile, on the other side of the Atlantic, Stephen LaBerge (1980) had the very same insight about using eye movements as a signal. But whereas Hearne had only one dreamer, LaBerge studied five. Their lucid dreams also occurred during REM sleep and without any sign of micro-awakenings (LaBerge et al., 1981, 1986). Further discoveries followed; that lucid dreams usually occur during phasic REM in periods of heightened arousal, increased breathing rate and more eye movement compared to average REM sleep.

Collecting more accounts of lucid dreams and studying more dreamers in the sleep lab, LaBerge and his colleagues identified two types of lucid dream. The majority, perhaps 80 per cent, they called DILDs or 'dream initiated lucid dreams'. These occur right in the middle of REM sleep, as confirmed by the polygraph. The other 20 per cent are WILDs or 'wake initiated lucid dreams' in which dreamers report waking briefly before directly entering a dream with no break in awareness.

Some dream reports suggested that WILDs included more OBE-like content, so they checked 107 lucid dreams from fourteen different dreamers and classified them into DILDs or WILDs according to whether the physiological measures showed a brief awakening or not. Ten of the lucid dreams included body distortions, vibrations, paralysis, floating or flying, being aware of being in bed, or the sensation of leaving the body and these were four times more likely to occur in WILDs than DILDs. Concerned that this might only be true for lab conditions, they sent questionnaires to nearly six hundred people interested in lucid dreaming. Eighty-five per cent were able to return to a dream after waking up, which would make it likely they could have WILDs, and these people reported not only more lucid dreams but more OBEs and more sleep paralysis (Levitan & LaBerge, 1991).

When Hearne and LaBerge first tried to publish their findings, they were not met with enthusiasm. The journals *Science* and *Nature* both rejected LaBerge's first paper in 1980 (LaBerge, 1985) and it was a long time before other scientists realised that once lucid dreams could be studied in the sleep lab all sorts of previously unanswerable questions could be investigated.

For example, how long do dreams take? Do the events play out in normal time as they seem to do, or do they happen in a flash? For centuries this has been a live question with many speculating that dreams might be entirely concocted in the moment of waking, taking almost no time at all. In 1865, the French physician, Alfred Maury, had his famous 'guillotine dream'. It was Maury who coined the term 'hypnagogic hallucination', and he strongly disagreed with his contemporary, Saint-Denys, about the nature of dreams: he thought they were caused by external events. In this particular dream he was chased, through a long series of events, to the guillotine, where, as the blade fell, he awoke to find the bedpost fallen on his neck.

This seemed to confirm that long dreams can be created instantaneously. But Maury was wrong. Once EEG recording could be used to identify REM sleep, researchers could wake dreamers and ask about their dreams. Those who had been longer in REM reported longer dreams. But it was the discovery of signalling from lucid dreams that really settled the matter. In his early research, LaBerge (1985) asked dreamers to signal when they became lucid, then count a ten-second interval and signal again. Their average was thirteen seconds, which was the same as their estimate when awake. Alan Worsley also gave accurate estimates of the length of whole dreams or segments of dreams (Schatzman et al., 1988).

Later research found a more complex picture. Counting the time taken does indeed seem to be the same as when awake but physical actions take longer. In one study, dreaming of doing squats took 40 per cent longer than they would in reality (Erlacher & Schredl, 2004). In another, lucid dreamers had to walk ten, twenty or thirty steps and do a gymnastics routine that would take the same time as walking ten steps. Both these actions took longer in the dream than they would in real life (Erlacher et al., 2014).

Are the same nerves and muscles involved? Yes. In early experiments Worsley dreamed of drawing triangles and small muscle movements were detected in his forearm. When he kicked a ball or snapped his fingers relevant muscles were slightly activated, and his eye movements tracked the movements he said he was watching in his dreams (Schatzman et al., 1988). When LaBerge breathed extra fast or held his breath the changes happened physically as well, and when he sang in a lucid dream his right hemisphere increased activation, but when he counted it was the left, as we would expect when awake (LaBerge & Dement, 1982a,b).

Could practising a skill during a lucid dream improve that skill for real? Early experiments showed that people could improve existing skills and even learn new ones by deliberately dreaming about them (Tholey, 1990). More recently, 57 per cent of a group of 840 German athletes reported having lucid dreams and 9 per cent claimed to use lucid dreaming to practise their sport (Erlacher et al., 2012). Other experiments tested practising simple skills such as finger tapping or throwing coins into a cup during lucid dreams and found this works better than actual waking practice (Stumbrys et al., 2016). This makes sense because imagining an action uses much of the same brain areas as actually carrying it out; the value of lucidity is presumably the greater control it gives. If I want to get better at playing my snare drum, I must first practise lucid dreaming and then dream that our whole village samba band is playing brilliantly and I am not making all my usual mistakes.

Are we getting closer to answering the questions I began with – why lucid dreams feel so different and why I feel 'more myself' or 'more conscious'? Back in 1988, LaBerge speculated that high levels of cortical activation might provide the memory access and cognitive abilities needed to realise it's a dream (LaBerge, 1988). It was a good guess but impossible to reject or confirm until nearly twenty years later when he and his team could use physiological measures to explore the differences in brain activation between lucid and non-lucid dreams (Holzinger et al., 2006).

Using EEG, they found differences in the beta frequency band (13–19Hz), which is usually associated with waking activity, and the largest difference was in the left parietal lobe, suggesting a link with language and self-awareness. They concluded that lucid dreaming as a conscious act is based on understanding the words 'I am dreaming'.

Increased activity in the gamma range has also been found, especially at 40Hz, which is often associated with consciousness. A mixed state with some features of waking and some of REM sleep has been found, along with a large increase in 'global networking' across the brain. In other words, more long-range connections are made during lucid dreaming, which might mean more links between self-processing, memory and thinking (Voss et al., 2009).

If this seemed to be creeping towards answers, the picture was made far clearer with the first ever study of lucid dreaming in an fMRI brain scanner (Dresler et al., 2012). In REM sleep the dorsolateral prefrontal cortex (DLPFC) is normally deactivated compared with waking. This recently evolved and slow maturing brain area is part of a functional network that includes the TPJ. Its functions include planning, working memory and cognitive flexibility so its inactivation could explain why ordinary dreams are so bizarre and illogical and we have so little insight. Knowing this led to the prediction that the DLPFC should be more active in lucid than ordinary dreams and this is exactly what was found: one of four dreamers had two long and stable lucid dreams in the early hours of the morning, both signalled with eye-movements and both reported on waking. During those dreams the DLPFC was more active.

Further links with prefrontal cortex were found by applying transcranial direct current stimulation, a method similar to TMS but using direct current instead of magnetic stimulation. Although not a large effect, this stimulation increased lucidity in frequent lucid dreamers (Stumbrys et al., 2013). Other hints come from research showing that intellectually more able school students report more lucid dreams (Voss et al., 2012), and frequent lucid dreamers do better than non-lucid dreamers at a problem-solving task designed to measure insight (Bourke & Shaw, 2014).

What then of the sense that I become more 'myself' when lucid? An area called the precuneus, on the inside of the parietal lobes, is known to be deactivated during REM (Dresler et al., 2012). Since this area relates to self-referential processing, including first-person perspective and the sense of agency, this nightly deactivation could explain why 'I' am not myself in ordinary dreams, so it is especially interesting to learn that the parietal lobes are more active during lucid dreaming than ordinary REM sleep (Holzinger et al., 2006).

All this needs caution and a lot more research, especially because the scanner results depended on just one lucid dreamer and two dreams, but the principle emerging is clear enough: the areas of the brain that are especially active in lucid as opposed to non-lucid dreaming are the ones involved in decision making, logical thinking and the construction of self.

It seems that we need no speculations about astral worlds or souls leaving the body to understand the extraordinary sensations and exhilarating control we find in lucid dreaming. Instead we are creeping towards the slightly discomforting idea that what we call our mind or consciousness is constructed by an integrated set of brain structures that models selves and worlds, provides more or less clarity and insight, and can induce both lucid dreams and OBEs.

If you're a lucid dreamer you'll recognise this wonderful feeling of waking up in your dreams. If not, perhaps it's time to try.

# CHAPTER 11

# How to Get There

You want to have an OBE? First, become lucid! This is a lot harder than it sounds unless you are a natural lucid dreamer. In that case you may wonder why others find it so hard. But it's not impossible to learn and then, if you want, to convert the lucid dream into an OBE.

Simple preparations can help. High levels of physical and emotional activity during the day tend to precede lucidity at night, as do playing video games (Gackenbach, 2006). Even reading about lucid dreams sometimes provokes them and students have often told me they had their first ever lucid dream after my lecture on the topic. Waking during the night and carrying out some kind of activity before falling asleep again also encourages lucidity during the next REM period, as can napping during the day, and these hints form the basis of some well-known induction techniques. Whichever method you decide to try, it is helpful to keep a dream diary before you begin to help you remember your dreams and alert you to your own recurring dream themes. There are many methods but I will briefly outline just four main types.

*Waking awareness.* Throughout the day keep asking yourself, 'Am I awake or am I dreaming?' This builds on the idea that we spend most of our lives in a waking daze; if only we were more aware in waking life, we would become more aware while dreaming. The problem is getting distracted away from the present moment, which is why meditation and mindfulness are supposed to increase lucid dreaming (Gackenbach & Bosveld, 1989). A quicker trick is to write a big 'C' on your hand and every time you notice it, ask, 'Am I conscious now?' or 'Am I dreaming?' (Tholey, 1983). If you practise really hard, you may find yourself looking at your hands in a dream and asking, 'Am I dreaming now?' Even then you might say 'no', but it's a good start.

*MILD or Mnemonic Induction of Lucid Dreaming.* In its simplest form all you need do is use a mnemonic, or memory aid, while falling asleep. You might say, for example, 'I will have a lucid dream tonight', or 'I will realise I'm dreaming'. Knowing the common themes that recur in your dreams helps the shift into lucidity. I often dream of crawling along crumbling cliffs or dangerous ledges, or of wanting to go skiing and being prevented, but it's amazing how often I have dreams like this and still don't realise I'm dreaming. Whatever your themes are, keep them in mind as you fall asleep. LaBerge developed MILD in the 1970s, suggesting you set an alarm for the early hours of the morning when most lucid dreams occur, then get up and walk around or do some other activity, before going back to bed and imagining yourself asleep and dreaming. Rehearse the dream from which you awoke and remind yourself, 'Next time I dream this, I will know I'm dreaming.'

*Technology.* Many gadgets are available, most aimed at getting you into a half-asleep state, using lights, sounds or vibrations. Hearne experimented with spraying water onto sleepers' faces or hands but although some dreamed of water, they rarely became lucid. His more successful 'Dream Machine' detected the changes in breathing rate which accompany the onset of REM and then gave a weak electric shock to the wrist (Hearne, 1990). LaBerge tried recorded voices and vibrations but settled on flashing lights for the first version of his 'DreamLight'. Out of forty-four subjects tested in the lab, 55 per cent had a lucid dream and two had their first-ever lucid dream (LaBerge, 1985). Following this, the NovaDreamer used goggles that detected

REM and flashed lights in different patterns to encourage lucidity. Since then other systems have been developed, including a sleep mask called Remee and a phone app called Dream:ON designed to collect mass data for research into dreaming.

*WILD.* Said to be based on Tibetan dream yoga, WILD, like some of the methods above, means holding yourself in a state just short of falling asleep. You relax and just watch as you drift into a hypnagogic state, perhaps seeing or hearing hallucinations, feeling vibrations or drifting into paralysis without reacting. From there you invent a dream scene, looking beyond the hypnagogic imagery and immersing yourself in the scene while resisting the temptation of falling asleep. With this method you can imagine dreaming of your own room and seeing yourself in bed, so converting the lucid dream into an OBE. Any lucid dream can be used this way but other methods for inducing OBEs begin from the waking state.

## Inducing an OBE

There is no shortage of books and websites to tell you the amazing benefits of learning to 'go OB': you might gain access to other planes of reality, meet your spirit guide or guardian face-to-face, discover the purpose of your life, meet people who have 'passed away', increase your psychic abilities, extend the boundaries of perception, gain healing powers, learn defences against etheric or astral attack, visit friends in faraway places, explore the solar system and beyond, and prove your immortality.

If you are sceptical about astral worlds and immortality, just ignore the wilder claims and choose a method you think will suit you. The trouble is the vast number, all claiming to be the quickest and best, with some charging large fees for courses of varying quality that promise rapid success.

Apparently you can *Have an Out-of-body Experience in 30 Days* (Harary & Weintraub, 1990, Jacobs, 2013) or *30 Days to the Most Exciting Experience of Your Life* (Stack, 1988). A Kindle book promises *Astral Projection In 3 Days Or Less,* (Naiken, 2015) and a competitor boasts *Astral Projection Within 24 Hours* (Quentin, 2013). A video goes one better with *Astral Projection in Less Than 3 Minutes*. The truth, as far as I can tell, is that deliberately inducing an OBE is hard, so don't expect to turn into a Sylvan Muldoon, Oliver Fox or Blue Harary overnight, and remember it took Fox about five years to master the skill. That said, many people have succeeded and some have learned to initiate and control OBEs at will. The trick is probably to choose a method that suits the skills you already have and then persist.

When I first studied these techniques my sole aim was to return to that wonderful state that I remembered so clearly. I lapped up occult theories and immersed myself in ideas that might help my astral body leave its physical shell and fly into other planes. Now, although I still practise some of them, my interest is quite different. I enjoy trying to work out how each relates to what is going on in our bodies and brains. Some encourage relaxation and reduce sensory input so as to confuse the vestibular system and produce OB feelings; others overload the senses for the same purpose; some cleverly manipulate the body schema to help create a duplicate; some emphasise concentration to avoid lapsing back into normality; and others emphasise imagery to aid the switch from OB feelings to OB vision. The methods may look superficially very different but all can create a dramatic shift in our constructed sense of self.

## Relax, concentrate, imagine

Almost every method begins by combining physical relaxation with mental alertness and producing a state similar to hovering between waking and sleeping. This encourages vivid imagery and reduces signals from the body, confusing the vestibular system and allowing the body schema to drift. Muldoon & Carrington (1929) advocates lying down but the danger then is that it's so easy to fall asleep. At the other extreme, however, being uncomfortable interferes with concentration and brings your attention back to the body, which is what you are trying to avoid. This is why an alert but comfortable posture is best. You are then ready to relax, concentrate and imagine.

If you find it hard to relax, recordings with a soothing voice will guide you step by step, but you can easily do this on your own using progressive muscular relaxation. The idea is to go slowly around the body, alternately tensing and relaxing the muscles: tensing brings your attention to that part of the body; relaxing lets it go. You may find tension in muscles you didn't even know you had. There is no right way to do this but you might begin at the feet, tense and relax each toe, flex and relax each toe, tense and relax the whole foot, flex and twist the foot and let go. Then carry this on to the ankles, calves, knees, thighs and so on, slowly tensing and relaxing every muscle you can find. Thinking about the whole process as you go along should keep you alert while your muscles relax.

When Palmer tried to test for ESP, he used a similar method, along with disorienting sounds and images, to induce OBEs in the lab. Placing target pictures in another room, he asked regular OBErs to travel there and report what they saw (Palmer & Vassar, 1974). Twenty-one (42%) of them achieved an OBE but their ESP scores were below the chance guessing level. A second experiment gave more promising results but they could not be repeated (Palmer & Lieberman, 1975, 1976) and similar disappointments followed when other researchers looked for ESP during OBEs (Alvarado, 1982, Osis, 1975, Rogo, 1978).

Concentration and imagery skills are also important and both can be improved with practice. Meditation entails both. Indeed learning to meditate is all about training attention (Austin, 2006) so this provides an ideal foundation. My own meditation practice has been mostly in Chan, the Chinese forerunner of Zen, in which the main method is the stark practice of 'just sitting', but I've also trained in Tibetan techniques which involve conjuring up the most wonderfully complex and colourful images of deities with multiple arms and elaborate surroundings. Many occult traditions use special imagery techniques too. These may be designed for performing magical operations, reading Tarot cards or developing clairvoyance, as well as for astral projection. Back in the 1970s, when I took classes in Wiccan magic, I learned to cast spells and joined a coven. We studied Conway's

*Occult Primer* (1974) and Brennan's *Astral Doorways* (1971), prepared ourselves for dangers on the higher planes with Dion Fortune's *Psychic Self Defence* (1930) and spent a lot of time sitting around in dark rooms, training our imaginations.

Here's the hardest task I remember: first, imagine a solid cube with textures and colours of your choice. Make these very vivid in your imagination. Then rotate the cube, watching from many different angles and distances. Finally, view it from all sides at once. This sounds impossible but in the end requires a fascinating flip, something like seeming to become much larger than the cube and looking in on it from all around. At least, that's the best way I can describe it, although whether it helps with magical operations I cannot say.

Since the nineteenth century psychologists have tried to measure two main aspects of imagery: vividness and control. Vividness was first tested in 1883, when Francis Galton asked a hundred of his acquaintances to summon up a mental image of their breakfast table and was amazed to discover that while some of them reported rich and vivid images, others saw scarcely anything at all. Modern tests include the VVIQ (Vividness of Visual Imagery Questionnaire, Marks, 1973), Gordon's Test of Visual Imagery Control (Gordon, 1949) and other, more recent measures devised to explore all the senses rather than just visualisation (Andrade et al., 2014). There's little evidence that scores on any of these are related to having spontaneous OBEs or lucid dreams (Irwin, 1980, Blackmore, 1982b). Even so, most induction techniques emphasise imagery, whether visual, bodily or any other sense.

If you try any of these methods an obvious question is going to bother you: what is the difference between imagining you are having an OBE, and really having one? If you practise hard and get a wonderful sense of leaving your body, is this the real thing or only a fantasy?

Perhaps it's unhelpful to say that if you 'seem to be' out of your body then you are, by definition, having an OBE. But I think this is actually quite reasonable. If you can still feel your physical position and your vision is cloudy and dim then you won't really feel you are 'out-of-the-body'. Some adepts state categorically that the distinction is clear; ordinary imagination is nothing like the extraordinary clarity of the OBE. But other experts describe states ranging from cloudy, dim and unstable to brightly conscious and realistic, referring to all of them as out-of-body.

For astral projection theorists a clear distinction must exist: either the astral body is exteriorised, or it is not. So they deal with in-between states by saying that the astral body has not fully separated, or the etheric double is not providing enough energy, or the astral vision is blurred. The trouble is that these *ad hoc* explanations can be multiplied forever and cannot be tested. If we could detect these other bodies or 'subtle energies' we could test whether the astral body has really left or not, or measure the energy coming from the etheric, and relate these to the clarity of astral vision, but we cannot.

What is the alternative? You might say that all OBEs are just imagination anyway and there is nothing more to be explained. This does not satisfy me. OBE vision can seem realer than real and be extraordinarily vivid. Even the best mental-imagers rarely say that of their imagination. There is also that odd mental flip that I remember so well from my own OBE. It seems as though your vision suddenly clears and you are 'there'. There is even sometimes an audible sound, Fox's 'cerebral click', when this happens.

This sudden switch to clarity suggests what Fox, among others, refers to as 'seeing with eyes closed'. Many people experience this on the verge of sleep, when ordinary hypnagogic imagery suddenly clears to produce a stunningly vivid picture that can be scanned with eye movements as though it were real. This is quite distinct from ordinary imagery and seems to me to have the same quality as OB vision. Indeed, in my 1984 survey the people who had OBEs also had this experience more often. I have been trying to induce it on the verge of sleep for many years and with increasing success, but as far as I know there is no research that even begins to investigate it.

Is there something interesting going on here in the brain? Could it be that the visual system is flipping into a different mode and if so, what is it doing and why? This is the kind of question I think we need to ask, and indeed I *will* ask when we return to the neuroscience of OBEs.

## Training your imagination

Imagine you are looking down on a pale blue plate with a bright orange orange on it. For some people the colours will be feeble and the shapes unstable while others will imagine them so clearly that they are almost as vivid as looking at the real thing. Wherever you lie on this spectrum, you can improve with practice.

To extend into other senses and learn control, imagine reaching out one hand to grasp the orange, feeling the movement, touch and weight of your arm. Feel texture of the orange's rough skin and the way it squishes when you gently squeeze it. Now scratch the skin and smell the sharp juice given off. Begin peeling the orange, pulling away the skin from the pith and exploring how it feels, looks and smells. When the peel is all lying on the plate, pull the orange apart and lay the segments out in a pleasing pattern. Eat one.

Some people can barely get through this procedure without their mind wandering off. Others find the process almost overwhelming as the sharp, tangy smell assails them and their mouth waters freely as it would when peeling a real orange. If you are one of the former, try exercises like this again and again until they become easier, even if you don't quite get to the mouth-watering stage. If you are already swallowing all that unnecessary saliva, try doing visualisations like this with your eyes open. This is harder for most people and is good practice.

Here's a task more directly relevant to inducing an OBE.

Sit upright in a comfortable chair, shut your eyes and imagine someone standing a metre in front of you. Imagine their back, their hair, their clothes, the way they are standing and any other details you can conjure up. Hold that image for a while and then have them walk slowly away from you. Now do the same but this time imagine yourself, with your own hair, clothes and posture. Hold the image for a while before 'you' walk away into the distance.

If you get good at this, try the same exercise lying down. This is harder because when you imagine something the same parts of the brain are active as when you are actually seeing, hearing or feeling it. In the first exercise both you and the imagined figure were standing and facing in the same direction but now they are not. Even harder is to imagine the person turning round to face you. For me this is nigh on impossible because I'm so bad at face recognition. I can fail to recognise someone I have known for years if they have changed their hair or grown a beard. In the pathological condition of prosopagnosia, usually caused by brain injury, people cannot recognise faces at all but we all lie along a continuum and however hard you find it, this exercise is still good practice for seeing yourself in an OBE.

Another trick can be done on a moving bus or train by shutting your eyes, feeling the movements and vibrations, and imagining you are travelling in the opposite direction. Or when lying in bed with your eyes closed, imagine you are sitting up, or when lying on your front that you are on your back. This will help to get you used to ignoring the signals coming from your muscles, joints and skin and should make you feel drifty and peculiar. If you don't like these vestibular sensations, just open your eyes and move so you can feel where your body really is. This shows that you can control the feelings and will give you the confidence to keep practising.

These three basic skills, relaxation, concentration and imagery, can all help induce an OBE. Beyond that there are too many methods to cover them all so I have chosen seven types that are relatively easy to follow and cover the whole range although there are plenty of others available (e.g. Brennan, 1989, Harary & Weintraub, 1990, Rogo, 1983).

## Seven ways to an OBE

### 1. Just imagery

Using imagery alone requires real skill but here are three basic methods.

(a) Lie on your back and relax as deeply as you can. Feel your body as clearly as possible, so you have a real sense of its shape and position from head to toe. Now imagine you are very slowly drifting upwards. Don't move as this will bring you straight back down. You can also imagine the ceiling coming closer to you as you rise up or imagine other details of the room as they would look from this elevated position. Hold this sensation until you lose all feeling from the bed or floor. Once this is stable, move slowly into an upright position and begin to move away from your body and around the room.

Look carefully at the objects and details around the room. Only when they seem vivid and stable should you turn round and look at your own body. It's likely to give you a shock and an instant return to where you started.

Although I have often heard this method suggested, it requires extremely good and steady imagery skills and it seems to me to be too difficult for anyone but a practised OBEer. However, it can be useful in conjunction with other methods.

(b) In any comfortable position, sitting or lying down, close your eyes and imagine a duplicate of yourself standing about a metre in front of you, including as much detail as you can. As in the exercise above, it is easier to imagine this double with its back to you. Once it seems solid and realistic you may begin to feel unsure about your physical position. This is the feeling you want, and you can encourage it by contemplating questions like, 'Where am I?', 'Who am I?' or, 'Which one is me?'

When you feel ready, imagine transferring your consciousness into the double. This is the hard part, but if you succeed you can then look around the room from this new position.

(c) As a variant of (b), imagine your double is facing you, either when you are lying down with the double floating above you, or sitting or standing with it facing you. Then ask those questions, 'Where am I?', or 'Who am I?' or, 'Which one is me?' You should feel great uncertainty about which one it is. You can imagine how the room looks from the position of your body or from that of the imagined double, and then flip between the two views. Once they are both strong and stable, forget the view from the body and adopt the double's view.

## 2. Ophiel's 'little system'

'Ophiel' was the pseudonym of a prolific writer and occultist, Edward Peach, who died in 1988. In *The Art and Practice of Astral Projection* (1961) he urges you to express your artistic nature, forget all your expectations about higher planes and prepare to transfer your consciousness into another body. He provides four methods, including creating a body of light, using an occult symbol, and a dream method similar to those below. The imagery method he calls the 'Little System'.

Pick a familiar route inside your house, perhaps taking a regular walk between two rooms, and choose at least six points along the way. Spend several minutes each day looking at each one and memorising it. You might even place a special 'symbol object' at each point to reinforce the image. Then remember all the sights, sounds, smells and the way objects feel to the touch at each spot. Once you have these firmly in mind you can begin.

Sit or lie in a comfortable position and relax while imagining your first point-spot. Stay there for some time before moving on. Ophiel claims you are now looking at the 'etheric image' of that point, whatever that means. Move on to the next and progress through each one before returning in reverse order. When you can do this easily you are ready to project.

Begin from your chair or bed and imagine yourself lifting up and beginning to move along your route. At first it will seem as though you are looking at yourself performing the action. You can then try to 'transfer your consciousness, you, yourself, to the image of yourself that you are watching' (p.31), seeing through the eyes of the image and feeling yourself into it. This image, he says, is the etheric body that you are watching through the eyes of your astral body. Eventually the two will fuse and 'you will open another kind of an eye' and find you are 'really there'. When you want to return, simply go back the way you came and transfer your consciousness to the physical body.

Forgetting all the theory about different bodies, this is a simple and practical way of using multi-sensory imagery to deflect attention from the physical body and induce an OBE. Ophiel also mentions opening 'another kind of eye' and I suspect this is the same 'seeing with eyes closed' that I find so fascinating.

## 3. The Christos technique

This method, popularised by Australian journalist Gerald Glaskin (1974), was originally designed for contacting 'past lives' and only later adapted for inducing OBEs by Alastair McIntosh (1979), who once guided me through the experience. Although it may sound quite odd, and even unpleasant, it's a good way of confusing the body schema and inducing vestibular sensations. You need two helpers and a warm and relaxing atmosphere, perhaps with gentle music and soft lighting, and a bed where you can lie comfortably on your back. One helper massages your feet and ankles, quite firmly, even roughly, while the other massages your forehead, rubbing it vigorously with a clenched fist for several minutes. This rather odd kind of massage may make your head buzz and hum, your feet tingle and your whole body feel light and floaty, so that you soon begin to feel disorientated. Now the helpers start guiding your imagery and telling you what to do.

First, imagine your feet stretching out and becoming longer by about an inch, then do the same with your head. Then alternate back and forth between head and feet, gradually increasing the distance until both are stretched by two feet or more. Now imagine stretching both at once, making yourself very long. Then swell up, filling the room like a huge balloon. These exercises remind me of the bizarre distortions I experienced with Persinger's 'God helmet' and of similar distortions reported by some astral projectors.

Next, imagine you are outside your own front door. Describe out loud everything you can see or hear or touch in as much detail as you can, solidifying the imagery until it is as convincing and realistic as possible. Finally, lift up from by the front door into the sky. From there you should be able to go anywhere you wish.

Back in the 1970s we used to experiment with the Christos technique, finding that it works very quickly for some people but not others – you have to take it at each person's own pace. Yet even those who thought it could never work often found the sensations of swelling and growing quite powerful. There is no need to do anything to end the experience because you'll just find yourself 'back', but it is worth taking a few minutes to relax and gently bring back the usual sense of your body before you get up.

What interests me most about this technique is how the massage confuses bodily sensations and the imagery of stretching is used to manipulate the body schema, before attempting the move to some-where else.

## 4. Ritual magic

Occultists and magicians use a wide variety of rituals and tools to achieve their magical aims, which may include having OBEs. They use symbols, ritual objects, human circles and dances, chants and mantras, tarot cards or cabbalistic path-workings. Yet underlying all the differences they also rely on the basics of relaxation, concentration and imagery to induce altered states.

Magical rituals often include opening, purifying and closing ceremonies that keep the ordinary world distinct from the altered states, which makes good sense from a psychological point of view. They may use 'doorways' of various kinds, which are reminiscent of the tunnels and dark spaces of some OBEs and of Fox's and Monroe's symbolic doorways (see also Chapter 4). Magical ways of dealing with trouble (e.g. Fortune, 1930) are also similar to those advocated by Fox.

The theories involved in magic range from comprehensible attempts to work with one's own mind without invoking the supernatural to wild and extravagant theories of multiple planes and other worlds, angels, demons and evil forces, thought forms to be counteracted, and so on. These methods are usually learned as part of a magical training and this is certainly not for everyone. I mention them here only to point out that undergoing magical training and using magical rituals relies just as much as many other OBE techniques on the use of carefully trained imagery.

## 5. Hypnosis

In the early days of psychical research, hypnosis was used to induce 'travelling clairvoyance'. Spirit mediums were sent to distant places to view events or try to to influence them. In what was called 'exteriorisation of sensitivity' some claimed to feel touches, heat or even pricking with pins at a distance from their body (de Rochas, 1906, Durville, 1908). Sadly, like so many experiments in early psychical research, a few mediums were caught cheating and the dramatic effects were not repeated under tighter conditions. Muldoon & Carrington (1929) even tried to test this by making a board with needles sticking out above his bed. But when projecting, he just passed right through his own 'pricker' and concluded it was hypnosis, not astral projection, that caused the earlier results.

Close connections between hypnosis and OBEs have continued ever since, not only because OBErs tend to be higher in absorption and suggestibility but because OBE-like experiences can occur during hypnosis. Highly hypnotisable people often report vestibular sensations such as spinning or floating, and visual imagery spontaneously increases along with increased activation in visual cortex (Terhune & Cardeña, 2009). In one group of highly suggestible individuals, everyone experienced vestibular sensations and disembodiment and some even reported seeing the room from a different position although none actually saw their own body (Cardeña, 2005). Perhaps it's not surprising that from his extensive surveys Hart (1954) suggested that hypnosis induced a state more like spontaneous OBEs and was therefore the most promising way to induce them.

If you want to try this method, in principle all you need is a good hypnotist who can get you into an extremely relaxed but alert state. Guided imagery can then be combined with suggestions of leaving the body, floating or flying, disembodiment and shifts in visual perspective. At the end of the session it is important that the hypnotist brings you carefully back into feeling your body in the normal way.

The last two methods also depend on imagery but using the hypnagogic state; that special state hovering between waking and sleeping.

6. *The Rope method*

This popular technique is promoted by Robert Bruce in his books and website *Astral Dynamics* (1999). Bruce, also known as 'AstralBob', says it took him 'literally years' to figure out that astral projection does not work through visualisation alone but needs tactile and kinaesthetic feelings as well. This is a distinctly odd remark because traditional methods like those above all entail multi-sensory imagery, and AstralBob's method uses about as much visualisation as they do. Even so, he is right that you mustn't neglect the body.

The first step is to get into a comfortable position and relax, using any method you know, such as breathing exercises, meditation or progressive muscular relaxation. Once relaxed, you need to bring yourself closer to sleep without actually falling asleep. Bruce suggests focusing on an imagined object and watching as other thoughts and images arise. Light patterns will appear and you need to keep watching until they go. You should now start losing awareness of your physical body and possibly feeling paralysed as well. In other words, you may drift into sleep paralysis.

If you can stay mentally alert in this state you should soon feel vibrations throughout your body. These are presumably the same vibrations as those reported by Oliver Fox, Yram, Monroe and some spontaneous OBErs. According to Bruce, you must learn to control these vibrations by varying their speed or stopping and starting them. When you can do this you are ready for the rope.

Imagine there is a long rope hanging down right above you. Then reach up to grasp it with one hand. You may need to stop at this point, put the hand down again, relax and then do it again, this time going on to pull yourself up, climbing hand over hand up the imaginary rope. Ignore any change in the vibrations or feelings of being paralysed and keep on climbing until you feel yourself separating from your body.

These vibrations are used in other methods too. I have taught myself to induce them and tried to measure their rate, which is usually several per second. Initially I thought they might reflect the eye movements of REM sleep but they do not seem to go at the same rate as eye movements and they can, as Bruce suggests, be deliberately speeded up or slowed down. I would love to know what is going on here but there has been no research that I know of to find out.

These vibrations play an even more central role in the final method.

### 7. Monroe's method

In his books, *Journeys Out of the Body* (1971) and *Far Journeys* (1985), Monroe recounts his personal explorations of 'nonphysical reality' and describes a complicated-sounding technique for inducing OBEs. Although in some ways this is similar to other imagery methods, he puts the 'vibrational state' first.

Lie down in a warm, darkened room in any comfortable position, but with your head pointing to magnetic north and wearing no jewellery or metal objects. Begin by relaxing and breathing with your mouth half-open and eyes closed. Now look into the blackness at a spot about a foot from your forehead, concentrating your awareness on that point and bringing it back whenever your mind drifts away. When you can keep steadily concentrating on this point, move it gradually to three feet away, then six, and then turn your attention ninety degrees upwards, reaching right up above your head.

You should now be feeling the vibrations or shaking. 'It is as if a surging, hissing, rhythmically pulsating wave of fiery sparks comes roaring into your head,' says Monroe. 'From there it seems to sweep throughout your body, making it rigid and immobile' (1971, p.205). You must reach for the vibrations and mentally pull them down into your head, and once you have achieved the vibrational state, learn to control it and to smooth out the vibrations by 'pulsing' them.

Monroe warns that at this point it is impossible to turn back and you are ready to leave the body. For the 'lift-out' method, think of getting lighter and floating upwards; for the 'rotation' method, imagine turning over in bed, twisting first the top of your body, head and shoulders until you turn right over and float upwards. After this you can move away and explore wherever you like.

The Monroe Institute in Virginia was founded in the 1970s and runs courses using his techniques. Monroe invented a process he calls 'Hemi-Sync', which uses binaural beats. These are created when two slightly different frequencies are played, one to each ear, producing a new sound at a frequency corresponding to the difference between them. This is heard as though it's coming from inside the head, and by 'auditory driving' or 'neural entrainment' can synchronise the underlying brainwaves to that frequency. The full Hemi-Sync method adds other soothing and relaxing sounds or audio instructions to the beats. You can buy CDs or find sounds online but note that for genuine binaural beats you must play different frequencies into each ear.

Monroe's description of surging, hissing and pulsating sounds far more dramatic than most descriptions of simple vibration and more like the 'peculiar and rather terrifying preliminary sensations' that made Fox so afraid of using his 'pineal door' method. He said it was 'like a great outrush or uprush of all my being' (Fox, n.d., p.86). Sadly, although Fox (1920) describes many adventures he had through the pineal door, he does not tell us how to do it.

CHAPTER 12

# Out on Drugs

I watched as I fell not only out of my body but out of this version
of the world . . . I found myself in a long tunnel like if I was in the
middle of a tunnel running through the center of the earth. . . .
surrounding me was an infinite bookcase and I was led to believe
it held the entirety of human experience, including everything
that is yet to happen and has happened in parallel universes, so
essentially everything, everywhere, all the time and access to these
planes was granted by reading these books.

Wouldn't it be wonderful if there were a cheap and perfectly safe
'magic astral pill' you could take and – hey presto – have an
instant OBE? I think it would, not only because many people would
like to try it, including me, but because of all the research we could do.
Just imagine being able to answer some of our trickiest questions
about OBEs. We might use a scanner to find out what's happening in
the brain when people enter the tunnel, or when they float, fly, or 'fall
out' of their body. We could test for psychic powers by giving people
the pill, asking them to signal when they felt out-of-body and then
visit a distant room, where we could put pictures, videos and objects.
We could test for the existence of a double by having their friends or
lovers in another room to see whether they could detect it or use the

latest technology to look for subtle energies or signs of an astral form. Of course such tests have been tried with Miss Z, Robert Monroe, Blue Harary and others and with little or no success, but a magic pill would give us so much more control.

Such a pill does not exist. Even if it did there would always be the awkward question of whether spontaneous OBEs and drug-induced OBEs are the same thing or not. When I told people about my experience all those years ago, many derided it as a 'drug induced fantasy' or a 'stoned hallucination' and not 'the real thing'. So we have to ask, as we did with dream-induced OBEs, and will with near-death experiences (NDEs), whether drugs can induce a 'genuine' OBE or not.

The experience above was described by a frequent ketamine user (Jones, 2016), although on this occasion she was taking DPT (N,N-dipropyltryptamine), a powerful and reputedly unpredictable psychedelic related to DMT and known as 'the light'. Was this too weird to count as an OBE? Using our usual definition it's dubious. The writer 'fell out' of her body but landed in another world, not this one. She reports the familiar tunnel, but what about the library of infinite books? We need to find out more.

There are two ways in which psychoactive drugs can affect OBEs, either inducing or suppressing them. Barbiturates and alcohol suppress OBEs, which makes sense because they tend to dull sensory experience and reduce control over imagery. In contrast, cannabis, morphine, psychedelics and the major hallucinogens can be helpful (Eastman, 1962, Monroe, 1971, Masters & Houston, 1967). In addition, people who take certain drugs more often report OBEs even if those OBEs do not happen when actually taking the drug. This is the case with cannabis and we can start there.

## Cannabis

Cannabis is a drug like no other. The name 'cannabis' refers to a group of flowering plants that contain a bewildering number of ingredients. Nearly five hundred have been identified and over one hundred are psychoactive of which the main one is THC (delta-9-tetrahydrocannabinol). This is one of many cannabinoids which act on receptors in the brain's endocannabinoid system. Also important is cannabidiol, a neuroprotector which occurs in high concentrations in natural cannabis but has been systematically bred out of modern 'skunk' types to increase the immediate effect. This unwanted consequence of drug prohibition may be why modern cannabis is proving more dangerous than the wild varieties and types used back in the 1960s and 70s.

The leaves and buds are usually dried and smoked as weed, grass or marijuana. Hash is a resin extracted from female flowers that can be smoked or eaten, and other extracts can be smoked in a vaporiser. Smoking gives an effect that comes on fast, is highly controllable and lasts about two to four hours. When eaten alone or cooked in cakes or sweets the effect may not begin for an hour or more and then lasts for several hours. Either way the effects include euphoria, laughter and enhanced enjoyment of music, colours, tastes and other sensations (Tart, 1971a, Earleywine, 2002). These are probably the main effects people want but others, like me, use cannabis for the way it changes thought processes and gives a different view on the world and the self. This is partly because short-term memory is reduced while episodic memory (memory for past events) is enhanced and these effects are also related to the time distortions that can work in both directions. Synaesthesia and hallucinations can occur with high doses and some people can become frightened or paranoid.

Being such a complex and variable plant, cannabis nicely illustrates the difference between natural psychoactive mixtures, such as those in mushrooms or the peyote cactus, and the simpler or starker effects of synthetic compounds. When active ingredients are isolated for medicinal or research purposes the rich and varied psychological effects are usually lost (Weil, 1998). There is really no other drug quite like cannabis and it is often classified, all on its own, as a 'minor hallucinogen'. It is definitely my favourite drug.

So what is the connection between OBEs and cannabis use?

In his pioneering book *On Being Stoned*, psychologist Charles Tart (1971a) surveyed 150 experienced marijuana users (they'd used the drug at least a dozen times) and found that 44 per cent reported OBEs, which is much higher than found in surveys of the general public or even of students. Of these, nearly a quarter (23%) had had one OBE and about a fifth (21%) had had many. But most OBEs did not occur when they were stoned and most users had never had an OBE while high.

Some OBEs were set off by accidents, such as this from a 36-year-old assistant manager:

> Knocked unconscious in fall—saw crowd collect around own body from above, saw self lying on pavement. Perception and cognition very sharp for three days afterward.

Others sound more like just a normal part of life, such as this comment from a 26-year-old teacher:

> I sometimes view my body and the sequence of functions it follows in a particular environment from some operator's or observer's vantage above and behind my body. 'The whole scene' is then more obvious to me in that I have a sense of 360° perception rather than 180–200°. I am now conscious of what is actually behind me.
>
> Tart, 1971a, p.104

Why should cannabis users have more OBEs even if few of the OBEs occur when they are stoned? One possibility is that the type of people who are prone to having OBEs are also those who enjoy smoking dope. For example, healthy cannabis users score higher on schizotypy than non-users (Dumas et al., 2002, Williams et al., 1996) and we know that OBErs do too, but the causal connections are unknown. It might be that schizotypal traits incline people both to having OBEs and enjoying cannabis.

Alternatively, cannabis use might increase schizotypy or change people's brains in other ways that make an OBE more likely. From what we know so far, this might include loosening the body schema, reducing own-body imagery, or increasing the ability to relax, concentrate or control imagery, but there is little evidence exploring these and the causal connections are likely to be complicated.

But what about OBEs during cannabis use? Many users report changes in bodily sense, including familiar-sounding vibrations. 'I feel a vibration or tingling sensation in some or all of my body that I can tell is not an actual muscle tremor by looking at my body' (Tart, 1971a, pp.118–19). Others describe becoming larger or smaller, as I did; others become heavier or lighter. 'My body may feel very light or even feel as if I float up into the air when stoned' (Tart, 1971a, p.111). Full OBEs also occur and drug-use websites are full of fascinating descriptions. Here are just a few:

> i filled a hot bath and had a smoke of some mid's, nothing special. as i got stoned i felt very focused in my concentration. i heard a ringing in my ears. as i focused on the ringing it brought me to an even deeper sense of relaxation and concentration. i started hearing a buzzing in my ears. it reminded me of some things i had read about OBE's earlier though i have no practical experience with it. so i pictured my 'astral' legs lifting out, then my arms, then my torso. i felt no different. as i pictured my 'astral' head coming free i started feeling tingling all over my skin especially in my face. it was like 'whoa!' i then pictured/willed my astral body to lean backwards and as i did that i felt my 'mind' peel away from my physical senses. i then found 'my mind' floating several feet behind where i sensed my physical body.

Among comments to this post, one pointed out that the description sounded like the 'vibrational state'. Another, a regular yoga and meditation practitioner, said that whenever he got stoned, he felt as if he was vibrating. He went on:

> I had just gotten done meditating (stilling your mind is a very important skill to learn if you're going to get into this) and was still stoned so I decided to lay down and try to leave my body. I was determined this time and was going to do it. I entered into a 'waking sleep' state and just thought myself out of my body. Opening your eyes in this state is extremely difficult. You cannot think your eyes

open, you just have to believe that they are already open. So I thought myself out of my body and felt the ceiling of my room. I felt my back against something hard and bumpy and 'believed' my eyes open and I was staring back at the couch I was on. Strangely, I couldn't see my body for some reason, but I was there floating.

Once again there is this hint of 'seeing with eyes closed'. I think what he means here is not opening his physical eyes, but making that flip to seeming to have them open and being able to scan the scene as you would if they were.

After enjoying smoking for fun for six months or so, this man decided to take his experience to 'the next level'.

> My brother and I decided not goof off and instead focus on the simple state of mind that weed makes you drift into. We didn't do anything but relax and focus on the state of mind that we were in. This smoke session changed my life.
>
> We stumbled on something absolutely beautiful. Simply put, when you focus on the high and only the high (let all other thoughts go), the high intensifies deeper and deeper and eventually results in out of body experiences. I know this might sound ridiculous, but I have gotten to the point where the high is so intense that I am completely free from my body and I am simply a soul.

Responders to this Reddit post agreed that 'the next level' can be achieved by just focusing on the high or 'exploring the high'. One explains how to do it, emphasising letting go of thoughts and describing weed as 'a "gateway" to meditative practices':

> Close your eyes and put all your focus into it. . . . Don't fear and follow the high as much as you can. Don't lose focus of the high, and let all thoughts go. . . . you will get deeper and deeper and deeper and deeper into the high and eventually you will have an amazing (some may say spiritual) out of body experience that is impossible to explain.

Why does cannabis encourage OBEs? Being such a complex mix of constituents, and with its illegal status making research difficult, it is hard to find out. There is a little evidence of increased reactivity in the TPJ of young cannabis users (Spechler et al., 2015), but most research is either designed to test long-term harmful effects of cannabis or THC for medical purposes. I imagine we have to wait for cannabis to be legalised before research will become easier and we can find out just what happens inside the brain of someone high on weed and enjoying a drug-induced OBE. Whatever we do find out, cannabis is far from being our 'magic OBE pill'. Perhaps the closest any drug comes is the synthetic dissociative anaesthetic, ketamine.

## Ketamine

If anyone wants to take a drug to try to have an OBE they are likely to choose ketamine or 'Special K'. Classified as a dissociative anaesthetic, it is an N-methyl-D-aspartate (NMDA) receptor antagonist that also affects opioid receptors and the transport of some neurotransmitters. In high doses it induces anaesthesia with paralysis, reduced pain, sedation and memory loss. In lower doses it leads to euphoria, possibly by inhibiting dopamine reuptake, and to strange bodily changes, vestibular sensations of flying or falling, and a dissociated state of derealisation and depersonalisation in which things seem altered, distant or unreal. When injected, the effects begin within a few minutes and last about half an hour; when taken as a pill, the effect is much slower and longer-lasting, with after-effects lasting several hours.

Although these effects don't sound especially enticing, ketamine has become a popular recreational drug. Some use it as a rave or dancing drug while others treat it as therapeutic or even sacred, using it to explore deep issues of birth, life and death (Jansen, 2001). There is even evidence that it can alleviate severe depression, possibly because it reduces activity in brain areas involved in sensory processing and selective attention, as well as decreasing functional connections between important brain networks (Musso et al., 2011, Scheidegger et al., 2012).

Ketamine is not the only dissociative drug said to induce OBEs. Others include PCP (phencyclidine or 'angel dust'), nitrous oxide and

*Salvia divinorum*, a South American member of the sage family containing salvinorin A. One user, having smoked two heavy doses of salvia, writes:

> I started to feel a tingle start in my limbs. The next thing I know my astral body is being pulled out the back of my physical body and then through the wall of my house. Down my block I went, being pulled by an unseen force. . . . I had to fight with all my might to travel back into my house and back into my body sitting in a chair.

Another describes the following experience, calling it 'A true OBE'.

> I remember looking out the window and being sucked out of it, as half my body got ripped off and I looked back at . . . the lower half of my body as I was forcibly sucked out of the window by some intangible force.

These tales made me laugh because of their similarity to my own first experience of salvia. I seemed to be dragged out of the room where a friend was acting as sitter to find myself in a dream-like state, clawing at the walls outside and trying in vain to climb back into the room. I hated that experience and it was the only time I have, if briefly, lost all insight into the fact that I was taking a drug, yet the similarities are interesting. Is there something about this specific chemical and its action on the brain that induces this particular feeling? If so, we are far from understanding it.

Although in one sense these experiences are 'out-of-body', they are hardly akin to the clarity and joy of many spontaneous OBEs. But let's return to ketamine. In a study comparing frequent, infrequent and ex-users, two-thirds said that the most appealing aspects of ketamine were 'melting into the surrounding', 'visual hallucinations', 'out-of-body experiences' and 'giggliness'. Against that, half worried about 'memory loss', 'decreased sociability' and addiction (Muetzelfeldt et al., 2008, Morgan & Curran, 2012). Then, in high doses, there is the famous

'K-hole', an experience of extreme dissociation, derealisation, bodily dissolution and, in many cases, OBEs or NDEs. Described as anything from a place of extreme horror to the best time ever, the K-hole is sought by some and feared by others.

Perhaps surprisingly, OBEs seem more likely during the first few occasions of taking ketamine (Corazza &Schifano, 2010), suggesting it's futile to go on taking lots of ketamine in the hope of achieving one. Many other experiences associated with OBEs are reported with ketamine, including dark tunnels, bright lights, floating and hovering, time distortion, insights into self, noises like those of SP, the vibrational state, and bodily distortions (Dillon et al., 2003). Taking ketamine in experimental settings, people report bodily distortions as well as OBEs (Curran & Morgan, 2000). One said, 'My hands look small, but the fingers are really long'; another observed, 'My legs look very big and funny shaped, like another person's' (Pomarol-Clotet et al., 2006). These could well be preludes to an OBE and a survey of users found the typical progression from illusory movements to OB feelings to full OBEs (Wilkins et al, 2012).

I desperately wanted to take ketamine to find out and, more importantly, to answer a most obvious personal, if not scientific, question – would an OBE induced by ketamine be like my own OBE or different? I might also be able to test for ESP. If this drug could induce an OBE and I could travel away from my body then maybe I would be able to see events at a distance or appear to people far away.

Back in the 1980s I worked in the Brain and Perception Lab, founded by Richard Gregory at the University of Bristol. Famous for his work on visual illusions, Gregory was interested in everything from the origins of the universe to the problems of consciousness. Applying the theory that you can learn about something by switching it on and off, he embarked on a 'Journey to unconsciousness with ketamine' (Gregory, 1986). He chose to be in an operating theatre in case anything went wrong, and was given psychological tests throughout. Enduring feelings of floating and unreality and a loud buzzing sound like being in an engine room, he entered a world of 'brilliant supersaturated colours and shapes' and experienced synaesthesia for the only time in his life when the bristles of a brush felt like an orange, green and red tapestry, 'clear like hypnagogic images'.

Gregory never wished to repeat his unpleasant experience but, as with any psychoactive drug, the experience depends critically on the set and setting in which it's taken – the 'set' meaning your attitude and state of mind; the 'setting' meaning the environment and other people. Being in hospital with psychologists giving you tests is far from an ideal set or setting.

Another of my deeply curious scientific heroes, the physicist Richard Feynman, chose a far better setting for his explorations, the isolation tanks created by researcher and psychonaut, John Lilly. Longing to experience hallucinations without taking drugs, Feynman immersed himself in the warm, dark tanks many times but it wasn't until after he'd had a tiny dose of ketamine that one day he felt as though he was an inch to one side. Wondering why we assume our 'ego' (as he called it) is behind our eyes he began teaching himself to move further away and then down inside his own body, as I had done. With practice this got easier and easier until, as he described it, 'everything else was exactly the same as normal, only my ego was sitting outside, "observing" all this'. In what sounds very much like that flip into OB vision, he said, 'the entire imagery would suddenly appear.' In this way he achieved his goal of inducing hallucinations at will, and had many types of OBE along the way.

My own ketamine adventure was in neither an operating theatre nor an isolation tank but lying on a huge, warm waterbed. There was soft music playing, a good friend close by and no chance of interruption, let alone psychological tests to complete. A dose just short of anaesthesia was injected and in a few moments I was off.

Some of the effects would have been terrifying, had I not felt comfortable and safe. At this high dose, close to the anaesthetic level, my whole body was completely paralysed except for my eyes, which I could just about move with difficulty. All sensation from my body disappeared and I could only tell where it was from faintly glimpsing my feet. But then I was slipping deep into a wonderful floaty, yielding softness. I began to disintegrate into pieces and then into nothing at all – a 'no-body experience' you might say. But I was determined to try to get out of body, so I imagined lifting up in a second body and was soon flying through a deep blue sky to my home, hundreds of miles away. I flew inside the house and saw someone working in the kitchen and my children asleep in bed. Then I flew back to find the effect wearing off and some sense of a physical body returning.

Before it wore off my friend tried some simple ESP tests. He held up several fingers, asking me each time how many I could see. I got the first guess right, but thereafter all were wrong. Had these succeeded we would have tried properly controlled tests, but there seemed no point if I couldn't even count a few fingers. Later, I learned that I was wrong about what was happening in my house at the time so one of my questions was answered, if not very helpfully. There was no hint of ESP.

Another was answered too; this experience was emphatically unlike my original OBE. I felt I was flying and floating, but not clearly, smoothly and in control as before. During that first OBE everything was wonderfully vivid. Even when I saw strange things such as my own body without a head, or a perfectly star-shaped island with a hundred trees, they were vivid and realistic. Indeed my mind and vision felt absolutely clear, clearer than in ordinary life. With ketamine, they were blurred and unstable. There was none of the joy of that first experience either, and none of the sense of 'rightness' or insight that accompanied it. So was this an OBE at all? Some might say it was, but by my definition I would personally say no. I did not really 'seem to perceive the world from a location outside my body'. The floating self was hardly me, being so confused and unstable, and the world I saw was vague. There was no 'flip' into clarity.

Despite my personal disappointments, there is clearly a special relationship between OBEs and ketamine. In a large online survey of poly-drug users, researchers at the University of Waterloo in Canada found that frequency of ketamine use correlates strongly with lifetime OBE frequency, more so than for any other recreational drug, and some of the correlations they found between OBEs and other drugs could, they concluded, be explained by associated ketamine use (Wilkins et al., 2011).

Most of their drug users (73%) reported having experienced OB feelings and rather fewer (42%) had experienced OB autoscopy. This fits well with Cheyne and Girard's suggestion from their neurobiological model of OBEs (Chapter 9, page 155) that OB feelings are more fundamental and can then lead on to OB vision and autoscopy.

## Psychedelics

> I smoked ~30mg of very pure DMT about 10 hours into a ~300ug LSD trip. After taking three hits of the DMT, the walls in my room began to rearrange themselves in a rotating fashion. Once the movement ceased, I stood up and left my body behind, entering a wholly psychedelic world. From there, I encountered dozens of entities who made me view a simulation of a perfect life, using small puppets to symbolize myself and my partner. Once the play was over, they 'killed' me, or rather my ego.
>
> Jones, 2016

This woman was using, one after the other, two of the most potent psychedelics and probably the two most likely to be associated with OBEs. Many people use multiple drugs either in combination or separately and in his survey of cannabis users, Tart (1971a) found that those who used psychedelics as well as cannabis reported more OBEs and more multiple OBEs. Yet these OBEs did not necessarily occur when taking the psychedelics. Perhaps, as with cannabis, they may change the brain in ways that make an OBE more likely rather than specifically inducing OBEs at the time. The major psychedelics include naturally occurring ingredients of plants such as mescaline from the Peyote cactus, psilocybin found in magic mushrooms and DMT, which occurs in a wide variety of plants. Then there are synthetic versions of these compounds as well as the entirely synthetic drug, LSD (lysergic acid diethylamide). Most of them belong to two families of compounds, the tryptamines and the phenethylamines, both of which work through their effects on serotonin, although there are many other and more complex effects as well. If you want to know more about these families of drugs, the ultimate authorities are husband-and-wife team, Sasha and Ann Shulgin. Sasha was a chemist who designed hundreds of new drugs, which the pair systematically tested on themselves. They lovingly describe the effects in two books (1991, 1997) but they do not mention OBEs.

LSD is often called the ultimate psychedelic. Synthesised in 1938 by Albert Hofmann at the Sandoz labs in Basel, he discovered its psychoactive properties in 1943 by famously experimenting on himself and then riding his bike home on the first ever LSD trip (Hofmann, 1980). In 2006 the route he took that day was renamed 'Albert Hofmann Weg' in honour of his hundredth birthday. During the celebrations he described his 'problem child' as giving him 'an inner joy, an open mindedness, a gratefulness, open eyes and an internal sensitivity for the miracles of creation.' Even at one hundred he had bright eyes and a magnetic personality. As he climbed the steps to the stage for his speech, he apologised for needing a stick, saying, 'I have to remind myself that I am no longer in my nineties.' All I could do when I met him was, like everyone else there, thank him for his wonderful gift.

LSD is effective in minute doses; a typical dose of only one hundred micrograms induces a trip that begins within half an hour to an hour and lasts anywhere from eight to twelve hours depending on dose, set and setting. Although non-addictive, LSD is extremely powerful and not to be undertaken lightly for it can throw apart everything you ever thought you knew about yourself and the world.

The classic work on LSD is *The Varieties of Psychedelic Experience* by Robert Masters and Jean Houston (1967), who observed 206 drug sessions and describe accounts from more than two hundred people who had taken LSD or peyote in experiments, during therapy or on their own. Among bodily distortions are those when, 'A subject may lie on his back and look at his feet, which may seem to be five yards away or just under his chin.' The whole body might be elongated or shortened, or just an arm or leg might be stretched. Some users could project an image of themselves onto a wall or into a crystal and one claimed to be able to multiply himself and see several doubles at once.

They go on, 'There is also a fairly common experience where the subject seems to himself to project his consciousness away from his body and then is able to see his body as if he were standing off to one side of it or looking down on it from above.' The second body was described as diaphanous and almost immaterial. One subject, after lying down for some minutes, 'reported himself able to travel in his astral body and to pass through walls and other solid obstacles. He had just been down on the street, he said, and described very vividly what he had seen there. But asked to pass through the wall into the neighboring apartment, with which he was not familiar, and to describe its furnishings, he declined' (Masters & Houston, 1967, pp.86–7).

After that, little serious research was possible because, like most psychedelics, LSD was made illegal in most countries in the 1960s. However, Stanislav Grof (1975), the American psychiatrist and founder of transpersonal psychology, described OBEs occurring in early experiments and during LSD therapy for the dying, concluding that this extraordinary drug may have contributed to the reduction in fear and death anxiety that these experiments revealed (Grof & Halifax, 1977). Half a century later research on LSD for the terminally ill has at last begun again with similarly encouraging results (Gasser et al., 2014).

Other exciting discoveries are being made too now that limited amounts of LSD research are being licensed in the UK. In the first ever brain scanning studies, subjects took seventy-five micrograms of LSD and lay in an fMRI scanner. Functional connectivity increased right across the brain, and higher cerebral blood flow in visual areas was associated with stronger visual hallucinations. Connectivity decreased between some areas and the decrease between the parahippocampus and the retrosplenial cortex correlated strongly with reports of 'ego dissolution' and the sense of altered meaning, 'implying the importance of this particular circuit for the maintenance of "self" or "ego" and its processing of "meaning"' (Carhart-Harris et al., 2016, p.4853). No one had an OBE but increased functional connectivity in the temporo-parietal junctions also correlated with ego dissolution (Tagliazucchi et al., 2016).

If this all sounds a bit too complicated, its significance is that we're beginning to map out the circuits that build up the sense of self. When those self circuits break apart they create the OBE. Alternatively, if they fail in a different way, the self dissolves. This is why OBEs and LSD trips can be close to mystical experiences. They reveal the self as a model the brain builds up, not a little conscious nugget living inside and controlling its body, and this realisation is at the heart of the mystical experience.

Some people believe that taking LSD has changed them permanently so it's significant that some of the brain changes found in scanners predicted personality changes two weeks later. 'Openness to experience' increased and increased more in those who reported ego dissolution during their trip (Lebedev et al., 2016). It's rather scary to know that taking a drug whose effects last just a few hours can change your personality but we do not know how long the change persists and perhaps many users would welcome becoming more open to experience.

## Ayahuasca and DMT

Another psychedelic that deserves special mention is DMT (N,N-dimethyltryptamine). Sometimes called the 'spirit molecule', DMT is often said to induce OBEs, as well as lights, tunnels, strange sounds and, above all, vivid visions. American mystic and psychonaut, Terence McKenna, reputably said, 'You cannot imagine a stranger drug or a stranger experience.'

Smoked in its pure form, DMT acts very fast, the effects coming on almost immediately and lasting only fifteen to twenty minutes, inviting comparisons with an eight-hour LSD trip compressed into fifteen minutes. The friend who gave me my first DMT experience warned that someone he knew had said, in the midst of the trip, it was so horrendous that nothing that ever happened in the future could make things right again. Well – it's good to get an honest opinion before trying something new! Is this 'openness to experience'?

I sat on the floor of my study, propped up comfortably with a big cushion, and was told to take two drags of a pipe. The first, my friend said, would have little effect; the second would make me drop the pipe, which he would catch. He was exactly right: the first drag gave me a gentle lightness and a tingly feeling in my hands and legs. The second hurled me instantly into another world of screeching noise and colour. The carved legs of the table in front of me whirled like manic barber's poles in horrific bright pink and lime green. The carpet became a seething mass of horrible green and orange creatures – snakes, serpents, penises and rats' tails, all vibrating to the sound of loud machinery and crawling over each other in a seething mass.

How did I react? I remember thinking that I must just stay mindfully with whatever happened, however disturbing it was. I don't remember much else except that I sat there with a ridiculous grin on my face, saying, 'Terrible, terrible!' I had nothing like an OBE, and reading many online accounts the consensus seems to be that DMT when smoked produces a completely different experience from the OBE. People talk of the DMT 'breakthrough' and take high doses to achieve it, but this is hard to describe. Some say it's a transition out of this world into DMT Hyperspace and is very obvious. Others say it cannot be described and you just have to experience it.

What about eating DMT? The problem is that it is quickly destroyed in the stomach by enzymes called monoamine oxidase (MAO) that break down monoamines such as adrenaline, dopamine, serotonin and melatonin. Yet Amazonian shamans have been brewing and drinking DMT in the form of the traditional healing brew called ayahuasca or yagé for hundreds, and possibly thousands, of years. How is this possible?

Ayahuasca is based on the vine *Banisteriopsis caapi* (the spirit vine, soul vine or vine of the dead). Mixed with the leaves of various shrubs (e.g. *Psychotria viridis* or *Psychotria carthagenensis*), it provides 'one of the most sophisticated and complex drug delivery systems in existence' (Callaway, 1999, p.256, Metzner, 1999). The secret is that the caapi vine contains MAO inhibitors, the β-Carbolines, harmine, harmaline and tetrahydroharmine, while the other plants contain DMT. This might seem rather magical, that ancient peoples could have developed this mixture so long ago when you need both chemicals to make it work, but the truth is probably simpler. The caapi vine alone can have psychoactive properties by increasing the levels of monoamines such as dopamine and serotonin so it's possible that this was discovered first and other DMT-containing plants added later. In any case, the effects of ayahuasca are legendary.

Traditionally a healing drug, ayahuasca is sometimes used by the healer alone, sometimes by the patient, and sometimes by the whole community. The plant itself is the teacher, claim healers, and they trust in her wisdom to guide meetings with other plants, animals and spirits. One frequent effect is powerful vomiting, giving the drug another of its common names: the 'vomit drug'. Otherwise, after anything from a few minutes to an hour come a bewildering variety of bodily sensations, transformations, visions and insights (Luna & White, 2016, Metzner, 1999, Shanon, 2002).

Does ayahuasca induce OBEs? Many people claim so but their descriptions sound more like total self-body-dissolution than OBEs. I have drunk ayahuasca just four times, in a safe and carefully prepared environment with experienced users and an expert guide. One of the first visions I had was of rows and rows of beautifully perfect bright green trees, or skeletons of trees, disappearing into the distance. Although simple and fleeting, there was something peculiarly wonderful about the clarity and vividness of these visions. And the effects were magical and long-lasting. I felt healed in a profound way, as though emptied out or cleansed through for many days afterwards, but I experienced nothing like an OBE. Other people with me, more used to the drug than I was, were transformed into butterflies, birds or snakes and visited other worlds, but none of these sounded like OBEs either.

Yet there are some distant connections with OBEs worth exploring. Apart from the disruption of the normal bodily sense, there is the nature of the visions. Many users report tunnels, spirals and the vast void reported in some NDEs. Luis Luna, director of a research centre for studying visionary plants, has drunk ayahuasca hundreds of times. 'Colorful lights dancing, whirlpools, tunnels, and geometric patterns may cover my whole field of vision,' he says. He sees temples, magnificent cities and strange futuristic worlds reminiscent of Monroe's

'Locale 2' or the visions of the great astral projectors (Luna & White, 2016).

So there is that tunnel again. Because it was my own stepping-off point for an OBE I would dearly love to understand it. I'm sure that tunnel can give us clues to what is happening on the edges of an OBE.

CHAPTER 13

# Tunnels to Virtual Reality

I was floating through a tunnel . . . When I say tunnel, the only thing I can think of is – you know, those sewer pipes, those big pipes they put in? It was round like that, but it was enormous.

I remember going through a tunnel, a very, very dark tunnel . . . I wasn't afraid because I knew there was something at the other end waiting for me that was good.

## Into the tunnel

I knew nothing of such experiences when I entered my tunnel of leaves but there are many routes into the magical tunnel and many variations; light or dark, wide or narrow, like sewer pipes or subway tunnels, or spiralling water slides in multi-coloured skies. Although tunnels are a classic feature of near-death experiences, including the two above from Kenneth Ring's NDE collection (Ring, 1980), they have been studied since long before the term 'NDE' was even invented.

Psychical researcher Ernest Dunbar (1905) described tunnels experienced with ether, chloroform and hashish (cannabis) more than a century ago. In the 1960s, Crookall linked OBEs to tunnels, reporting one woman who nearly died 'seemed to float in a long tunnel' (Crookall, 1961a, p.8), while another went into 'an opening, like a tunnel, and at the far end a light' (Crookall, 1961a, p.13).

In 1981, Kevin Drab studied 815 people who reported 1,112 visionary encounters which included seventy-one tunnel experiences. Defining the tunnel as a realistic enclosed space longer than it is wide, he found descriptions of everything from scintillating darkness and luminous vapour to realistic tunnels of bricks and cobblestones. Many were associated with cardiac arrest, severe trauma, pain, fatigue, fear or migraine. Others occurred in relaxing conditions, including sleep, meditation and hypnosis. Interestingly, it was tunnels in this latter group, not the trauma group, that were most often associated with OBEs.

Most of Drab's informants described their tunnels as dark or dimly lit; nearly half saw a light at the end, with three-quarters saying the light was growing larger or they were moving towards it. This light was often described as extremely bright but without hurting the eyes, and the same is often said by NDErs who 'enter the light'.

Please note that these 'tunnel experiences' are nothing to do with 'tunnel vision'. Tunnel vision is a well-documented effect caused by eye disease or by lack of oxygen to the eyes themselves. The visual field narrows down to a small central circle and this is all the person can see. The impression may resemble being inside a tunnel but the 'walls' of the tunnel itself are blank: there are no sewer pipes, trees or colourful spirals, just nothingness. Unfortunately, some NDE sceptics conflate tunnel vision with the tunnel experience, creating much confusion (Nelson, 2010, Woerlee, 2004).

We now have two questions to answer that may be related or may be quite separate: why the tunnel and why the light at the end?

Occult theories abound in explanations. Some say there is an actual tunnel that leads from one world to the next, from the physical to the astral or higher worlds, although it's hard to imagine what it's made of or how the transition between totally different 'vibration rates' or 'levels of reality' can meaningfully be connected by a tunnel. In *Astral Dynamics*, Bruce describes the 'astral tube-type entrance structure'. Entering it, you will 'feel a sensation of great speed and often hear a rushing sound like air whooshing past you. Grid lines and colors and patterns and tones and musical notes change as you move through it.' He urges his readers to 'hang on, enjoy the astral tube roller-coaster ride, and see where you end up' and, reassuringly, 'The tube will not hurt you no matter what you do' (Bruce, 1999, p.160).

Others avoid such material difficulties by saying that the tunnel is not actual but symbolic. Crookall (1964) said it represented the blacking out of consciousness as we shed the physical body and gave many examples, arguing 'that in this symbol a genuine experience of a surviving soul is indicated' (Crookall, 1961b, p.106). Others see it as representing a long journey (Green, 1968a), a flow of 'vital force' through the 'astral cord', the mind's experience of transitions through states of consciousness, or its shift to a holographic or four-dimensional consciousness of pure frequencies (Ring, 1980).

A popular theory is that the tunnel re-enacts something we've all experienced just once – being born. 'Do not the astral body and the astral cable afford striking similarities to the new-born physical body and the umbilical cord?' asked Muldoon and Carrington (1929, p.80). Um, I'm not sure. Newborns are tiny, with heads far larger in proportion to their bodies than adults' heads, yet I have never heard anyone say that their astral double was like a baby. And the umbilical cord is not silvery, transparent and so elastic that it can stretch across the world. But let's grant that there are indeed similarities and perhaps the idea is just symbolic.

This is what Czech psychiatrist Stanislav Grof proposed, fifty years later; that moving through a tunnel towards the light is a symbolic re-experience of being born – a memory of the 'near-birth experience' (Grof & Halifax, 1977). That same year, no less a scientist than Carl Sagan (1977) endorsed the idea, arguing that the universality of imagery in near-death experiences, including OBEs, could be accounted for only by reference to the one experience we all share – our birth. Parapsychologist Barbara Honegger (1983) made the analogy even more explicit, likening the tunnel to the passage down the birth canal, the vibrations to the contractions of labour, the light to the lights of the delivery room and the silver cord to the umbilical cord.

As soon as I read this I realised that the idea was testable (Blackmore, 1983b). If the experience is a re-enactment of birth, it should vary with the way in which people are born. In particular, those born by Caesarean section should not experience tunnels because they never did pass down that birth canal towards the light of the outside world. So I contacted 254 people, of whom thirty-six had been born by Caesarean, and asked them about tunnel experiences. The answer was simple; exactly the same proportion of both groups, 36 per cent in each, had experienced the tunnel. A person's actual birth experience makes no difference.

Of course this might not matter on the weaker theory that the experience is symbolic of births in general. Yet even this idea is fraught with difficulties (Becker, 1982). Imagine yourself as a baby being born and it's obvious that the birth canal is nothing like a tunnel. The foetus is being forced through a tight space, usually with the top of its head emerging first and its eyes tight shut. It would not see a tunnel, let alone the light of the outside world coming closer. Nor would it have any sight or knowledge of the umbilical cord unless it could feel its pull or maybe even feel the cord being cut, but I have never heard of an OBE or NDE in which this cutting is represented. Birth theories get us nowhere. Much better ideas, also going back a long way, come from a different direction: the study of hallucinations.

## Constant forms in hallucinating minds

In 1926, German psychologist Heinrich Klüver acquired some Peyote buttons to explore the hallucinogenic effects of mescaline. Comparing his own experiences with those in various traditional cultures as well as in modern America, he described four commonly-recurring 'form constants' that arise again and again in hallucinations, whether caused by migraines, epilepsy, hypnagogic imagery or psychedelic drugs. The four types are:

(a) Grating, lattice, fretwork, filigree, honeycomb, or chessboard
(b) Cobweb
(c) Tunnel, funnel, alley, cone or vessel
(d) Spiral.

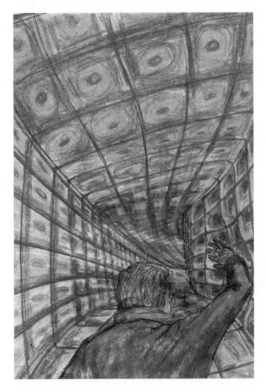

**Figure 13.1: A tunnel experienced during 'alien abduction'.** David Howard suffered from narcolepsy, falling uncontrollably asleep and having repeated experiences in which he seemed to be abducted by aliens and taken, sometimes through a tunnel, to a distant planet called Dut. This is one of the many paintings he gave me. The tunnel and checkerboard design are typical of the form constants which he knew nothing about.

He found that a wide range of hallucinations are transformations or reduplications of these four basic forms, turning them into geometrical designs of great complexity and even into landscapes or cities made up of the same designs (Klüver, 1926,1966). Drug inspired art, whether modern psychedelic painting or the ornamentation of pots and clothing in traditional cultures, uses these forms repeatedly. I even found similar tunnels in a case of alien abduction (see Figure 13.1).

American psychopharmacologist Ronald Siegel (1977) asked people to describe their visions while taking marijuana. At first they saw mostly simple geometric forms, sometimes pulsating or moving, and often with a bright light in the centre creating a tunnel-like perspective. Later, complex imagery took over, including small animals or caricature people. With THC, psilocybin, LSD and mescaline the forms became more organised as the experience progressed, until after one and a half to two hours most were lattice-tunnels, often incorporating complex imagery and fantastical scenes. At the peak of the experience 'The subjects reported feeling dissociated from their bodies'.

Why these same forms should occur in so many different situations became clearer with the work of mathematical biologist Jack Cowan (Cowan, 1982, Ermentrout & Cowan, 1979). He noted that the images do not move with the eyes and must therefore be generated in the cortex. So what could be happening in the cortex to produce such repeatable patterns? He realised that those conditions that typically create form constants all involve increased random firing of cortical neurons. This can be set off by epilepsy, fever or anoxia, or by drugs that affect inhibitory neurons. These are nerve cells that inhibit other, excitatory, neurons. If their activity is reduced the resulting disinhibition leads to widespread random firing, and when neurons in visual cortex fire they produce visual experiences with no information coming in from the eyes.

What Cowan worked out was the consequences of such disinhibition for visions. The random firing of an excitatory neuron increases the chances of others firing too and this produces waves of excitation propagating across the visual cortex. To work out what kind of visions this would create we need to know how the arrangement of neurons in primary visual cortex (area V1) maps onto images on the retina (see Figure 13.2). Cowan showed that straight lines of cells in the cortex correspond to concentric rings on the retina, straight lines at right angles to these correspond to radiating lines, and those at other angles to spirals. If waves of excitation spread across the cortex, the experience will be visions of expanding rings, radiating lines or spirals. Cowan elaborated his findings with mathematical modelling and computer simulations of the cortex, showing that 'the various patterns of activity that spontaneously emerge when V1's spatially uniform resting state becomes unstable correspond to the form constants when transformed to the visual field using the retino-cortical map' (Bressloff et al., 2002, p.474).

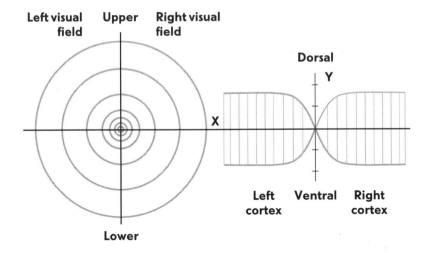

**Figure 13.2: The mapping from retina to primary visual cortex.**
Rings seen in the visual field are shown on the left and the corresponding representation in visual cortex on the right. If waves of excitation pass across a hyper-excited visual cortex they will appear as though there are concentric rings in the visual field. (After Cowan, 1982)

This could explain why tunnels are so common; radiating lines and spirals can form into tunnels; expanding rings can invoke the impression of moving through a tunnel. Early experiments with LSD show that, with eyes closed, the primary visual cortex behaves as if it's seeing such localised visual inputs (Roseman et al., 2016) so perhaps now that LSD research is tentatively being licensed we'll soon find out much more.

But all this prompts another question: if disinhibition in visual cortex induces cobwebs and checkerboards as well as tunnels, why do we find only tunnels in OBEs?

To find out we need to consider the effects of disinhibition on the rest of the visual system and ask what this should look like in the person's experience. The whole visual system devotes far more processing to the centre of the visual field than to the periphery. The fovea in the centre of each retina has very high acuity because of its densely packed light-sensitive cones with tiny receptive fields – the area to which they respond. Out towards the edges acuity gets much lower with larger receptive fields, although we still respond to movement further out.

You can test this by looking straight ahead and holding an object to one side, almost at ninety degrees from where you are looking, or try reading this page while looking even slightly away. As long as you don't move your eyes or the page you will find it hard to identify any details but if it moves, you'll detect the movement instantly.

Think now about what kind of visions would result from disinhibition and hyperactivity in a system like this. Excited cells will signal light where really there is none, and because far more of them are devoted to the centre of the visual field there will seem to be a bright light in the centre fading out to dark towards the edge. If random activity increases, this light will seem to get larger and larger, giving the sense of moving towards or into the light, an illusion that might even be enhanced by excited movement-sensitive cells signalling movement when really there is none. This means the tunnel experience itself might contribute to vestibular sensations and OB feelings.

Back in the 1980s I tried to test the basic idea with simple computer simulations of what disinhibition and random excitation should look like based on the known distribution of cells in the visual system (Figure 13.3). I think tunnel experiences and bright lights that don't hurt your eyes are just what we should expect of a hyper-excited visual system (Blackmore & Troscianko, 1989).

I still haven't answered my question about why we find tunnels with OBEs but not cobwebs or checkerboards, but here's a suggestion. I tried to imagine what an expanding light getting brighter in the middle of a checkerboard or lattice would look like. It just wouldn't have the same dynamic effect. It wouldn't create an appearance of depth and movement or draw me into the middle because checkerboards and lattices don't have a middle. Movements signalled on the periphery would just make the lattices or checkerboards jiggle about rather than pulling me forwards. Indeed I have often experienced fluttering or wriggling lattices and geometrical patterns with hallucinogenic drugs, but they did not lead to vestibular sensations, let alone an OBE.

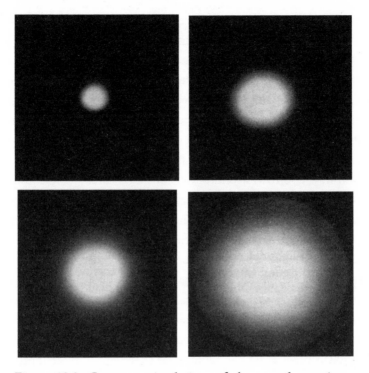

**Figure 13.3: Computer simulations of the tunnel experience.**
**Simulating the tunnel experience.** A simple computer simulation of
the expected effect of random excitation in the visual system, based
on the density of neurons devoted to processing different parts of the
visual field. With eyes closed there would be no reference point so
the light would appear to come closer as it got larger until the whole
visual field is flooded with light.

We can now pull this together with something else we know about
OBEs, the importance of illusory movement experiences (IMEs) in
initiating them. As we discovered in the previous chapter, Cheyne and
Girard (2009) showed that IMEs typically precede both OB feelings
and OB autoscopy. So now it makes sense. When conditions in the
brain are right for producing the form constants, any of them may
appear but it is only tunnels that induce an IME and so set the stage
for an OBE. At last I think we can answer the question.

This all sounds rather complicated, but what I have enjoyed about
studying these ideas is the way science always draws us on. Occult

theories change only when one person disagrees with another; they argue and there's nothing that can be done to adjudicate between them, so no progress is ever made. When we start making testable theories and looking for evidence we get answers, and those answers lead to more questions, and delving into those questions we finally, sometimes, explain something that once seemed utterly mysterious – the OBE at the end of the tunnel.

## Out in virtual reality

Can you imagine a devious experimenter convincing you that a pink rubber hand, lying flabbily in front of you on a table, is your own? It seems unlikely but this is what happens in the 'rubber hand illusion' (RHI). As the story goes, this now-famous trick was hit upon by a student, Matthew Botvinick, at a Halloween party while messing about with one of the spooky props. Along with psychologist Jonathan Cohen at Princeton, he had the wits to turn what some might consider an idle trick into a proper experiment (Botvinick & Cohen, 1998).

In the lab they asked people to place their left hand on a table but then hid it with a screen and placed a rubber hand just next to it and in full view. They took two small paintbrushes and stroked both the hidden real hand and the visible rubber hand at exactly the same time. The stroking had to be synchronous, i.e. done in the same way and at the same time on both. After about ten minutes some people began to feel the touch as though it was on the rubber hand and some even said they felt as though the rubber hand had become their own. The experiment had set up a conflict between vision and proprioception – between where the brushing was seen to happen and where it was felt – and vision won.

The feeling of owning our body parts is something we take for granted, but, as this effect shows, we should not: it is a decision made by the brain and it can be tricked. To measure the size of the effect volunteers closed their eyes and pointed with their right hand to where they thought their (hidden) index finger was. On average they pointed closer to the rubber hand. This is called 'proprioceptive drift' because the feeling of the hand's position drifts towards where the

**Figure 13.4: A set-up for inducing the rubber hand illusion.** If the experimenter strokes both the hidden hand and the visible rubber hand in synchrony, people often begin to feel that the rubber hand is their own.

fake hand is seen. Despite disagreements about exactly what is being measured with proprioceptive drift, this illusion has opened up new ways of finding out how we come to locate our own body parts and feel they are 'mine' (Rohde et al., 2011, Tsakiris et al., 2006).

And here are some interesting findings. First, when TMS is applied over the right TPJ (the spot Blanke discovered) the rubber hand illusion is reduced (Tsakiris et al., 2008). Second, ketamine, the closest we have to an OBE-inducing drug, increases the RHI (Morgan et al., 2011). Third, positive (but not negative) schizotypes are more susceptible to the illusion (Asai et al., 2011, Germine et al., 2013).

So are schizophrenics. In one study, a schizophrenic patient even had an OBE while doing the experiment. He had had many OBEs before, either when falling asleep or when awake, and they always preceded a psychotic episode. Each time he turned over and looked down on his own body, describing what he saw as vivid and accurate. During testing with the rubber hand he again found himself looking down from near the ceiling and was afraid it presaged another psychotic episode but, to his relief, nothing happened. When an OBE happened a second time he found it pleasant and wanted the sensation to return (Thakkar et al., 2011).

These findings with the rubber hand illusion might imply that people who have spontaneous OBEs should be more susceptible to the illusion but Braithwaite and his colleagues (2014) found that the illusion takes longer to induce in people who have many anomalous experiences. So this is an obvious question for future research. But is this connection between the artificial situation of the RHI and OBEs really as close as it seems? After all, the RHI affects only people's hands and not the rest of their body, and they are still looking out from behind their eyes. But what if it were possible to shift location or ownership for a whole body?

The first experiment to try this difficult trick used not a pink, flabby rubber body but a virtual body and was devised by neuropsychologist Bigna Lenggenhager and her colleagues in Zurich (Lenggenhager et al., 2007). The set-up is rather hard to explain but it helps if you try to imagine what it would feel like to take part. Volunteers were asked to stand two metres in front of a video camera wearing head-mounted 3D video displays. The cameras were pointed at their backs so what they saw was a view of their own back as if it were two metres in front of them. The experimenter then stroked their back with a stick (Figure 13.5).

What would this feel like? You stand still and can feel someone stroking your back while you watch a video of your back being stroked as though it were someone else two metres in front of you. What would happen?

The participants had the strange impression of feeling the touch almost as though it were on the virtual body rather than on their own

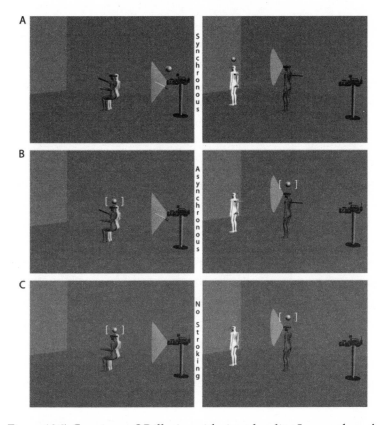

**Figure 13.5: Creating an OB illusion with virtual reality: Lenggenhager's method.** Wearing a head-mounted display, the participant sees his own virtual body in 3D standing 2m in front of him and having his back stroked synchronously or asynchronously. The self seems to move forwards towards the seen body. (Lenggenhager et al 2007)

back. Again there was proprioceptive drift; when asked to pinpoint their own position they chose a spot closer to the virtual body than where they really were. This happened only when the stroking was synchronous, and not when a block of wood was filmed instead of the person's own back. Once again, there was 'visual capture', with vision overruling touch. This is why the authors called their paper 'Video ergo sum' – I see therefore I am.

Does this experiment really tell us anything about OBEs? No participants experienced a full OBE or even reported feeling disembodied.

They did not fly around the room or float above themselves. Indeed, the authors suggest that these experiences were more like heautoscopy than an OBE. Should we conclude that these tricks induce nothing more interesting than an irrelevant quirk of the body sense? Some further explorations of virtual reality take us deeper into 'out-of-body illusions' and from there to the nature of self.

## Four aspects of self

Sitting here at my desk I feel unambiguously that I'm inside my body. I am inside my head, positioned roughly between my eyes and looking out at the world. This sense of being a discrete, located self changes with different drugs and even disappears in deep meditation, but it is the norm for me in everyday life.

Does everyone feel this way? In lectures I often ask people this question and although some say they are in their throat or heart, or spread throughout their whole body, most feel they are behind their eyes, and this is common in other cultures too (Chapter 7, page 119). Regardless of the precise position, this self is remarkably unified. We do not feel like one self who is looking and another who is hearing or feeling, or moving; one who is in control of the body and another who owns it. We just feel unified – this is 'me' and this is 'my' body.

Taking a closer look, though, we can discern four distinct aspects to being a self (Blanke, 2012, Blanke & Arzy, 2005, Lopez et al., 2008). The first three create what Metzinger calls 'minimal phenomenal selfhood' or the minimum that is needed for a person to experience self-consciousness (Blanke & Metzinger, 2009, Metzinger, 2013, Limanowski, 2014). The four are:

1. Embodiment or self-location – the position where I feel myself to be.

2. Body ownership or self-identification – the sense that this is 'my' body.

3. First-person perspective – the position from which I am observing the world.

4.  Agency – the sense that I am an agent in control of my body.

Thinking about these as separate functions may feel rather weird as it threatens the sense of unity, but this scheme provides new ways of understanding the full-body illusions: OBEs, autoscopy, heautoscopy and the sense of a presence. All involve a double but they differ in how the four components split apart.

In OBEs, self-location, first-person perspective and agency all shift to the double. I still own my physical body but 'I' am not in there; when 'I' want to move, the disembodied self or point of view moves. In autoscopy, ownership shifts to the double or splits in two while embodiment, perspective and agency remain with the physical body. In heautoscopy, embodiment and first-person perspective can both shift and even alternate. And with the sense of a presence nothing changes except that a double is felt close by.

The lab-based illusions can be thought of this way too. In the rubber hand illusion, first-person perspective remains unaffected while embodiment and ownership shift for just the hand. In Lenggenhager's experiment, first-person perspective is unaffected but embodiment and ownership move towards the whole virtual body.

If these four aspects are really distinct this implies a somewhat uncomfortable idea of self, that I am the result of several interacting brain mechanisms that construct an illusion of unity. If this is correct, for example if the four depend on different brain mechanisms, then it should possible to separate them out, and even produce the right changes to induce a full OBE. Some further experiments with virtual reality have attempted just this.

## That's my body!

Neuroscientist Henrik Ehrsson leads the Brain, Body and Self Lab at the Karolinska Institute in Sweden, where he tries to understand how we come to own our bodies. Like Lenggenhager, he induces OB illusions using virtual reality but he uses a method that is subtly different from hers and produces a different experience.

**Figure 13.6: Creating an OB illusion with virtual reality: Ehrsson's method.** Wearing a head-mounted display, the participant sees his own back as well as a stick appearing and disappearing close to him as he would if his chest were being stroked. Simultaneously he feels the other stick stroking his chest. The self seems to move backwards towards the position of the camera. (From Ehrsson 2007.)

In the first experiment (Ehrsson, 2007) the subject sat in a chair wearing a pair of head-mounted displays. Two metres behind him were two video cameras pointed at him so he would seem to be looking at his own back from behind but this time the experimenter did two things at once: he stroked the subject's chest with a plastic rod and at the same time stroked the air just below the cameras (Figure 13.6).

This sounds rather complicated. So if it doesn't make sense, try this: pick up a pen or stick and hold it in front of your face. Look straight ahead and now repeatedly stroke your own chest with the stick. I guess you will see the stick appearing in front of you and then disappearing as it drops below your line of vision. This movement is what the cameras filmed when Ehrsson stroked the air close to them. The cameras could not see the other rod that was stroking the subject's chest because this was concealed by his body.

This meant that the display showed a rod appearing and disappearing close to the camera as if it were stroking a chest below it. Beyond that the subject could see his own back, and he could feel the rod stroking his chest. How would this feel? You might like to try to imagine the effect before reading on.

After just two minutes of synchronous stroking, the participants reported a sense of having moved location. But rather than moving forwards they had moved back to sit at the position of the cameras, behind their actual body and watching its back. This trick was a new way of inducing an OB illusion.

All this seems very strange. By manipulating vision and touch in slightly different ways the sense of self can be moved in opposite directions. With Lenggenhager's method the self seems to move forwards towards the seen body; with Ehrsson's method it moves backwards towards the position of the camera. Both show how flexible our sense of location is, but they are not strictly comparable in other ways. So as a next step Lenggenhager's lab tried to produce both effects in one go (Lenggenhager et al., 2009).

For this experiment, twenty-one healthy young men took part, lying face down on a special table that had a hole cut in it through which their chests could be stroked as in Ehrsson's method. Cameras were fixed two metres above the table, pointing down, and projecting images to a HMD as before. This meant that the two different experiences could be induced in the same setting by stroking either the man's back or his chest.

In both cases powerful illusions of touch and location were created. When the men's backs were stroked they seemed to remain lying on the table, looking down at a body beneath them, and with synchronous stroking they moved closer. In contrast, when their chests were stroked they seemed to move up nearer the cameras, looking down on their bodies and feeling the stroking on an imaginary, floating body. This sounds much more like an OBE and the men reported stronger sensations of floating and of identifying with the floating self. One even said it was, 'as if the self and the body were in different locations' (Lenggenhager et al., 2009, p.114).

Were they really disidentifying with their own body, or was this just a faint sense of being distant from it? If the real body were threatened, how would they react? If it were hurt, would they feel the pain?

The same out-of-body illusion was used to find out. Once again, participants felt they were located near the cameras and not in their own body, only this time 'the experimenter threatened the participant's real body with a knife, by making a slow, well-controlled stabbing motion towards the upper back'! (Guterstam & Ehrsson, 2012, p.1039). Their skin conductance response was measured (a standard way to measure arousal by detecting sweat on the skin) and was far lower when the illusion was strong. Conversely, when the illusory body was 'hurt' by hitting it with a hammer, the skin conductance response was stronger when the illusion was stronger (Ehrsson, 2007). In other experiments, participants' body temperature even dropped during synchronous stroking (Salomon et al., 2013).

To induce pain an electronic 'algometer' gradually increased pressure on their index finger until they pressed a stop button to say that it was painful. When the illusion was induced using Lenggenhager's method, the pain was felt less strongly the more they identified with the illusory body (Hänsell et al., 2011). This all suggests that when embodiment shifts to an imagined body, this is not only a high-level cognitive shift but involves physiological changes throughout the body.

This reduction in pain is most interesting. Many OBEs happen to people in stressful or painful situations. This is not just near death or in serious accidents but in frightening or painful situations such as war, hostage taking and rape. Children who are physically or sexually abused report many dissociative phenomena, including alterations in bodily perception and OBEs (Briere & Elliott, 1994). It's as though someone else is enduring the abuse, not them. These reactions are often described as merely an emotional escape or pretence, but if pain is reduced when first person perspective shifts beyond the body then these dissociations are more than that. The pain really is reduced, not because it has forced a soul or astral body to leave, but because the shift in embodiment reduces felt pain.

If it's possible to shift to inhabiting a virtual body, could it be possible to swap bodies? I mean, could I be made to feel that I was inside someone else's body? This reminds me of when I was a child and tried to work out what would happen if I could swap with my

**Figure 13.7: The body swap illusion.** The set-up for the body-swap illusion. The participant wears a head-mounted display and stands opposite a life-size mannequin. The mannequin has a camera on its head pointing down to view its own body. When the experimenter strokes both at once the participant feels the stroking and can look down on the mannequin's body as though it is his own. (After Petkova & Ehrsson 2008).

sister. I never thought that any experiment could approximate to this but it can.

In Ehrsson's lab, participants stood in front of a life-size mannequin, looking down at their own body. Only they did not see it. Instead they saw the view from two cameras located where the mannequin's eyes would be and also looking down. So where their own body should be, they saw this other body (Figure 13.7). When both were stroked at once they felt as though the other body was their own and reacted less to a knife threatening their real body (Petkova & Ehrsson, 2008).

The final experiment aimed at a real body swap. This time participants directly faced the experimenter and the display showed the view from the experimenter's eyes, so they were looking straight at the cameras. When they reached out as if to shake hands and repeatedly squeezed each others' hands, the vivid illusion was created that the experimenters' arm was the participant's own arm. Afterwards some said things like, 'Your arm felt like it was my arm, and I was behind it', and, 'I was shaking hands with myself'.

Pulling all this research together tells us a lot about our normal in-body experience. The illusions show that touch tends to be felt where the stroking is seen, and self location moves to where the touch is felt rather than where it really is. This confirms that our normal sense of location – when not disturbed by trauma or tricked by fiendish experimenters – depends on multisensory integration. The reason I normally feel unified and firmly embodied is that this brain is successfully integrating vision, touch, vestibular sensations and every other sense to give the impression of a conscious person located inside this body and looking out.

This means that my in-body experience is as much a construction of the brain as any out-of-body experience might be.

## Virtual reality in the brain

Imagine you are playing an online role-playing game, watching your avatar from a third-person perspective, exploring a virtual environment, interacting with others and becoming completely engrossed. The sense of agency and control you have over the avatar will suck you into identifying with it. Indeed, some gamers identify more closely with their avatar than their own body, others alternate between the two rather as happens in heautoscopy, and others seem to bilocate, identifying with both (Furlanetto et al., 2013). Is this anything like an OBE?

Researchers in the Netherlands noted the difference; in OBEs the sense of self, first-person perspective and agency all move out to the double, but in this kind of gaming first-person perspective stays with the physical body while self and agency move to the avatar. So the two experiences are different, but both can be understood in terms of self-identification. And what of the brain? Studying gamers with fMRI showed more activity in the left angular gyrus at the TPJ for avatar referencing than for self- and other-referencing (Ganesh et al., 2012). So we find the same part of the brain implicated once again.

Could this be investigated for the full-body illusions? This is technically extremely demanding but has actually been achieved by psychologist Silvio Ionta and his colleagues in Switzerland. They managed to induce out-of-body illusions in more than twenty volunteers when lying in an fMRI scanner (Ionta et al., 2011).

This time the volunteers had to lie on their backs inside the machine, which makes for a good comparison with OBEs because so many OBErs report lying on their backs (Zingrone et al., 2010). The table was adapted to include a custom-built robotic stroking device that moved a rod up and down the participant's back. A video projected to their goggles showed the same rod stroking the back of a person lying face down and this seen stroking was either exactly in synchrony with the felt stroking, or delayed and out of synchrony. The moving rod could also be shown moving without a body as a control condition.

To measure how high the participants felt they were, they were given a ball to hold and asked to estimate how long it would take to fall to the floor – a method previously tested for this purpose – and their brain activity was monitored throughout.

Something very strange happened. In a pilot study, done to test the procedures, several said that they found themselves flipping over and looking down on the body whose back they saw being stroked. In other words, although they were actually lying on their backs inside the scanner, they felt as though they had floated up, flipped over and were looking down instead, just as happens in many OBEs. For the main experiment participants had to say whether they were looking up or down, and this created two groups with eleven in each.

As before, synchronised stroking caused movement towards the body in the video but the up-group started low before rising towards the body seen above them, while the down-group initially rose higher but then came down towards the body seen below them. Once again, many identified themselves with the virtual body and said the stroking seemed to be happening to that body, not to their own.

Some reported floating or flying, even when the stroking was not synchronised. One said, 'I felt as if I were "rising" in a strange way towards the roof,' and another, 'I had the impression of being in two places at the same time as if I had two bodies.' Some sounded very much like OBEs: 'the vision from above was very bizarre because I was looking downwards at my own body.' 'I had the impression of forgetting my body as if my eyes were leaving my body and were going upwards. I was "watching" myself, "my real me", from above,' 'I had the impression of being two people at the same time. One myself was flying, and was watching the other (real) myself being touched by the stick.'

While all this was happening, rich data were collected from the scanner. This revealed that seven different cortical regions were involved but the authors wanted to pin down the part responsible for self-location (the height above the ground indicated by the ball-dropping test). The two groups showed slightly different responses but only one region showed changes in activity that reflected the changes in self-location (Ionta et al., 2011). That was, on both sides, the TPJ – the same area originally discovered by Blanke's stimulation.

What fascinates me about this illusion is something that might shed light on spontaneous OBEs. That is, half the participants spontaneously flipped over to look down at their own body while the others did not, even though they watched the same videos and experienced the same stroking. What made the difference?

To explore this question, further experiments varied the strength of the conflict between vision and vestibular feelings from the body (Pfeiffer et al., 2013). In one video people saw the back of someone standing, i.e. at 90 degrees different from their own position; in the other it was lying face down, i.e. 180 degrees from their own position, but this made no difference to their up or down perspective. Perhaps people differ in how they resolve the conflict between vision and vestibular sense and some just find it easier to flip over. In this case I wonder whether they are more likely to have a spontaneous OBE.

These experiments seem to be homing in on the same brain areas and creating experiences increasingly similar to OBEs. But are they really OBEs? They're close. I defined the OBE as an experience in which a person seems to perceive the world from a location outside their physical body. This illusion fits the definition. Yet the world seen in virtual reality is produced by video; in an OBE there is no video providing the pictures. The OB world must come either from the person's own memories and imagination or from another world.

Is there another world? Some people who have come close to death are completely sure: they *know* there is another world because they have been there.

# CHAPTER 14

# On the Verge of Death

A man is dying and, as he reaches the point of greatest physical distress, he hears himself pronounced dead by his doctor. He begins to hear an uncomfortable noise, a loud ringing or buzzing, and at the same time feels himself moving very rapidly through a long dark tunnel. After this, he suddenly finds himself outside of his own physical body, but still in the immediate physical environment, and he sees his own body from a distance, as though he is a spectator . . .

Imagine my surprise when, in 1975, I read *Life After Life* by American physician Raymond Moody. While studying psychical research I had read many Victorian accounts of 'death-bed experiences', in which a dying person describes a world beyond, filled with light and love, and their dead loved ones beckoning them on (Barrett, 1926, Myers, 1903). But by the 1970s modern medicine was bringing people back from states further into death than ever before and they were living to tell their own tales. Many doctors must have heard such accounts but it seems they dismissed them as fantasy, or feared ridicule if they mentioned them, so they said nothing. Moody was therefore a real pioneer in systematically collecting these stories and putting together his now-famous account of a typical NDE, which begins with the excerpt above.

From gathering over a hundred accounts Moody created the first of many lists of typical NDE features. This list of nine provides a good overview.

1. Sounds; buzzing or ringing noises
2. Peace; reduced pain, peace, contentment and even joy
3. OBE; sensations of rising or floating and looking down on the physical body below, often with vivid vision and the ability to pass through walls and other objects
4. Tunnel; being drawn into and through a dark tunnel towards a radiant golden-white light
5. Rising to heaven; seeing earth as though from space or entering heavenly worlds
6. Meeting others; seeing and sometimes speaking silently with deceased friends or relatives
7. Being of light; a spiritual entity, sometimes without form or identified as God, Jesus or another religious figure
8. Life review; the person's life re-enacted in panoramic view
9. Reluctance to return; the Being of light may tell the person that it is not their time to die, or they may have to decide for themselves, perhaps returning for the sake of others.

Why was I so surprised? Because Moody's list so closely matched my own experience that had happened just five years earlier. My noise was a thunderous drumming like the hooves of a galloping horse, my tunnel was a tunnel of leaves, the light bright and welcoming. I left my body and travelled in other worlds of great vividness, seeing more clearly than I had ever seen before. I met beings who seemed to teach me without speaking, I felt watched by some being greater than myself and finally I made the difficult decision to go back down into that heavy body and get on with ordinary life. I was nowhere near death, yet the only part of Moody's account that I had not experienced was the life review. I was amazed. Until then the only concept I knew to apply to my experience was 'astral projection' so I suppose I ignored all the other details as just too weird to name or even think about. Now I knew that others, many others, had experienced the same series of events. But why?

Once Moody had set the ball rolling, research on NDEs began in earnest. Psychologist Kenneth Ring (1980) collected 102 accounts from people who had nearly died through illness, accidents or attempted suicide. Confounding many vociferous critics, he broadly confirmed Moody's findings, concluding, 'there is a consistent and remarkable experiential pattern that often unfolds when an individual is seemingly about to die. I will call this reliable near-death pattern the "core experience"' (Ring, 1980, p.22).

He described five stages:

1. Peace
2. Body separation (the OBE)
3. Entering the darkness (including dark tunnels)
4. Seeing the light
5. Entering the light (and other worlds).

You will immediately recognise familiar experiences on both these lists; ones that we know can be caused by disinhibition or hyperactivity in various areas of the brain: the humming and grinding noises by random activity in auditory cortex, the tunnel and lights by hyperactivity in visual cortex, and the other beings, sense of presence and OBE by disruption to self-systems at the TPJ. This same disturbed brain activity is likely to occur close to death, whether that's through stress and fear, low blood pressure or lack of oxygen.

What also stands out from both schemes is the order in which the stages occur. Moody acknowledged that his collection was neither systematic nor scientific but he had the impression that events usually unfolded in a similar order and that the closer to death someone came, the deeper their experience. Ring at least partly confirmed this, showing that the earlier stages were also the most common. Peace was reported by 60 per cent, body separation by 37 per cent, but far fewer entered the darkness or saw the light (Figure 14.1). A simpler scale revealed the same effect (Kohr, 1983), as did a much later and better

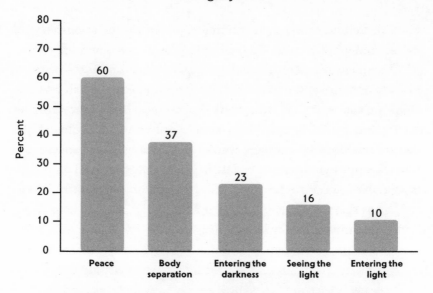

**Figure 14.1: The stages of the NDE according to Ring (1980), based on 102 survivors of NDEs.** Note that the earlier stages also tend to be the most frequently reported.

Fig 14.2

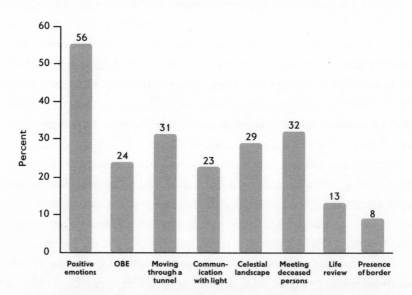

**Figure 14.2: Elements of the NDE from van Lommel's prospective study based on 62 respondents (van Lommel et al 2001).**

controlled study in which 56 per cent had positive emotions, 31 per cent a tunnel, 24 per cent an OBE and just 13 per cent a life review (van Lommel et al., 2001, Figure 14.:2).

In reality the order is not always the same; tunnels can precede OBEs or vice versa, and the light can be seen before the OBE or tunnel, but generally this order stands up, with peacefulness and positive emotions being the most commonly reported, and sometimes being the only memory from a close brush with death (van Lommel et al., 2001, Parnia et al., 2001).

Why is this significant? Because, if true, it might suggest something more than a random collection of effects in a disturbed brain; something more like a series of deep changes unfolding as death approaches. Could there be a natural order to the way the brain responds to trouble?

Some people are sure they know the answer; they *know* that NDEs are the soul's journey towards the next world, or the self leaving the prison of its temporary physical body. They *know* this because they have been there and seen that everything is completely real; they have no doubt. Yet I have seen this too and I have plenty of doubts. I want to know a lot more about NDEs before jumping to conclusions.

## Measuring the NDE

Among the necessary tools is a way to decide what counts as an NDE. Ring used his findings to develop the 'Weighted Core Experience Index' (WCEI), giving different weights to each feature to provide an NDE score between zero and twenty-nine. A few years later, psychiatrist Bruce Greyson (1983) developed another scale, starting with eighty features and testing his questionnaires through several stages until he had sixteen questions in four clusters to provide a score between zero and thirty-two. Finding that the tunnel experience did not correlate with other features he left it out of his scale. The average score among a large group of NDErs was fifteen, and a score of seven or above (one standard deviation below the mean) is counted as an NDE for research purposes.

Out of interest I completed these scales myself, trying to be as truthful as I could. My score on Ring's scale is fourteen and on

Greyson's twenty-three. This means I had a very deep NDE, despite not being close to death or even afraid I might die. This may seem odd but many people have NDEs when not close to death. These are sometimes called 'fear-death experiences' – for example, when people think they are about to die in accidents that prove less serious than they seemed or when falling from cliffs only to land safely on soft ground or deep snow.

In 1892, Albert Heim, a Swiss geologist and mountain climber, collected accounts from climbers who had survived serious falls. Many described joy and 'profound acceptance, and a dominant mental quickness'. His discoveries helped him console the families of fellow climbers who had died. The author Arthur Koestler (1954) describes how he benefited from 'split consciousness' when he thought he was about to be executed. This is significant, not only because it makes defining NDEs difficult, but because it weakens the argument that NDEs and other OBEs are fundamentally different.

To study such differences, Gabbard and Twemlow analysed hundreds of cases, finding that people who really were close to death slightly more often reported noises, tunnels, and non-physical entities, but the differences were small (1984, Gabbard, Twemlow & Jones, 1981). A Belgian team compared what they called 'real NDEs', reported after pathological comas, with 'NDE-like experiences', finding them very similar in both features and intensity (Charland-Verville et al., 2014). And one more study compared NDEs in twenty-eight people who would have died without medical intervention with thirty who only thought they were dying. The only significant difference was that those close to death more often reported enhanced light, and this was correlated with tunnels, enhanced cognitive function and positive emotions (Owens et al., 1990).

These findings show that you need not be near death, let alone have a cardiac arrest or clinical death, to experience all the basic features of an NDE. This may be problematic for people who are convinced that NDEs are something special and not dependent on a functioning brain but it suggests to me that we probably won't need a different explanation for NDEs near death than for all the tunnels, lights and OBEs we have met so far. But we need to know a lot more to be sure.

## How common are NDEs?

Don't believe those claims in the popular literature that 15 per cent of Americans have had an NDE. This idea comes from a notoriously unreliable poll that counted an NDE if people said 'yes' to having had 'a close call with death' (Gallup & Proctor, 1982). Other surveys of the general population give wildly different estimates (Blackmore, 1993a). But really this is not the most useful question. Using Ring's and Greyson's scales we can answer a more pertinent one – of all those people who come close to death, how many have an NDE?

Of Ring's (1980) 102 near-death survivors, forty-eight had NDEs. Of Sabom's one hundred hospital patients forty-three reported an NDE (Sabom & Kreutziger, 1978), and Melvin Morse (1990) found that 85 per cent of children who came close to death had NDEs. But this early research asked people to remember events that had sometimes happened a long time before, introducing many possible errors. To answer the question accurately requires prospective studies, meaning that researchers select their sample in advance, for example by interviewing every patient who undergoes a given procedure or is admitted to a certain hospital or cardiac unit within a given time frame.

The first and largest study of this kind was carried out in the Netherlands by cardiologist Pim van Lommel (van Lommel et al., 2001). He and his colleagues recorded every patient who was successfully resuscitated in coronary care units in ten Dutch hospitals between 1988 and 1992, collecting data on their health, background, religion, education and many other variables. Within a few days of the resuscitation they interviewed all those who were well enough and gave them the WCEI. Two years later they interviewed any remaining survivors more fully and finally followed them up again after eight years. The vast majority of the 344 patients remembered little or nothing. Just 12% had a core experience (including 5% with a WCEI score of 6 to 9, 5% 10 to 14 and 2% a very deep NDE with a score of

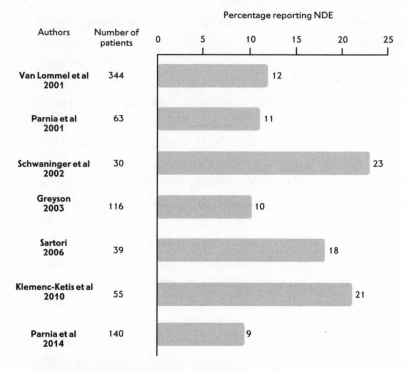

**Figure 14.3: The incidence of NDEs.** The percentage of patients suffering a cardiac arrest who reported an NDE, from seven studies in the Netherlands, UK, USA, and Slovenia.

15 to 19). So the answer is clear thus far: not everyone who comes close to death remembers an NDE, but some do.

Other prospective studies confirm this, with data coming from Slovenia (Klemenc-Ketis et al., 2010), Wales (Sartori, 2006), the USA (Schwaninger et al., 2002, Greyson, 2003), the UK, USA and Austria (Parnia et al., 2001, 2014), with their results summarised in Figure 14.3. Reviewing these studies and considering their sizes and methods, French (2005) gives a best estimate of 10–12%.

## Who are the NDErs?

If not everyone who nearly dies has an NDE, who does? Right from the start Ring speculated about what he called the 'NDE-prone personality' suggesting it had to do with how, as children, people learn to cope with life. He found that NDErs had more often been abused as children; they were not more fantasy prone but did report greater sensitivity to 'nonordinary realities' as children and scored higher on psychological dissociation than a control group (Ring & Rosing, 1990). Greyson (2000) found that dissociative tendencies were higher among a group of NDErs compared with a control group and this correlated with the depth of their NDEs. In a later study (Greyson, 2003), NDErs reported more previous psychic experiences, déjà vu, and altered states of consciousness, none of which is surprising given what we already know about dissociation and OBEs.

This may seem a trivial point but the nature of the control group is important. Ring's non-NDEr control group was just people who were interested in NDEs. What we really need is people who have come as close to death as the NDE group, but had no NDE and are matched on such variables as age, sex and time since their cardiac arrest. This is precisely what some more recent studies have achieved.

These prospective studies (van Lommel et al., 2001, Parnia et al., 2001, Klemenc-Ketis et al., 2010) all used appropriate control groups and none found that education or religion made any difference. Age did matter though, with younger patients more likely to report NDEs. As van Lommel pointed out, researchers such as Sabom and Morse used much younger samples, which might explain their higher rates of NDEs, possibly because younger patients are more likely to recover well and to remember what happened.

Surprisingly, medical differences including any drugs given and the duration of cardiac arrest have never been found to explain who has NDEs and who does not. Greyson (2003) did find that 10% of those who had a cardiac arrest had NDEs as compared with only 1% of those who had other heart problems, but their social support, quality of life, cognitive function, objective proximity to death and coronary prognosis made no difference.

Is there then no 'NDE-prone personality'? There may yet be, because one persistent finding is that people who have one NDE are more likely to have another, suggesting there is something different about them (Klemenc-Ketis et al., 2010, van Lommel et al., 2001) – but what?

A possible clue comes from the similarities between sleep paralysis, REM intrusion and NDEs, and on this basis Nelson suggested that 'REM consciousness and wakefulness blending into each other as death approached could explain many of the major features of near-death experiences' (Nelson, 2010, p.9). This is not only because borderline sleep states entail strange noises, tunnels, floating and OBEs, but because the regions of the brain that generate REM are known to respond strongly to pain, lack of oxygen and low blood pressure. These regions are way down in the brain stem, which, he rightly argues, have generally been neglected by NDE researchers, who concentrate only on the cortex, the most recently evolved part of our brains. But it is the reticular activating system in the brain stem that controls sleep-waking cycles and the shift into REM. The important point for NDEs is that this shift can also be triggered by signals coming from a failing respiratory system or from the heart via the vagus nerve. So Nelson suggests that the reason some people are more prone to having NDEs is that their REM switch is more apt to stick between REM and waking.

If he is right, people who are more prone to REM intrusion should be more likely to have an NDE and this is just what he and his team found when they compared fifty-five NDErs with an age- and sex-matched control group. The NDErs reported having experienced more sleep paralysis, sleep-related hallucinations and sleep-related OBEs before their NDE than the control group did. In addition, REM intrusion was more common in NDErs who had an OBE as part of their experience (Nelson et al., 2006). Along similar lines, a study of forty-three NDErs found that they had shorter sleep and more delayed REM sleep than controls, as well as more temporal lobe signs (Britton & Bootzin, 2004).

Sadly, though, neither of these control groups is good enough. It's possible that the effect works the other way round – that coming close to death changes the temporal lobes or brain stem in some way that makes REM intrusion more likely. So susceptibility to REM intrusion might be an after-effect of a close brush with death rather than a cause of NDEs. To avoid this problem we would need to compare NDErs with people who also came close to death but did not have an NDE. Until that is done, and other problems with this research are cleared up (Long & Holden, 2007), we cannot be sure whether susceptibility to REM intrusion really does explain why only some people have NDEs when close to death.

## Gases in the blood

If you've read somewhere that Sue Blackmore says all NDEs are caused by lack of oxygen (and she is wrong), please don't believe it. I do *not* think that all NDEs are caused by lack of oxygen, even if some are! My argument is that all the classic NDE features are caused by excessive random or disorganised neural activity in different parts of the brain. This random activation has many potential causes; stress and fear, lack of sensory input, vestibular disturbance, REM intrusion and electrical or magnetic stimulation. Cerebral hypoxia (reduced oxygen) and anoxia (no oxygen) are just two more potential causes.

Lack of oxygen is a possible cause because it significantly disrupts both the TPJ and the prefrontal cortex (Arzy et al., 2005). It also, at least in rats, damages inhibitory neurons more easily than excitatory ones (Wang, 2003). As we saw with tunnels (Chapter 13, page 218), this results in disinhibition, creating the hyperactivity that I have proposed underlies all NDEs. Indeed one idea is that hypoxia explains why so many religious revelations have occurred on mountain tops – the altitude and low oxygen levels leading to mystical and religious experiences of transcendence and oneness (Arzy et al., 2005). But do NDErs' brains actually suffer hypoxia during their experiences?

Few studies of blood gases have been done while someone is having an NDE because obviously doctors are concentrating on trying to save lives. But in one well-known case a man who had a cardiac arrest and OBE watched from above as his doctors inserted a needle (Sabom, 1982). The blood removed at the time had slightly *elevated* oxygen and lowered carbon dioxide. Then in Parnia et al's (2001) prospective study of cardiac arrest survivors, levels of potassium, sodium, oxygen and carbon dioxide were measured and the only significant finding was *higher* partial pressure of oxygen in the NDE group. Although this might seem to go against any role for lack of oxygen, an obvious alternative explanation is that patients with higher oxygen levels were better able to remember their experiences.

The picture becomes even more confused with another prospective study of cardiac arrest survivors at the University of Maribor in Slovenia (Klemenc-Ketis et al., 2010). In this case, blood levels of oxygen made no difference but the NDErs had higher levels of carbon dioxide and their scores on the Greyson Scale positively correlated with $CO_2$ levels. Yet, as Greyson (2010) pointed out, higher carbon dioxide indicates a better functioning heart and this too may allow for better memory of any experiences. Add to this the problem that levels of gases in blood may not truly reflect levels in the brain and we clearly need a lot more evidence. But this does not change the basic point that NDEs are caused by specific changes in brain activity, and lack of oxygen may or may not contribute.

## Heaven and hell

The impression so far is that NDEs are delightful experiences, characterised by great peace and calm, acceptance, happiness and joy. Scenes are often heavenly and the beings in the light are warm and loving. Why?

One of the brain's natural responses to stress, fear or trauma is to release its own morphine-like chemicals, the endorphins and enkephalins. These 'endogenous opiates' reduce pain and promote positive emotions in many situations from childbirth and extreme sports to the horrors of battle when wounded soldiers may carry on running or fighting apparently heedless of the pain. So a flood of endorphins is only to be expected in life-threatening situations and might explain the emotionally positive effects. Not only do endorphins reduce pain; they also, like the opiates to which they are closely related, induce hallucinations. These hallucinations can be blocked by a drug called naloxone – an opioid antagonist that blocks the pain-relieving and positive emotional effects of opioids, including morphine and heroin as well as these endorphins.

But are all NDEs happy ones? Moody (1975), Ring (1980) and Sabom (1982) reported no hellish experiences and in the Dutch prospective study, 'No patients reported distressing or frightening NDE' (van Lommel et al., 2001, p.2,041). The British study was rather different, asking about a wide range of memories from the resuscitation; many were nothing like classic NDEs and major themes were fear, violence or persecution, animals and plants, bright light, déjà vu and family (Parnia et al., 2014). We rarely hear about these more varied and less pleasant recollections so perhaps we get too rosy an impression.

In 1978, the cardiologist and born-again Christian Maurice Rawlings described plenty of nasty NDEs. One man kept yelling that he was in hell every time Rawlings ceased his efforts at resuscitation. A woman met elves and imps and a grotesque giant who beckoned her on into the dark, with people moaning all around her. Another went down a tunnel that ended not in a brilliant light but in a hideous cave filled with half-human creatures and a revolting smell of decay. Rawlings describes the pure terror that will meet the wicked as they die, along with quotes from the Bible and the message that only Jesus saves. It seems his purpose may have been more evangelical than informative (Bush, 2002). Indeed Ring (1980) called Rawlings' book a 'proselytizing Christian tract'.

Yet hellish NDEs do happen. Some negative experiences might be expected, such as when people emerge from locked-in syndrome. In this rare condition patients with brainstem damage are awake and aware but unable to speak or move, and unlike sleep paralysis this doesn't quickly wear off. Researchers in Liège collected NDE reports from fourteen such patients, comparing them with those of other coma patients. Eight had NDEs according to the Greyson Scale and their experiences were similar to the other groups except for having less positive emotions (Charland-Verville et al., 2015).

British psychologist Margot Grey had an intense NDE while travelling in India, in which she encountered the light and had 'a feeling of being very close to the "source" of life and love, which seemed to be one' (Grey, 1985, pp.xiii–xiv). Inspired by her own experience, she collected thirty-eight cases of core experiences including five terrifying ones (12%). This account is from a woman overcome by heat while working in a nursing home. She rushed out of the kitchen, down some steps and fell.

> I found myself in a place surrounded by mist. I felt I was in hell. There was a big pit with vapour coming out and there were arms and hands coming out trying to grab mine . . . I was terrified that these hands were going to claw hold of me and pull me into the pit with them.
>
> Grey, 1985, p.63

Other researchers have amassed collections of distressing NDEs, the largest being by Bruce Greyson and Nancy Bush (1992, Bush, 2012), who detected three different types among their fifty accounts. Some were like typical NDEs but without the positive feelings; some consisted mainly of a terrifying void or bleak non-existence; others involved traditional hellish worlds. Sometimes the terrified person accepted and gave in to the horror, whereupon it changed into a more conventionally pleasant NDE; resisting just made it worse, as happens in sleep paralysis. Bush (2002) extended this idea to whole societies, arguing that when a culture misunderstands any experience, including NDEs, SP or OBEs, everyone is more likely to be frightened. Having had three NDEs herself, American writer P. M. H. Atwater (1992) interviewed numerous NDErs, including those with hellish experiences, and argued for these to be more readily accepted and researched.

So what causes negative NDEs? Rawlings (1978) claimed they are found more often when people are interviewed immediately after their brush with death but other researchers strongly disagreed, arguing that there's no solid evidence to back him up (Grey, 1985, Sabom, 1979). Also, this would imply that people quickly repress memories of traumatic events but we know that survivors of abuse, war, torture and other traumas rarely forget their ordeals. As Ring points out, LSD trips can be either blissful and enlightening or terrifyingly hellish, but people remember both types without selectively repressing the bad trips.

Yet there is one reason why people may be less likely to report a visit to hell, even if they can remember it. In both Christianity and Islam believers are taught that the faithful go to heaven while sinners are eternally damned. So imagine finding yourself close to death, in a dark tunnel, hearing strange sounds and afraid. In your fearful state you might imagine you are on your way to hell, hearing the chattering of demons or the screams of the damned. Afterwards you may hesitate to tell anyone because it seems to imply that you deserve to go to hell.

To Catholics, taking your own life is a grave sin, regardless of the suffering endured; the Koran forbids suicide, as do some Hindu and Buddhist teachings. If NDEs are a true glimpse of the afterlife then people who attempt to kill themselves should more often have hellish NDEs: they don't. Jumping from the Golden Gate Bridge in San Francisco Bay is nearly always fatal but in the 1970s the neuropsychiatrist David Rosen tracked down seven of the known ten survivors (Rosen, 1975). All reported peaceful feelings during their fall as well as some kind of transcendence or spiritual renewal. Ring (1980) described suicide NDEs as truncated or damped-down, but with a feeling of relief and peace. He found entirely positive emotions in twenty-four suicide NDEs although their experiences tended to be brief and without tunnels, lights or transcendent worlds (Ring & Franklin, 1982). Could these positive NDEs encourage people to attempt suicide again? Apparently not (Greyson, 1981). When Moody asked one survivor whether he would try again, he replied,

> No. I would not do that again. I will die naturally next time, because one thing I realized at that time is that our life here is just such a small period of time and there is so much which needs to be done while you're here. And when you die it's eternity.
>
> Moody, 1975, p.46

Summing up, hellish NDEs seem to be a mirror image of blissful ones. Fear replaces joy and peace, a dark void replaces the welcoming tunnel, leaving the body is terrifying, and the world beyond is full of evil instead of light, implying that both have the same underlying structure but with different emotional states.

Could this difference come down to the presence or absence of endorphins? One clue clearly points this way: naloxone, the opioid antagonist discussed above, is sometimes given to the terminally ill if they've had too much morphine to control their pain. In one such case a cancer patient reported an NDE after being found in a coma and injected with naloxone (Judson & Wiltshaw, 1983).

At first he found himself in a blissful state, standing on a high plateau in the shadow of a rock.

> I am a living being, and my life is bliss and utter rightness, but a greater bliss and discovery of being are imminent. I rest in and open myself to the power which is within and about me.

A group of beings with kind and compassionate faces then appeared, but suddenly he knew that something was wrong and the beings began closing in on him.

> I beg them to go away. To my horror, they lay hands upon me and try to pull me out of shape. The pain is unbearable . . . Please, please let me alone. You are destroying me.
>
> Judson & Wiltshaw, 1983, p.561

As he began to despair a powerful rhythm or vibration overtook him, along with a cloying, astringent smell that was even worse than the pulsing rhythm. Then he was back. The outdoor landscape was gone and he was in bed in a small room with a curtained door and agitated comings and goings. Looking up into the eyes of two beings he realised he was back in the world of doctors, nurses and drips, still struggling and still afraid.

There are so many familiar details in this brief account: the vibrations, the pulling feeling and bodily distortion, the other beings and even the high plateau that reminds me of the great plain at the very end of my own experience. The unique feature of this case is that it began with bliss and 'rightness' but on the injection of naloxone it turned to hell. This is at least one clue that the endorphin theory may be correct: our brain's own drugs create the bliss and joy. They may also trigger memories.

## The life review

> Though the senses were ... deadened, not so the mind; its activity seemed to be invigorated, in a ratio which defies all description, for thought rose above thought with a rapidity of succession that is not only indescribable, but probably inconceivable by any one who has not himself been in a similar situation ... travelling backwards, every past incident of my life seemed to glance across my recollection in retrograde succession ... the whole period of my existence seemed to be placed before me in a kind of panoramic review, and each act of it seemed to be accompanied by a consciousness of right or wrong, or by some reflection on its cause or its consequences.

This excerpt comes from the famous description by Sir Francis Beaufort, who nearly drowned in Portsmouth Harbour in 1795. The popular idea that when you are drowning 'your whole life flashes before you' may contain some truth because life reviews are more common with drowning than cardiac arrest (Noyes & Slymen, 1979). This difference might be significant if the slow effects of drowning cause life reviews more often than the sudden crisis of a cardiac arrest.

In Moody's classic scheme the life review comes near the end and may be revealed or guided by the Being of Light but it can happen at other stages too. Early estimates suggested that about 25 to 30 per cent of NDEs include a life review (Noyes & Kletti, 1972, Ring, 1980, Greyson & Stevenson, 1980), but this is probably an over-estimate. In a later study only 9 per cent of fifty-eight NDErs reported a life review (Owens et al., 1990) and a recent prospective study gave 13 per cent (van Lommel et al., 2001).

I have sometimes heard it said that these life reviews are 'non-judge-mental' but that is not my impression from reading many accounts and meeting people who have experienced them. Rather, they seem to involve a kind of self-judgement that is completely different from self-criticism or self-hatred. People watch their childhood self being kind or unkind in the school playground, or their adult self helping or harming others and they see all this in a compassionate way, accepting, as Beaufort said, the causes and consequences of their actions without self-blame.

This acceptance reminds me of the passivity or the surrender to a higher power that is a common theme in mystical experiences (James, 1902). It relates also to beliefs about the power of free will. As a teenager I began to think that free will must be illusory because all our actions have to be caused by existing conditions such as our genes, personality, brain state and past experiences. If this is so, I reasoned, I must live my life without believing in it (Blackmore, 2013). This undoing of the illusion of a self who acts is found in many spiritual traditions, including Advaita Vedanta and Zen Buddhism, both of which culminate in 'non-action' or 'not-doing'. This does not mean there are no actions but that the sense of an inner self who 'does' things is lost. I think this change happens to some NDErs as they watch their past actions with compassion and, at last, see that everything happened as it had to happen; that what is needed is not blame but acceptance.

A profound case came from a prisoner who deliberately made himself ill by eating soap and suffered acute pain (Lorimer, 1990). He went into a state of terror as a scroll or movie appeared before him with a stream of vivid pictures showing all the victims he had injured in his long criminal career; 'every pang of suffering I had caused others was now felt by me as the scroll unwound itself' (Lorimer, 1990, p.23). His agonising life review led to weeks of anguish until he was able to imagine and remember the hurt with love and forgiveness. This kind of 'perspective taking', or experiencing events from someone else's point of view, was a prominent feature of seven in-depth interviews done with people who'd seen 'life flash before their eyes' and can be a profound consequence of such remembering (Katz et al, 2017).

So what explains this review of one's life? Ring thought that the Being of Light is really one's own higher self manifesting as a brilliant golden 'astral light' to which we are only sensitive in a fourth dimension or 'holographic reality'. David Lorimer (1990) describes the life review as an expansion of the individual into a realm in which all are one. Other theories are similar to ideas I began my PhD with, but then abandoned, such as Rupert Sheldrake's theory of 'morphic resonance', in which memories are accessed through similarity to past events rather than depending on physical changes in the brain.

The most recent version comes from none other than Pim van Lommel who proposes that 'our endless consciousness with declarative memories finds its origin in, and is stored in, a non-local dimension as wave-fields of information, and the brain only serves as a relay station' (van Lommel, 2013, p.38). Theories like this may once have seemed plausible but now, with neuroscience effectively revealing the physical basis of memory, ideas of distributed memories in an astral plane or wave-field seem, at best, superfluous. That doesn't mean they cannot be true but perhaps the life review can be explained without us overturning everything we know about how memory works.

The explanation may lie with those same endorphins and enkephalins that are responsible for positive emotions. These are found predominantly in the brain stem and reticular activating system which regulates sleep-wake cycles and the switch into REM. They are not found widely in the cortex except for in the temporal lobes but they are active throughout the limbic system, including the fear-inducing amygdala and the hippocampus, which is critical to laying down memories.

Why would they cause a fast flood of personal memories? Because one of their effects is to reduce the seizure threshold in the limbic system and temporal lobes. Reducing the seizure threshold means making it easier for cells to go into uncontrolled or random firing. In addition, enkephalins can actually suppress neural activity in some areas but in the hippocampus they suppress inhibitory cells, which means they provoke disinhibition leading to hyperactivity instead. Given the importance of both hippocampus and temporal lobes in memory formation and storage, the effect of this uncontrolled activity is a flood of memories – memories pouring up as if all at once, with their inhibitory controls inactivated.

This can be frightening if the disinhibition is caused by hallucino-genic drugs, but when caused by endorphins, the flood of memories is experienced, along with joy, positive emotions and acceptance. This explains why even memories of one's own cruel past deeds can be seen with equanimity, and thus real personal growth can come about.

Once again I come back to one underlying cause of all OBEs whether close to death or not – the disinhibition that results in random or disorganised brain activity. When this happens in visual cortex it produces tunnels and lights; in the TPJ and associated areas, the OBE; in the brain stem REM intrusion; and in the hippocampus and temporal lobes a life review.

Is this enough to dispel the mystery? Can we now rule out the idea that there are two types of OBE, 'real' and 'fake', and conclude that Type-A theories have won; that nothing leaves the body in any OBE, whether it happens close to death or not?

Not quite. Many NDErs, and even some researchers, are convinced that this misses the whole point – for NDEs prove that consciousness exists beyond the brain.

CHAPTER 15

# Consciousness
# Beyond the Brain

I was encountering the reality of a world of consciousness that existed *completely free of the limitations of my physical brain* . . . My experience showed me that the death of the body and the brain are not the end of consciousness, that human experience continues beyond the grave . . . The place I went was real. Real in a way that makes the life we're living here and now completely dreamlike by comparison.

Alexander, 2012, p.9

If this were true it would be the most amazing and science-shattering discovery I can imagine. Psychology, philosophy and neuroscience as we know them would be overthrown. We would have to conclude, even though everything we have learned over the centuries points ever more clearly to non-duality – to the interconnectedness and interdependence of self, mind and brain – that we are wrong. And what then? We would somehow have to incorporate the discovery that consciousness, whatever that really means, exists independently of all that messy brain-stuff.

Really? This is the dualist message shouted loudly by a long series of people who have come close to death, had deep experiences and wanted to proclaim their discoveries to the world. If they are right, we should listen to them and work out the consequences. If they are wrong, we should make clear why.

The example above comes from *Proof of Heaven* by American neurosurgeon Eben Alexander, who contracted a rare form of bacterial meningitis, causing serious brain damage and a week-long coma. When he gradually awoke to find himself alive and fully conscious, he was a changed man. From being proud of his medically based 'materialist and reductionist' views, he had become a believer in life after death.

*Proof of Heaven* is a great read; lively, pacy and full of interesting anecdotes. Alexander hears pounding sounds and smells horrible smells, becomes a lone point of awareness in the 'Realm of the Earthworm's-Eye View', enters 'an inky darkness that was also full to brimming with light' (p.48), meets a girl on a butterfly wing who guides him into 'the Core', to meet 'Om' and 'the Orb'. He learns to move through 'the green brilliance of the Gateway and into the black but holy darkness of the Core' (p.70). He finds that love is the basis of everything and that 'our eternal spiritual self is more real than anything we perceive in this physical realm' (p.146). The book has sold millions of copies and was on bestseller lists for months. It fits with the dualist intuitions we all begin with as children; it fits with religious doctrines of heaven and hell, and it conveys touching ideas about love and compassion. Despite heavy criticism, and exposés of his 'troubled history', including five malpractice cases (Dittrich, 2013), a great many people clearly want to believe him. But what really happened?

My starting point with any such tales, whoever they are told by, is to believe what they experienced but doubt their interpretations. I don't mean that I summarily reject their interpretations, I mean I listen with an open and questioning mind. The distinction between experience and interpretation is never absolute (arguably, we lay interpretations on all our experiences), but this is still a reasonable starting position. I took this approach to tunnels, lights, sleep paralysis and OBEs. It is this approach that revealed the similarities across ages, cultures and belief systems and led to the discovery that these similarities depend on us all having similar brains, not on astral bodies, spirits or souls.

Does this apply to nearly dying as well? Or could it be that when people come close to death something altogether stranger happens and consciousness really does survive without a functioning brain? This is the great question underlying forty years of research, debates and deep divisions in the world of near-death studies.

The three main arguments for consciousness beyond the brain are (1) the realness and clarity of thinking during NDEs, (2) the profound transformations people undergo and (3) the paranormal ability to gain true information. I'll leave paranormal claims for the next chapter and begin with that striking 'realness'.

## It was absolutely real

> I had a life-changing preview of eternity, visiting heaven's gate . . .
> I was reunited with loved ones; saw babies, children, and angels;
> peeked at the throne of God and Book of Life; and had a
> conversation with the apostle Peter . . . I knew that it was true,
> and that it hadn't been a dream or a hallucination.
>
> Besteman, 2012, p.11

I know just how that 'realness' feels. NDErs often say their brief experience was more real than anything that happened to them before or since; that their mind was clear and their vision vivid and bright. I said the same and would say so still, despite the intervening half century. Vision is wonderfully vivid and colourful, sounds are clear and bright, touch is strangely weird as your hand passes through a wall or table and yet even this feels utterly real. Why?

The 'obvious' answer is that the other world seems real because it is real. American retired banker Marvin Besteman gets to the gates of heaven (yes, he saw outer and inner gates), where he chats with his favourite Bible hero. Peter has 'a scrubby beard, shaggy hair, and clothes that looked like he had been wearing them for 1,000 years of hauling in nets and gutting fish' (Besteman, 2012, p.88). Peter searches for the names of those destined for heaven in an antique leather-bound book resting on a stone shelf about three foot high, taking about forty seconds for each person in the queue, but he cannot find Besteman's name and tells him to go back. When Besteman protests, Peter says, 'Okay, the only thing I can do is go talk to God' (p.118), and off he goes, leaving Besteman glimpsing through the inner crystalline gate, to a world where the grass is greener than any golf course and the water bluer than any earthly sea.

I guess he sincerely believes he went to a real place called heaven, and will return there when he dies. From the multitude of online comments, his readers agree. How can I be confident he is wrong? Because nothing adds up. Take the countless tiny babies and the gloriously happy adults (I'll leave aside the singing angels and 'winged creatures'). His grandparents 'had both died in their old age, bedridden and withered versions of who they had once been. Yet, here they stood before me, just sixty feet away, flourishing and vibrant, with rosy cheeks and a spring in their steps' (p.145). So when we die in old age we are transformed into perfect versions of ourselves. But what about the millions of foetuses and stillborn infants he saw? 'I knew these babes would grow and bloom here, perfectly safe, entirely happy, and wholly loved.' He wonders what kind of people they would grow up to be. What? How could anyone become a truly human being if they were brought up without challenges or achievements, failures or fears, losses or sadness? None of this makes any sense at all.

Most chokingly cloying in the 'heaven tourism' genre is *My Time in Heaven* by the Revd. Richard Sigmund, who began preaching as a child in Iowa. In his heaven, the book at the gate was a mile high and three quarters of a mile wide, with Sigmund's own name in three-inch golden letters outlined in crimson red. He sees a baby arrive through the veil at one of 'heaven's receiving areas' and with 'the full power of speech', the baby says, 'Jesus said that I could remain a baby and that Mommy could raise me in heaven' p.18. To be fair, many Christians have rejected his claims as incompatible with scripture, but do people really believe this 'heavenly home' will be theirs when they die?

Besteman mentions that some of his Christian friends had difficulty 'getting their heads round' some of his story. And so they should. Indeed they should have so much trouble 'getting their heads round' it that they reject the whole idea. Yet they don't.

There's an important question here. Why, you might reasonably ask, is this any different from having trouble 'getting our heads round' quantum mechanics or evolutionary theory? Just because I cannot understand something without years of training doesn't mean it's untrue. The difference lies between the methods of science and personal conviction. Quantum mechanics and evolutionary theory make clear predictions about how the world behaves, and time and again they are proved right, or if they are not right their failure leads to abandoning one hypothesis and asking new questions. Besteman's vivid experiences cannot be tested by any means at all, except perhaps by comparing them with others'.

From the leather-covered books to the crystal gate and Saint Peter's clothes, Besteman's details are just what a twenty-first century Christian ex-banker from Michigan might expect of heaven and not at all what an Indian Hindu, British Muslim or Japanese atheist might expect. So how much do the contents of NDEs come down to expectation and wishful thinking?

## Does culture matter?

I would love to be able to tell a simple story something like this: tunnels, lights, OBEs and life reviews depend on brain function and are therefore common to all ages and cultures, while the heavens and other worlds depend on people's upbringing, religion and expectations.

This may not be too far off the mark, but the evidence is woefully confusing. Early cross-cultural studies found no tunnels in India (Osis & Haraldsson, 1977, Pasricha & Stevenson, 1986), prompting me to collect cases of my own. Advertising in an Indian newspaper for close brushes with death I received eight descriptions of NDEs; among them tunnels, dark spaces and bright lights, as well as peace and love. One woman 'felt I was going through complete blackness and there was a tingling sound of tiny bells.' A 63-year-old man after a cardiac arrest wrote, 'I travelled a few million miles away . . . to a space of brilliant light where I was being loved,' (Blackmore, 1993b, pp.210–1) and this came from a 39-year-old man, who passed out while playing badminton.

> I seemed to be floating in a dark space. I distinctly remember
> having an unusual peace of mind state for some brief moments. I
> felt totally at peace.
>
> Blackmore, 1993b, p.211

No tunnels or lights were found in Thailand and India (Belanti *et al*
2008) or in an overview of Chinese NDEs (Becker 1984) although one
NDEr emerged from a dark tubular calyx and a monk passed through a
void, both of which might count as tunnel forms. Also in China, Zhi-
ying and Jian-xun (1992) surveyed eighty-one survivors of an earthquake.
Thirty-two reported NDEs including OBEs, tunnels, peace, life reviews,
deceased beings and unearthly realms, so Chinese NDEs seemed to be
similar to Anglo-European NDEs (Kellehear, 2008).

A collection of ten NDEs in Thailand included completely different
forms, including harbingers of death, visions of hell and realising the
benefits of making generous donations to Buddhist monks and
temples (Murphy, 2001). Some met Yama, the Lord of the Dead, who
asked one man whether he would like to see hell and when he said yes,
the entrance to the first level was made 'by opening a tunnel'.

Meeting other beings may be common but the beings themselves differ widely. Long ago Osis and Haraldsson (1977) found that Americans
and Indians met their own religious figures, with Americans mostly
willing to go with them while those in India more often refused. This
suggests that the traditional 'being of light' seen by many Westerners
may have the same origin as Thai Buddhist yamatoots, Hindu yam-
doots and Christian visions of Jesus, Saint Peter and the angels.

As for life reviews, they are widely reported even if not in the
panoramic, all-at-once form of the classic Moody-type NDE. For
example, one Chinese man had to face all his sinful deeds (Becker,
1984), some Indians follow Hindu tradition by hearing the record of
their life being read out (Pasricha & Stevenson, 1986), and many
glimpse a book in which their name is written only if it is their time
to die. A man from the Mapuche people of south America was said to
have been 'dead for two days', entering a volcano where he met dead
relatives and a German man writing names in a book but in this and

other Mapuche and Hawaiian accounts there were no life reviews (Belanti *et al* 2008). Across Asia, Africa and the Pacific area, Kellehear (2008) found no life reviews in hunter-gatherer societies, which he suggests may be because individual ethical behaviour is not emphasised, rewarded or punished as it is in Judaism, Christianity, Buddhism and Hinduism. So the common underlying experience of facing up to one's past may present itself in very different ways.

Despite the uncertainties, many cross-cultural researchers agree that neurobiological mechanisms underpin the NDE and there are 'iconic images, which are influenced by the experient's culture and religion' as well as language (Belanti et al., 2009, p.117, Augustine 2007c). Indeed, recurring NDE features may provide a foundation for folk religious beliefs about spirits, souls, life after death and magical abilities (McClenon, 2009, Metzinger, 2005).

I think it's safe to conclude that no NDE, however real it seems, is actually 'Proof of heaven'.

## Deciding what's real

Why then do NDEs and the other worlds visited seem so very real? Why was Besteman so convinced by meeting Saint Peter, and Alexander by his girl on the butterfly wing?

The answer is that our judgements of what is real or unreal are just that – judgements. It is the brain's job, in other species as well as ours, to distinguish between our own imaginings and what is real and needs acting upon. You might think that brains evolved to get the most accurate impression possible of everything around them but this is not so. Accurate perception is expensive in time and processing capacity; catching prey, escaping from predators or picking a mate may have to be done fast. So brains have evolved to notice what's relevant to survival, take shortcuts, make guesses and generally decide what is real on the fly. Mostly we get it right. Often we get it wrong, as in visual illusions or when I mistake the cushion on that chair for my cat.

The skill of distinguishing perception from imagination is called reality discrimination or reality monitoring (Johnson & Raye, 1981) and we need checks on our memories too. Memory depends on continual small changes being made in neural connections so it is fluid and adaptable and not like a camera or computer with fixed images stored in specific locations. Research on false memories has shown how easily we can come to 'remember' something that never happened, especially if others keep telling us it did, or if we keep telling and retelling a story and changing it as we go (Loftus & Pickrell, 1995). It is the last version we told that is most likely to be remembered and comes to seem more real and this is highly relevant to reporting NDEs (French, 2001, 2003). So how do we get these distinctions right?

Stability is an important clue. If something remains the same when our eyes move, or doesn't change from day to day, we usually conclude it is real. Memories that are more vivid or more easily brought to mind seem more real, and if the context makes sense we are more likely to trust them as we juggle imagined and real worlds. For example, when reading a book we can be immersed in the plot but never confuse it with the actual room around us. We can do the washing or cook dinner while listening to the radio without confusing reality and imagination.

We can think of this in terms of models of reality (Blackmore, 1984b, 2009). At any time we maintain just one 'model of reality' despite everything else that is going on in our busy minds. This integrates the body schema and self-image into the immediate world of vision, touch and hearing. When something new appears, if it fits this context it's likely to be really there in the world; if not, it's probably imagined.

Now think about the situation in which NDEs occur. Typically, the input from the person's senses is confused or completely cut off, whether through cardiac arrest, traffic accident or near drowning. Their brain will be trying to do its job of finding a stable model of current reality but cannot do so. It then has little option but to take the most stable and convincing model currently being constructed and take that as reality. And what will that be? If there's hyperactivity in primary visual cortex (V1), it will be tunnels and spirals; if it is in higher visual areas, it will be visions of people, objects or scenes; if in temporal lobes, memories.

The effect will be strongest if there is little else competing with these visions. German philosopher and long-term meditator Thomas Metzinger has had OBEs himself and describes them as happening 'within a window of presence'. There is no remembering the past or planning the future, 'an OBE is something that is happening *now*' (Metzinger, 2005, p.67). This, he says, explains the 'hyperpresence' or 'hyperrealism' of the experience, especially in those OBEs that blend into 'religious ecstasy'. I guess mine would count as one of those as my OB self became indistinguishable from everything else in a state of wonder and oneness.

No wonder people entering 'other worlds' are so convinced they are real. No wonder a devout Christian can believe that the heaven he saw is the same real heaven that awaits after death. But both evidence and logic proclaim that it is not.

## Life transformed

It was a blessing in a way, because before that heart attack I was too busy planning for my children's future, and worrying about yesterday, that I was losing the joys of the present. I have a much different attitude now.

Following this experience, it almost seemed as if I were filled with a new spirit. Since then, many have remarked to me that I seem to have almost a calming effect on them, instantly, when they are troubled. And it seems that I am more in tune with people now.

Right from the start of NDE research it was clear that people's lives could be forever changed by an NDE, as in these two examples from Moody (1975, pp.91–2). In *Transformed By the Light*, Melvin Morse (1992), best known for his studies of NDEs in children, describes how those who return from the brink of death live healthier and happier lives, have stronger family ties, better relationships, give more money to charity and, above all, lose their fear of death. Concern for others may increase (Flynn, 1982) and motivations, values and conduct change (Ring, 1980). Van Lommel (2013) concluded that NDErs gain more interest in spirituality, greater acceptance of and love for themselves and others, and less interest in possessions and power.

How and why could such a brief experience have such profound effects?

Lots of people *know* they know the answer and are keen to tell the world. *Proof of Heaven* proclaims a miraculous God-given transformation in which 'seeing the light' and meeting Jesus opens people's hearts to the truth. *To Heaven and Back* exudes similar Christian confidence from a doctor who describes herself as 'analytical, scientific, and sceptical by nature' (Neal, 2011). Her final chapter, 'Logical Conclusions', says that faith sets us free, dissolves fear, replaces worry with hope and allows us to walk confidently with God into a future filled with joy. I can see why a dramatic NDE can be so emotionally convincing, but can this really be called 'logical'?

We need to ask what causes what. Are lives transformed specifically by having an NDE, or does just coming close to death have the same effect? Is being close to death even necessary, or do OBEs, tunnels and lights bring about equivalent changes with no threat of death?

My own experience changed my life and I was nowhere near death. Without that single event I would never have embarked on parapsychology nor devoted the rest of my research life to trying to understand consciousness and altered states, and I doubt I would have taken up Zen practice and done thirty years of daily meditation.

Gabbard, Twemlow and Jones (1981) tried to find out by comparing OBErs who came close to death with those who did not. Those who came close to death more often found purpose in their experience and said it changed their lives but two-thirds of all the OBErs became more convinced of life after death, whether they had come close to death or not.

What about coming close to death and having no NDE? When I was writing *Dying to Live* (Blackmore, 1993a), I interviewed many patients from our local hospital in Bristol. One woman told me that her husband remembered nothing from a medical crisis following a burst artery yet both their lives were changed.

Certainly I did not have a NDE – the most life threatening thing I did was to drink hospital coffee. Yet both of us found that the experience had a profound and lasting effect ... simply coming very close to dying also shakes the very foundation of your existence – with or without NDE.

So the question narrows down to this: does having an NDE, or the depth of that NDE, add anything more to life transformations over and above proximity to death? Ring (1980) explored this question by comparing cases with and without an NDE.

One woman who was nearly killed in a car explosion remembered no NDE but said:

My priorities have definitely changed ... it suddenly made me realize that nothing is important unless you have people around you that you love ... I just feel that I have a greater appreciation of being here.

Ring, 1980, p.142

Another was clinically dead for about three minutes after a heart attack and had a core experience.

I love people now ... I've never had the ability to love before ... the ability to accept people as they are and to love them for what they are and not for what you want them to be, this has all come about – and I think that God has done this for me.

Ring, 1980, p.157

As you might guess from this comparison, Ring (1984) found changes in both groups, including an enhanced sense of purpose, greater appreciation for life and increased empathy for others, but his was not a prospective study with matched groups; two later studies were (Greyson, 2003, van Lommel et al., 2001). Van Lommel used Ring's inventory of life-change questions as well as interviewing survivors after two and eight years. At two years the NDErs claimed more reduced fear of death and more belief in an afterlife than those who had no NDE. After eight years the differences were smaller although changes in motivation, interest in nature and deeper involvement in family life intensified in both groups while reduced fear of death was more specific to NDErs. These positive changes were long-lasting and even more apparent at eight years, and Greyson (2007) found that after all this time the NDErs still remembered their experiences clearly and could describe them almost as they did before.

Could we ever find out what it is about NDEs that reduces fear of death? Virtual reality might seem an odd place to look but some experiments with immersive virtual reality have created simulations of full OBEs, giving the impression of lifting up and looking down on a virtual body below. When participants were manipulated to feel no connection with the virtual body they reported less fear of death afterwards. It seems that even being tricked into feeling you are outside your body can have a profound effect (Bourdin et al., 2017).

All this is good to know but no one ever seems to ask whether the effects can go the other way. And yes, they can. Survivors of cardiac arrest may suffer memory loss, cognitive impairment and post-traumatic stress disorder (Parnia et al., 2007). Even before Moody's famous research, studies explored the difficulties survivors may face in adjusting to life after cardiac arrest, with some who had no NDE being confirmed in their atheism and others led to conclude that death must be the end (Dobson et al., 1971, Druss & Kornfeld, 1967).

This effect can be as life-changing as the popularly touted increases in religious belief. I interviewed one man who had been a keen member of his local church and editor of its newsletter until he had a cardiac arrest.

> I know now that you don't see the pearly gates or anything. I know you just pass out. At least that's the way it was with me. I just stopped living.

This not only affected him but challenged his wife's faith at a time when she needed it the most. We have no idea how many people lose their faith this way but since 80 to 90 per cent of survivors report no NDE he cannot be alone. Yet it doesn't make such a good story: 'Man returns from death to declare there is no God' or 'Woman loses her faith after encounter with nothing'.

Claims of atheists converting to Christianity, or 'closed-minded, materialist scientists' being forced to 'admit the truth', make far better headlines, as when philosopher A. J Ayer described his own NDE (Ayer, 1988). This famous atheist apparently choked on a piece of smoked salmon smuggled in by visitors (although the attending doctor could find no trace of fish in his throat), and had a cardiac arrest with no heartbeat for four minutes.

Reading the news at the time one could easily be convinced Ayer had seen God and become a believer. But reading his long, rather turgidly philosophical article in the *Sunday Telegraph* gives a different impression. He describes crossing a river and confronting an exceedingly bright and painful red light which seemed to be responsible for the government of the universe. The ministers in charge of inspecting space had not done their job properly and he tried to help by using his knowledge of Einstein's theory of general relativity. 'It was most extraordinary,' he said. 'My thoughts became persons.' Although he agreed that 'on the face of it' these experiences imply 'death does not put an end to consciousness,' it does not necessarily follow that there is a future life. After all the fuss in the media he tried to clear up the gross misunderstandings, writing that 'the most probable hypothesis is that my brain continued to function although my heart had stopped.'

This brings us to the crunch. If tunnels, lights, OBEs and real-seeming other worlds are all caused by random activation in different parts of the brain, that means they cannot happen if that brain is dead.

## Consciousness with a silent brain?

As NDEs become ever better explained in natural terms, the possibility of consciousness without a functioning brain becomes less and less plausible. So the question we must ask is quite simple – have any NDEs really occurred with absolutely no brain activity?

Pim van Lommel says they can and have. In the most extraordinary leap of illogic, he jumps from describing his research findings to this: 'we reached the inevitable conclusion that patients experienced all the aforementioned NDE elements during the period of their cardiac arrest, during the total cessation of blood supply to the brain' (van Lommel, 2013, p.16).

Was this 'inevitable'? No. His reasons for reaching this conclusion may or may not be valid and we need to find out because this is a most dramatic, contentious and important claim. If he is right about this then he is also right that our 'current materialistic view' of consciousness must be overthrown. And there are many who agree with him that NDEs prove the continuity of consciousness and therefore the current 'materialist paradigm' must go (Laszlo, 2014, Rivas et al., 2016).

Van Lommel (2010, 2013) hopes to replace it with his theory of 'Non-local Consciousness', mentioned in the last chapter (page 253), in which memory is stored outside the brain in a 'wave-field of consciousness'. Using the familiar old metaphor of the TV set he compares the function of the brain to that of 'a transceiver, a transmitter/receiver, or interface', and the function of neuronal networks to 'receivers and conveyors, not retainers of consciousness and memories'. This is the same tired old idea with which I began my PhD and which many, many others have toyed with and rejected. It seems even less plausible now that we are beginning to understand just how the brain constructs the sense of self and stores a lifetime of memories.

But – and this is the crucial 'but' – if NDEs really happen when there is no brain activity at all then we *have to* turn to ideas like van Lommel's 'Endless Consciousness', Ring's Holographic theory, or Morse's 'Universal Mind', or we have to invent other new theories because NDEs would be inexplicable on any kind of brain-based theory of any kind. So do they?

The question really amounts to this: what state are brains in during NDEs? We already know that every aspect of NDEs can happen without threat to life or serious brain trauma so we need to focus on NDEs in which people really are clinically dead and their brain function is compromised. This includes van Lommel's, Greyson's and

Parnia's cardiac arrest survivors as well as some of the 'I went to heaven' stories. Do these NDEs happen in the deepest state when there is no brain function that could possibly sustain thinking, imagining, remembering and feeling? Or do they occur either before brain function fails or when it is returning after the crisis? The timing of the experience is the crucial question and that is very often hard to determine.

First, consider what death means. Death is a process, not a sudden change from being alive to being dead. 'Clinical death' is defined as when both heartbeat and breathing have stopped. So resuscitation can bring someone back from clinical death and frequently does so, but 'brain death' is defined as irreversible, and once neurons are dead they do not start firing again. Legal definitions vary, with some allowing continuing function in the brain stem, but all require that the cortex is irreversibly dead. So if someone comes back to health and recounts an NDE, either their brain was not actually dead, even if it looked that way, or something truly extraordinary has happened.

To answer our question we need to understand the brain states before and after clinical death. For a start, the heart does not always stop suddenly but often begins to pump erratically before stopping altogether. This means blood flow is poor, oxygen levels drop slowly, the brain begins to suffer hypoxia and this may continue for some time. Once the heart has completely stopped beating it takes just ten to twenty seconds for blood pressure to drop to zero, the EEG to become abnormal and the person to lose consciousness, but this still does not mean there is suddenly no brain activity at all. There may still be a little oxygen in the static blood and in the brain cells themselves. How quickly this is used up depends on the temperature (people can survive much longer in very low temperatures) and the type and size of the brain cells affected. So even with a sudden cardiac arrest some brain activity may continue while the person loses consciousness and again while they regain consciousness during resuscitation.

What happens in such a brain? Happily there is plenty of evidence of both the physical and psychological effects of hypoxia and anoxia, coming from medical studies, lab experiments and the effects of altitude in climbers and acceleration in fighter pilots. Medical studies reveal which parts of the brain are most sensitive to anoxia. The retina at the back of the eye is really an extension of the brain and this is the most sensitive, followed by the cortex and then the thalamus and brain stem. Other especially sensitive areas include the hippocampus, which is vital for memory, and the basal ganglia and cerebellum, which are both concerned with controlling movement.

Anoxia is also experienced by healthy people at high altitudes, and climbers have reported many strange effects, including bodily distortions such as changing size or shape, the sense of presence, visions of animals or people who aren't there, hearing ringing bells, music or voices, and sensations of flying through the air. In one study of eight extreme-altitude climbers, five reported OBEs lasting between a few seconds and, in one case, twelve hours (Brugger et al., 1999). The OBEs occurred mostly in times of high emotion or danger, so factors other than anoxia may be relevant here. Lab experiments can, however, isolate the effects of anoxia.

Some of these experiments are truly extraordinary and would never be permitted now but we can still learn from the discoveries they made. During the Second World War planes began flying higher, manoeuvres got faster and some pilots suffered sudden loss of consciousness, now known as G-LOC or Gravity-induced Loss of Consciousness. This happens because the heart cannot pump effectively against the extreme G-forces induced by swooping and turning and so the brain is quickly starved of oxygen.

During the Second World War a team in Minnesota, led by Lieutenant Rossen, tried to find out what was happening by designing an inflatable cuff, a collar that goes around the neck and is attached to a compressed air tank (Rossen et al., 1943) (Figure 15.1). It could be inflated very fast to cut off blood flow through the veins and arteries to the head, and quickly deflated by either the subject or experimenter. Once they had used it on themselves with no ill effects they tested it not on volunteers but on prisoners, young offenders and schizophrenics, which is one reason why it could never be done now (Smith et al., 2011).

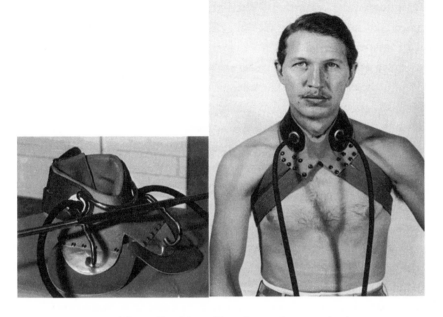

**Figure 15.1: The inflatable cuff used to induce cerebral anoxia.**
This photograph shows the KRA cuff being worn in 1942 (in its
uninflated state) by John P. Anderson, who designed it. When
inflated to 600 mmHg, the cuff shuts off blood flow to the brain. It
can quickly be deflated when needed.

Within four to ten seconds the subjects became unconscious but
about a second before that their eyes became fixed in mid position.
They saw spots or twinkling lights and their vision became blurred or
grey and narrowed to a small area directly in front of their eyes. Note
that this is 'tunnel vision', not the 'tunnel experience' associated with
sleep paralysis, OBEs and NDEs (see page 214). Some were paralysed
but could still hear what was going on.

Further experiments tested pilots by flying very high or using
decompression chambers to reduce oxygen levels at different rates
(Goldie, 1941). With rapid onset anoxia the pilots began twitching
and convulsing before quickly becoming unconscious, often failing to
realise, afterwards, that they had ever lost consciousness. With slower
onset they became irritable and agitated, and were unable to carry out
simple tasks even though they insisted they could – a very dangerous

state for a pilot. Some said the light dimmed at the start but more often they reported a bright light or an increase in brightness as they were recovering.

Long after WW2 was over, and with better techniques available, James Whinnery, at the Naval Air Development Center in Pennsylvania, studied G-LOC using a human-sized centrifuge to simulate high G-forces. He made himself unconscious ten times in fifteen minutes, likening it to the auto-erotic effect some people induce by partially hanging themselves. More than five hundred G-LOC episodes were recorded over twelve years with unconsciousness lasting between two and thirty-eight seconds, subjects averaging twelve seconds and often followed by convulsions (Whinnery & Whinnery, 1990). Many reported tunnel vision due to the loss of oxygen to the retina. A few had something vaguely like a tunnel experience, such as being in a dark closet with a red light at the top or being pushed along a supermarket aisle. Others reported 'dreams' with radiantly bright colours, beautiful surroundings and even loved ones coming to meet them. Many felt floating sensations and at least two had OBEs.

Whinnery (personal communication, 1990b) wrote to me about his own OBE, experienced after his intensive multiple G-LOC episodes. He suggested that a more severe insult to the brain is required to induce an OBE than just floating sensations, which fits perfectly with recent evidence that OB feelings usually come before OB vision (Chapter 9, page 155). One G-LOC volunteer felt he was propelled along by a magic carpet while paralysed; a terribly frustrating experience because he could hear the G-LOC warning sound and couldn't turn it off. An important finding was that during recovery hearing was restored before motor function returned. This is significant for understanding NDEs because a clinically dead patient may appear completely unconscious but still be able to hear what is going on.

These experimental results also illustrate the difference between the psychological and objective effects of anoxia (Woerlee, 2013). Objectively, attention and concentration are badly affected, reaction times slowed, and ability to do simple tasks drastically reduced. Old memories are retained but laying down new ones is interfered with (presumably because anoxia affects the hippocampus). By contrast, little of this is realised by the person involved, who may initially feel elated with an unusually clear mind and a sense of enhanced well-being. This means that we should be careful when interpreting what people say about mental clarity after a cardiac arrest. It's like Metzinger's 'window of presence'. Perhaps when only very limited thinking is possible this feels like clarity compared with our usual multi-tasking minds – just as clarity arises in meditation when excessive thoughts are let go and the 'monkey mind' is stilled.

## The very last moments

Even so, you might argue, brief hypoxia is not the same as nearly dying. NDErs experience complex life reviews, deep emotions, and mystical insights when surely their brain activity must have almost entirely stopped. So must it?

No. As we have seen, anoxia affects some brain areas more quickly than others but this does not mean that activity there stops immediately. If inhibitory cells are selectively impaired then a period of hyperactivity will ensue before the excitatory cells are also affected. This is the hyperactivity that I have suggested as the underlying cause of all the tunnels, lights, OBEs and life reviews. And if oxygen levels are not too low and the hippocampus not too badly affected, the person will be able to remember the experiences afterwards.

So is there any evidence for such a brief rush of activation on the verge of death?

Stories have long been reported of unexpected brief spikes of activation as a person dies, but only recently has a formal experiment been done. Seven critically patients had their EEG recorded when the decision was made to stop life-support and let them die (Chawla et al., 2009). EEG was measured as part of the 'comfort care protocol' to ensure they were comfortable. In each case brain activity decreased as blood pressure fell but once it reached zero, there was a brief burst of brain activity before ceasing altogether. They call it a 'brief burst' but in fact these bursts lasted between thirty seconds and three minutes, which is plenty of time to support detailed conscious experiences.

The researchers attributed this burst to a cascade of neural activity that starts once a critical level of anoxia is reached. They speculated that 'in those patients who suffer cardiac arrest who are successfully revived, they may recall the images and memories triggered by this cascade' (Chawla et al., 2009, p.1099).

In some remarkable experiments with rats, cardiac arrest was induced while their EEG was monitored (Borjigin et al., 2013). After their hearts stopped, normal EEG patterns lasted for about three seconds and then within thirty seconds a surge of synchronous gamma oscillations was observed in all the animals. Interestingly, the previous study of EEG spikes in human patients (Chawla et al., 2009) also reported high gamma activity. These fast (over 25Hz) brainwaves are found in alert waking states as well as REM sleep and especially in deep meditation. There has been much speculation about their possible role in binding brain pro-cesses together to produce a sense of unified consciousness, and their long-range synchronisation is thought to underlie unified perceptions. The researchers also looked at connectivity between the front and back of the brain, which underlies conscious perception in the waking state. This connectivity decreased with anaesthesia but after cardiac arrest it increased, not just for gamma waves but for other frequencies too, last-ing for thirty seconds in the gamma range and up to sixty seconds in other bands. Overall, the level of directed connectivity exceeded that seen during the normal waking state.

These are extraordinary findings and might potentially explain why cardiac arrest survivors report clear consciousness during NDEs. Critics point out that we cannot ask rats what they experienced; human brains might differ from rats' and all the rats exhibited the same brain patterns whereas only a fraction of human survivors report NDEs (Greyson et al., 2013). Even so, the results show that brain activity does not just stop after cardiac arrest; highly synchronised activity still goes on and could potentially support conscious experience.

Is our question now answered? Can we conclude that all these amazing NDEs depended on active, functioning brains, so there is no need even to consider the possibility of consciousness beyond the brain?

No, not yet. There is one final argument with potentially profound implications. In just a very few cases NDErs claim to have seen or heard something they could not possibly have known about. In other words, they claim paranormal powers. Even fewer claim that these perceptions occurred at precisely the time when they had no brain activity at all so they must, they claim, have seen, heard and been conscious without a functioning brain. If they are right consciousness must be independent of the brain, dualism must be true, materialism must be false, and survival beyond death is assured.

Are they?

CHAPTER 16

# Incredible!

B ased on the incredible true story ...

Colton, not yet four years old, told his parents he left his body
during the surgery – and authenticated that claim by describing
exactly what his parents were doing in another part of the hospital
while he was being operated on. He talked of visiting heaven and
relayed stories told to him by people he met there whom he had
never met in life, sharing events that happened even before he was
born. He also astonished his parents with descriptions and
obscure details about heaven that matched the Bible exactly,
though he had not yet learned to read.

Yes, this is 'incredible'. If true as described, it is evidence for mind
beyond the body; for paranormal ability on the verge of death. The
story matches what some Christians would love to believe about a
glorious heaven in which, as Colton himself puts it, 'Nobody is old and
nobody wears glasses'. Even atheists living in this unfair world may
sometimes wish that goodness will eventually be rewarded and evil
punished. These, and many other factors, may explain why *Heaven is
For Real* (Burpo, 2010) was a No. 1 *New York Times* bestseller, sold 10
million copies within a few years and had a major movie made about it.

The book was written by Colton Burpo's pastor father and a Christian journalist. The excerpt above comes from the back cover. Even this extract rings warning bells for me. The word 'exactly' is often a giveaway, as it was in the Wilmot case (Chapter 5, page 71–77). Did little three-year-old Colton see 'exactly' what his parents were doing at the time? We cannot tell. Assuming he reported his experience as truthfully as he could, he left his body, spoke with angels and told his father, 'You were in a little room by yourself praying, and Mommy was in a different room and she was praying and talking on the phone' (Burpo, 2010, p.61). Neither of these actions is remotely surprising for a pastor and his wife in a time of crisis and there is no indication that the little boy gave any further description of the rooms or 'exactly' what his mother was doing. As for his descriptions 'exactly' matching the Bible, he couldn't read but his mother and father read Bible stories to him at bedtime.

In 2015 the young author of another Christian heaven story, Alex Malarkey, recanted the tale he had told in *The Boy Who Came Back from Heaven* (2010), describing the angels who took him to heaven after a terrible car crash. Left paralysed, he later admitted he had invented the story to get attention – 'I did not die. I did not go to heaven' – and as a result Christian bookshops all over America withdrew copies. In the furore, Colton Burpo, now fourteen, reaffirmed the truth of his own account. He may indeed have been telling his story as accurately as he could but there is no real evidence of supernatural perception and none to confirm his brain state at the time. For that kind of evidence we need better attested cases.

## Maria and the shoe

My first attempt to find such evidence was inspired by the famous story of Maria and the tennis shoe. Kimberly Clark was a social worker in the critical care unit of a Seattle hospital when she met her first NDEr (Clark, 1984, Clark Sharp, 1995). Maria was a migrant worker visiting friends in the city when she had a severe heart attack, was brought into hospital at night by ambulance and then, a few days later, had a cardiac arrest. Later that day, Clark found Maria agitated and wanting to talk. She said that when the doctors and nurses were trying to resuscitate her she had found herself 'looking down from the ceiling at them working on my body' (Clark, 1984, p.242). Clark dismissed this on the grounds that Maria had been in the hospital for some time and would have known what the room and the procedures looked like. Since hearing is the last sense to go, she reasoned, Maria might have heard what was going on.

Her opinion changed when Maria told her that she'd been distracted by something on a ledge over the emergency room driveway. She found herself outside, 'thought her way' up, and saw a tennis shoe on a third-floor ledge at the north end of the building. So Clark set off to find it. From outside she couldn't see much at all so she 'began going in and out of patients' rooms and looking out their windows, which were so narrow that I had to press my face to the screen just to see the ledge at all' (p.243). Finally, she found the shoe and brought it back, concluding, 'My vantage point was very different from what Maria's had to have been for her to notice that the little toe had worn a place in the shoe and that the lace was stuck under the heel . . . The only way she would have had such a perspective was if she had been floating right outside and at very close range to the tennis shoe . . . it was very concrete evidence for me' (p.243).

What impresses me now, more than thirty years on, is how badly Clark wanted this confirmation and why. She describes thoroughly rational thoughts about what Maria could and could not have known about the emergency room, doctors and equipment there. But her only alternative to this being a 'real' NDE (i.e. Maria's spirit left her body) was to say that Maria 'confabulated'. In other words, it was either 'real' or Maria was making it up. She did not have, as we do now, any explanation of how Maria's NDE could have been absolutely realistic and life-changing even though her spirit never actually floated outside the hospital windows.

Remember, this was the early 1980s, not long after the term NDE was coined, and most people knew nothing about OBEs or NDEs. There were no TV programmes, no radio discussions and certainly no Internet. Indeed, the main thrust of Clark's article, entitled

'Clinical interventions with near-death experiencers', concerns how to help fearful patients and their families. In this context, and given that apparent choice, I can understand why Clark wanted that evidence. Add to that her own later comment that, 'I was doubting Maria's account because I had not dealt with my own NDE' (Sharp, 2007, p.248) and we can imagine the importance of the evidence to her.

Sadly, people seem to get stuck in that same false dichotomy today and without the excuse they had then. Time and again I read people claiming that OBEs or NDEs are not 'real' unless there is concrete evidence. They seem unable to grasp the possibility that everything we ever experience in life is because of what our brains and bodies are doing and OBEs are no different – they are just a much more remarkable and strange manifestation of what it is to be a conscious human being. But I must get back to Maria's shoe and the 'concrete evidence' . . .

At the time I tried to find out more by writing to Clark via her publishers but despite several attempts I received no response. I wanted to know whether Maria had described the worn patch and the lace under the heel before Clark found the shoe. She certainly does not say so in the article. To be 'concrete evidence' for anyone other than Clark, we need some record of the conversation before the shoe was found. That would be convincing indeed, as it would if Maria had drawn a sketch of the shoe or told other people about it beforehand. Less convincing, but still helpful would be if Maria could later confirm what happened. But as far as I know she left the hospital and was never traced again. Above all, the whole story is told by just one person, Clark herself. And however truthful Clark tried to be, one person's story is not enough to challenge our entire understanding of the world.

Ring declared the story of Maria and the shoe one of the most convincing cases on record (Ring & Lawrence, 1993). Others repeated the story, often distorting it in weird ways. In Morse's bizarre version which, as far as I can tell is baseless, Clark opens the window of Maria's room. Seeing no shoe and with Maria insisting it was round the corner, 'Courageously, Clark crawled onto the ledge of her fifth-floor window and around the corner. There sat a shoe, just as Maria had described' (Morse, 1990, p.19). This version, too, is repeatedly cited as evidence for life after death (Varga, 2011).

Other researchers did more thorough investigations than I had. In an article, delightfully subtitled 'Waiting for the other shoe to drop' (Ebbern et al., 1996), two young students, Ebbern and Mulligan, visited the hospital, placed a shoe on a similar ledge and tried to see how difficult it was to see. Although there were building works going on at the time, they could easily see it and when they returned to the hospital a week later someone had removed it. So presumably it was quite conspicuous. They also had no difficulty either placing a shoe on the ledge or seeing it from the inside without, like Clark, having 'to press my face to the screen just to see the ledge at all'.

Many years later, Keith Augustine (2007a) included Maria's shoe in his critical survey of paranormal claims in the *Journal of Near-death Studies*. Clark Sharp (as she became) responded with 'The other shoe drops' (Sharp, 2007), castigating him for basing his analysis, 'not on my original description of the case but rather on a distorted account in a magazine written by two college students who misrepresented the facts and made unwarranted assumptions to support their beliefs'. That does sound shoddy, but that magazine was *Skeptical Inquirer*, which is a respected journal even if biased towards sceptical investigations. Arguments can get quite heated when such deep beliefs are under scrutiny.

In this rebuttal Sharp makes much of the fact that the actual shoe appeared in a TV programme and only when this resurfaced some years later did she remember the Nike logo on the side. But this adds absolutely nothing to the case because we have no knowledge, even from Clark herself, of how Maria described the shoe *before* Clark went to retrieve it. After all this time I guess I can only reach the same conclusion about Maria's shoe as I did in *Dying to Live*: 'fascinating but unsubstantiated' (1993a, p.128).

## Pam Reynolds

I chose to write about Maria's shoe in such detail because it was the first case that piqued my interest. Since then the most famous case is undoubtedly that of Pam Reynolds who, back in 1991, reported an apparently veridical OBE after her brain was cooled and her heart deliberately stopped to remove an aneurysm from her brain. This has attracted more debate than any other, both constructive and pointless, since its first publication by Michael Sabom (1998). Some excellent recent reviews discuss what she actually said, what happened in the operating theatre, the state of her brain at the time and whether any experiences or memory would be expected in the circumstances (Augustine, 2007a, Woerlee, 2005 a, b, 2011, French, 2009, Palmer, 2009).

In the end, as so often happens, this case comes down to one question – when did her OBE occur? Was it when there was no activity being recorded from her brain or was it before or after this state? Augustine (2007a) constructed a helpful timeline based on Sabom's original text, which seems to show that her OBE happened well before her induced cardiac arrest, when she was anaesthetised but not clinically dead, a conclusion then challenged by Sabom (2007). Personally, I am most impressed by the view of John Palmer, a parapsychologist and believer whom I have known since the 1980s. Even he concludes, 'we cannot be confident that any of these experiences in fact occurred during the part of the procedure in which Pam was clinically dead' (Palmer, 2009, p.166).

Timing is critical. So how could Pim van Lommel and his team write, in that most respected peer-reviewed journal, *The Lancet*, 'this patient proved to have had a very deep NDE, including an out-of-body experience, with subsequently verified observations *during the period of the flat EEG*' (my italics, van Lommel et al., 2001, p.2044)? Whatever the truth of the Pam Reynolds' case, this claim about verification is untrue.

Are any other claims in this important paper also untrue? Remember, this paper presented the results of one of the best and most carefully conducted prospective studies of NDEs ever done and then jumped to what seem to be completely unwarranted conclusions about 'Endless consciousness'. Are there more problems to come?

## The teeth in the drawer

'During the pilot phase in one of the hospitals, a coronary-care-unit nurse reported a veridical out-of-body experience of a resuscitated patient' (van Lommel et al., 2001, p.2041). We might have expected van Lommel and his colleagues to be a little more cautious, perhaps saying 'a purported veridical OBE' or 'an apparently veridical OBE' before actually checking its veridicality, but here is a little oddity, a small point but a rather telling one for assessing the value of this work.

I guess anyone reading the statement about the nurse would assume that this 'veridical OBE' occurred during the pilot phase, and perhaps even in the same hospital. I certainly assumed this the first few times I read it. But they do not actually say this: they say that during the pilot phase a 'nurse reported a veridical OBE'. What is not clear from van Lommel's report, and was uncovered later by others, is that the events took place in 1979. Since data collection for the study didn't begin until nine years later, in 1988, it makes more sense to take the statement literally, i.e. the nurse merely *reported*, during the pilot study, something that had happened a long time before.

It later emerged that this case was described in a Dutch magazine in 1991, not by the nurse involved, but by someone who had heard it second-hand (Craffert, 2015). Add to this that the major interview with the nurse was not done until after this was published, and indeed twenty-nine years after the events occurred (Smit, 2008), and the case already begins to look a little shaky for one that is meant to shatter scientific opinion and 'induce a huge change in the scientific paradigm in western medicine' (van Lommel, 2006, p.148).

So here's the story. A comatose man was found in a meadow by passers-by and brought into the cardiac unit, where artificial respiration was started. When trying to intubate him, the nurse removed his dentures and put them on the crash cart. It took about an hour and a half for the patient to gain sufficient heart rhythm and blood pressure to be moved and he was still intubated, ventilated and comatose. More than a week later the nurse met him again for the first time since his resuscitation, and to his surprise the man immediately said, 'Oh, that nurse knows where my dentures are,' and proceeded to describe the cart and the sliding shelf on which the nurse had put them.

Van Lommel uses this story of 'Dentures man', as he became known, to back up his claim for 'endless consciousness' and memory outside the brain. He uses it not only in this article but elsewhere too, writing, 'The story of the dentures that were removed and stored during a resuscitation, which was published in *The Lancet* and told earlier, is inexplicable to most scientists' (van Lommel, 2010).

Of course it is inexplicable if it were true as told – but is it? That is the question no one can answer for sure and, like the Maria and Pam Reynolds' cases, this one has been amply debated (Craffert, 2015, French, 2005, Smit, 2008, Woerlee, 2010, Smit & Rivas, 2010). What was his brain state during resuscitation, both in the ambulance and in hospital? Could his hypothermia have contributed to preserving brain activity? Exactly when were the dentures removed? What did the crash cart really look like and how close was his description? Could he have heard the nurse's apparently distinctive husky voice during the resuscitation and recognised him that way? So long after the events consensus on any of these questions is impossible.

What are we to conclude about 'Dentures man'? Rudolf Smit (2008) tried to 'set the record straight' and provided the most thorough account of the story so far. Smit is no avowed sceptic but an NDE researcher and co-author of *The Self Does Not Die: Verified Paranormal Phenomena from Near-Death Experiences* (Rivas et al., 2016). Yet he concluded, 'this case cannot constitute definitive proof of continuation of consciousness, let alone survival of death. But it does provide corroborating testimony that something extraordinary happened at the time, an event that should not be dismissed out of hand as a ridiculous story made up by naïve believers' (Smit, 2008, p.61).

There are two interesting things about this conclusion. The first is that even this case, so often trumpeted as evidence for consciousness beyond the brain and used by van Lommel for that purpose, does not stand up to careful scrutiny. The second is that it reveals, even as late as 2008, that people still tend to think in terms of just two opposing possibilities – that either the story is true as told and is therefore amazing evidence for souls, life after death or consciousness without the brain, or is made up.

The most likely truth in this as in so many other famous cases is neither of these. It is that 'Dentures man' really did have an out-of-body experience, really did seem to see the room from up near the ceiling and described it as faithfully as he could but this, like every other OBE we know about, was caused by the state of his body and brain; not by his spirit leaving his body. Yes, it was 'something extraordinary' and no, it wasn't 'made up by naïve believers' but nor is it evidence for the soul.

Van Lommel's unwarranted reliance on this old case set me looking more carefully into his famous *Lancet* paper. And there I found more serious problems with his attempts to convince us that consciousness can leave the brain and that 'mainstream scientists' and 'materialists' are all wrong. I will point out just four.

(1) *The Lancet* paper states, 'blind people have described veridical perception during out-of-body experiences at the time of this experience' (2001, p.2044). This is a bold claim that van Lommel repeats elsewhere (e.g. 2009, p.179) without giving any references to how contentious this claim has been (Irwin, 1987). It goes back at least to 1967 and a lecture given by Elisabeth Kübler-Ross (1967) but she was heavily criticised for not publishing any cases to back up her claims. I was therefore terribly excited when, in 1991, I read what sounded like a perfect case; the story of a blind woman called Sarah who had seen in minute detail the doctors who were trying to revive her, their clothes, what they said and even the scribbles on the board outside. I wrote immediately to the author of *Recovering the Soul* (Dossey, 1989), hoping to find out more and maybe even to contact Sarah herself (Blackmore, 1993). Apparently Kenneth Ring did the same and we both got the same answer: Dossey had made it up!

Dossey's reasoning was all too common in this field. He wrote, 'My reasons for composing her were to dramatically illustrate the key features of non-local ways of knowing – ways that seem (to me) fully documented in the experiences of diverse numbers of human beings'

(Dossey, 1991). In other words, he was so sure it was true that he was willing to make up a story, presented as a real case, to illustrate his beliefs.

I wrote to Ring, who was as troubled by this as I was and tried to find other cases but failed. He wrote back, 'In short, as much as this is the lore of NDEs, there has never, to my knowledge, been a case of a blind NDEr reported in the literature where there was a clear-cut or documented evidence of accurate visual perception during an alleged OBE (And you can quote me.) I wish there were such a case' (Ring, 1991). Ring eventually went on to make a serious study of thirty-one accounts of OBEs and NDEs in the blind (Ring & Cooper, 1997, Ring & Cooper, 2008).

This threw up some fascinating insights into the mental worlds of the blind. Sighted people sometimes imagine that a blind person must stumble around in blackness as they themselves would with a blindfold on, but this is not so. Blind people have rich spatial awareness based on sound, touch and other senses, and a body schema just like anyone else, which means they can also have an OBE like anyone else. They can experience OB feelings and vestibular sensations, have life reviews, feel joy and love, and, if their primary visual cortex remains undamaged (for example, if only their eyes or optic nerve are damaged), experience tunnels and lights. This is because hyperactivity in visual cortex will still produce the wonderful bright light and the tunnel as it would with anyone else. Maybe this explains what seems to be a remarkable statement from one of Ring's NDErs, 'This was the only time I could ever relate to seeing and what light was, because I experienced it.' Ring interpreted his findings in terms of 'transcendental awareness', but I think they tell us more about the mental worlds of the blind.

(2) The second problem is how badly van Lommel misrepresents current understanding of the mind. He writes, 'For decades, extensive research has been done to localize consciousness and memories inside the brain, so far without success' (2009, p.180). He made this identical statement in 2004 and continues to repeat it (in 2006, 2011a and b).

This is ridiculous because few researchers would ever try to 'localise consciousness'; even those who are searching for the neural correlates of consciousness do not expect to find a specific location. Consciousness is not that sort of thing (Blackmore, 2010). As for memory, progress has been stunning and the mechanisms underlying the formation, storage and retrieval of memory are being understood in ever more detail – but you cannot say that memory is 'localized inside the brain' other than by pointing to the many areas involved in different aspects of memory processing, such as the hippocampus, prefrontal cortex and parts of the parietal and temporal lobes.

(3) With similar seeming confidence van Lommel writes, 'We cannot measure what we think or feel. There are no known examples of neural-perceptual matches, and hence reasons to doubt the truth of the "matching content" doctrine' (2009, p.181). Van Lommel is a retired cardiologist, not a neuroscientist, so he cannot be expected to know about all the latest research but he might be expected to know that he does not know and so avoid making such ignorant claims.

The fact is that with fMRI (functional magnetic resonance imaging) and the massive computing power now available it is possible to do exactly what he says we cannot do – find out what is going on in someone's head. At the Gallant Lab at the University of California at Berkeley, scientists recorded hours of scan data while subjects were watching videos (Nishimoto et al., 2011) and created a huge 'dictionary' relating the shapes, edges and movements in the videos to activity at several thousand points in the viewer's brain. When they then showed a new video to the same person they could reconstruct what he was seeing. The computational power required was vast and early reconstructions hazy but they were recognisable as the scenes in the video and are getting better all the time. A similar method has been applied to people sleeping inside a scanner and woken from REM sleep so as to create a video revealing what they are dreaming about (Horikawa et al., 2013). Van Lommel is simply wrong yet he has gone on repeating this same claim again and again (2009, 2011 a and b, 2013).

(4) Perhaps most troubling is what seems like a throwaway remark van Lommel makes when discussing the work of Parnia and Fenwick (Parnia et al., 2001 and again repeated in several articles). He writes, 'They found in their study that 11 per cent reported an NDE: 6.3 per cent reported a core NDE, and 4.8 per cent a superficial NDE. They write that the NDE-reports suggest that the NDE occurs during the period of unconsciousness. This is a surprising conclusion in their view' (2009, p.179).

I was puzzled because I couldn't remember Parnia and Fenwick finding any such evidence. So I checked. What they actually say is, 'Some patients do appear to have obtained information which they could not have obtained during unconsciousness [35]' (Parnia et al., 2001, p.154). Please note the superscript [35] – Parnia and Fenwick are not referring to their own collection of NDEs but to a popular book by Michael Sabom called *Recollections of Death*, published nearly twenty years before. Van Lommel should make this clear and not distort other people's work to make his own case.

Some of these tiny details may seem tedious but I keep delving because I so badly want to know whether people really can see without a functioning brain; it would be so important if they could. But I have found nothing yet to convince me. I agree with OBE researcher Jason Braithwaite, who, after a thorough and scathing review of van Lommel's work, concludes, 'Despite its impact in NDE circles, the van Lommel et al. study provides no evidence that human consciousness survives bodily death'; it 'poses no serious challenge at all to current neuroscientific accounts of the NDE' (Braithwaite, 2008, p.15). I would add that Pim van Lommel has misrepresented both neuroscience in general and other people's work in particular to bolster his own dubious theory. He is doing a serious disservice both to scientists and to everyone else and has no justification for saying, 'Obviously, during NDE enhanced consciousness is experienced independently from the normal body-linked waking consciousness' (van Lommel, 2009, p.179, and identically in 2006, 2011b, and 2013, p.25). There is nothing obvious about this repeated claim. But could he still be right – and could we find out?

# AWARE

First hint of "life after death" in biggest ever scientific study.
*Daily Telegraph*, 7 October 2014

Back in the 1980s, when I first began research into NDEs, I wrote a novel. It was terrible and never published, but the story revolved around a scientist who, rather like van Lommel, was totally convinced that consciousness could exist outside the body and determined to prove it. His innocent young research assistant fell in love with him (of course!) only to discover that he was cheating on his results, this unenviable situation being based on my own horrible experiences of uncovering fraud in ESP experiments (Blackmore, 1987a, 1996). I mention this only because my fictional scientist placed targets above the beds of cardiac patients, hoping they might have an OBE, see the target words or numbers, and so prove his theory.

I was not the first to think of this idea. It is the obvious way to test claims of veridical perception during NDEs but at that time it seemed impossible. Now it is not only possible but has been done in a huge, multi-national study lasting four years (2008–12) called 'AWARE; AWAreness during REsuscitation' (Parnia et al., 2014). This is the prospective study I referred to in which nearly half of cardiac arrest survivors had memories of some kind, 9 per cent experienced NDEs, 2 per cent recalled '"seeing" and "hearing" actual events related to their resuscitation' and 'One had a verifiable period of conscious awareness during which time cerebral function was not expected' (Parnia et al., 2014, p.1799). The results were published to a flurry of media excitement and exaggeration, like the headline above from one of Britain's top broadsheets.

The main aims of the study, as described in the academic paper, were to explore the relationships between awareness during CPR (cardiopulmonary resuscitation) and the cognitive deficits and post-traumatic stress suffered by some survivors of cardiac arrest. However, the researchers also looked for 'objective verification of claims of awareness' – in other words, they wanted to find out whether any patient who had an OBE could observe something that was impossible for them to see while lying on the bed.

They installed between fifty and one hundred shelves in each of fifteen hospitals where they thought CPR might be needed and on each one placed a single image of national or religious symbols, people, animals and major newspaper headlines. These could be seen only from a position close to the ceiling. Why they chose these varied images they do not explain, nor how they were chosen. I know from all my years in parapsychology that the correct randomisation of targets is crucial and often the weakest link in experimental designs: targets must be chosen randomly to avoid using popular targets more often or creating other opportunities for lucky guessing. They also fixed a triangle on the underside of the shelves to test whether patients had their eyes open during CPR. Any with memories of visual or auditory awareness were invited for a further in-depth interview.

Sadly, this resulted in only two patients and both suffered ventricular fibrillation in areas of the hospital that had no shelves. So the researchers couldn't even test whether anyone saw the images. However, they report in detail the NDE of one 57-year-old man who described watching events from the top corner of the room: 'He accurately described people, sounds, and activities from his resuscitation [. . .]. His medical records corroborated his accounts and specifically supported his descriptions and the use of an automated external defibrillator' (Parnia et al., 2014, p. 1802). In the interview the man described talking to the nurse, feeling pressure on his groin and then seeing, up in the corner of the room, a woman beckoning him. He felt that she knew him and was there for a reason and 'the next second, I was up there, looking down at me, the nurse, and another man who had a bald head' (Parnia et al., 2014, p. 1803). The next thing he remembers is waking up, feeling quite euphoric.

The authors conclude, 'our verified case of VA (visual awareness) suggests conscious awareness may occur beyond the first 20–30 s after CA (cardiac arrest) . . . The case indicates the experience likely occurred during CA rather than after recovery from CA or before CA' (p. 1803). They go on, 'similar experiences have been categorized using the scientifically undefined and imprecise term of out of body experiences (OBE's), and further categorized as autoscopy and optical illusions' (p. 1803), rejecting the idea that the man's experiences were hallucinations on the grounds that they corresponded with reality.

Yet this whole description sounds to me exactly what you would expect of an OBE in which the man could still hear and feel what was going on and incorporate it into a bird's-eye view. The critical question is whether his brain was active enough to have supported and then recalled an OBE. The authors believe not because the events took place more than twenty or thirty seconds into the three-minute period without heartbeat. Yet this is exactly the time at which those unexpected bursts of activity were reported in dying patients (Chawla et al., 2009). My guess would be that during that brief period his brain was active but was sufficiently disturbed to create a displaced body schema and hallucinations such as the woman beckoning him. But of course there was no EEG or other measure to tell us for sure.

I have such mixed feelings about the AWARE project. On the one hand it was a most ambitious and difficult study to undertake and I can only congratulate the authors on all their hard work. This is exactly the kind of study we need if we are ever to find out whether NDErs really can see things that would be invisible to their physical eyes and I hope they will continue. On the other hand I am frustrated by the way this single case has been made out to be evidence for life after death.

In a footnote, Parnia et al. say that if large numbers of patients with the ability to observe events from above consistently fail to identify the images this would suggest the experiences were some kind of illusion. I agree. My simple prediction is that, if the experiment is repeated with adequate controls, no patient will ever be able to see the image. I do hope we'll have the chance to find out.

## What do NDErs really see?

These claims of true perception would be so important if true that they have beguiled me as well as everyone else into failing to ask the opposite, but equally pertinent, question – do people see *untrue* things during NDEs? The answer is, of course, a resounding yes.

# Incredible!

Whenever veridical observations are claimed they are typically mixed in with a far greater number of invented or imagined things. We know that already. Fox saw his beloved Elsie and two exam questions but most of what he saw in a lifetime of astral projection was wrong. Monroe got the details of Tart's house wrong, Apsey got his mother's position wrong, the Canadian architect saw non-existent houses in Fulham. Even in the case just described, the patient saw a woman beckoning to him from the top corner of the room. Clearly she was not really there. And if you argue that she was a ghost or spirit appearing in the actual room, then why do so many NDErs meet living, not dead, people beckoning them into a tunnel or telling them it is not their time to die?

Peter and Elizabeth Fenwick (1995) collected 350 NDE reports, in which 14 per cent met living people and others had details that were wrong, such as a woman who saw her own heart lying beside her body during an operation when in fact it remained inside. Morse (1994) describes a young boy who saw his living playmates on the other side of a river, and Keith Augustine (2007b) elaborates on this point, giving many examples of NDErs seeing things that are not there, missing things that are, experiencing clearly hallucinatory imagery and meeting fictional characters.

Then there's my own experience all those years ago. Vicki's room looked convincingly real, as did Oxford city and the surrounding countryside, but the only details I was able to check up on proved to be wrong. I think, now, that everything I saw was a product of my own life experience and a functioning brain. Everything looked as I expected because what I saw was based on what I expected.

The fact is we don't hear about the many mistakes nearly as much as the very, very few details that turn out to be correct. This is obvious, really: when someone has an NDE they may, and often do, fear no one will believe them or even that they are going mad. So they understandably emphasise any small details that were correct and these tales are told and retold by their family and friends, getting into popular books and even into the scientific literature. The result is a total distortion of the truth. As far as I can see, the answer is clear: lots of people have

NDEs and OBEs with wonderful visions of places, scenes and people, but there is no reliable evidence that they have actually seen anything at a distance or that consciousness survives beyond death.

I will admit that I find this terribly depressing – not that death is the end of me and my little personal consciousness but the misuse of the evidence. The trouble with NDE research, and the main reason I find it depressing, is the levels of emotional commitment. Or perhaps that's too polite a way of putting it. Let me say instead that the trouble with NDE research is how unwilling people are to change their minds in the face of the evidence. I know this is hard to do but it is the absolutely most fundamental tenet of scientific inquiry. You invent a hypothesis, ask a question, devise a way to answer it and then base your understanding of the world on that answer.

I know how hard this is because I've had to do it myself, and do it big time (Blackmore, 1996). After my dramatic experience my original hypothesis was clear: *obviously* my soul or astral body or spirit had left its body and gone travelling. I was totally and completely convinced and that's why I can understand why others are too. Yet I was wrong and I had to change my mind. Now I ask different questions – I don't ask whether there is consciousness beyond the brain but how modern science can help me understand what really happened.

It's time, at last, to go back to 1970.

CHAPTER 17

# Back to That Night
# in November

I was sitting cross-legged on the floor late one evening. Sleep deprivation had upset my vestibular system, making me feel I was drifting and floating, and had interfered with my right TPJ, disturbing my body schema (Chee & Chuah, 2007, Quarck et al., 2006). Nearly four hours of holding out my arm for the Ouija board had confused my bodily sense even more. REM intrusion threatened (Nelson, 2010) and I was on the verge of hallucinating even without that puff of cannabis; with it my short-term memory was reduced to a brief window in the present moment (Earleywine, 2002).

In the near darkness, with my eyes shut, primary visual cortex (V1) was deprived of useful information. With my hyperexcitable cortex (Braithwaite et al., 2013) already disinhibited by sleep deprivation and cannabis it went into random firing, producing an illusory central light and the form constants of spirals and tunnels (Cowan, 1982). As the light increased, I seemed to move towards it, disinhibited motion detectors adding further illusory movement experiences (IMEs). Memories of that day's cycling through autumn trees drifted by. I was moving through a tunnel of leaves.

My auditory cortex was similarly hyperactive, producing random low-frequency repetitive sounds that drowned out the music, making sounds like the pounding of horses' hooves; I had visions of galloping down the tunnel towards the light.

When Kevin asked, 'Where are you, Sue?' I was brought up short. I tried to picture my own body and its real location but my disturbed TPJ could no longer combine vestibular and sensory input to create a firm sense of an embodied self (Blanke et al., 2002). Confused, I tried to work out where I was but my logical prefrontal cortex was deactivated as my brain hovered on the edge of sleep (Muzur et al., 2002). As I struggled to look harder to see where I was, a sudden shift from OB feelings to OB vision took place and with the view from above being easiest to construct from memory (Blackmore, 1987b), this became my model of reality: I was near the ceiling and looking down.

The scene became intensely vivid, with the images coming from inside visual cortex, unclouded by defects in my eyes (Luna, 2016). The ordinary world of the senses became ever more remote, while thoughts in the present moment were hyper-present and real (Metzinger, 2005). This new view seemed real because it was the best model of reality my brain could create (Blackmore, 1984b) and with Kevin repeatedly asking questions, my attention was kept on the imagined world. He asked if I could see a silver cord so I saw one and enjoyed playing with it in this flexible, thought-controlled world (Leadbeater, 1895, Muldoon & Carrington, 1929).

My free-floating body seemed quite normal at first, based on the brain's intrinsic model of the human body schema (Melzack, 1989), but dissociated from the senses it began to drift, changing shape along with imagined worlds and actions as I set off and flew above the town. The roofs, gutters and chimneys I saw were just as I imagined them, not as they were. So too were the cities, lakes, oceans and islands I saw. I laughed at the vivid 'star-shaped island with a hundred trees' believing it was a thought form in the astral plane (Besent, 1896, Findlay, 1931) because that was the only theory I knew.

By the time I tried to return all sense of coherent bodily self had gone so I tried to reconstruct an image of myself sitting in the room as I remembered it. After two hours without a functioning body schema this was impossible. Trying to get inside the body it became too small, producing internal heautoscopy (Blanke & Mohr, 2005). Trying to compensate, it became larger and larger, taking in the room, the world and ultimately everything I could imagine. Self and other became one and all aspects of self dissolved; embodiment, agency and body ownership no longer held any meaning. Without a body to provide a stable first-person perspective, space became meaningless. Without attention to past or future, time became meaningless. Although I did not know it, this was a mystical experience (James, 1902). Everything was perfect, as it must be without a self to give either perspective or desires: the classic experience of nonduality.

With what little thinking ability remained I assumed this was 'it'; this was all that ever was or ever could be, until Kevin asked what more I could see and something strange opened up, a sense of vast consciousness all around. I was too tired to do more than glimpse this new vastness. In exhaustion I seemed to face a choice; stay in this marvellous, right-seeming, perfect state, or return to ordinary life? The choice made itself and the struggle began. After more than two hours of serious disturbance this brain took some time to reinstate both body schema and self-image and even then confused my own body with others. When I opened my eyes I felt and saw greyish body-shapes around the others as well as myself; displaced body schemas that gradually faded until I was (more or less) back to normal. Yet nothing was ever quite the same again.

## Science over speculation

Today I find myself writing happily again, the depression of dealing with NDEs is over. And now the reason seems clear: I loved trying to rewrite my own experience in light of what I've learned from the science; doing so only pushed me to find out more. And I found more. For example, I kept wondering where the cannabis fitted in and whether or not it contributed to the effects. I soon discovered that cannabis shifts the inhibition-excitation balance and can cause cortical disinhibition (den Boon et al., 2015, Yoshino et al., 2011). *Yes!* I tried to work out why my sleep deprivation might have been important and learned that sleep deprivation affects both the vestibular system and, of all things, the right TPJ (Quarck et al., 2006). *Of course!*

These discoveries are a joy to me but quite the opposite to others. When my long-time friend, NDE researcher Ken Ring read my two accounts he wrote, 'The first is gripping; the second, at least to me, is rather boring. The first experience changed your life; the second seems to have satisfied your quest to understand what happened to you.' (Ring, 2016)

Yes, indeed! But for me, the scientific analysis only adds to the pleasure. It encourages me to keep learning, keep meditating, and keep trying new techniques and drugs. It motivates me to explore further the potential of a mind utterly entwined with body and brain. It reminds me of the words I was left with at the very end of my experience 'However far you go, there's always somewhere further.' This is what happens with science too; the more you learn the more you realise how much you still don't know.

This is what so rarely happens in NDE research. Again and again the arguments come back to whether someone actually saw something they should not have been able to see, or consciously saw anything at all when their brain was silent. And then what? Then, you might believe from reading Morse, Parnia, Fenwick, Rivas or van Lommel, we have 'proof' that the scientists are all wrong, that the materialist, reductionist (and heartless and anti-spiritual?) Western scientific paradigm must be overthrown. And then?

Then nothing. The 'new paradigm' and the 'visions of a new science of consciousness' (Parnia & Fenwick, 2002) are empty. We are told that a few special cases prove the reality of the human soul and its survival of bodily death, that memory is stored outside of the brain and consciousness does not depend upon having a body. And then? What do these new 'theories' predict? If I take them seriously, I want to ask questions such as, 'What is the soul made of?', 'What capabilities does it have and not have? And how can we find out?', 'If memory is stored outside the brain, how is it stored, and what does this tell us about learning, forgetting, or retrieving old memories?', 'What is consciousness and what is left of it when the eyes and ears, visual and auditory cortices, vestibular system and self-systems are all dead?' And I get no answers. It is not that the research has yet to be done, it is that these theories don't tell us what research needs to be done. They provide no predictions, no interesting questions that can be answered with experiments, and no ways of finding out which of them fits the data better. Like the theory of astral projection, they are empty.

In the philosophy of science there are many descriptions of how science does or should operate: Karl Popper's falsificationism, Thomas Kuhn's idea of paradigm shifts or the anarchism of Paul Feyerabend. But I find Imre Lakatos's (1978) ideas about scientific research programmes most helpful. In asking what makes one scientific theory better than another he describes all theories as having a hard, inflexible core and a more flexible protective belt of ideas and ways of solving problems. Successful research programmes are progressive even if they hang onto a rigid core – that is, they keep moving on. Failed programmes fail to change; they never give up on refuted ideas and never move on.

The new science of OBEs, I am so happy to say, is a thoroughly progressive research programme. From the discovery of how to stimulate OBEs, through the use of brain scans and virtual reality to the neuroscience of the self, research keeps moving on, asking new questions and finding new answers that just raise more questions. Yes, this paradigm more or less depends on an inflexible core of what the critics call 'the Western materialist paradigm' but perhaps it will throw this off, or not. We have to wait and see.

For myself I am not a materialist (though many people seem to assume I must be). I reject dualism because it does not work so I could better be described as a neutral monist (though that term too has its confusions). All I mean is that I believe the universe consists of only one kind of stuff and I do not know what that stuff is – is it ultimately material, is it purely mental, is it mind and matter in some way combined, or is it something else altogether from which mind and matter emerge? I do not know – hence my endless struggles with the mind-body problem and the mystery of consciousness (Blackmore, 2005, 2010, 2011). Whatever the solution to this mystery, OBE research is moving on apace.

Endless consciousness, non-local consciousness, notions of souls and astral bodies may pander to the way many people would like things to be, but they inspire no exciting new questions that can be answered by experiment. They keep searching for evidence to prove that the current scientific paradigm is false but put nothing in its place. This is the sure sign of a failing research programme.

## Back to those three theories

I am finally going to reject the Type A theories I described at the start – those dualist *something leaves the body* theories that invoke a soul or astral body; and accept Type B – that *nothing leaves the body* in an OBE because both logic and the evidence (or lack of it) firmly tell us so.

Should we still consider that third possibility, Type C, that there might be two quite different kinds of OBE: the 'fake' sort which are hallucinations, and the 'real' sort in which a spirit or soul travels free in this world or the next?

No, because whether we look at classic astral projectors such as Sylvan Muldoon and Oliver Fox, modern astral projectors such as Robert Bruce and Robert Monroe, the OBE and SP accounts of ordinary healthy people, or the NDEs of people who nearly drowned or suffered a cardiac arrest, we find far more similarities than differences. Even those few special NDEs that seem to provide evidence for life after death do not stand out from the rest as any different. All can include tunnels and lights, and be tinged with fear or joy. All can begin with bodily distortions and vestibular sensations. All describe their experiences as extraordinarily real and vivid, whether they saw this world, visited fantastical scenes in the 'astral plane', or 'went to heaven'. All can lead to lives transformed.

Separating 'real' OBEs from 'fake' OBEs is impossible.

I can understand why people are unwilling to accept this conclusion and move on; why they want to hang on to the natural and ancient idea of a soul or spirit or inner conscious self. The consequences of giving it up are terrifying. There is no heaven awaiting us after death. None of our loved ones will be there to greet us, they are dead. We will be dead. There will be no retribution for the murderers, rapists and torturers who caused such terrible human misery and suffering, and no reward for the kind, quiet people who selflessly devoted themselves to others all their lives. We are biologically evolved creatures on a small planet revolving around an ordinary star and our consciousness arises and falls away as our little bodies are born, live and die.

Douglas Adams puts it better than I can, in *The Hitchhiker's Guide to the Galaxy*, when he talks about our 'insignificant little blue green planet' and our primitive love of digital watches.

Yes, it's that stark. But the proponents of life after death use a strange inversion of logic that we find again and again in NDE research. Take this widely repeated comment from Kübler-Ross's (1975) introduction to Moody's famous book: 'It is research such as Dr. Moody presents in his book that will enlighten many and will confirm what we have been taught for two thousand years – that there is life after death'.

They imply that we will be amazed and surprised, that we will be enlightened by the wonderful discovery that 'we', our real and everlasting conscious selves, will survive. But there is nothing surprising or enlightening about this ancient idea: people have believed it for two thousand years because it comes naturally to us as children to think this way, and major religions have built on this to encourage their believers and capture new ones. Their threats of hell and promises of heaven have no power without a dualist belief in life after death so our scientific discoveries are overturning an old and pernicious view of human importance. This is what is truly enlightening.

Yet rejecting the conventional belief is still hard – indeed painful – until you get used to it and accept the consequences. The Buddha knew this when, more than two thousand years ago, he taught that enlightenment comes in the realisation that self is as impermanent as everything else. A monk once asked him, 'Sir, is there a case where one is tormented when something permanent within oneself is not found?'

Indeed, replied the Buddha. When someone realises, '"I will be annihilated, I will be destroyed, I will be no more", he mourns, worries himself, laments, weeps, beating his breast, and becomes bewildered.

Thus [ ... ] there is a case where one is tormented when something permanent within oneself is not found,' (Rahula, 1959, p.56).

So Morse, Ring, Parnia, Fenwick, van Lommel and many more are following in the footsteps of ancient people who found it hard to relinquish their idea of self and sought to defend it. Of course they might be right but I shall not believe them unless and until they provide a new and progressive research paradigm to challenge that of the new science of OBEs.

## Remaining mysteries

Have we come to the end of the journey? Have I come to the end of my own personal journey to understand completely that one experience that changed my life? No, not yet. The new theories are far better than what went before. In my 'psychological theory of the OBE' (Blackmore, 1984b, 1993) I was right to emphasise the reduction in sensory input and proprio-ception; to see OB worlds as 'reflections of the structure and organization of the brain' (1993, p.251), and that 'What is needed is a split between the imagined position of the self and the input from the senses' (1993, p.247), but I was wrong in thinking this depends on having especially vivid imagery. It doesn't; it depends on disruption to self-processing at the TPJ. This is just a small example of the importance in science of giving up ideas that don't work and moving on to new ones. Modern neuroscience has given us the tools that none of us had back then.

Yet some fascinating questions remain. For example, what causes those vibrations of astral projection lore? The same sensations were reported by Blanke's patient when her TPJ was stimulated too weakly to produce a full OBE (Blanke et al., 2002). They also appear when the vestibular system is upset during space missions and parabolic flights (Whinnery & Whinnery, 1990). Are they just the result of a failed attempt to find a stable location for the body schema? Are they something to do with REM? I doubt the latter because from my own assessment the vibration is not at the same rate as rapid eye movements. So there is more to be discovered here.

What about another of my long-unanswered questions: why do so many OBErs rise up and then flip over, ending up about two metres above the body and looking down? This happens with vestibular disruptions and in virtual reality as well as OBEs. Perhaps it is no more mysterious than that we tend to find views from above easier to adopt than ones from the floor looking up – or that as soon as we seem to leave the body we want to turn over and look to see if it's there, but we do not know. I bet there is a lot more to learn about that mental flip-over.

And what about the other self – the floating one? Why do some people have another body, sometimes complete with clothes and glasses and shoes, while others are just a floating point of view – a formless perceiving self? In my own case I progressed from a parasomatic OBE, complete with arms, legs and head, to an asomatic OBE with no other body, and then to no self. What determines these shifts? I guess when we learn more about self-systems and the models they construct we may find out.

Another fascinating question concerns that shift from OB feelings to OB vision. Is this the same as that delightful flip from ordinary imagination into 'seeing with eyes closed'? And what casues this shift that feels like the opening of an inner eye? Irwin (1986) suggested that disembodied feelings are translated into visual form by synaesthesia. I am weakly synaesthetic and enjoy seeing colours to music or thinking with complex moving 3-D structures, but these are not the vivid visions of that OBE. Yet synaesthesia might be relevant because people who have visual OBEs are more often weak synaesthetes than those who have only OB feelings (Terhune, 2009). Indeed there's an interesting possibility here; since synaesthesia is thought to depend on hyperconnectivity between different sensory areas of the cortex it is possible that something similar underlies OBEs too; that global disinhibition means activity in one brain area spilling over into others with OB feelings immediately translated into visual impressions. There are a lot of 'maybes' and 'possiblys' here, but that means lots of exciting possibilities too.

## An obsession with realness

One further question still obsesses me after all these years: why is the OBE so utterly vivid and realistic? My own experience was probably the most intense of my whole life and I have never forgotten it. This intense realness was partly to do with vision, with a wonderful visual quality that is hard to describe. In addition was a wider sense of realness: I seemed more alive, more awake, more really 'me' than ever before. There was a 'rightness' and immediacy about everything that made ordinary waking life seem dreamlike in comparison.

Let's take that extraordinary visual quality first. This is nothing like imagination, nor like ordinary dreaming, nor like most hypnagogic or drug induced hallucinations. When some sceptics claim that OBEs are 'just hallucination' or 'only imagination' they completely miss this point.

Lucid dreams are closer but, at least in my experience, not quite the same. The only two states that really compare are first, hallucinations with DMT, and second, 'seeing with eyes closed'. In both cases the images are not only extremely colourful and vivid but they can be scanned with eye movements as though they were real. The OBE world is like this too: you can shift your attention and look around in a most realistic way. What is going on?

Luis Luna (2016), an expert in ayahuasca both through long personal experience and through research, suggested an answer: when we look at a green tree we see it with all the imperfections of our visual system; light scattered inside the eye, imperfect lenses, chromatic aberration, less than perfect combining of the two images, haze in the atmosphere or dust in our eyes. Luna explains, 'since visions are not mediated by the cornea, iris and lens, everything in the inner field of vision seems to be equally sharp, which may contribute to the "more real than real" feeling that is so frequently reported in ayahuasca experiences' (Luna, 2016, p. 259).

My brief and simple ayahuasca visions also had this other odd quality of seeming fully three-dimensional. Luna goes much further, describing how he moves into the visions, not letting them remain as though on a screen in front of his eyes, but going right inside them. Then, he says, he can look all around, even turning right round to see what lies behind him. I hope one day I might have the chance to learn to do this for myself – this really does sound like the OBE world.

There is so much I still don't understand about this kind of vision. I think it's the same as what I have been calling 'seeing with eyes closed' and some just call 'Seeing'. I think it's the same as that flip into clarity that was such a feature of my OBE. Fox reported it when projecting from the waking state, and Whiteman (1956), who writes about the mystical life and higher transformations, described 'seeing through the eyelids' when 'separating' from his physical body. In occult circles it may be described as the opening of the 'third eye'.

Where in the brain is this being generated? My first guess was extrastriate visual areas such as V4, which has orientation-selective cells and processes both colour and forms associated with colour. It is easy to see how rows of bright green trees might be generated in such cells. I thought of this because primary visual cortex, V1, is suppressed during dreaming but then this isn't like dreaming and I may be quite wrong. A clue for a different idea comes from a paper interestingly entitled 'Seeing with the eyes shut' (de Araujo et al., 2012). Using fMRI, a research team in Brazil investigated the vivid 'seeings' after drinking ayahuasca. They found increased activation in temporal and frontal areas (both of which are relevant to OBEs) and levels of activity in V1 were as high as during normal vision with open eyes. They concluded, 'By boosting the intensity of recalled images to the same level of natural image, Ayahuasca lends a status of reality to inner experiences' (de Araujo et al., 2012, p.2550).

I think we may be creeping up on the occultists' 'opening of the third eye' and the vividness and 3D quality of the OBE world, but we've a long way to go.

## An unfolding experience

Here's another question I cannot yet answer: why do OBEs and NDEs so often unfold in a particular sequence? My own experience was fairly typical, beginning with vestibular sensations, moving on to the tunnel leading towards the light, then to an OBE and to other worlds and finally, a mystical experience of no time, space or self. As we saw with NDEs, the sequence is not fixed but there is a tendency for the earlier features also to be the most common (Ring, 1980) and for OB feelings

303

to precede OB vision (Cheyne & Girard, 2009), suggesting some driving force behind this sequence.

Something similar appears in descriptions of mystical and religious experiences. They can begin with a trance or deep meditation state leading to visions, being enveloped in light, 'wrapped in a flame-coloured cloud', or taken up out of the body, but once they begin the mystic feels as though his own will is in abeyance (James, 1902); that states unfold as they will, whether this leads to the 'transcendent' type of mystical experience with God, spirits, or a completely impersonal being, or to the 'immanent' type which involves the complete loss of self or its fusion with everything else (Fontana, 2007).

Another unfolding sequence is found in the Buddhist jhanas, a series of eight increasingly absorbed states said to be reached through deep concentration. From their descriptions they sound like a series of 'discrete altered states of consciousness' (Tart, 1975), each deeper than the next. When I first read about them I was intrigued by the idea that thousands of years ago people had developed techniques for inducing particular mental states, but I didn't imagine I would ever be able to learn them myself. Then I met the American jhanas teacher Leigh Brasington, decided I had to learn and sat two ten-day retreats with him. Even in this short time I began to learn that if you follow the instructions these states do indeed unfold as described.

The first jhana involves raising a kind of energy called, in the ancient suttas, *piti*. This is very much like descriptions of kundalini in the occult literature and like Fox's 'Pineal door' method for inducing OBEs. It can come in a rush with shaking, vibrating, hot flushes and noises in the ears. The skill is then to drop down from this hyper-excited and joyful state into a happy but calmer state, and then to an equanimous state, converting the *piti* into *sukha*, and then to a deep, emotionally neutral state without thoughts. All these states are rooted in the body but the next four are referred to as the 'immaterial' or 'formless' states and for me they ring loud bells, even if I cannot reach them.

The first of these is limitless, infinite or boundless space and one technique for reaching it is to imagine expanding. Forms are said to slip away, leaving only the space as the object of concentration.

Cannabis can have this same effect, as well as shrinking and expanding, with one user saying, 'I have lost all consciousness of my body and the external world and just found myself floating in limitless space' (Tart, 1971a, p.106).

Was this where I found myself after I'd expanded and expanded into everything? At the time I thought this was all that could ever be, but when Kevin urged me on I found I was wrong. I entered a new state in which there seemed only to be a vast, impersonal awareness all around. The sixth jhana is that of infinite consciousness. Had I been led inexorably from one to the next in some kind of naturally unfolding sequence?

I might be completely deluding myself and I certainly intend to keep on with my jhana practice to learn more. But I mention this not only because of the unfolding nature of these states but because of Brasington's (2015) speculations that the techniques amount to self-stimulating the reward system. This begins with a flood of dopamine, leading to increased noradrenaline and then to endorphins, each neurotransmitter accounting for the various emotions and sensations of what the ancients called *piti* and *sukha*. Finally, the opioids fade, leaving the neutral state of the fourth jhana.

Although speculative, these ideas can and have been tested. When meditating in the lab, both EEG and fMRI scans showed different patterns corresponding closely to when Brasington entered and left each jhana (Hagerty et al., 2013). In further studies, increased activation of the nucleus accumbens was found to correspond to the extreme joy, which makes sense because this is part of the dopamine/opioid reward system. If it turns out that the jhanas are a naturally occurring sequence of brain-based states perhaps the same is true of OBEs and NDEs and we might one day work out why each stage leads to the next.

Perhaps global disinhibition affects some areas more quickly than others. Perhaps a disturbance in one brain system spreads in a particular order to others. Perhaps release of a certain neurotransmitter affects some areas more quickly than others. Perhaps there is a cascade of neurotransmitters, with one breaking down into another to cause the sequence of events. We simply do not know. At least, *I* do not know. But this is just the kind of constructive exploration that the science of OBEs can embark on, and the hunt for consciousness beyond the brain cannot.

People sometimes ask whether I am not upset to think my amazing experiences all come down to the firing of this set of neurons or the release of this or that neurotransmitter. Not at all. Everything in my life and yours, from making a cup of tea to falling in love, has to have some kind of basis in the body and brain. That does not belittle the experiences one jot.

I am so grateful for those strange few hours all that long time ago; hours during which 'I' felt more real, more thoroughly alive, more really 'me' than in ordinary waking life. How can this be? That of course depends on who or what 'I' am.

CHAPTER 18

# Who am I?

This morning I sat meditating at the end of the garden by the river. It was early and the air was cold and still except for the songs of a hundred different birds, all advertising their springtime wares. Breaths came gently and slowly, mingling with birdsong, the rushing river, the distant traffic and the moos and bleats of animals on the hill above. Hearing them all but reacting to none, everything felt real, immediate and fresh. As ever, the fundamental koan was not far away: who am I? It hovers there, unspoken but sensed, after so many years of Zen practice. I lose my balance, thinking of something, but gently return to the present. To the body.

There it is, underlying everything else — a solid, physical, warm and breathing creature. Is this me? No, it's all me — all this stuff. There's no separate 'me' observing it all any more, it just is.

I was surprised, long ago, when my Zen teacher kept going on about the importance of the body. I never liked those 'body scan' exercises where you go ever so slowly over each finger, wrist, arm and leg one by one, feeling and sensing every part until your whole body seems alive and irritatingly present. I suppose I thought the body was unimportant, to be transcended or overcome by the mind. Surely, I might have thought, this meditation training is about the mind, isn't it? Aren't I to practise and practise and practise until I can see clearly through all the mess and worry and fear and hatred and horribleness of my own mind? Enlightenment, if such a thing exists, is surely nothing to do with the itch on my knee or the heaviness of muscle, bone and subcutaneous fat, is it?

How my ideas have been forced to change – for two intertwined reasons. One is the science that has transformed our understanding of human nature; the other is the ancient practices of Zen which, curiously enough, have the same effect. For most of my life I thought these two were separate disciplines; the science was my work and Zen was a private matter, almost a hobby. Yet as it turns out they both lead in the same direction: they both take 'me' down from its pedestal and show it in quite a different light.

I began to learn meditation in the 1970s but it was some years later that I took up Zen as a daily practice of paying attention (Blackmore, 1995). The reason was simple: I was desperate. I was unhappy and confused, and the world around me seemed increasingly distant and unreal. I would pinch myself to feel something. I would look out of the window at the trees opposite and blink and squint, trying to make the world seem real. It did not work.

At a conference I helped to organise with some friends I came across the idea of mindfulness for the first time and it struck me hard. From that moment on I threw myself into intense mindfulness practice for several weeks and then established a daily meditation practice that still continues. It's a slow process, like untangling the most contorted and impenetrable ball of wool that keeps winding itself up again, or fighting an army of slithery monsters that keep attacking you when you least expect it. But the results are a gradual waking up. The world no longer seems distant and unreal but the opposite – bright and real and vivid and alive – a little more like that original OBE. It's been a long road and I don't suppose I would ever have embarked on it if not for all the questions forced upon me by that brief experience.

Paying attention clearly and steadily to what is here right now banishes the tangly wool and disarms the slithery monsters. All those disparate thoughts, emotions and worries that otherwise keep running in our heads float through one vast space and seem to lose their power. This is called 'one mind' or 'one-pointedness' and is quite different from our usual harried, messy confusion. The world comes to seem more and more real and immediate. Body, self and world come together. They are all the same stuff – there is no longer a conscious me looking out at a real physical world but just all of this – whatever it is.

This is the slow change from duality to nonduality; from a world in which minds inhabit bodies towards one in which minds and bodies are fundamentally the same; from a world in which 'I' am in control of 'my' body towards one in which decisions just happen because they must. This is a radical change and a scary one. But we can cope! We can give up our childhood dualism; give up the idea of a unified and continuing inner self who is the wielder of free will and the subject of our experiences, and accept the scary view that neuroscience provides. Just as we have given up thinking of the earth as the centre of the universe, so we can give up our very natural but false intuitions about ourselves.

This is not easy because those intuitions are deeply ingrained. From a very young age children are mind-body dualists. For example, 3-year-olds readily distinguish between an object and an idea. When asked about either a cookie or a boy thinking about a cookie they can correctly reply that the cookie can be seen, touched and eaten while the thought of a cookie cannot. Three- to 5-year-olds appreciate that thoughts can be about impossible, non-existent things, such as a dog that flies, while real objects cannot (Wellman & Estes, 1986). Young children play with dolls and talk to teddy bears, they pretend tea-time and hospital, and some have imaginary playmates, but they don't confuse them with real people.

Modern children learn about brains at a young age but they still seem to imagine a 'me' whose brain it is and who is helped along by its clever powers. Psychologist Paul Bloom asked his 6-year-old son Max what the brain does. Max replied that it does 'millions of things', like seeing, hearing, smelling and thinking. But he said it is Max, not his brain, who goes to sleep, dreams, loves his brother and feels happy or sad. Bloom concludes that the natural conception of the brain by children is as a useful tool; 'a cognitive prosthesis, added to the soul to increase its computing power' (Bloom, 2004, p.201).

Many adults think like this too – believing that 'I' am the feeling, thinking person in charge. In this way, we turn our self into a supreme conscious entity living in, owning and controlling our bodies. It is no surprise, then, that having an OBE seems to confirm this ready illusion: 'I' have left my body so I must be an independent thinking and feeling soul. The reverse may also be true, that throughout the ages OBEs have inspired the idea of the soul (Tart, 1972, Metzinger, 2005). Either way, it's a quick jump to the false belief that the supreme conscious entity called 'me' can leave its bodily shell behind and go travelling. But it cannot: nothing can leave the body in an OBE because there is nothing there that could leave.

## Self as illusion

To call something an 'illusion' is not to say it does not exist, it means that it is not what it seems to be. My self *seems* to be a continuing conscious entity, a subject of experience and possessor of free will, but this is not true. The self is a representation or model of something that does not exist – but the model itself exists.

We now know a lot more about how this model is constructed, with processes in the TPJ building the body schema and linking to self-other distinctions and empathy. We are learning how this body schema is integrated into a full and rich model of 'myself' through its interactions with other parts of the brain, including the thalamus, limbic system and prefrontal cortex. It is this ability of a living system to model itself, not a soul or spirit, that is the foundation of self and consciousness.

This brings us back to the visions and insights of mystical experience and the effects of long-term meditation. In several religions the self is said to be illusory, including Advaita Vedanta in Hinduism and the Buddhist concept of anatta or 'no-self'. This is especially interesting here because the Buddha apparently told some people 'there is no self' and others 'there is a self' depending on their understanding.

Modern neuroscience says the same. In one sense there is a self – or, rather, lots of different selves. They are useful mental models of a continuing conscious entity. In another sense there is no self because these models are ephemeral constructions that arise and fall away, change and decay, and no such continuing powerful and unified conscious entity actually exists.

In *Buddha's Brain*, American psychologist and meditation teacher Rick Hanson explains that,

> the various aspects of the apparent self – and the intimate and powerful experience of *being* a self – exist as patterns in the mind and brain. The question is not whether those patterns exist (but) does that which those patterns seem to stand for – an "I" who is the unified, ongoing owner of experiences and agent of actions – truly exist? Or is the self like a unicorn, a mythical being whose representations exist but who is actually imaginary?
>
> Hanson, 2009, pp.208–9

I go for unicorns.

As well as mystics and meditators there have long been philosophers and scientists arguing against our self-centred intuitions. One of my great heroes, the 'founding father of American psychology', William James, claimed that *'thought is itself the thinker*, and psychology need not look beyond'. He believed that, 'The same brain may subserve many conscious selves' (James, 1890, i, 401). He rejected the idea of a 'substantial soul' and tried to understand how a 'stream of passing thoughts' becomes the one who thinks. But he did not have the benefit of the science we have today.

An even more challenging rejection is made by American philosopher Dan Dennett, who explicitly demands that we give up our intuitions and our lazy, easy ways of thinking (1991, and in Blackmore, 2005). He knows how hard it is to escape these false intuitions and proposes a series of 'intuition pumps' as tools for overthrowing them (Dennett, 2013). There is no 'Cartesian theatre' inside the brain, he says. This mythical place where 'I' reside, controlling 'my' actions and enjoying 'my' stream of consciousness is ever so easy to imagine. Yet neither the theatre nor its audience of one exists. The self is 'a benign user illusion', a necessary and effective illusion but an illusion none-theless (Dennett, 1991). Contrary to Dennett, I have argued that this self-illusion is far from benign and is ultimately the root of suffering, greed, hatred and delusion (Blackmore, 2000). Either way it's not what it seems to be.

In his famous 1979 book, *Gödel, Escher, Bach*, mathematician and cognitive scientist Douglas Hofstadter played with paradoxical self-referential sentences in 'a metaphorical fugue' on minds, machines, maths and music. In *I Am a Strange Loop* (2007) he describes the brain as a tangled hierarchy of loops; loops that turn back on themselves and paradoxical feedback loops that switch from level to level. So 'I' am just one of those; a strange loop, 'a mirage that perceives itself'.

In *The Illusion of Conscious Will*, psychologist Daniel Wegner (2002) demolishes the idea that our conscious thoughts cause our actions. We think they do only because thoughts often precede actions, making us jump to the conclusion that one caused the other when in reality both arise from underlying neural processes. This is why 'Our sense of being a conscious agent who does things comes at a cost of being technically wrong all the time' (2002, p.342). So the 'agent self' is a fabrication, a virtual agent, and 'The sense of *being an agent* creates our sense of subjective self and identity' (Wegner, 2002, p.263). This, of course, is the agent self who seems to leave the body.

These are just some of the ways in which today's scientists and philosophers are exploring the illusion of self but most draw no connection between the science and spiritual practice. Among those who do is American neuroscientist, atheist, meditator and philosopher Sam Harris. For him, the sense of being a subject or locus of consciousness inside the head makes no neuro-anatomical sense. 'There is no place for a soul inside your head' (Harris, 2014, p.205). Yet far from being diminishing, this realisation frees us from temptations that are so often exploited by oppressive religions; the idea of an eternal soul, the hope for life after death and the fear of punishment in hell. It directs us to live our lives learning and accepting who we are.

Another is German philosopher and long-term meditator Thomas Metzinger, whose book, *Being No One*, proclaims, 'Nobody ever was or had a self' (Metzinger, 2003). Selves just seem to be real and continuous because we confuse our Phenomenal Self Model (PSM) with what it represents. In this way we are trapped in our own 'ego tunnel' (Metzinger, 2009). Can we accept this un-religious view of ourselves and still have spiritual lives? Can we combine a secular spiritual practice with the scientific ideal of intellectual honesty? Metzinger points to the many bridges connecting spirituality with science and hopes that such honesty and self-knowledge can lead us to act well and 'perhaps even with inner affection and joy' (Metzinger, 2010).

V. S. Ramachandran was born in India and raised in the Hindu tradition, taught that the concept of the self – the 'I' within me that is aloof from the universe – is an illusion, a veil called *maya*, that when lifted reveals a self that is, 'One with the cosmos'. He says that, ironically, after all his extensive training in Western medicine and his research on neurological patients and visual illusions, he has come to think of free will as a 'post hoc rationalisation' and realises 'that the notion of a single unified self "inhabiting" the brain may indeed be an illusion' (Ramachandran & Blakeslee, 1998, p.227).

Does he find this hard to accept? Or depressing? No, not at all, he told me.

> I think it's a bit like the whole dance of Shiva thing, that you think you're an aloof spectator watching the universe . . . but if you think you're part of the ebb and flow of the cosmos, and there's no separate little soul, inspecting the world, that's going to be extinguished – then it's ennobling . . .
>
> (in Blackmore, 2005, p.196)

Although many people fear the consequences of accepting this idea, there really is no need. Giving up free will and living without its burden may be hard but is not impossible – I know, because that's how I live.

Oddly, I think this may have been a consequence of my OBE too. That amazing experience threw everything into question and left me pondering; Who am I? What's the point of it all? Who is in control? What is consciousness? And among the many other consequences of this determined questioning was the conclusion that free will cannot be what it seems to be and I would have to give it up. It really is possible to live happily and morally without free will (Blackmore, 2013).

## Bringing science and the OBE together

Something has finally happened that I hoped for but never really expected. From languishing far out on the fringes of science, studied by a few lone parapsychologists and rejected as fantasy by the majority of scientists and philosophers, the OBE is now fully involved in the science of mind and self.

OBE research, claims Metzinger, 'helps unveiling the fine-grained functional architecture underlying the conscious self-model of human beings' (Metzinger, 2005, p.75). OBEs show that you can represent something as being 'my body' even when 'you', your first-person perspective and your sense of agency are located elsewhere. And when Metzinger speaks of agency he means not just the ability to move and control a body but also cognitive and attentional agency – the ability to think and to direct attention. For him 'the experience of attentional agency may be the core of phenomenal selfhood and perspectivalness and the origin of all consciously experienced intentionality' (2005, p.77). This is a grand claim and one that brings research on OBEs right to the forefront of our attempts to understand self and consciousness.

Metzinger expands on my notion of how our 'model of reality' changes in OBEs (Blackmore, 1984b, 2009) to argue that when a self-model cannot be anchored in internal somatosensory input (for example, through disruption of the body schema), the brain searches for a maximally coherent global model of reality. Thinking and attention take over to stabilise that model and we experience ourselves as being outside it. No wonder people believe in souls, says Metzinger, for 'The soul is the OBE-PSM' (Metzinger, 2009, p.85). His 'self-model theory of subjectivity' comes close to something else I concluded

– that it is not physical human beings or cats, dogs or bats that have subjective experiences but the models they create of themselves. It is models of selves that are conscious, models of self that experience being out of the body.

We have come a long way from believing that having an OBE proves the existence of a soul or a conscious 'me' that can abandon its body and live on without it. Instead we find that our notions of self and consciousness have been, and are being, transformed. What seems so wonderful to me, after all these years, is that OBEs can now contribute to that transformation.

For me it's been a long journey. As Metzinger says, 'For anyone who actually had that type of experience it is almost impossible not to become an ontological dualist' (Metzinger, 2005, p.78) and I did. Like so many others who have OBEs I jumped to the obvious conclusion that my soul or astral body had left its physical shell and could think and feel and travel without it. It has taken a lot of thinking, experiencing, meditating and science for me to travel from that dualism to its utter rejection – to seeing the duality of body and mind, or physical and mental, as a feature of the way we model the world, not of the world itself. I no longer think that my soul left my body; that my astral body separated from its physical shell to travel on the astral planes or that my deep and unforgettable experience has anything to do with life after death. Thanks to decades of science and philosophy I have a far better idea of what happened to me during those special few hours back in 1970.

I am alive here and now in a vivid and colourful world. Yet the models that make up 'me' and my world will cease once this body dies. While it's alive they will carry on arising and falling away, arising and falling away to give the impression of a continuing and unified inner self that does not really exist. It is not this human being that is conscious. There is nothing it is like to be a bat, cat, dog or human being. There is only something it is like to be the stories we tell, or the models we construct, about what it's like to be me now. And that's enough.

# References

Adams, D. (1979). *The Hitchhiker's Guide to the Galaxy*. London, Pan.

Alcock, J. E. (1981). *Parapsychology: Science or Magic?* Oxford, Pergamon.

Alexander, E. (2012). *Proof of Heaven: A Neurosurgeon's Journey into the Afterlife*. New York, Simon & Schuster

Alsmith, A. J., & Longo, M. R. (2014). Where exactly am I? Self-location judgements distribute between head and torso. *Consciousness and Cognition, 24*, 70–74.

Alvarado, C. S. (1982). ESP during out-of-body experiences: A review of experimental studies. *The Journal of Parapsychology, 46:3*, 209.

Alvarado, C. S. (1984). Phenomenological aspects of out-of-body experiences: a report of three studies. *Journal of the American Society for Psychical Research, 78*, 219–240.

Alvarado, C. S. (2000). Out-of-body experiences. In *Varieties of Anomalous Experience*, Ed. E. Cardeña, S. J. Lynn, S. Krippner. Washington DC, American Psychological Association, 183–218.

Alvarado, C. S. (2001). Features of out-of-body experiences in relation to perceived closeness to death. *Journal of Nervous and Mental Disease, 189*, 331–332.

Alvarado, C. S. (2007). On the use of the term Out-of-Body Experience. *Journal of the Society for Psychical Research, 71*, 100–103.

Alvarado, C. S. (2012). Explorations of the features of out-of-body experiences: An overview and critique of the work of Robert Crookall, *Journal of the Society for Psychical Research, 65–82*.

Alvarado, C. S., & Zingrone, N. L. (1999). Out-of-body experiences among readers of a Spanish New Age magazine. *Journal of the Society for Psychical Research, 63*, 65–85.

# References

Alvarado, C. S., & Zingrone, N. L. (2015). Features of out-of-body experiences: Relationships to frequency, wilfulness and previous knowledge about the experience. *Journal of the Society for Psychical Research, 79*, 98–111.

Andrade, J., May, J., Deeprose, C., Baugh, S. J., & Ganis, G. (2014). Assessing vividness of mental imagery: the Plymouth sensory imagery questionnaire. *British Journal of Psychology, 105:4*, 547–563.

Anzellotti, F., Onofrj, V., Maruotti, V., Ricciardi, L., Franciotti, R., Bonanni, L., ... & Onofrj, M. (2011). Autoscopic phenomena: case report and review of literature. *Behavioral and Brain Functions, 7*(1), 2.

Arnold-Forster, H. O. (1921). *Studies in Dreams.* London, Allen and Unwin.

Arzy, S., Idel, M., Landis, T., & Blanke, O. (2005). Why revelations have occurred on mountains? Linking mystical experiences and cognitive neuroscience. *Medical Hypotheses, 65:5*, 841–845.

Arzy, S., Seeck, M., Ortigue, S., Spinelli, L., & Blanke, O. (2006). Induction of an illusory shadow person. *Nature, 443*, 287.

Asai, T., Mao, Z., Sugimori, E., & Tanno, Y. (2011). Rubber hand illusion, empathy, and schizotypal experiences in terms of self-other representations. *Consciousness and Cognition, 20:4*, 1744–1750.

Aspell, J. E., & Blanke, O. (2009). Understanding the out-of-body experience from a neuroscientific perspective, In *Psychological Scientific Perspectives on Out-of-body and Near-Death Experiences.* Ed. C.D. Murray, New York, Nova, 73–88.

Atwater, P. M. H. (1992). Is there a hell? Surprising observations about the near-death experience. *Journal of Near-Death Studies, 10*,149–160.

Augustine, K. (2007a). Does paranormal perception occur in near-death experiences? *Journal of Near-Death Studies, 25:4*, 203–236.

Augustine, K. (2007b). Near-death experiences with hallucinatory features. *Journal of Near-Death Studies. 26*, 3–31.

Augustine, K. (2007c). Psychophysiological and cultural correlates undermining a survivalist interpretation of near-death experiences. *Journal of Near-Death Studies, 26:2*, 89–125.

Austin, J. H. (2006). *Zen-brain Reflections: Reviewing Recent Developments in Meditation and States of Consciousness,* Cambridge, Mass, MIT Press.

Ayer, A. J. (1988). What I saw when I was dead, *Sunday Telegraph,* August 28th 1988.

Barrett, D. (1991). Flying dreams and lucidity: An empirical study of their relationship. *Dreaming, 1:2*, 129.

Barrett, W. F. (1926). *Death-bed Visions: The Psychical Experiences of the Dying.* London, Methuen.

Beauregard, M., & Paquette, V. (2006). Neural correlates of a mystical experience in Carmelite nuns. *Neuroscience Letters, 405*, 186–190.

Becker, C. B. (1982). The failure of Saganomics: Why birth models cannot explain near-death phenomena. *Anabiosis: Journal of Near-Death Studies*, 2, 102–109.

Becker, C. B. (1984). The Pure Land revisited: Sino-Japanese meditations and near-death experiences of the next world. *Anabiosis: The Journal of Near-Death Studies*, 4, 51–68.

Belanti, J., Perera, M., & Jagadheesan, K. (2008). Phenomenology of near-death experiences: a cross-cultural perspective. *Transcultural Psychiatry*, 45(1), 121–133.

Belanti, J., Jagadheesan, K., & Perera, M. (2009). Prevalence, phenomenology and biosocial aspects of the near-death experience. In *Psychological Scientific Perspectives on Out-of-body and Near-death Experiences*. Ed. C. D. Murray, New York, Nova, 117–27.

Bergson, H. (1896). *Matière et Mémoire*. Translated by Paul, N. M., & Palmer, W. S. as *Matter and Memory: Essay on the Relation of Body and Spirit*. Courier Corporation. 2004.

Bertossa, F., Besa, M., Ferrari, R., & Ferri, F. (2008). Point zero: a phenomenological inquiry into the seat of consciousness 1, 2. *Perceptual and Motor Skills*, 107:2, 323–335.

Besent, A. (1896). *Man and His Bodies*. London, Theosophical Publishing House.

Besteman, M. J. (2012). *My Journey to Heaven*. Grand Rapids, MI, Revell.

Blackmore, S. J. (1980a). A study of memory and ESP in young children. In: *Research in Parapsychology 1979* Ed. W. G. Roll, Metuchen, NJ, Scarecrow Press, 152–154.

Blackmore, S. J. (1980b). Correlations between ESP and Memory. *European Journal of Parapsychology*, 3, 127–147.

Blackmore, S. J. (1980c). *ESP as a cognitive process*, PhD thesis, University of Surrey.

Blackmore, S. J. (1981a). Errors and confusions in ESP. *European Journal of Parapsychology*, 4, 49–70.

Blackmore, S. J. (1981b). A survey of OBEs. *Research in Parapsychology 1980*. Ed. W. G. Roll and J. Beloff, Metuchen, NJ, Scarecrow Press, 105–106.

Blackmore, S. J. (1982a). *Beyond the Body*. London, Heinemann.

Blackmore, S. J. (1982b). Out-of-body experiences, lucid dreams, and imagery: Two surveys. *Journal of the American Society for Psychical Research*, 76, 301–317.

Blackmore, S. J. (1983a). Are out-of-the-body experiences evidence for survival? *Anabiosis*, 3, 137–155.

Blackmore, S. J. (1983b). Birth and the OBE: an unhelpful analogy. *Journal of the American Society for Psychical Research*, 77, 229–238.

Blackmore, S. J. (1984a). A postal survey of OBEs and other experiences. *Journal of the Society for Psychical Research*, 52, 225–244.

# References

Blackmore, S. J. (1984b). A psychological theory of the OBE. *Journal of Parapsychology, 48,* 201–218. Also reprinted, with new postscript, in *Psychological Scientific Perspectives on Out of Body and Near Death Experiences.* Ed. Craig D. Murray. New York, Nova, 2009.

Blackmore, S. J. (1986a). *The Adventures of a Parapsychologist.* Buffalo, New York, Prometheus.

Blackmore, S. J. (1986b). Where am I?: Perspectives in imagery, memory and the OBE. In: *Research in Parapsychology 1985.* Ed. D.Weiner and D.Radin, Metuchen, NJ, Scarecrow, 163–164.

Blackmore, S. J. (1986c). Out-of-body experiences in schizophrenia: a questionnaire survey. *Journal of Nervous and Mental Disease, 174,* 615–619.

Blackmore, S. J. (1986d). Spontaneous and deliberate OBEs: a questionnaire survey. *Journal of the Society for Psychical Research, 53,* 218–224.

Blackmore, S. J. (1987a). Where am I?: Perspectives in imagery, and the out-of-body experience. *Journal of Mental Imagery, 11,* 53–66.

Blackmore, S. J. (1987b). A report of a visit to Carl Sargent's laboratory. *Journal of the Society for Psychical Research, 54,* 186–198.

Blackmore, S. J. (1993a). *Dying to Live: Science and the Near Death Experience.* London, Grafton.

Blackmore, S. J. (1993b). Near-Death Experiences in India: They have tunnels too. *Journal of Near-Death Studies, 11,* 205–217.

Blackmore, S. J. (1994). Alien abduction. *New Scientist,* 19 November, 29–31.

Blackmore, S. J. (1995). Paying attention. *New Ch'an Forum, 12,* 9–15.

Blackmore, S. J. (1996). *In Search of the Light: The Adventures of a Parapsychologist.* Amherst, New York, Prometheus Books.

Blackmore, S. J. (1998). Abduction by aliens or sleep paralysis? *Skeptical Inquirer, 22,* 23–28.

Blackmore, S. J. (2000). Memes and the malign user illusion (abstract). *Consciousness and Cognition, 9,* S49.

Blackmore, S. J. (2005). *A Very Short Introduction to Consciousness.* Oxford, Oxford University Press.

Blackmore, S. J. (2009). A psychological theory of the OBE (reprinted, with new postscript) in *Psychological Scientific Perspectives on Out of Body and Near Death Experiences.* Ed. Craig D. Murray. New York, Nova, 23–36.

Blackmore, S. J. (2010). *Consciousness: An Introduction, Second Edition.* London, Hodder Education, and New York, Oxford University Press, 2011.

Blackmore, S. J. (2011). *Zen and the Art of Consciousness.* Oxford, Oneworld Publications.

Blackmore, S. J. (2013). Living without free will. In *Exploring the Illusion of Free Will and Moral Responsibility*. Ed. G. Caruso, Lanham, M.D., Lexington Books, 161–175.

Blackmore, S. J., & Cox, M. (2000). Alien abductions, sleep paralysis and the temporal lobe. *European Journal of UFO and Abduction Studies, 1,* 113–118.

Blackmore, S. J., & Harris, J. (1983). OBEs and perceptual distortions in schizophrenic patients and students. In *Research in Parapsychology 1982*. Ed. W. G. Roll, J. Beloff & R. A.White, Metuchen, NJ, Scarecrow, 232–234.

Blackmore, S. J., & Rose, N. J. (1997). Reality and Imagination: A psi-conducive confusion? *Journal of Parapsychology, 61,* 321–335.

Blackmore, S. J., & Troscianko, T. S. (1989). The Physiology of the Tunnel. *Journal of Near-Death Studies, 8,* 15–28.

Blanke, O. (2012). Multisensory brain mechanisms of bodily self-consciousness. *Nature Reviews Neuroscience, 13:8,* 556–571.

Blanke, O., & Arzy, S. (2005). The out-of-body experience: disturbed self-processing at the temporo-parietal junction. *The Neuroscientist, 11,* 16–24.

Blanke, O., Landis, T., Spinelli, L., & Seeck, M. (2004). Out-of-body experience and autoscopy of neurological origin. *Brain, 127:2,* 243–258.

Blanke, O., & Metzinger, T. (2009). Full-body illusions and minimal phenomenal selfhood. *Trends in Cognitive Sciences, 13:1,* 7–13.

Blanke, O., & Mohr, C. (2005). Out-of-body experience, heautoscopy, and autoscopic hallucination of neurological origin: Implications for neurocognitive mechanisms of corporeal awareness and self-consciousness. *Brain Research Reviews, 50*(1), 184–199.

Blanke, O., Mohr, C., Michel, C. M., Pascual-Leone, A., Brugger, P., Seeck, M., ... & Thut, G. (2005). Linking out-of-body experience and self processing to mental own-body imagery at the temporoparietal junction. *The Journal of Neuroscience, 25:3,* 550–557.

Blanke, O., Ortigue, S., Landis, T., & Seeck, M. (2002) Stimulating illusory own-body perceptions. *Nature, 419,* 269–70.

Bloom, P. (2004). *Descartes' Baby: How the science of child development explains what makes us human.* London, Heinemann.

Borjigin, J., Lee, U., Liu, T., Pal, D., Huff, S., Klarr, D., ... & Mashour, G. A. (2013). Surge of neurophysiological coherence and connectivity in the dying brain. *Proceedings of the National Academy of Sciences, 110,* 14432–14437.

Botvinick, M., & Cohen, J. (1998). Rubber hands 'feel' touch that eyes see. *Nature, 391:6669,* 756.

Bourdin, P., Barberia, I., Oliva, R., & Slater, M. (2017). A virtual out-of-body experience reduces fear of death. *PloS one, 12*(1), e0169343.

# References

Bourke, P., & Shaw, H. (2014). Spontaneous lucid dreaming frequency and waking insight. *Dreaming, 24*(2), 152.

Braithwaite, J. J. (2008). Towards a cognitive neuroscience of the dying brain. *Skeptic, 21,* 8–16.

Braithwaite, J. J., Samson, D., Apperly, I., Broglia, E., & Hulleman, J. (2011). Cognitive correlates of the spontaneous out-of-body experience (OBE) in the psychologically normal population: evidence for an increased role of temporal-lobe instability, body-distortion processing, and impairments in own-body transformations. *Cortex, 47*(7), 839–853.

Braithwaite, J. J., Broglia, E., Bagshaw, A. P., & Wilkins, A. J. (2013a). Evidence for elevated cortical hyperexcitability and its association with out-of-body experiences in the non-clinical population: new findings from a pattern-glare task. *Cortex, 49*(3), 793–805.

Braithwaite, J. J., Broglia, E., & Watson, D. G. (2014). Autonomic emotional responses to the induction of the rubber-hand illusion in those that report anomalous bodily experiences: Evidence for specific psychophysiological components associated with illusory body representations. *Journal of Experimental Psychology: Human Perception and Performance, 40*(3), 1131.

Braithwaite, J. J., James, K., Dewe, H., Medford, N., Takahashi, C., & Kessler, K. (2013b). Fractionating the unitary notion of dissociation: disembodied but not embodied dissociative experiences are associated with exocentric perspective-taking. *Frontiers in Human Neuroscience, 7,* 719.

Braithwaite, J. J., Mevorach, C., & Takahashi, C. (2015). Stimulating the aberrant brain: evidence for increased cortical hyperexcitability from a transcranial direct current stimulation (tDCS) study of individuals predisposed to anomalous perceptions. *Cortex, 69,* 1–13.

Braithwaite, J. J., Samson, D., Apperly, I., Broglia, E., & Hulleman, J. (2011). Cognitive correlates of the spontaneous out-of-body experience (OBE) in the psychologically normal population: evidence for an increased role of temporal-lobe instability, body-distortion processing, and impairments in own-body transformations. *Cortex, 47*(7), 839–853.

Brasington, L. (2015). *Right Concentration: A Practical Guide to the Jhanas.* Boston, Shambala.

Brennan, J. H. (1971). *Astral Doorways,* Wellingborough, Northants, Aquarian Press.

Brennan, J. H. (1989). *The Astral Projection Workbook.* Wellingborough, Northants, Aquarian Press.

Bressloff, P. C., Cowan, J. D., Golubitsky, M., Thomas, P. J., & Wiener, M. C. (2002). What geometric visual hallucinations tell us about the visual cortex. *Neural Computation, 14*(3), 473–491.

Briere, J. N., & Elliott, D. M. (1994). Immediate and long-term impacts of child sexual abuse. *The Future of Children*, 54–69.

Britton, W. B., & Bootzin, R. R. (2004). Near-death experiences and the temporal lobe. *Psychological Science, 15*(4), 254–258.

Brooks, P. L., & Peever, J. H. (2012). Identification of the transmitter and receptor mechanisms responsible for REM sleep paralysis. *The Journal of Neuroscience, 32*(29), 9785–9795.

Browne, S. (2002). *Sylvia Browne's Book of Dreams*. London, Piatkus.

Bruce, R. (1999). *Astral Dynamics: A New Approach to Out-of-body Experiences*. Newburyport, Mass, Hampton Roads.

Brugger, P. (2002). Reflective mirrors: perspective-taking in autoscopic phenomena. *Cognitive Neuropsychiatry, 7*(3), 179–194.

Brugger, P. (2006). From phantom limb to phantom body. In *Human Body Perception from the Inside Out*, Ed. G. Knoblich, Oxford, Oxford University Press, 171–209.

Brugger, P., Agosti, R., Regard, M., Wieser, H., & Landis, T. (1994). Heautoscopy, epilepsy and suicide. *Journal of Neurology, Neurosurgery and Psychiatry, 57*, 838–839.

Brugger, P., Regard, M., & Landis, T., (1996). Unilaterally felt 'presences': the neuropsychiatry of one's invisible Doppelgänger. *Neuropsychiatry, Neuropsychology, and Behavioral Neurology, 9*, 114–122.

Brugger, P., Regard, M., & Landis, T. (1997). Illusory reduplication of one's own body: phenomenology and classification of autoscopic phenomena. *Cognitive Neuropsychiatry, 2*(1), 19–38.

Brugger, P., Regard, M., Landis, T., & Oelz, O. (1999). Hallucinatory experiences in extreme-altitude climbers. *Cognitive and Behavioral Neurology, 12*(1), 67–71.

Bünning, S., & Blanke, O. (2005). The out-of body experience: precipitating factors and neural correlates. *Progress in Brain Research, 150*, 331–606.

Burpo, T. (2010). *Heaven is For Real: A little boy's astounding story of his trip to heaven and back*, Nashville, TN, Thomas Nelson.

Bush, N. E. (2002). Afterward: making meaning after a frightening near-death experience. *Journal of Near-Death Studies, 21*(2), 99–133.

Bush, N. E. (2012). *Dancing Past the Dark: Distressing near-death experiences*. BookBaby.

Callaway, J. C. (1999). Phytochemistry and neuropharmacology of ayahuasca. In R. Metzner (Ed) *Ayahuasca*, New York, Thunder's Mouth Press, 250–275.

Cardeña, E. (2005). The phenomenology of deep hypnosis: Quiescent and physically active. *International Journal of Clinical and Experimental Hypnosis, 53*(1), 37–59.

# References

Carhart-Harris, R. L., Muthukumaraswamy, S., Roseman, L., Kaelen, M., Droog, W., Murphy, K., ... & Leech, R. (2016). Neural correlates of the LSD experience revealed by multimodal neuroimaging. *Proceedings of the National Academy of Sciences, 113*(17), 4853–4858.

Carington, W. W. (1945). *Telepathy: An Outline of Its Facts, Theory, and Implications.* London, Methuen.

Carrington, H. (1919). *Modern Psychical Phenomena.* London, Kegan Paul.

Carroll, R. T. (2003). *The Skeptic's Dictionary: A Collection of Strange Beliefs, Amusing Deceptions, and Dangerous Delusions.* Wiley.

Carter, C. (2012). *Science and the Afterlife Experience: Evidence for the Immortality of Consciousness.* Vermont, Inner Traditions.

Chalmers, D. J. (1995). Facing up to the problem of consciousness. *Journal of Consciousness Studies, 2,* 200–219.

Charland-Verville, V., Jourdan, J. P., Thonnard, M., Ledoux, D., Donneau, A. F., Quertemont, E., & Laureys, S. (2014). Near-death experiences in non-life-threatening events and coma of different etiologies. *Frontiers in Human Neuroscience, 8.*

Charland-Verville, V., Lugo, Z., Jourdan, J. P., Donneau, A. F., & Laureys, S. (2015). Near-Death Experiences in patients with locked-in syndrome: Not always a blissful journey. *Consciousness and Cognition, 34,* 28–32.

Charman, R. A. (2013). Did Mrs Wilmot cross the sea during an OBE in the pre-dawn hours of 14th October 1863 to visit Mr Wilmot? *Journal of the Society for Psychical Research, 77,* 164.

Chawla, L. S., Akst, S., Junker, C., Jacobs, B. & Seneff, M. G. (2009). Surges of Electroencephalogram Activity at the Time of Death: A Case Series. *Journal of Palliative Medicine, 12,* 1095–1100.

Chee, M. W., & Chuah, Y. L. (2007). Functional neuroimaging and behavioral correlates of capacity decline in visual short-term memory after sleep deprivation. *Proceedings of the National Academy of Sciences, 104*(22), 9487–9492.

Cheyne, J. A. (2003). Sleep paralysis and the structure of waking-nightmare hallucinations. *Dreaming, 13*(3), 163.

Cheyne, J. A., & Girard, T. A. (2009). The body unbound: Vestibular–motor hallucinations and out-of-body experiences. *Cortex, 45*(2), 201–215.

Cheyne, J. A., Rueffer, S. D., & Newby-Clark, I. R. (1999). Hypnagogic and hypnopompic hallucinations during sleep paralysis: neurological and cultural construction of the night-mare. *Consciousness and Cognition, 8*(3), 319–337.

Clark, K. (1984). Clinical interventions with near-death experiencers. *The Near-Death Experience: Problems, prospects, perspectives.* Springfield, Charles C Thomas, 242–255.

Conway, D. (1974). *Magic: An Occult Primer.* London, Jonathan Cape.

Cook, A. M., & Irwin, H. J. (1983). Visuospatial skills and the out-of-body experience. *Journal of Parapsychology*, 47(1), 23–35.

Corazza, O., & Schifano, F. (2010). Ketamine use: a prospective study on the emergence of near-death states among a group of 50 ketamine recreational users. *Substance Use & Misuse*, 45, 916–924.

Cowan, J. D. (1982). Spontaneous symmetry breaking in large scale nervous activity. *International Journal of Quantum Chemistry*, 22(5), 1059–1082.

Craffert, P. F. (2015). Do out-of-body and near-death experiences point towards the reality of nonlocal consciousness? A critical evaluation. *The Journal for Transdisciplinary Research in Southern Africa*, 11(1), 1–20.

Critchley, M. (1950). The body image in neurology. *Lancet*, 1:335–340.

Critchley, M. (1953). *The Parietal Lobes*. New York, Macmillan.

Crookall, R. (1961a). *The Study and Practice of Astral Projection*. Wellingborough, Northants, Aquarian Press.

Crookall, R. (1961b). *The Supreme Adventure*. London: James Clarke.

Crookall, R. (1964). *The Techniques of Astral Projection: Denouement after Fifty Years*. Wellingborough, Northants, Aquarian Press

Crookall, R. (1968). *The Mechanisms of Astral Projection: Denouement after Seventy Years*. Moradabad, India: Darshana International.

Crookall, R. (1969). *The Interpretation of Cosmic and Mystical Experiences*. Cambridge, England, James Clarke.

Curran, H. V., & Morgan, C. (2000). Cognitive, dissociative and psychotogenic effects of ketamine in recreational users on the night of drug use and 3 days later. *Addiction*, 95(4), 57–-590.

Cytowic, R. E., & Eagleman, D. M. (2009). *Wednesday is Indigo Blue: Discovering the Brain of Synesthesia*, Cambridge, MA, MIT Press.

Dahlitz, M., & Parkes, J. D. (1993). Sleep paralysis. *Lancet*, 341(8842), 406–407.

Davies, O. (1996). Hag-riding in Nineteenth-Century West Country England and Modern Newfoundland: An Examination of an Experience-Centred Witchcraft Tradition. *Folk Life*. 35. 36–53.

De Araujo, D. B., Ribeiro, S., Cecchi, G. A., Carvalho, F. M., Sanchez, T. A., Pinto, J. P., ... & Santos, A. C. (2012). Seeing with the eyes shut: Neural basis of enhanced imagery following ayahuasca ingestion. *Human Brain Mapping*, 33(11), 2550–2560.

De Foe, A., Van Doorn, G., & Symmons, M. (2012). Auditory hallucinations predict likelihood of out-of-body experience. *Australian Journal of Parapsychology*, 12(1), 59.

De Ridder, D., Van Laere, K., Dupont, P., Menovsky, T., & Van de Heyning, P. (2007). Visualizing out-of-body experience in the brain. *New England Journal of Medicine*, 357(18), 1829–1833.

# References

De Rochas, A. (1906). New Experiments Relative to the Astral Body and the Magnetic 'Rapport'. *Annals of Psychical Science, 4,* 120–5.

De Saint-Denys, H. (1982). *Dreams and How to Guide Them.* London, Duckworth.

De Vesme, C. (1906). The sensation of flying during sleep. *Annals of Psychical Science, 4,* 325–331.

Decety, J., & Lamm, C. (2007). The role of the right temporoparietal junction in social interaction: how low-level computational processes contribute to meta-cognition. *The Neuroscientist, 13*(6), 580–593.

Delage, Y. (1919). *Le rêve: étude psychologique, philosophique et littéraire.* Paris, Les Presses Universitaires de France.

Den Boon, F. S., Werkman, T. R., Schaafsma-Zhao, Q., Houthuijs, K., Vitalis, T., Kruse, C. G., ... & Chameau, P. (2015). Activation of type-1 cannabinoid receptor shifts the balance between excitation and inhibition towards excitation in layer II/III pyramidal neurons of the rat prelimbic cortex. *Pflügers Archiv-European Journal of Physiology, 467*(7), 1551–1564.

Dennett, D. C. (1991). *Consciousness Explained.* London, Little, Brown & Co.

Dennett, D. C. (2013). *Intuition Pumps and Other Tools for Thinking.* New York, Norton

Dharani, N. E. (2005). The role of vestibular system and the cerebellum in adapting to gravitoinertial, spatial orientation and postural challenges of REM sleep. *Medical Hypotheses, 65*(1), 83–89.

Dillon, P., Copeland, J., & Jansen, K. (2003). Patterns of use and harms associated with non-medical ketamine use. *Drug and Alcohol Dependence, 69*(1), 23–28.

Dobson, M., Tattersfield, A. E., Adler, M. W., & McNicol, M. W. (1971). Attitudes and long-term adjustment of patients surviving cardiac arrest. *British Medical Journal, 3*(5768), 207–212.

Dossey, L. (1989). *Recovering the Soul: A Scientific and Spiritual Search.* New York, Bantam.

Dossey, L. (1991). Personal communication.

Drab, K. J. (1981). The tunnel experience: Reality or hallucination? *Anabiosis: The Journal of Near-Death Studies, 1,* 126–152.

Dresler, M., Wehrle, R., Spoormaker, V. I., Koch, S. P., Holsboer, F., Steiger, A., ... & Czisch, M. (2012). Neural correlates of dream lucidity obtained from contrasting lucid versus non-lucid REM sleep: a combined EEG/fMRI case study. *Sleep, 35*(7), 1017–1020.

Dittrich, L. (2013). The prophet, *Esquire,* 2.7.2013.

Druss, R. G., & Kornfeld, D. S. (1967). The survivors of cardiac arrest: A psychiatric study. *JAMA, 201*(5), 291–296.

Dumas, P., Saoud, M., Bouafia, S., Gutknecht, C., Ecochard, R., Daléry, J., ... & d'Amato, T. (2002). Cannabis use correlates with schizotypal personality traits in healthy students. *Psychiatry Research, 109*(1), 27–35.

Dunbar, E. (1905). The light thrown on psychological processes by the action of drugs *Proceedings of the Society for Psychical Research, 19,* 62–77.

Durville, H. (1908). New Experiments with Phantoms of the Living, *Annals of Psychical Science, 7,* 464–470.

Earleywine, M. (2002). *Understanding Marijuana: A New Look at the Scientific Evidence,* New York, Oxford University Press.

Eastman, M. (1962). Out-of-the-Body Experiences. *Proceedings of the Society for Psychical Research, 53,* 287–309.

Easton, S., Blanke, O., & Mohr, C. (2009). A putative implication for fronto-parietal connectivity in out-of-body experiences. *Cortex, 45*(2), 216–227.

Ebbern, H., Mulligan, S., & Beyerstein, B. (1996). Maria's near-death experience: Waiting for the other shoe to drop. *Skeptical Inquirer, 20,* 27–33.

Ehrsson, H. H. (2007). The experimental induction of out-of-body experiences. *Science, 317*(5841), 1048.

Erlacher, D., Schädlich, M., Stumbrys, T., & Schredl, M. (2014). Time for actions in lucid dreams: effects of task modality, length, and complexity. *Frontiers in Psychology, 4,* 1013.

Erlacher, D., & Schredl, M. (2004). Time required for motor activity in lucid dreams, *Perceptual and Motor Skills, 99,* 1239–1242.

Erlacher, D., Stumbrys, T., & Schredl, M. (2012). Frequency of lucid dreams and lucid dream practice in German athletes. *Imagination, Cognition and Personality, 31*(3), 237–246.

Ermentrout, G. B., & Cowan, J. D. (1979). A mathematical theory of visual hallucination patterns. *Biological Cybernetics, 34*(3), 137–150.

Faraday, M. (1853). Experimental investigations of table moving. *The Athenaeum,* 801–803.

Fenwick, P., & Fenwick, E. (1995). *The Truth in the Light.* London, Headline.

Findlay, A. (1931). *On the Edge of the Etheric or Survival after Death Scientifically Explained.* London, Psychic Press

Flynn, C. P. (1982). Meanings and implications of NDEr transformations: some preliminary findings and implications. *Anabiosis: The Journal of Near-Death Studies, 2,* 3-13.

Fontana, D. (1991). A responsive poltergeist: A case from South Wales. *Journal of the Society for Psychical Research,* Vol 57(823), 385–402.

Fontana, D. (2007). Mystical experience. In *The Blackwell Companion to Consciousness* Ed. Velmans, M. and Schneider, S. Oxford, Blackwell 163–172.

# References

Fortune, D. (1930). *Psychic Self-Defence: A Study in Occult Pathology and Criminality.* Wellingborough, Northants, Aquarian Press

Fox, O. (1920). The pineal doorway. *Occult Review, 31,* 256–264.

Fox, O. no date. *Astral Projection.* London, Rider & Co.

French, C. C. (2001). Dying to know the truth: Visions of a dying brain, or false memories? *Lancet, 358,* 2010–2011.

French, C. C. (2003). Fantastic memories: The relevance of research into eyewitness testimony and false memories for reports of anomalous experiences. *Journal of Consciousness Studies, 10*(6–7), 153–74.

French, C. C. (2005). Near-death experiences in cardiac arrest survivors. *Progress in Brain Research, 150,* 351–367.

French, C. C. (2009). Near-death experiences and the brain. In *Psychological Scientific Perspectives on Out-of-body and Near-Death Experiences.* Ed. C.D. Murray, New York, Nova, 187–203.

Fukuda, K., Miyasita, A., Inugami, M., & Ishihara, K. (1987). High prevalence of isolated sleep paralysis: Kanashibari phenomenon in Japan. *Sleep, 10,* 279–286

Furlanetto, T., Bertone, C., & Becchio, C. (2013). The bilocated mind: new perspectives on self-localization and self-identification. *Frontiers in Human Neuroscience, 7,* 71.

Gabbard, G. O., & Twemlow, S. W. (1984). *With the Eyes of the Mind.* New York, Praeger.

Gabbard, G. O., Twemlow, S. W., & Jones, F. C. (1981). Do 'Near Death Experiences' Occur Only Near Death?. *The Journal of Nervous and Mental Disease, 169*(6), 374–377.

Gackenbach, J. (2006). Video game play and lucid dreams: Implications for the development of consciousness. *Dreaming, 16*(2), 96.

Gackenbach, J., & Bosveld, J. (1989). *Control your dreams.* New York, Harper.

Gallup Jr, G., & Proctor, W. (1982). *Adventures in Immortality.* New York, McGraw-Hill.

Ganesh, S., van Schie, H. T., de Lange, F. P., Thompson, E., & Wigboldus, D. H. (2012). How the human brain goes virtual: distinct cortical regions of the person-processing network are involved in self-identification with virtual agents. *Cerebral Cortex, 22*(7), 1577–1585.

Gasser, P., Holstein, D., Michel, Y., Doblin, R., Yazar-Klosinski, B., Passie, T., & Brenneisen, R. (2014). Safety and efficacy of lysergic acid diethylamide-assisted psychotherapy for anxiety associated with life-threatening diseases. *The Journal of Nervous and Mental Disease, 202*(7), 513.

Germine, L., Benson, T. L., Cohen, F., & Hooker, C. I. L. (2013). Psychosis-proneness and the rubber hand illusion of body ownership. *Psychiatry Research, 207*(1), 45–52.

Gissurarson, L. R. and Gunnarsson, A. (1997). An experiment with the alleged human aura. *Journal of the American Society for Psychical Research, 91,* 33–49.

Glaskin, G. M. (1974). *Windows of the Mind: The Christos Experience.* London, Wildwood.

Goldie, E. A. G. (1941). The Clinical Manifestations of Oxygen Lack, *Proceedings of the Royal Society of Medicine, 34*(10), 631.

Gordon, R. (1949). An investigation into some of the factors that favour the formation of stereotyped images. *British Journal of Psychology, 39,* 156–167.

Gow, K., Lang, T., & Chant, D. (2004). Fantasy proneness, paranormal beliefs and personality features in out-of-body experiences. *Contemporary Hypnosis, 21*(3), 107–125.

Green, C. E. (1966). Spontaneous 'Paranormal' Experiences in Relation to Sex and Academic Background, *Journal of the Society for Psychical Research, 43,* 357–63.

Green, C. E. (1967). Ecsomatic Experiences and Related Phenomena. *Journal of the Society for Psychical Research, 44,* 111–31.

Green, C. E. (1968a). *Out-of-the-body Experiences.* London, Hamish Hamilton.

Green, C. E. (1968b). *Lucid Dreams.* London, Hamish Hamilton.

Green, C. E., & McCreery, C. (1994). *Lucid Dreaming: The Paradox of Consciousness During Sleep.* London, Routledge.

Gregory, R. L. (1986). *Odd Perceptions.* London, Routledge.

Grey, M. (1985). *Return from Death: An Exploration of the Near-Death Experience.* London, Arkana.

Greyson, B. (1981). Near-Death Experiences and Attempted Suicide. *Suicide and life-threatening behavior, 11*(1), 10–16.

Greyson, B. (1983). The Near-Death Experience Scale: Construction, Reliability, and Validity. *The Journal of Nervous and Mental Disease, 171*(6), 369–375.

Greyson, B. (2000). Dissociation in people who have near-death experiences: out of their bodies or out of their minds? *The Lancet, 355*(9202), 460–463.

Greyson, B. (2003). Incidence and correlates of near-death experiences in a cardiac care unit. *General Hospital Psychiatry, 25*(4), 269–276.

Greyson, B. (2007). Consistency of near-death experience accounts over two decades: Are reports embellished over time? *Resuscitation, 73*(3), 407–411.

Greyson, B. (2010). Hypercapnia and hypokalemia in near-death experiences. *Critical Care, 14*(3), 1.

Greyson, B., & Stevenson, I. (1980). The phenomenology of near-death experiences. *The American Journal of Psychiatry. 137*(10), 1193–1196.

Greyson, B., & Bush, N.E. (1992). Distressing near-death experiences. *Psychiatry, 55*(1), 95–110.

# References

Greyson, B., Fountain, N. B., Derr, L. L., & Broshek, D. K. (2014). Out-of-body experiences associated with seizures. *Frontiers in Human Neuroscience, 8.*

Greyson, B., Kelly, E. F., & Dunseath, W. R. (2013). Surge of neurophysiological activity in the dying brain. *Proceedings of the National Academy of Sciences, 110*(47), E4405.

Griffith, R. M. (1958). Typical dreams: A statistical study of personality correlates. *Dissertation Abstracts, 18,* 1106.

Grof, S. (1975). *Realms of the Unconscious: Observations from LSD Research,* New York, Viking Press.

Grof, S., & Halifax, J. (1977). *The Human Encounter with Death.* Dutton, New York.

Gurney, E., Myers, F.W., & Podmore, F. (1886). *Phantasms of the Living.* London, Trubner & Co.

Guterstam, A., & Ehrsson, H. H. (2012). Disowning one's seen real body during an out-of-body illusion. *Consciousness and Cognition, 21*(2), 1037–1042.

Hagerty, M. R., Isaacs, J., Brasington, L., Shupe, L., Fetz, E. E., & Cramer, S. C. (2013). Case study of ecstatic meditation: fMRI and EEG evidence of self-stimulating a reward system. *Neural plasticity.*

Hall, C., & Van de Castle, R. (1966). *The Content Analysis of Dreams.* New York, Appleton-Century-Crofts.

Hänsell, A., Lenggenhagerl, B., Känell, R., Curatolol, M., & Blankel, O. (2011). Seeing and identifying with a virtual body decreases pain perception. *European Journal of Pain, 15*(8), 874–879.

Hanson, R. (2009). *Buddha's Brain: The practical neuroscience of happiness, love, and wisdom.* Oakland, CA, New Harbinger.

Haraldsson, E. (1985). Representative national surveys of psychic phenomena: Iceland, Great Britain, Sweden, USA and Gallup's multinational survey. *Journal of the Society for Psychical Research, 53,* 145–158.

Haraldsson, E. (1988). *Modern Miracles: The Story of Sathya Sai Baba, a Modern Day Prophet.* New edition 2013, Hove, Sussex, UK, White Crow Books.

Haraldsson, E., Gudmundsdottir, A., Ragnarsson, A., Loftsson, J., & Jonsson, S. (1977). National survey of psychical experiences and attitudes towards the paranormal in Iceland. In *Research in Parapsychology 1976,* Ed. J. D. Morris, W. G. Roll, and R. L. Morris. Metuchen, NJ, Scarecrow Press, 182–186.

Harary, K. and Weintraub, P. (1990). *Have an Out-of-body Experience in 30 Days: The Free Flight Programme.* Wellingborough, Northants, Aquarian Press.

Harris, S. (2014). *Waking Up: A Guide to Spirituality Without Religion.* New York, Simon & Schuster.

Hart, H. (1954). ESP projection: spontaneous cases and the experimental method. *Journal of the American Society for Psychical Research, 48,* 121–146.

Hartmann, E. (1975). Dreams and other hallucinations: An approach to the underlying mechanism. In R. K. Siegel and L. J. West (Eds) *Hallucinations: Behaviour, Experience and Theory*. New York, Wiley, 71–79.

Hartwell, J., Janis, J., & Harary, S. B. (1975), A Study of the Physiological Variables Associated with Out-of-Body Experiences, In *Research in Parapsychology 1974*, Ed. J. D. Morris, W. G. Roll and R. L. Morris, Metuchen, NJ, Scarecrow Press, 1975, 127–129.

Hearne, K. M. T. (1978). *Lucid Dreams: An Electrophysiological and Psychological Study*. Unpublished PhD thesis, University of Liverpool.

Hearne, K. M. T. (1981). Lucid Dreams and ESP: An Initial Experiment Using One Subject *Journal of the Society for Psychical Research*. 51, 7–11.

Hearne, K. (1990). The dream machine. *Lucid Dreams and How to Control Them*. Wellingborough, Northants, Aquarian Press.

Heydrich, L., Lopez, C., Seeck, M., & Blanke, O. (2011). Partial and full own-body illusions of epileptic origin in a child with right temporoparietal epilepsy. *Epilepsy & Behavior, 20(3)*, 583–586.

Hill, J. A. (1918). *Man is a Spirit, a Collection of Spontaneous Cases of Dreams, Vision, and Ecstasy*. London, Cassell.

Hofmann, A. (1980). *LSD: My Problem Child*. New York, McGraw-Hill.

Hofstadter, D. R. (1979). *Godel, Escher, Bach: An Eternal Golden Braid*. Penguin.

Hofstadter, D. R. (2007). *I am a Strange Loop*. New York, Basic Books.

Holzinger, B., LaBerge, S., & Levitan, L. (2006). Psychophysiological correlates of lucid dreaming. *Dreaming, 16(2)*, 88.

Honegger, B. (1983). The OBE as a near-birth experience. In *Research in Parapsychology 1982*. Ed. Roll, W. G., Beloff, J., & White, R. A. Metuchen, NJ, Scarecrow Press, 230–231.

Hopkins, B., Jacobs, D. M., & Westrum, R. (1992). *Unusual Personal Experiences: An analysis of data from three National surveys conducted by the Roper Organization*. Bigelow Holding Corporation, Nevada.

Horikawa, T., Tamaki, M., Miyawaki, Y., & Kamitani, Y. (2013). Neural decoding of visual imagery during sleep. *Science, 340(6132)*, 639–642.

Hufford, D. J. (1982). *The Terror That Comes in the Night*. Philadelphia, University of Pennsylvania Press.

Inugami, M., & Ma, T. I. M. (2002). Factors related to the occurrence of isolated sleep paralysis elicited during a multi-phasic sleep-wake schedule. *Sleep, 25(1)*, 89.

Ionta, S., Heydrich, L., Lenggenhager, B., Mouthon, M., Fornari, E., Chapuis, D., ... & Blanke, O. (2011). Multisensory mechanisms in temporo-parietal cortex support self-location and first-person perspective. *Neuron, 70(2)*, 363–374.

# References

Irwin, H. J. (1980). Out of the body Down Under: Some cognitive characteristics of Australian students reporting OOBEs. *Journal of the Society for Psychical Research*, 50, 448–459.

Irwin, H. J. (1985). *Flight of Mind*. Metuchen, NJ, Scarecrow.

Irwin, H. J. (1986). Perceptual perspective of visual imagery in OBEs, dreams and reminiscence. *Journal of the Society for Psychical Research*, 53, 210–17.

Irwin H. J. (1987). Out-of-body experiences in the blind. *Journal of Near-Death Studies*, 6, 53–60.

Irwin, H. J. (2000). The disembodied self: an empirical study of dissociation and the out-of-body experience. *Journal of Parapsychology*, 64(3), 261–278.

Irwin, H. J., & Watt, C. A. (2007). *An Introduction to Parapsychology*. Jefferson, NC, McFarland.

Jacobs, S. (2013). *Astral Projection: How to have an out-of-body experience in 30 days*. CreateSpace Independent Publishing Platform.

Jalal, B., Simons-Rudolph, J., Jalal, B., & Hinton, D. E. (2014a). Explanations of sleep paralysis among Egyptian college students and the general population in Egypt and Denmark. *Transcultural Psychiatry*, 51(2), 158–175.

Jalal, B., Taylor, C. T., & Hinton, D. E. (2014b). A Comparison of Self-Report and Interview Methods for Assessing Sleep Paralysis: Pilot Investigations in Denmark and the United States. *Journal of Sleep Disorders*, 3: 1, 9–13.

James, W. (1890). *The Principles of Psychology*. London, MacMillan.

James, W. (1902). *The Varieties of Religious Experience: A Study in Human Nature*. London, Longmans, Green & Co.

Jansen, K. (2001). *Ketamine: Dreams and Realities*. Sarasota, FL, Multidisciplinary Association for Psychedelic Studies.

Johnson, M. K., & Raye, C. L. (1981). Reality monitoring. *Psychological Review*, 88(1), 67.

Johnstone, B., & Glass, B. A. (2008). Support for a neuropsychological model of spirituality in persons with traumatic brain injury. *Zygon*, 43(4), 861–874.

Jones, L. (2016) Final year dissertation, University of Plymouth.

Judson, I. R., & Wiltshaw, E. (1983). A near-death experience. *The Lancet*, 322(8349), 561–562.

Kahan, T. L., & LaBerge, S. (1994). Lucid dreaming as metacognition: Implications for cognitive science. *Consciousness and Cognition*, 3(2), 246–264.

Katz, J., Saadon-Grosman, N., & Arzy, S. (2017). The life review experience: Qualitative and quantitative characteristics. *Consciousness and Cognition*, 48, 76–86.

Kellehear, A. (2008). Census of non-Western near-death experiences to 2005: Overview of the current data. *Journal of Near-Death Studies*, 26(4), 249–265.

Kelly, E. F., Kelly, E. W., Crabtree, A., Gauld, A., Grosso, M., & Greyson, B. (2007) *Irreducible Mind: Toward a Psychology for the 21st Century*. Lanham, MD, Rowman & Littlefield.

Kessler, K., & Braithwaite, J. (2016). Deliberate and spontaneous sensations of disembodiment: capacity or flaw? *Cognitive Neuropsychiatry*, 21(5), 412–428.

Klemenc-Ketis, Z., Kersnik, J., & Grmec, S. (2010). The effect of carbon dioxide on near-death experiences in out-of-hospital cardiac arrest survivors: a prospective observational study. *Critical Care*, 14(2), 1.

Klüver, H. (1926). Mescal visions and eidetic vision, *American Journal of Psychology*, 37, 502–515.

Klüver, H. (1966). *Mescal and Mechanisms of Hallucinations*. Chicago, University of Chicago Press

Koestler, A. (1954). *The Invisible Writing*. London, Collins & Hamish.

Kohr, R. L. (1980). A survey of psi experiences among members of a special population. *Journal of the American Society for Psychical Research*, 74, 395–411.

Kohr, R. L. (1983). Near-death experiences, altered states, and psi sensitivity, *Journal of Near-Death Studies*, 3, 157–176.

Kölmel, H.W. (1985). Complex visual hallucinations in the hemianopic field. *Journal of Neurology, Neurosurgery and Psychiatry*, 48, 29–38.

Kroth, J., Mann, S., Cervantes, C., Jaffe, M., & Ristic, V. (2010). Financial stress, attitudes toward money, and scores on a dream inventory. *Psychological Reports*, 107, 173–176.

Kübler-Ross, E. (1967). Life, death and life after death, recorded lecture distributed by Friends of Shanti Nilaya, London.

Kübler-Ross, E. (1975). Foreword. In Moody, R. A. *Life after Life*. Atlanta, GA, Mockingbird.

LaBerge, S. P. (1980). *Lucid Dreaming: An Exploratory Study of Consciousness During sleep*. PhD thesis, Stanford University.

LaBerge, S. (1985). *Lucid Dreaming: The power of being awake and aware in your dreams*. Los Angeles, Tarcher.

LaBerge, S. (1988). The psychophysiology of lucid dreaming. In *Conscious Mind, Sleeping Brain*, Ed. J. Gackenbach, Springer New York, 135–153.

LaBerge, S., & Dement, W. C. (1982a). Voluntary control of respiration during REM sleep. *Sleep Research*, 11, 107.

LaBerge, S., & Dement, W. C. (1982b). Lateralization of alpha activity for dreamed singing and counting during REM sleep. *Psychophysiology*, 19, 331–332.

LaBerge, S., Levitan, L., & Dement, W. C. (1986). Lucid dreaming: Physiological correlates of consciousness during REM sleep. *Journal of Mind and Behavior*, 7, 251–258.

LaBerge, S. P., Nagel, L. E., Dement, W. C., & Zarcone Jr, V. P. (1981). Lucid dreaming verified by volitional communication during REM sleep. *Perceptual and Motor Skills*, 52(3), 727–732.

# References

Lakatos, I. (1978). The methodology of scientific research programmes. *Philosophical Papers* Vol. 1, Cambridge, Cambridge University Press.

Laszlo, E (2014). *The Immortal Mind: Science and the Continuity of Consciousness beyond the Brain*, Inner Traditions, New York, Simon & Schuster.

Leadbeater, C. W. (1895). *The Astral Plane: Its scenery, inhabitants and phenomena.* London, Theosophical Publishing Society.

Lebedev, A. V., Kaelen, M., Lövdén, M., Nilsson, J., Feilding, A., Nutt, D. J., & Carhart-Harris, R. L. (2016). LSD-induced entropic brain activity predicts subsequent personality change. *Human Brain Mapping 37*(9), 3203–3213.

Lenggenhager, B., Mouthon, M., & Blanke, O. (2009). Spatial aspects of bodily self-consciousness. *Consciousness and Cognition, 18*(1), 110–117.

Lenggenhager, B., Tadi, T., Metzinger, T., & Blanke, O. (2007). Video ergo sum: manipulating bodily self-consciousness. *Science, 317*(5841), 1096–1099.

Levitan, L., & LaBerge, S. (1991). Other worlds: out-of-body experiences and lucid dreams. *Nightlight, 3* (2–3).

Limanowski, J. (2014). What can body ownership illusions tell us about minimal phenomenal selfhood? *Frontiers in Human Neuroscience, 8.*

Limanowski, J., & Hecht, H. (2011). Where do we stand on locating the self? *Psychology, 2*(4), 312.

Loftus, E. F., & Pickrell, J. E. (1995). The formation of false memories. *Psychiatric Annals, 25*(12), 720–725.

Long, J., & Holden, J. M. (2007). Does the arousal system contribute to near-death and out-of-body experiences? A summary and response. *Journal of Near-Death Studies, 25*(3), 135–169.

Lopez, C., Halje, P., & Blanke, O. (2008). Body ownership and embodiment: vestibular and multisensory mechanisms. *Neurophysiologie Clinique/Clinical Neurophysiology, 38*(3), 149–161.

Lorimer, D. (1990). *Whole in One.* London, Arkana.

Luke, D. P., & Terhune, D. B. (2013). The induction of synaesthesia with chemical agents: a systematic review. *Frontiers in Psychology, 4*, 753.

Lukianowicz, N. (1958). Autoscopic phenomena. *Arch Neurol Psychiatry, 80,* 199–220.

Luna, L. (2016). Some observations on the phenomenology of the ayahuasca experience. In Luna, L., & White, S. (Eds) 2016 *Ayahuasca Reader: Encounters with the Amazon's Sacred Vine.* Santa Fe, Synergetic Press, 690–771.

Luna, L., & White, S. (Eds) (2016). *Ayahuasca Reader: Encounters with the Amazon's Sacred Vine.* Santa Fe, Synergetic Press.

Malarkey, A., & Malarkey, K. (2010). *The Boy Who Came Back From Heaven.* Carol Stream, IL,Tyndale House.

Malcolm, N. (1959). *Dreaming.* London, Routledge & Kegan Paul.

Marks, D. F. (1973). Visual imagery differences in the recall of pictures. *British Journal of Psychology, 64*, 17–24.

Markwick, B. (1978). The Soal-Goldney experiments with Basil Shackleton: new evidence of data manipulation. *Proceedings of the Society for Psychical Research, 56*, 250–277.

Masters, R. E., & Houston, J. (1967). *The Varieties of Psychedelic Experience*. London, Anthony Blond.

Mavromatis, A. (Ed.). (1987). *Hypnagogia: The Unique State of Consciousness Between Wakefulness and Sleep*. London, Routledge.

McClenon, J. (2009). Near-death experiences, out-of-body experiences and social scientific paradigms. In *Psychological Scientific Perspectives on Out-of-body and Near-death Experiences*. Ed. C. D. Murray, New York, Nova, 129–143.

McCreery, C., & Claridge, G. (2002). Healthy schizotypy: The case of out-of-the-body experiences. *Personality and Individual Differences, 32*(1), 141–154.

McIntosh, A. (1979). The 'Christos' procedure: A novel ASC induction technique. *Psychoenergetic Systems, 3*, 377–392.

McNally, R. J., & Clancy, S. A. (2005). Sleep paralysis, sexual abuse, and space alien abduction. *Transcultural Psychiatry, 42*(1), 113–122.

Mead, G. R. S. (1919). *The Doctrine of the Subtle Body in Western Tradition*. London, Watkins.

Melzack, R. (1989). Phantom limbs, the self and the brain. *Canadian Psychology, 30*, 1–16.

Metzinger, T. (Ed.) (2003). *Being No One: The Self–Model Theory of Subjectivity*. Cambridge, MA, MIT Press.

Metzinger, T. (2005). Out-of-body experiences as the origin of the concept of a 'soul'. *Mind and Matter, 31*, 57–84.

Metzinger, T. (Ed.) (2009). *The Ego Tunnel: The science of the mind and the myth of the self*. New York, Basic Books.

Metzinger, T. (2013). Spirituality and Intellectual Honesty. *A Conference on 'Meditation und Wissenschaft'*. Berlin, 27 November 2010, 1–58.

Metzinger, T. K. (2013). Why are dreams interesting for philosophers? The example of minimal phenomenal selfhood, plus an agenda for future research. *Frontiers in Psychology, 4*, 746.

Metzner, R. (Ed) (1999). *Ayahuasca: Human Consciousness and the Spirits of Nature*. New York, Thunder's Mouth Press.

Milán, E. G., Iborra, O., Hochel, M., Artacho, M. R., Delgado-Pastor, L. C., Salazar, E., & González-Hernández, A. (2012). Auras in mysticism and synaesthesia: A comparison. *Consciousness and Cognition, 21*(1), 258–268.

Mitchell, J. (1973). Out-of-the-Body vision, *Psychic*, 4. Also in Rogo, D. S., Ed. *Mind Beyond the Body*. New York, Penguin, 1978, 154–169.

# References

Mitson, L., Ono, H., & Barbeito R. (1976). Three methods of measuring the location of the egocentre: Their reliability, comparative locations and inter-correlations. *Canadian Journal of Psychology, 30,* 1–8.

Monroe, R. A. (1971). *Journeys Out of the Body.* New York, Doubleday.

Monroe, R. A. (1985). *Far Journeys.* London, Souvenir Press.

Moody, R. A. (1975). *Life after Life.* Atlanta, GA, Mockingbird.

Morgan, C. J., & Curran, H. V. (2012). Ketamine use: a review. *Addiction, 107*(1), 27–38.

Morgan, H. L., Turner, D. C., Corlett, P. R., Absalom, A. R., Adapa, R., Arana, F. S., ... & Fletcher, P. C. (2011). Exploring the impact of ketamine on the experience of illusory body ownership. *Biological Psychiatry, 69*(1), 35–41.

Morris, R.L., Harary, S.B., Janis, J., Hartwell, J., & Roll, W.G. (1978). Studies of communication during out-of-body experiences *Journal of the American Society for Psychical Research, 72,* 1–22.

Morse, M. (1990). *Closer to the Light.* London, Souvenir.

Morse, M. (1992). *Transformed by the Light: The powerful effect of near-death experiences on people's lives.* New York, Villard.

Morse, M. (1994). Near-death experiences of children. *Journal of Pediatric Oncology Nursing, 11*(4), 139–144.

Muetzelfeldt, L., Kamboj, S. K., Rees, H., Taylor, J., Morgan, C. J. A., & Curran, H. V. (2008). Journey through the K-hole: phenomenological aspects of ketamine use. *Drug and Alcohol Dependence, 95*(3), 219–229.

Muldoon, S. (1936). *The Case for Astral Projection: Hallucination or reality?* Eden, NY, Aries Press.

Muldoon, S., & Carrington, H. (1929). *The Projection of the Astral Body.* London, Rider & Co.

Muldoon, S., & Carrington, H. (1951). *The Phenomena of Astral Projection.* London, Rider & Co.

Murphy, T. (2001). Near-death experiences in Thailand. *Journal of Near-Death Studies, 19*(3), 161–178.

Murray, C. D., & Fox, J. (2005). Dissociational body experiences: Differences between respondents with and without prior out-of-body-experiences. *British Journal of Psychology, 96*(4), 441–456.

Musso, F., Brinkmeyer, J., Ecker, D., London, M. K., Thieme, G., Warbrick, T., ... & Winterer, G. (2011). Ketamine effects on brain function – simultaneous fMRI/EEG during a visual oddball task. *Neuroimage, 58*(2), 508–525.

Muzur, A., Pace-Schott, E. F., & Hobson, J. A. (2002). The prefrontal cortex in sleep. *Trends in Cognitive Sciences, 6*(11), 475–481.

Myers, F. W. H. (1903). *Human Personality and its Survival of Bodily Death.* London, Longmans, Green, and Co.

Naiken, H. (2015). *Astral Travel: Perform Astral Projection in 3 Days or Less* (Kindle only).

Neal, M. C. (2011). *To Heaven and Back.* Colorado Springs, CO, WaterBrook Press.

Neher, A. (2011). *Paranormal and Transcendental Experience: A Psychological Examination.* New York, Dover Publications.

Nelson, K. (2010). *The Spiritual Doorway in the Brain.* New York, Dutton.

Nelson, K. R., Mattingly, M., Lee, S. A., & Schmitt, F. A. (2006). Does the arousal system contribute to near death experience? *Neurology, 66*(7), 1003–1009.

Newberg, A., & D'Aquili, E. G. (2001) *Why God Won't Go Away: Brain Science and the Biology of Belief.* New York, Ballantine.

Newberg, A., Pourdehnad, M., Alavi, A., & D'Aquili, E. G. (2003). Cerebral blood flow during meditative prayer: preliminary findings and methodological issues. *Perceptual and Motor Skills, 97*(2), 625–630.

Nishimoto, S., Vu, A. T., Naselaris, T., Benjamini, Y., Yu, B., & Gallant, J. L. (2011). Reconstructing visual experiences from brain activity evoked by natural movies. *Current Biology, 21*(19), 1641–1646.

Noyes, R., & Kletti, R. (1972). The experience of dying from falls. *OMEGA-Journal of Death and Dying, 3*(1), 45–52.

Noyes, R., & Slymen, D. J. (1979). The subjective response to life-threatening danger. *OMEGA-Journal of Death and Dying, 9*(4), 313–321.

Ophiel (1961). *The Art and Practice of Astral Projection.* New York, Samuel Weiser.

Osis, K. (1975). Perceptual Experiments on Out-of-Body Experiences. In *Research in Parapsychology 1974.* Morris, J. D., Roll, W. G., & Morris, R. L. eds. Metuchen, NJ, Scarecrow Press, 53–55.

Osis, K. (1979). Insiders' Views of the OBE: A Questionnaire Survey. In *Research in Parapsychology 1978.* Ed. W.G. Roll, Metuchen, N J, Scarecrow Press, 50–52.

Osis, K., & Haraldsson, E. (1977). OBEs in Indian Swamis: Sathya Sai Baba and Dadaji, In *Research in Parapsychology 1976,* Ed. Morris, J.D., Roll, W.G., & Morris, R.L., Metuchen, NJ, Scarecrow Press, 147–150.

Osis, K., & Mitchell, J. L. (1977). Physiological Correlates of Reported Out-of-Body Experiences. *Journal of the Society for Psychical Research, 49,* 525–536.

Owens, J. E., Cook, E. W., & Stevenson, I. (1990). Features of 'near-death experience' in relation to whether or not patients were near death. *The Lancet, 336,* 1175–1177.

Oxenham, J., & Oxenham, E. (1941). London, Longmans Green.

# References

Palmer, J. (1978a). Consciousness localized in space outside the body: in D. Scott Rogo (Ed.), *Mind Beyond the Body: The Mystery of ESP Projection*. New York, Penguin Books, 35–42.

Palmer, J. (1978b). The out-of-body experience: A psychological theory. *Parapsychology Review*, 9, 19–22.

Palmer, J. (1979). A community mail survey of psychic experiences. *Journal of the American Society for Psychical Research*, 73, 221–252.

Palmer, J. (2009). Out-of-body and near-death experiences as evidence for externalization or survival. In *Psychological Scientific Perspectives on Out-of-body and Near-death experiences*. Ed. C. D. Murray, New York, Nova, 159–169.

Palmer, J., & Dennis, M. (1975). A Community Mail Survey of Psychic Experiences. In *Research in Parapsychology 1974*. Ed. R. L. Morris & W. G. Roll, Metuchen, NJ, Scarecrow Press, 130–133.

Palmer, J., & Lieberman, R. (1975). The Influence of Psychological Set on ESP and Out-of-Body Experiences. *Journal of the American Society for Psychical Research*, 69, 193–214.

Palmer, J., & Lieberman, R. (1976). ESP and Out-of-Body Experiences: A Further Study. In *Research in Parapsychology 1975*. Morris, J. D., Roll, W. G. & Morris, R. L. eds. Metuchen, NJ, Scarecrow Press, 1976, 102–106.

Palmer, J., & Vassar, C. (1974). ESP and Out-of-the-Body Experiences: An Exploratory Study. *Journal of the American Society for Psychical Research*, 68, 257–280.

Parker, A. (1975). *States of Mind: ESP and Altered States of Consciousness*. London, Malaby Press.

Parker, J. D., & Blackmore, S. J. (2002). Comparing the content of sleep paralysis and dream reports. *Dreaming*, 12(1), 45.

Parnia, S., & Fenwick, P. (2002). Near death experiences in cardiac arrest: visions of a dying brain or visions of a new science of consciousness. *Resuscitation*, 52(1), 5–11.

Parnia, S., Spearpoint, K., de Vos, G., Fenwick, P., Goldberg, D., Yang, J., ... & Wood, M. (2014). AWARE – AWAreness during REsuscitation – A prospective study. *Resuscitation*, 85(12), 1799–1805.

Parnia, S., Spearpoint, K., & Fenwick, P. B. (2007). Near death experiences, cognitive function and psychological outcomes of surviving cardiac arrest. *Resuscitation*, 74(2), 215–221.

Parnia, S., Waller, D. G., Yeates, R., & Fenwick, P. (2001). A qualitative and quantitative study of the incidence, features and aetiology of near death experiences in cardiac arrest survivors. *Resuscitation*, 48(2), 149–156.

Parra, A. (2010). Out-of-body experiences and hallucinatory experiences: A psychological approach. *Imagination, Cognition and Personality*, 29(3), 211–223.

Pasricha, S., & Stevenson, I. (1986). Near-death experiences in India: A preliminary report. *The Journal of Nervous and Mental Disease, 174*(3), 165–170.

Penfield, W. (1955). The twenty-ninth Maudsley lecture: the role of the temporal cortex in certain psychical phenomena. *Journal of Mental Science, 101,* 451–465.

Persinger, M. A. (1983). Religious and mystical experiences as artifacts of temporal lobe function: a general hypothesis. *Perceptual and Motor Skills, 57*(3f), 1255–1262.

Persinger, M. A., & Makarec, K. (1987). Temporal lobe epileptic signs and correlative behaviors displayed by normal populations. *Journal of General Psychology, 114,* 179–195.

Persinger, M. A., Saroka, K., Koren, S. A., & St-Pierre, L. S. (2010). The electromagnetic induction of mystical and altered states within the laboratory. *Journal of Consciousness Exploration & Research, 1*(7), 808–830.

Petkova, V. I., & Ehrsson, H. H. (2008). If I were you: perceptual illusion of body swapping. *PloS one, 3*(12).

Pfeiffer, C., Lopez, C., Schmutz, V., Duenas, J. A., Martuzzi, R., & Blanke, O. (2013). Multisensory origin of the subjective first-person perspective: visual, tactile, and vestibular mechanisms. *PLoS One, 8*(4), e61751.

Pomarol-Clotet, E., Honey, G. D., Murray, G. K., Corlett, P. R., Absalom, A. R., Lee, M., ... & Fletcher, P. C. (2006). Psychological effects of ketamine in healthy volunteers. *The British Journal of Psychiatry, 189*(2), 173–179.

Poynton, J. C. (1975). Results of an out-of-the-body survey. *Parapsychology in South Africa. Johannesburg: South African Society for Psychical Research,* 120–121.

Price, H. H. (1939). Haunting and the 'psychic ether' hypothesis: With some preliminary reflections on the present condition and possible future of psychical research. *Proceedings of the Society for Psychical Research, 45,* 307–374.

Quarck, G., Ventre, J., Etard, O., & Denise, P. (2006). Total sleep deprivation can increase vestibulo-ocular responses. *Journal of sleep research, 15*(4), 369–375.

Quentin, Q. (2013). *Astral Projection within 24 Hours: Your guide to astral travel if nothing has worked before,* (Kindle only).

Rahula, W. (1959). *What the Buddha Taught,* London, Gordon Fraser, and New York, Grove Press.

Ramachandran, V. S., & Blakeslee, S. (1998). *Phantoms in the Brain: Probing the Mysteries of the Human Mind,* New York, William Morrow.

Ramachandran, V. S., & Hubbard, E. M. (2001). Synaesthesia – a window into perception, thought and language. *Journal of Consciousness Studies, 8*(12), 3–34.

Rawlings, M. (1978). *Beyond Death's Door.* Nashville, Thomas Nelson.

Rhine, J. B. (1935). *Extrasensory Perception.* London, Faber & Faber.

# References

Ring, K. (1980). *Life at Death: A scientific investigation of the Near-Death Experience.* New York, Coward, McCann and Geoghegan.

Ring, K. (1984). *Heading toward Omega: In Search of the Meaning of the Near-Death Experience.* New York, Quill.

Ring, K. (1991). Personal communication.

Ring, K. (2016). Personal communication, email 16.09.2016.

Ring, K., & Cooper, S. (1997). Near-Death and Out-of-Body Experiences in the Blind: A Study of Apparent Eyeless Vision. *Journal of Near-Death Studies, 16,* 101.

Ring, K., & Cooper, S. (2008). *Mindsight: near-death and out-of-body experiences in the blind.* iUniverse.

Ring, K., & Franklin, S. (1982). Do suicide survivors report near-death experiences? *OMEGA-Journal of Death and Dying, 12*(3), 191–208.

Ring, K., & Lawrence, M. (1993). Further evidence for veridical perception during near-death experiences. *Journal of Near-Death Studies, 11*(4), 223–229.

Ring, K., & Rosing, C. J. (1990). The Omega Project: An empirical study of the NDE-prone personality. *Journal of Near-Death Studies, 8*(4), 211–239.

Rivas, T., Dirven, A., Smit, R. H., Mays, R.G., & Holden, J. M. (2016). *The Self Does Not Die: Verified Paranormal Phenomena from Near-Death Experiences.* Durham, NC, International Association for Near-Death Studies.

Roberts, U. (1975). *Look at the Aura – and Learn.* London, Greater World Association.

Rogo, D. S. (1976). Aspects of Out-of-the-Body Experiences. *Journal of the Society for Psychical Research, 48,* 329–335.

Rogo, D. S. (1978). Experiments with Blue Harary. In Rogo, D. S. ed. *Mind Beyond the Body.* New York, Penguin, 170–192.

Rogo, D. S. (1983). *Leaving the Body: A Complete Guide to Astral Projection.* Englewood Cliffs, NJ, Prentice Hall.

Rohde, M., Di Luca, M., & Ernst, M. O. (2011). The rubber hand illusion: feeling of ownership and proprioceptive drift do not go hand in hand. *PloS one, 6*(6).

Roll, W. G. (1966). ESP and memory. *International Journal of Neuropsychiatry, 2*(5), 505.

Rose, N. J., Blackmore, S., & French, C. C. (2002). Experiences and Interpretations of Sleep Paralysis. Parapsychological Association Conference, Paris, August 2002.

Roseman, L., Sereno, M. I., Leech, R., Kaelen, M., Orban, C., McGonigle, J., ... & Carhart-Harris, R. L. (2016). LSD alters eyes-closed functional connectivity within the early visual cortex in a retinotopic fashion. *Human Brain Mapping, 37*(8), 3031–3040.

Rosen, D. H. (1975). Suicide survivors. *Western Journal of Medicine, 122,* 289–294.

Rossen, R., Kabat, H., & Anderson, J. P. (1943). Acute arrest of cerebral circulation in man. *Archives of Neurology and Psychiatry, 50*(5), 510–528.

Rushton, W. A. H. (1976). Letter to the Editor, *Journal of the Society for Psychical Research, 48*, 412–413.

Saavedra-Aguilar, J. C., & Gómez-Jeria, J. S. (1989). A neurobiological model for near-death experiences. *Journal of Near-Death Studies, 7*(4), 205–222.

Sabom, M. (1979). Beyond Death's Door: A book review. *Anabiosis: The Journal of Near-Death Studies, 1*(3), 9.

Sabom, M. (1982). *Recollections of Death*. London, Corgi.

Sabom, M. (1998). *Light and Death*. Grand Rapids, MI, Zondervan.

Sabom, M. (2007). Commentary on Does Paranormal Perception Occur in Near-Death Experiences? *Journal of Near-Death Studies, 25*(4), 257–260.

Sabom, M., & Kreutziger, S. (1978). Physicians evaluate the near-death experience. *Theta, 6*(4), 1–6.

Sagan, C. (1977). *Broca's Brain: Reflections on the Romance of Science*. New York, Random House.

Salomon, R., Lim, M., Pfeiffer, C., Gassert, R., & Blanke, O. (2013). Full body illusion is associated with widespread skin temperature reduction. *Frontiers in Behavioral Neuroscience, 7*.

Sartori, P. (2006). The incidence and phenomenology of near-death experiences. *Network Review (Scientific and Medical Network), 90*, 23–25.

Schredl, M. (2007). Personality correlates of flying dreams. *Imagination, Cognition and Personality, 27*(2), 129–137.

Schredl, M., Ciric, P., Götz, S., & Wittmann, L. (2004). Typical dreams: stability and gender differences. *The Journal of psychology, 138*(6), 485–494.

Schredl, M., & Erlacher, D. (2011). Frequency of lucid dreaming in a representative German sample. *Perceptual and Motor Skills, 112*(1), 104–108.

Schatzman, M., Worsley, A., & Fenwick P. (1988). Correspondence during lucid dreams between dreamed and actual events. In *Conscious Mind, Sleeping Brain*, 155–179, ed. J. Gackenbach, & S. LaBerge. New York, Plenum.

Scheidegger, M., Walter, M., Lehmann, M., Metzger, C., Grimm, S., Boeker, H., ... & Seifritz, E. (2012). Ketamine decreases resting state functional network connectivity in healthy subjects: implications for antidepressant drug action. *PloS one, 7*(9), e44799.

Schwaninger, J., Eisenberg, P. R., Schechtman, K. B., & Weiss, A. N. (2002). A prospective analysis of near-death experiences in cardiac arrest patients. *Journal of Near-Death Studies, 20*(4), 215–232.

Shanon, B. (2002). *The Antipodes of the Mind: Charting the phenomenology of the ayahuasca experience*. Oxford, Oxford University Press.

# References

Sharp, K. C. (1995). *After the Light: What I discovered on the other side of life that can change your world.* New York, NY, William Morrow.

Sharp, K. C. (2007). The other shoe drops: Commentary on 'Does paranormal perception occur in near-death experiences?' *Journal of Near-Death Studies, 25*(4), 245–250.

Sharpless, B. A., & Barber, J. P. (2011). Lifetime prevalence rates of sleep paralysis: a systematic review. *Sleep Medicine Reviews, 15*(5), 311–315.

Sheils, D. A. (1978). Cross-cultural Study of Beliefs in Out-of-the-Body Experiences, *Journal of the Society for Psychical Research, 49,* 697–741.

Sheldrake, R. (1981). *A New Science of Life: The hypothesis of formative causation.* London, Blond & Briggs.

Shulgin, A., & Shulgin, A. (1991). *PiHKAL (Phenethylamines I Have Known and Loved): A chemical love story.* Berkeley, CA, Transform Press.

Shulgin, A., & Shulgin, A. (1997). *TiHKAL (Tryptamines I Have Known and Loved), The continuation.* Berkeley, CA, Transform Press.

Sidgwick, E. M. (1891). On the evidence for clairvoyance. In *Proceedings of the Society for Psychical Research, 7,* 30–99.

Siegel, R. K. (1977), Hallucinations. *Scientific American, 237,* 132–140.

Smit, R. H. (2008). Corroboration of the dentures anecdote involving veridical perception in a near-death experience. *Journal of Near-Death Studies, 27*(1), 47–61.

Smit, R. H., & Rivas, T. (2010). Rejoinder to 'Response to "Corroboration of the Dentures Anecdote Involving Veridical Perception in a Near-Death Experience"'. *Journal of Near-Death Studies, 28*(4), 193–205.

Smith, B. A., Clayton, E. W., & Robertson, D. (2011). Experimental arrest of cerebral blood flow in human subjects: the red wing studies revisited. *Perspectives in Biology and Medicine, 54*(2).

Spanos, N. P., Cross, P. A., Dickson, K., & DuBreuil, S. C. (1993). Close encounters: An examination of UFO experiences. *Journal of Abnormal Psychology, 102*(4), 624.

Spanos, N. P., McNulty, S. A., DuBreuil, S. C., Pires, M., & Burgess, M. F. (1995). The frequency and correlates of sleep paralysis in a university sample. *Journal of Research in Personality, 29*(3), 285–305.

Spechler, P. A., Orr, C. A., Chaarani, B., Kan, K. J., Mackey, S., Morton, A., ... & Cattrell, A. (2015). Cannabis use in early adolescence: Evidence of amygdala hypersensitivity to signals of threat. *Developmental Cognitive Neuroscience, 16,* 63–70.

Stack, R. (1988). *Out-of-Body Adventures: 30 Days to the Most Exciting Experience of Your Life.* New York, McGraw Hill.

Starmans, C., & Bloom, P. (2012). Windows to the soul: Children and adults see the eyes as the location of the self. *Cognition, 123*(2), 313–318.

Stokes, D.M. (2007). *The Conscious Mind and the Material World: On Psi, the Soul and the Self.* Jefferson, NC, McFarland.

Stumbrys, T., Erlacher, D., Johnson, M., & Schredl, M. (2014). The phenomenology of lucid dreaming: An online survey. *The American Journal of Psychology, 127*(2), 191–204.

Stumbrys, T., Erlacher, D., & Schredl, M. (2013). Testing the involvement of the prefrontal cortex in lucid dreaming: a tDCS study. *Consciousness and Cognition, 22*(4), 1214–1222.

Stumbrys, T., Erlacher, D., & Schredl, M. (2016). Effectiveness of motor practice in lucid dreams: a comparison with physical and mental practice. *Journal of Sports Sciences, 34*(1), 27–34.

Tagliazucchi, E., Roseman, L., Kaelen, M., Orban, C., Muthukumaraswamy, S. D., Murphy, K., ... & Bullmore, E. (2016). Increased global functional connectivity correlates with LSD-Induced ego dissolution. *Current Biology, 26*(8), 1043–1050.

Takeuchi, T., Miyasita, A., Sasaki, Y., Inugami, M., & Fukuda, K. (1992). Isolated sleep paralysis elicited by sleep interruption. *Sleep,* 15:217–225.

Takeuchi, T., Ogilvie, R. D., Murphy, T. I., & Ferrelli, A. V. (2003). EEG activities during elicited sleep onset REM and NREM periods reflect different mechanisms of dream generation. *Clinical Neurophysiology, 114*(2), 210–220.

Tart, C. T. (1967). A Second Psychophysiological Study of Out-of-the-Body Experiences in a Gifted Subject. *International Journal of Parapsychology, 9,* 251–258.

Tart, C. T. (1968). A Psychophysiological Study of Out-of-the-Body Experiences in a Selected Subject. *Journal of the American Society for Psychical Research, 62,* 3–27.

Tart, C. T. (1971a). *On Being Stoned: A psychological study of marijuana intoxication.* Palo Alto, CA, Science and Behavior Books.

Tart, C. T. (1971b). Introduction, In *Journeys Out of the Body* by R. A. Monroe. New York, Doubleday.

Tart, C. T. (1972). Concerning the scientific study of the human aura. *Journal of the Society for Psychical Research, 46*(751), 1–21.

Tart, C. T. (1975). *States of Consciousness.* New York, Dutton.

Tart, C. T., & Palmer, J. (1979). Some psi experiments with Matthew Manning. *Journal of the Society for Psychical Research, 50,* 224–228.

Tellegen, A., & Atkinson, G. (1974). Openness to absorbing and self-altering experiences ('absorption'), a trait related to hypnotic susceptibility. *Journal of Abnormal Psychology, 83*(3), 268.

# References

Terhune, D. B. (2009). The incidence and determinants of visual phenomenology during out-of-body experiences. *Cortex*, 45(2), 236–242.

Terhune, D. B., & Cardeña, E. (2009). Out-of-body experiences in the context of hypnosis: Phenomenology, methodology, and neurophysiology. In *Psychological Scientific Perspectives On Out of Body And Near Death Experiences*, Ed. C.D. Murray, New York, Nova, 89–104.

Thakkar, K. N., Nichols, H. S., McIntosh, L. G., & Park, S. (2011). Disturbances in body ownership in schizophrenia: evidence from the rubber hand illusion and case study of a spontaneous out-of-body experience. *PloS one*, 6(10), e27089.

Tholey, P. (1983). Techniques for inducing and manipulating lucid dreams. *Perceptual and Motor Skills*, 57(1), 79–90.

Tholey, P. (1990). Applications of lucid dreaming in sports. *Lucidity Letter*, 9(2), 6–17.

Thonnard, M., Charland-Verville, V., Brédart, S., Dehon, H., Ledoux, D., Laureys, S., & Vanhaudenhuyse, A. (2013) Characteristics of near-death experiences memories as compared to real and imagined events memories. *PloS one*, 8(3), e57620

Tsakiris, M., Costantini, M., & Haggard, P. (2008). The role of the right temporo-parietal junction in maintaining a coherent sense of one's body. *Neuropsychologia*, 46(12), 3014-3018.

Tsakiris, M., Prabhu, G., & Haggard, P. (2006). Having a body versus moving your body: How agency structures body-ownership. *Consciousness and cognition*, 15(2), 423–432.

Twemlow, S. W., Gabbard, G. O., & Jones, F. C. (1982). The out-of-body experience: A phenomenological typology based on questionnaire responses. *American Journal of Psychiatry*, 139(4), 450–455.

Tyrrell, G. N. M. (1943). *Apparitions*. New York, Pantheon Books.

van Eeden, F. (1913). A study of dreams. *Proceedings of the Society for Psychical Research*, 26, 431–461.

van Lommel, P. (2004). About the continuity of our consciousness. In *Brain Death and Disorders of Consciousness*, 115–132. Springer US.

van Lommel, P. (2006). Near-death experience, consciousness, and the brain: A new concept about the continuity of our consciousness based on recent scientific research on near-death experience in survivors of cardiac arrest. *World Futures*, 62(1–2), 134–151.

van Lommel, P. (2009). Endless consciousness: A concept based on scientific studies on near-death experience. In *Psychological Scientific Perspectives on Out of Body and Near Death Experiences*. Ed. Craig D. Murray. NY, Nova, 171–186.

van Lommel, P. (2010). *Consciousness Beyond Life.* New York, HarperCollins.

van Lommel, P. (2011a). Near-death experiences: the experience of the self as real and not as an illusion. *Annals of the New York Academy of Sciences, 1234*(1), 19–28.

van Lommel, P. (2011b). Endless Consciousness: A Concept Based on Scientific Studies of Near-Death Experiences. In *Neuroscience, Consciousness and Spirituality.* Springer Netherlands, 207–227.

van Lommel, P. (2013). Non-local Consciousness: A Concept Based on Scientific Research on Near-Death Experiences During Cardiac Arrest. *Journal of Consciousness Studies, 20*(1–2), 7–48.

van Lommel, P., van Wees, R., Meyers, V., & Elfferich, I. (2001). Near-death experience in survivors of cardiac arrest: a prospective study in the Netherlands. *The Lancet, 358*(9298), 2039–2045.

Varga, J. (2011). *Visits to Heaven.* Virginia Beach, VA, 4th Dimension Press.

Voss, U., Frenzel, C., Koppehele-Gossel, J., & Hobson, A. (2012). Lucid dreaming: An age-dependent brain dissociation. *Journal of Sleep Research, 21*(6), 634–642.

Voss, U., Holzmann, R., Tuin, I., & Hobson, A. (2009). Lucid dreaming: a state of consciousness with features of both waking and non-lucid dreaming. *Sleep, 32*(9), 1191–1200.

Wang, J. H. (2003). Short-term cerebral ischemia causes the dysfunction of interneurons and more excitation of pyramidal neurons in rats. *Brain Research Bulletin, 60*(1), 53–58.

Wegner, D. (2002). *The Illusion of Conscious Will.* Cambridge, MA, MIT Press.

Weil, A. (1998). *The Natural Mind: An investigation of drugs and the higher consciousness.* New York, Houghton Mifflin Harcourt.

Wellman, H. M., & Estes, D. (1986). Early understanding of mental entities: A reexamination of childhood realism. *Child Development,* 910–923.

Whinnery, J. E., & Whinnery, A. M. (1990). Acceleration-induced loss of consciousness: a review of 500 episodes. *Archives of Neurology, 47*(7), 764–776.

Whinnery, J. E. (1990b). Personal communication.

Whiteman, J. H. M. (1956). The process of separation and return in experiences fully 'out-of-the-body'. *Proceedings of the Society for Psychical Research, 50,* 240–274.

Wilkins, A., Nimmo-Smith, I., Tait, A., McManus, C., Della Sala, S., Tilley, A. ... & Scott, S. (1984). A neurological basis for visual discomfort. *Brain, 107*(4), 989–1017.

Wilkins, L. K., Girard, T. A., & Cheyne, J. A. (2011). Ketamine as a primary predictor of out-of-body experiences associated with multiple substance use. *Consciousness and Cognition, 20*(3), 943–950.

# References

Wilkins, L. K., Girard, T. A., & Cheyne, J. A. (2012). Anomalous bodily-self experiences among recreational ketamine users. *Cognitive Neuropsychiatry, 17*(5), 415–430.

Williams, J. H., Wellman, N. A., & Rawlins, J. N. P. (1996). Cannabis use correlates with schizotypy in healthy people. *Addiction, 91*(6), 869–877.

Wing, Y. K., Lee, S. T., & Chen, C. N. (1994). Sleep paralysis in Chinese: Ghost oppression phenomenon in Hong Kong. *Sleep, 17,* 609–613.

Woerlee, G. M. (2004). Darkness, tunnels and light, *Skeptical Inquirer, 28*(3), 28–32.

Woerlee, G. M. (2005a). An anaesthesiologist examines the Pam Reynolds story; Part 1: Background considerations. *The Skeptic, 18,* 14–17.

Woerlee, G. M. (2005b). An anaesthesiologist examines the Pam Reynolds story; Part 2: The experience. *The Skeptic, 18,* 16–20.

Woerlee, G. M. (2010). Response to 'Corroboration of the Dentures Anecdote Involving Veridical Perception in a Near-Death Experience'. *Journal of Near-Death Studies, 28*(4), 181–191.

Woerlee, G. M. (2011). Could Pam Reynolds hear? A new investigation into the possibility of hearing during this famous near-death experience. *Journal of Near-Death Studies, 30*(1), 3–25.

Woerlee, G. M. (2013). *Illusory Souls*, self-published.

Yoshino, H., Miyamae, T., Hansen, G., Zambrowicz, B., Flynn, M., Pedicord, D., Blat, Y., Westphal, R. S., Zaczek, R., Lewis, D. A., & Gonzalez-Burgos, G. (2011). Postsynaptic diacylglycerol lipase mediates retrograde endocannabinoid suppression of inhibition in mouse prefrontal cortex. *Journal of Physiology, 589*(20), 4857–4884.

Yram (1935). *Practical Astral Projection* (translated from the French *Le Medecin de L'Ame*), London, Rider.

Zhi-ying, F., & Jian-xun, L. (1992). Near-death experiences among survivors of the 1976 Tangshan earthquake. *Journal of Near-Death Studies, 11*(1), 39–48.

Zingrone, N. L., Alvarado, C. S., & Cardena, E. (2010). Out-of-body experiences and physical body activity and posture: responses from a survey conducted in Scotland. *The Journal of Nervous and Mental Disease, 198*(2), 163–165.

# Websites

**Chapter 2** astral projection (http://dictionary.reference.com/browse/astral-projection 6.11.15)

Christian website https://carm.org/out-of-body-experience 4.11.15

Islamic website http://islamqa.org/hanafi/qibla-hanafi/36763

http://www.astralpulse.com/forums/welcome_to_world_religions/souls_travel_out_of_the_body_an_islamic_viewpoint-t26024.0.html;wap2=

**Chapter 3** Auras

http://paranormal.lovetoknow.com/Aura_Colors_and_Their_Meaning

http://www.reiki-for-holistic-health.com/auracolormeanings.html

http://in5d.com/how-to-read-auras-what-is-the-meaning-of-each-color/

**Chapter 8** Inside the Brain

TV programme 'Close Encounters' https://www.youtube.com/watch?v=cbJoPuLsntk

**Chapter 10** Lucid dreams

https://islamqa.info/en/182280

http://www.gotquestions.org/lucid-dreaming.html

**Chapter 11** Drugs

http://boards.cannabis.com/threads/
cannabis-and-out-of-body-experiences.143722/

https://www.reddit.com/r/trees/comments/2b30xx/
the_next_level_of_smoking_marijuana_out_of_body/

https://www.erowid.org/experiences/exp.php?ID=9903

http://www.salvia.net/exp_joshua.htm

# Index

# Index

# Index

# Index

# Index